Governing from the Bench

Law and Society Series
W. Wesley Pue, General Editor

The Law and Society Series explores law as a socially embedded phenomenon. It is premised on the understanding that the conventional division of law from society creates false dichotomies in thinking, scholarship, educational practice, and social life. Books in the series treat law and society as mutually constitutive and seek to bridge scholarship emerging from interdisciplinary engagement of law with disciplines such as politics, social theory, history, political economy, and gender studies.

A list of titles in the series appears at the end of the book.

Emmett Macfarlane

Governing from the Bench
The Supreme Court of Canada
and the Judicial Role

UBCPress · Vancouver · Toronto

21 20 19 18   5 4

Printed in Canada on FSC-certified ancient-forest-free paper
(100% post-consumer recycled) that is processed chlorine- and acid-free.

Library and Archives Canada Cataloguing in Publication

Macfarlane, Emmett
   Governing from the bench : the Supreme Court of Canada and the judicial role /
Emmett Macfarlane.

(Law and society, ISSN 1496-4953)
Includes bibliographical references and index.
Issued also in electronic formats.
ISBN 978-0-7748-2350-0 (bound); ISBN 978-0-7748-2351-7 (pbk.)

   1. Canada. Supreme Court – Decision making. 2. Judicial process – Canada.
3. Law – Political aspects. I. Title. II. Series: Law and society series (Vancouver, B.C.)

KE8259.M33 2013	347.71'035	C2012-906950-7
KF8764.ZA2M33 2013		

Canadä

UBC Press gratefully acknowledges the financial support for our publishing program
of the Government of Canada (through the Canada Book Fund), the Canada Council
for the Arts, and the British Columbia Arts Council.

This book has been published with the help of a grant from the Canadian Federation
for the Humanities and Social Sciences, through the Awards to Scholarly Publications
Program, using funds provided by the Social Sciences and Humanities Research
Council of Canada.

UBC Press
The University of British Columbia
2029 West Mall
Vancouver, BC V6T 1Z2
www.ubcpress.ca

For my parents,
Don and Eileen Macfarlane

Contents

Acknowledgments

This book is the culmination of research and thinking conducted over many years and was influenced, in various ways, by the contributions of many people. An earlier form of this project took the shape of my doctoral dissertation, which was completed at Queen's University under the supervision of Janet Hiebert. I owe an incalculable debt of gratitude to Janet, whose friendship, mentorship, and support has helped ensure whatever success I have had in the first stages of my career. Janet's own work on the *Canadian Charter of Rights and Freedoms* and the institutional relationships surrounding judicial review serves as a great inspiration, particularly for the way in which it engages with important questions with nuance and sophistication. Furthermore, as a supervisor, she was everything a graduate student could hope for.

I am especially indebted to Keith Banting and Scott Matthews for serving as members of my dissertation committee and for their support throughout the last several years. Being able to count on their support has been immensely rewarding, and I have learned much from both of them. I would also like to thank Christopher Manfredi and Mark Walters for serving as examiners on my committee and for their helpful comments.

One of the most important contributions this book makes is a result of the twenty-eight not-for-attribution research interviews conducted with current and former justices, former law clerks, and other staff members of the Supreme Court of Canada. I would like to thank those who participated for their willingness to do so and for being so generous with their time. I would also like to thank the anonymous reviewers of this book. Elements of previously published articles in the journals *Canadian Public Administration* (2009) and *Supreme Court Law Review* (2010) appear in this book, and I am grateful for the use of this material and to the anonymous reviewers of those articles. Finally, I would like to thank Megan Brand and Randy Schmidt of UBC Press for so expertly guiding me through the publication process. They made what could have been an intimidating process an extremely smooth one.

I have benefited from the advice and wisdom of several teachers and mentors without whom this book may never have seen the light of day. My thanks to Ian Brodie, Laura Janara, and Bob Young for getting an undergraduate – who spent many more hours invested in student journalism than his coursework – interested in political science. Thanks to Kathy Brock, Grant Amyot, and Jonathan Rose for furthering this interest during my time as a graduate student. I would also like to acknowledge Dennis Baker, Matt Hennigar, Grant Huscroft, Jim Kelly, Rainer Knopff, Peter McCormick, and Jeremy Webber for their support in various endeavours or for their fruitful discussions over the past few years. Finally, I would especially like to thank Mark Tushnet for his advice and support during my time as a post-doctoral fellow at Harvard University. The institutional support of Harvard Law School and the Weatherhead Center for International Affairs and the financial support of the Social Sciences and Humanities Research Council are also acknowledged.

I was fortunate to meet many friends and graduate school colleagues while working on this project. My thanks to Mira Bachvarova, Siobhan Byrne, Jordan DeCoste, Megan Gaucher, Holly Grinvalds, Nick Hardy, Rachael Johnstone, Laura Kelly, Hayden King, Simon Kiss, Robert Lawson, Rémi Léger, Allison McCulloch, Marcel Nelson, Sean O'Meara, Dimitri Panagos, Lucia Salazar, Dave Thomas, Erin Tolley, and George Wootten. A special note of thanks to Jeremy Clarke, my comrade-in-arms in studying the *Charter* at Queen's, for many great discussions and debates.

This book would not have been possible without my parents, Don and Eileen Macfarlane, and my sister Aingeal. I am grateful for being able to rely on an encouraging and supportive family.

I am also thankful for the love and support of the most wonderful partner in the world, Anna Drake. Having Anna in my life makes good days great and bad days bearable. I could not have completed this book without her.

Governing from the Bench

Introduction

The Supreme Court of Canada is one of Canada's most important – and least understood – governing institutions. This book describes, analyzes, and explains how it works. In doing so, it considers the dominant explanations of judicial behaviour in political science and legal scholarship. Although the book challenges fundamental methodological aspects of these leading approaches, it aims to integrate their key theoretical insights. Through a focus on how the Supreme Court of Canada's justices conceive of their role, this study explores the institution's internal environment, the different stages of its decision-making process, and the rules, conventions, and norms that shape and constrain the justices' behaviour. At the same time, the book situates the Court in its broader governmental and societal context by examining the institution's role as it relates to the elected branches of government, the media, and the public.

Created in 1875, the Court has spent most of its history in relative obscurity. Only in the last thirty years has the institution garnered regular media coverage or sustained attention by political scientists. Much of this interest was generated by the advent of the *Canadian Charter of Rights and Freedoms* in 1982, which transformed the institution's role and thrust its work into the national spotlight.[1] The Court has evolved from a largely legal, dispute-resolving body into a policy-making institution whose decisions have far-reaching implications for virtually all areas of Canada's political, social, cultural, and economic life. As the country's final court of appeal, the Supreme Court of Canada is the authority for all areas of law. As the chief arbiter of Canadian federalism disputes, it has answered questions relating to the patriation of the Constitution from Great Britain and the constitutionality of the unilateral secession of Quebec from the rest of Canada. Under the *Charter,* the Court makes decisions affecting vital government programs such as health care and welfare, controversial social policies such as abortion and assisted suicide, the rights of women, gays, and lesbians, and the criminally accused.

The nature and extent of the Court's involvement in public policy matters has been the subject of extensive criticism and debate. Conservative critics lament rulings that implicate social policies such as abortion or expand the rights of gays and lesbians,[2] while commentators on the left criticize the Court for pro-business outcomes or decisions that prioritize individual rights over group ones.[3] These detractors share the view that judicial decisions are merely discretionary choices rooted in legalistic camouflage. They question the legitimacy of unelected judges overruling the legislative choices of the public's representatives. In many respects, such criticism mirrors American debates about the supposed undemocratic nature of judicial review, something Alexander Bickel famously termed the "counter-majoritarian difficulty."[4] The Canadian Constitution allows courts to invalidate legislation that is inconsistent with the *Charter*'s provisions, but critics maintain that the Court has taken an unduly "activist" attitude in using its power.[5] They claim that rather than taking on a restrained role that reflects Canada's shift from parliamentary sovereignty to constitutional supremacy, the Court has used its powers of judicial review to expand its policy-making authority, effectively transforming Canada into a system of judicial supremacy.[6] Defenders of the Court have responded, arguing that judges are constrained by the law and guided by factors such as the text of the *Charter* and precedent.[7] More recently, supporters of the Court's role under the *Charter* have refuted the notion that judicial rulings reign supreme by contending that the *Charter* promotes an inter-branch "dialogue" that allows legislatures to respond to the Court's decisions.[8] The normative questions provoking these debates have spurred other scholars to explore more fully the respective institutional roles surrounding constitutional interpretation and the enforcement of rights.[9]

The Supreme Court of Canada's importance can be measured not only by its rulings' effects on the country's law and the immediate policy issues that come before it but also by the influence its decisions have on governance, political culture, and public discourse. A fundamental aspect of the "judicialization of politics,"[10] which is enacted by the *Charter* in Canada – in which the Court is a central actor – is not only the transfer of power to the courts but also, in Peter Russell's words, "a general transformation of the nature of political life."[11] The decision to entrench the *Charter* has had significant consequences. Ran Hirschl argues that the *Charter* has encouraged legislatures to abrogate political responsibility for the resolution of contentious national questions. He contends that the transformation of controversial and complex political issues into legal questions deprives most of the citizenry of the opportunity to address these issues through public deliberation and other forms of participation.[12]

The shift toward constitutionalism and its emphasis on rights has transformed the legislative process itself. The rights culture shapes not only legislative responses to Court rulings but also legislative initiatives from their inception. The "vetting" of legislation by governmental lawyers for consistency with the *Charter* is now a central component of the legislative process.[13] As Janet Hiebert notes, the Supreme Court of Canada has a powerful influence on this process. First, the Court's two-stage approach to *Charter* analysis, in which it first examines whether a particular right has been infringed and then investigates whether the restriction is reasonable, has meant that bureaucratic risk assessment occurs largely within a consideration of "reasonable limits." Second, because the Court has not shied away from exercising its power to invalidate laws under the *Charter*, its jurisprudence has encouraged governments to be more vigilant in their internal scrutiny of legislative development. While the development of a legislative rights-conscious culture might be viewed in a positive light, the potential downside is the risk that policy objectives are confined "to those which legal advisers can confidently predict legal 'success'" – that is, those that will pass muster before the Court – which, in turn, "may lead to risk-aversion that distorts policy objectives and undermines Parliament's ability to pursue legislative objectives effectively."[14]

In addition to its impact on governance and the legislative process, the Court's public prominence also affects political discourse. As the central player in determining the meaning of the *Charter*, courts are the primary avenues for individuals and groups pursuing rights claims. As a result, judicial pronouncements on *Charter* rights, particularly those put forward by the Supreme Court of Canada, play a prominent role in shaping discourse around rights. The positive and negative consequences of a rights-infused political culture and public discourse are the subject of considerable scrutiny. On the one hand, scholars hail the empowering effects that rights review has on citizens, particularly for historically disadvantaged groups and individuals.[15] On the other hand, some view as problematic the capacity for rights claiming to harm political discourse by rendering it absolutist, divisive, and uncompromising. Writing in the American context, Mary Ann Glendon contends that "rights talk" subjugates other considerations, values, and policy initiatives to the unbending demands of those invoking a right, which is hardly a straightforward proposition when there is no consensus of what values, interests, or needs should be classified as rights.[16] A number of critics have echoed Glendon's concerns in the Canadian context.[17] Empirical study of the impact that the Court's rulings have had on political discourse is limited, but it generally supports these assertions.[18]

Despite the institution's significance for Canadian society, and the many direct and indirect ways it influences the country's governance, less is known about how the Supreme Court of Canada actually works than one might think. There are surprisingly few studies that focus specifically on the Court's decision-making processes and the behaviour of its justices. This fact is noteworthy because a better understanding of how the Court actually works would not only clarify the impact the institution has on specific policies or on the broader governance of the country, but it would also inform normative debates about the Court's role and how the other branches of government should engage the *Charter* or respond to the Court's rulings.

The historic lack of empirical attention on the Court cannot be overstated. As recently as 1987, Russell, arguably the country's foremost scholar of constitutional politics, wrote:

> Judicial institutions are not regarded as an important item in the agenda of political science. The role of the judiciary is perceived as being essentially technical and non-political: it is there to apply the laws made by the political branches of government. Indeed, the most important normative expectations of judges and courts would seem to be a thorough-going impartiality requiring total independence of the political process.[19]

As the level of interest in research on judicial politics has mushroomed over the last two to three decades, this view has changed considerably. As the vast scholarship addressing questions of the Court's activism and the role of the various branches in dealing with *Charter* issues makes clear, the Supreme Court of Canada has come to be viewed as a pivotal governing actor. Yet, despite this recognition, empirical investigation of the institution itself has been comparatively sparse. Studies relating to the Court's operation and decision-making processes were for some time limited to single chapters or sections of monographs on the broader judicial system.[20] Other studies have explored broader trends in the Court's jurisprudence by presenting statistical information on judicial voting patterns or by examining the written reasons.[21]

More recent studies have drawn explicitly on the theoretical and methodological approaches of the American judicial behaviour literature, examining individual voting patterns based on the justices' ideologies or other characteristics.[22] The behaviouralist "attitudinal model" regards the ideological policy preferences of the individual judge as the main determinant in decision making. Attitudinal scholars seek to measure the justices' attitudes and, taking account of case facts, examine voting records to determine how consistent the justices' decisions are with these attitudes. Like attitudinalists, adherents of the "strategic model" or rational choice understanding of judicial decision making generally consider judges' policy preferences to be the main consideration in decisions, but they believe that judges must make strategic calculations about their choices given the institutional rules of the game and the preferences of other actors and branches of government. To enact the decisions most consonant with their preferences, strategic judges must make compromises to garner support from their colleagues on the bench and to avoid a backlash from legislatures.

Canadian judicial politics scholarship, like many of the other subfields in Canadian political science, has for some time been relatively descriptive and atheoretical.[23] Given that the long tradition of judicial review in the United States has resulted in extensive study on the workings of American courts and judicial behaviour, it makes sense that Canadian scholars looking for more theoretically rich explanations would look to the leading theories and methodologies south of the border. In fact, much of the new Canadian scholarship is actually the application of American approaches to the Canadian Court by American scholars. As explored in Chapter 1, these approaches have much to offer – and much to warn against – for the empirical study of courts in the Canadian context.

Approach of the Book

This book proceeds from the premise that the Supreme Court of Canada is a political institution and that its justices are important political actors. This is not to equate the institution with elected legislatures or its justices with politicians. Indeed, one of the main objectives of this study is to examine the multitude of ways in which the judges of the Court are bound by their conceptions of their appropriate role and that of the institution in which they work. Nevertheless, the analysis that follows supports the argument put forward by many political scientists that judicial policy making is not an accidental by-product of the Court's adjudicative function. Rather, it is a result of the justices' determination that one set of legal rules is more socially beneficial than another.[24]

This book's approach is consistent with historical institutionalism, a perspective that requires an analysis of organizational and institutional configurations, with specific attention to long-term processes and the "critical junctures" that help shape them. As Paul Pierson and Theda Skocpol write, "[r]esearching important issues in this way, historical institutionalists make visible and understandable the overarching contexts and interacting processes that shape and reshape states, politics, and public policymaking."[25] Drawing on historical institutionalism and American political development scholarship, a recent study by Miriam Smith examines the evolution of lesbian and gay rights and policy differences in Canada and the United States. Smith writes that "historical institutionalists start with state structures, with the field of political institutions and the legacies of previous policies, to explain divergent policy outcomes." Critical to the approach is that the state is treated "as an independent player" in the analysis.[26]

Where Smith's work – and much historical institutionalist work generally – centres on a comparative analysis of policy outcomes, this study focuses on understanding and explaining the work of a single institution. Never-theless, the logic of analysis remains the same. The approach is premised on the belief that studies of the Supreme Court of Canada that focus solely on broad statistical trends in jurisprudence or those that seek to explain judicial decision making solely by analyzing the votes of individual justices are limited in their ability to further our understanding of the Court because they treat the institution as a "black box." As Chapter 1 explores, the be-havioural and rational choice approaches described earlier lead to incom-plete accounts of decision making that almost always treat the justices' personal policy preferences as their primary, if not only, motivation. Such studies stress the "outputs" of the black box (judicial votes) and draw ques-tionable inferences about the "inputs" (judicial ideologies). Aside from the strategic model's consideration of the effect some of the Court's procedural rules have on judicial choices, these approaches generally fail to devote attention to the institutional environment or the broader structural forces that have implications for the Court's decisions. As Smith contends, in contrast to the attitudinal and strategic approaches of judicial behaviour, "historical institutionalism ... allows us to embed judicial behaviour within the larger structure of political institutions."[27]

The aim of this book is to open the black box. Even before the *Charter* was created, Paul Weiler cautioned against seeing the Court as just a group of nine people because "this picture leaves out one important dimension to the social reality of the [C]ourt. The Supreme Court of Canada is an *institu-tion,* something more than the immediate preferences and actions of its members at any one time."[28] Only by describing and analyzing the Court's decision-making processes and gaining an appreciation of how the justices conceive of their proper function both within the Court and in the context of the broader political system can we truly understand how the institution works. This approach does not discount the importance of judicial policy preferences. Rather, the objective is to place the justices' behaviour in the full context necessary for an accurate appreciation of the Court's work and its impact on the rest of the governing system.

This is not an easy task. Some commentators seem to dismiss the prospect of exploring the inner workings of the institution altogether. Heather MacIvor notes that the secret nature of decision making "makes it impossible to gauge the relative influence of legal principle and personal policy preference on policy outcomes."[29] Daved Muttart writes that "[w]hatever the decision-making processes a justice employs, they are almost entirely beyond direct study inasmuch as they occur almost exclusively within the private confines of the judicial cranium."[30] Despite changes during the *Charter* era to make the Court more transparent with regard to the media and the public, in several important ways the institution is less open than its American counter-part.[31] Where journalistic and other insider accounts of the Supreme Court of the United States have become commonplace,[32] Canada has not had the same tradition.[33] Based on interviews with the justices and law clerks, these accounts have caused considerable controversy within the American legal profession by revealing bargaining, lobbying, and outright political manoeuvring on the part of the US court's justices. The Canadian justices have no doubt been trepidatious at the prospect of similar books being written about their institution.

Another contributing factor to the lack of studies exploring the Supreme Court of Canada's internal operation stems from the historic failure of the Court to preserve its records. Few justices have donated private papers to the national archives, and those that did so prior to the *Charter* failed to include substantive documentation about judgments. *Charter*-era justices have been more careful to preserve their records, but the documents remain unavailable to the public for twenty-five years following their donation to the archives.[34] As a result, the assertions of those individuals skeptical of scholarly investigation into the Court's inner workings are likely true to the extent that they refer to direct observation or scientific precision.

The approach of this study, however, is grounded in an understanding of decision making at the Court as inherently complex, with a myriad of motivating factors and a host of structural conditions that both influence, and are influenced by, the justices' behaviour. Making sense of this complexity requires the historical institutionalist approach adopted in this book. It emphasizes the centrality of the justices' role conceptions in order to gauge the relative impact of factors such as ideology, strategic behaviour, and institutionally derived norms and values at different stages of the Court's decision-making process. The book does not aim to develop a new "model" of judicial behaviour or even refute the leading theories of judicial behaviour. Instead, my more modest aim is to develop a new perspective from which to consider how the Supreme Court of Canada and its justices operate. The goal is to demonstrate that judicial role conceptions can shed light on when and how particular factors – including those factors that are central to the other approaches – influence the justices' decisions while attending to the full complexity of the Court's processes.

In examining the role conceptions of Supreme Court of Canada justices, this book draws on several different sources of data. Twenty-eight not-for-attribution interviews were conducted from July 2007 to August 2008, including five with current and former justices of the Court, twenty-one with former law clerks, and two with senior staff members. It is worth noting that this is the only existing study of the Court that gains insights from interviews with a substantial number of former law clerks. The law clerks interviewed served on the Court from 1979 to 2005, for thirteen different judges, providing snapshots of the Court's working environment throughout its modern history.[35] The Court's law clerks are said to be "sworn to lifelong silence" about their year-long tenure with the institution.[36] The stringency of these confidentiality agreements and the great concern the institution has in enforcing them came to light in June 2009 when the Court's executive legal officer issued a warning to all former clerks that participation in a survey sent to them by an American political scientist would place them in breach of their agreements. In an e-mail to the clerks, the Court maintained that confidentiality obligations "are not limited to information about cases, but also extend to internal processes of each Justice's chambers."[37] As a result, until or unless the Court reassesses questions of access, this book is the first and last to take advantage of access to so many former law clerks.[38] Most of the interviews with former law clerks were from thirty minutes to an hour in length. The interviews with the justices and other staff members ranged from one hour to two-and-a-half hours.

Few empirical studies benefit from interviews with the justices.[39] A recent book by Donald Songer incorporates research interviews with former justices into a broad, quantitative analysis of trends in the Supreme Court of Canada's decision making.[40] He examines the type of litigants at the Court, which participants tend to win or lose, and how the Court's policy making (that is, the type of cases the Court hears) has evolved. Similarly to a recent study applying the attitudinal model to the Court, Songer also engages in analyses of the justices' behaviour based on their ideologies and personal attributes.[41] He finds these ideological factors are important but that the Court is politically moderate. Importantly, he also explains how the justices' views on Court process may help explain certain elements of the institution's behaviour, such as an ability to achieve unanimous outcomes.

This book takes such analysis further by focusing explicitly on such judicial role conceptions. Where Songer's largely quantitative analysis sheds light on broad trends in the Court's modern history, this study provides an in-depth qualitative examination of the judicial role. This approach allows for an explanation of judicial behaviour that not only identifies the various factors that influence the Court's decisions but also accounts for when and under what conditions certain variables come to dominate a particular part of the process. It also allows for the identification and analysis of variables that are not conducive to quantitative measurement. Understanding Court decision making by way of judicial role conceptions requires placing a focus on the *ideas* and *norms* that shape a justice's approach to her work. This focus permits insight into behaviour related to, but distinct from, personal values, such as collegiality, consensual norms, and personality.

The broad conception of the judicial role developed throughout this book has three components. The first relates to the justices' views of the proper role of the *institution* itself. These include a consideration of how the Supreme Court of Canada ought to address the political and policy-laden questions it often confronts, particularly under the *Charter*. Issues relating to the law of justiciability, the involvement of third party interveners in cases, and the type of evidence justices are willing to consider in the course of making decisions are all implicated by these normative perceptions of the Court's proper role.

The second component of the judicial role pertains to how the justices view their *individual* role within the institution. Although this perspective includes addressing relatively simple notions sometimes considered in the extant literature – such as whether the judges consider themselves "law interpreters" or "law makers" or even how much they may allow their personal values to intrude on decision making – it extends much further. A host of considerations play into the justices' individual roles when making decisions, including the extent to which they strive to achieve consensus (or unanimity) with their colleagues, the style or approach they take to collaboration, and the leadership style of the chief justice. Examining these individual role perceptions can demonstrate how role theory is also useful for identifying which stages of the decision-making process and under what conditions sites of activity for attitudinal or strategic behaviour are likely to emerge. The process of deliberation and negotiation on the Court is closely intertwined with norms of collegiality and rules of convention. This book will show that where attitudinal or strategic behaviour materializes, it usually coincides with those areas where consensus regarding such norms or conventions breaks down.

The third component of the judicial role involves a consideration of both the Court and the individual justice in relation to broader government and society. As is explored in Chapter 1, many studies of judicial behaviour emphasize the degree to which justices must consider the preferences and actions of the other branches of government. Often overlooked is judicial concern for the quality of the jurisprudence, media and public criticism tied to the legitimacy of the Court itself, personal reputation, esteem of the legal and wider community, and the relationship of the Court with the other branches of government. A role-centric approach shows how justices' normative understandings of the appropriate place of legislatures in making policy choices shapes not only the degree of deference they give to those institutional roles but also the reasons for, and the type of, action they choose to take. Further, by examining judicial considerations of the Court's institutional capacity or competence for dealing with complex matters of public policy, this book sheds light on understanding how the justices perceive of the limits or boundaries of judicial review. In Chapter 5, I examine the Court's *Charter* cases that implicate health policy in order to contrast these normative views with how questions of institutional capacity are ultimately addressed in the Court's jurisprudence. This section of the book finds that when the justices fail to explicitly consider the question of institutional roles in their reasoning, opportunities are created for them to impose their personal policy preferences on case outcomes on an issue-by-issue basis.

The major argument advanced in adopting this approach is that not only do the judges' policy preferences, values, or ideologies matter but also that judicial behaviour is governed by what the judges think about how they *ought* to approach their work. To obtain a sufficient understanding of these normative conceptions, the book incorporates, in addition to interview data, an analysis of the justices' speeches and writings, many of which provide insight into their approach to adjudication or their perceptions of their proper role. Other secondary sources provide insight into the operation of the Court. Particularly illuminating among these documents are several judicial biographies, the authors of which were given rare access to the private papers of the justices.[42] Although such biographies have been criticized as hagiographical, my analysis seeks to place those works as well as the interviews and judicial speeches into a broader context.[43]

Finally, any analysis of the Court's work is incomplete without an examination of its primary product – the case decisions. The most ardent behavioural scholars have dismissed written reasons as mere rationalizations of the justices' preferred policy outcomes.[44] Yet, the institution's legitimacy rests on the justifications for the outcomes it determines. As Russell writes,

> [t]he judicial decision is apt to find its strongest basis of public support in its capacity to persuade those whose rights and interests it affects that it is the correct decision – indeed, the legally required decision. In this sense the reasons which judges give for their decisions, although such reasons may be quite different from the psychological process through which they actually reach their conclusion, are, in our society, the prime basis of the judicial decision's moral authority.[45]

The written decisions also have a genuine impact on the citizenry as they carve out the scope of particular rights, issues, or policies at stake and set the guidelines for lower courts to settle the same issues in similar cases. Moreover, as a product of a distinctly collegial process, the reasons do much more than merely establish winners or losers. The internal procedures of the Court influence the character and quality of the final judgments.[46] Even if the language of reasons distorts or hides political or value-based motivations, they cannot be seen as mere proxies of individual votes because they are a product of deliberation and negotiation among a group of actors. Indeed, it would make little sense for the justices to expend so much of their time producing careful judgments if that is all they were. At a minimum, even if reasons are nothing more than sites of activity for the justices' attitudinally based or strategically minded behaviour, no study of the Court would be complete absent some inquiry into the content of these decisions. Nevertheless, this book is not intended to be a comprehensive analysis of legal doctrine or even of *Charter* jurisprudence. As such, it emphasizes decision-making processes rather than wide-ranging case analysis. Cases are used as illustrations of the Court's approach to particular institutional policies or those that reflect judicial considerations of the Court's appropriate role in matters of substantive policy under the *Charter*. The selection of cases hinged on their applicability to the specific themes examined throughout this book and follow a consideration of their relevance as reflected in existing political science and legal scholarship.

Emphasizing the *Charter*

Although *Charter* cases represent only one part of the Supreme Court of Canada's total caseload, much of this analysis focuses on *Charter* jurisprudence as well as on that document's impact on the institution's role. There are several reasons for this focus. First, the Court itself has determined that "*Charter* values" permeate decisions in all areas of the law.[47] Second, the arrival of the *Charter* is often described in revolutionary terms, not only in having transformed the judicial and legal system but also in having a significant impact on Canadian political culture.[48] As Allan Hutchinson writes, "not only has the Charter taken discrete issues out of the political forums of democratic debate and into the legal arenas of judicial pronouncement, but the whole ethos of rights-talk has saturated Canadian politics and society."[49] Thus, the *Charter* embodies the most prominent instrument of the "judicialization of politics" in Canada.

The Court's justices have themselves acknowledged the *Charter*'s significance for the judicial role. Several years after the first *Charter* cases reached the Court, former Chief Justice Antonio Lamer noted: "I've been a judge for 20 years. And all my professional life I've been used to not sitting in judgment of laws. And I've been chastised whenever I did. Suddenly we're told that every law can be measured to the Charter."[50] Prior to her appointment to the Supreme Court of Canada, current Chief Justice Beverley McLachlin wrote:

> The Charter means that judges are called upon to answer questions they never dreamed they would have to face, such as the right to abortion, the right to work after sixty-five and the right to practice one's profession as one wishes. To make matters more difficult, the Charter has deprived judges of their traditional methods of answering the questions that are put before them. Rules of construction, *stare decisis* and the doctrine of precedent are of limited value when one is not only confronted by new issues, but required to make fundamental value choices in deciding them.[51]

In a very real sense, particularly among members of the Canadian legal community, this understanding of the subjective or value-laden nature of judicial decision making was not fully appreciated until after the *Charter* was created.[52] In fact, Lamer CJ and McLachlin CJ ascribe it directly to the *Charter* itself.

The Supreme Court of Canada has always had the power of judicial review in its adjudication of federalism disputes. Yet, as Robert Sharpe and Kent Roach point out, issues under the *Charter* "are not only more open-ended and apparently less constrained by strict legal principles, but also of greater significance to the average citizen than those relating to federalism."[53] Further, although the 1960 statutory *Canadian Bill of Rights* gave the Court the authority to review federal legislation inconsistent with its provisions, the success of pre-*Charter* rights litigation was extremely limited.[54]

Outline of the Book

The book consists of six chapters. The three leading explanations of judicial decision making – the legal, attitudinal, and strategic approaches – are examined in Chapter 1. Each approach is marked by particular assumptions about the law. The most fundamental divide in this respect is, for the most part, between legal scholars and political scientists. The former tend to view law as being autonomous from politics and consider judges as generally impartial or objective arbiters, while the latter generally see law and legal interpretation as inherently political. Within political science, however, there is a considerable range of views as to what motivates judges, the extent to which legal rules and processes are considered influential, and the nature of judging more broadly. On their own, each of these approaches to explaining judicial behaviour is somewhat narrow and in some instances suffers from serious methodological problems. The chapter concludes by exploring how attention to judicial role conceptions can build bridges between the various understandings of judicial behaviour and account for the myriad of factors that come into play at the Court.

Chapter 2 provides a brief overview of the Supreme Court of Canada's history and its emergence from a relatively obscure component of government to one of the country's most prominent policy-making institutions. It explores this evolution by examining key trends and changes in the justices' conception of their role and the role of the Court. The Court has been altered not only by external political forces (the entrenchment of the *Charter*, for example) but also by decisions made by the justices themselves. Among these decisions are the loosening of the rules of justiciability (the set of legal doctrines that govern whether a matter is suitable for the courts to decide), the increased role of third party interveners, and an expansion of the type of evidence considered in settling cases. These changes have made the Court a distinctly more policy-driven and political institution. Chapter 2 then examines how the contemporary judge has also evolved. It explores how the justices conceive of their role, the law, and impartiality. These views are contrasted with how judicial scholars conceive of ideology. I argue that integrating an analysis of judicial role conceptions allows for a more robust and realistic consideration of the role ideology plays in the justices' decisions. Finally, certain factors have become prominent in the composition of the modern Court, particularly given gender diversity and the appointment of judges with academic backgrounds. The chapter explores how these factors might shape or interact with a justice's personal ideology and how they influence a justice's conception of her role more generally.

The book then provides a picture of the contemporary Court by detailing the role of the chief justice, law clerks, and executive legal officer in Chapter 3. It explores how pressures relating to institutional efficiency impact the Court's decisions and serve as a fundamental constraint on judicial discretion, something rarely explored in the scholarly literature. The third chapter then examines the "front end" of the Court's decision-making process. It analyzes changes in rules and institutional procedure governing the leave-to-appeal process (how the justices choose which cases to hear). It explores the factors that shape the "inputs" for the Court's decisions, including what the justices consider important when it comes to the written arguments put forward by the parties to the case (known as factums) and the work of the law clerks and the support they offer. Finally, this chapter examines the oral hearing and assesses its significance for the final outcome of cases. Placed in this institutional context, the chapter assesses how these various stages of decision making on the Court might be influenced by the justices' role perceptions as opposed to their ideological preferences and how and when certain aspects of these processes might permit strategic behaviour. It concludes that these processes are dictated largely by norms of collegiality, consensus, and legal rules.

The process of deliberation and collaboration that generate the Court's decisions is examined in Chapter 4. The analysis highlights the extent to which judicial conceptions of collegiality – to what extent a justice should work individually or in concert with colleagues, how to utilize law clerks, and what the proper limits of negotiation are – vary significantly among individual justices. These differences explain how the level of consensus on the Court can vary over time as well as the different degrees to which individual justices might pursue attitudinal or strategic behaviour. The chapter provides an in-depth, original analysis of the post-hearing conference negotiations, the drafting of reasons, the circulation of drafts and comments, and the acceptance or refusal of revisions and how these culminate to form the final reasons. It also examines the nature of one of the most controversial aspects of the collegial process – lobbying between justices. The chapter concludes with an exploration of the impact the goal of consensus – and, more specifically, of unanimity – has on the quality and meaning of the final judgments. Where other studies examine the development of unanimous cases on the Court, this chapter explores the effect a goal of unanimity has on decisions, a process virtually ignored in the extant scholarly literature.

Where the fourth chapter explores the justices' consideration of their role within the Court, Chapter 5 examines the justices' views on the role of the Court as a policy-making institution. Central to these considerations is their view on whether the Court is equipped to deal with the moral and policy-laden issues often entailed in judicial review of the *Charter*. The chapter explores how the justices' considerations of their appropriate role in relation to the elected branches of government become particularly pertinent when they must consider the Court's capacity or competence to deal with complex social policy matters. Specifically, it examines the Court's *Charter* cases involving health policy, finding that in practice the justices give surprisingly little consideration to the capacity issue, which in turn gives them wide latitude to decide such cases according to their personal policy preferences.

Chapter 6 explores the Court in relation to the rest of government and society. First, it examines the justices' views on the most prominent account of the inter-institutional relationship involved in *Charter* review – one of a "dialogue" between the Court and the legislatures. Turning to the Court's relationship with broader society, Chapter 6 assesses how justices respond to public opinion and what role it plays in decisions. Finally, it looks at the Court's evolving relationship with the media.

The concluding chapter explores the implications that the book's findings have for the dominant explanations of judicial decision making. It finds that attention to the justices' role perceptions permits a broader and deeper understanding of the sources of the Court's decisions. Where much existing empirical scholarship attempts to identify trends and patterns associated with ideological voting on the part of justices, this book identifies how and in what context such voting may be more or less likely to occur. The conclusion also explores the implications the book's findings have for normative debates about the appointments process, the response legislatures should take to Court rulings, and the role of the Court more broadly.

1
Studying Judicial Behaviour

On back-to-back days in June 2004, the Supreme Court of Canada heard arguments in two cases involving equality rights under the *Canadian Charter of Rights and Freedoms*.[1] In *Auton (Guardian ad litem of) v British Columbia (Attorney General)*, the judges were asked to rule on whether British Columbia was required to fund a particular type of behavioural treatment for children with autism.[2] In *Chaoulli v Quebec (Attorney General)*, they were asked to rule on the constitutionality of a Quebec law prohibiting the purchase of private medical insurance.[3] Both cases were heard by the same seven judges and both enmeshed the Court in a consideration of complex health policy issues. The similarities end there.

In the autism case, it took the justices five months to render a unanimous decision upholding the province's discretion not to fund the treatment. Writing for the Court, Chief Justice Beverley McLachlin explains that the legislation setting out delivery of "medically necessary" services in British Columbia was not discriminatory and that, despite whatever sympathies the justices may have for autistic children, the question of what the public health care system should provide is the proper purview of the legislature. By contrast, the *Chaoulli* decision featured a sharply divided Court that shocked observers by striking down Quebec's prohibition on private medical insurance (with six of the justices evenly split on the *Charter* issue, and the seventh invalidating the law on the basis of Quebec's *Charter of Human Rights and Freedoms*).[4] In written reasons the Court took a full year to produce, the justices disagreed on the equality issues surrounding the case and dove headfirst into the policy details and implications surrounding a law designed to protect the public health care system.

Why the justices exhibited such different behaviour in these two cases is unclear. Some might argue that the autism issue was an "easy" case, that it was so straightforward in terms of the law (or even common sense) that the consensus was obvious. Yet, the Court's ruling overturned decisions by both the original trial court and the provincial court of appeal forcing the province to fund the treatment, repudiating any notion that the correct answer was somehow readily apparent. Although *Auton* would have required the justices to impose positive obligations (and, most contentiously, direct spending) on the government, where *Chaoulli* would not, the Court's willingness to impose such costs in similar cases – such as in directing British Columbia to provide sign language interpreters for deaf hospital patients – makes this distinction an unsatisfactory explanation as well.[5] The risk that the Court would face criticism had it ruled in favour of the *Auton* claimants was minimal, especially in contrast to the firestorm that surrounded the *Chaoulli* decision.[6] It is doubtful that any of the judges would shy away from the autism issue to protect the Court from criticism in one instance, but stride so boldly into one of the most politically contentious issues in the country in the other.

The divergent outcomes in these two cases highlight some of the central questions scholars often confront about the Supreme Court of Canada and judicial behaviour. What are the sources of judicial decisions? Does "the law" matter? What conditions foster unanimous outcomes or divided ones? How do judges interpret the broadly worded, often ambiguous concepts enumerated in the *Charter*? Why does the Court sometimes exhibit "activist" behaviour and at other times appear deferential to legislative choices? Is the Court a legal institution or a political one?

Scholars have developed theories that purport to explain judicial motivations and decision making. Legal explanations of how judges make their decisions generally view questions of precedent, the language of constitutional and statutory provisions, and the application of legal rules to the facts of a given case as being essential to understanding case outcomes. Judges at the Supreme Court of Canada level have some discretion because they deal primarily with cases of "national importance" – those harder, more complex cases in which the law is less settled – and are thus more concerned with the development of principles for the lower courts to follow. Nevertheless, they are said to remain fundamentally constrained by the tenets of the legal approach. There is little evidence of these legal constraints in *Chaoulli*. The justices on either side of the decision cite different precedents to support their views and express divergent interpretations of the factual basis for the case.

Political science explanations of judicial behaviour tend to view judicial decision making as a primarily political and value-laden exercise, where case outcomes are determined largely by the justices' personal policy preferences (that is, their different ideologies or "attitudes"). The disagreement over the policy issues in *Chaoulli* would come as no surprise to anyone espousing this "attitudinal model" of decision making. Yet, the attitudinal perspective fails to account for the Court's decision in *Auton*. A panel of seven justices, the same ones who were presumably ideologically diverse enough to split over the issue of private medical insurance, was somehow able to coalesce around deference to a province refusing to fund treatment for a very sympathetic class of claimant.

A central argument of this book is that the leading approaches to the study of judicial behaviour have difficulty accounting for the differences illustrated in cases such as *Auton* and *Chaoulli* because the focus on judicial policy preferences often impedes attention to the institutional environment and, most importantly, the norms with which the judges approach their work. This chapter explores the basis for this argument through an examination of the dominant methods used in the explanation of judicial behaviour. The preceding discussion of these two cases is intended only to provide an illustration of the problems inherent in giving primacy to single-variable explanations of judicial decision making. While this chapter offers a strong critique of many of the methodological aspects of the dominant models, the book does not aim to refute the underlying theories inasmuch as it aims to supplement them, while providing a shift in focus for the study of judicial behaviour. The chapter develops the approach taken in the remainder of the book, one that accounts for these various perspectives but that provides a more comprehensive and institutionally grounded appreciation of how the Court works.

The Legal View

The classic legal or formalist conception of judicial decision making envisions judging as a mechanical process in which the law is applied in an objective fashion. The emergence of legal realism in the 1920s is often said to have called this view into question by advancing the notion that, rather than discovering or merely interpreting the law, judges create it and are influenced by their personal backgrounds and ideological predilections. Although legal formalism in its purest form has long been cast in doubt (if it ever existed), this traditional view of judging often appears influential in contemporary political rhetoric.[7] The controversy that erupted in 2009 over the fact that then nominee of the Supreme Court of the United States (US Supreme Court) Sonia Sotomayor dared to connect "empathy" to her vision for the role of a judge is illustrative. In order to secure her appointment, Sotomayor avoided defending her previous use of the term during her appearance before the Senate Judiciary Committee as well as not expressing disagreement when its members repeatedly invoked the rhetoric of judge as "neutral umpire," a description Chief Justice John Roberts used at his own committee hearing in 2005.[8] Such rhetoric is surprising, if not completely absurd, given the partisan and openly ideological debates that surround appointments to the American court.

While few contemporary legal theorists would invoke the umpire analogy to describe a judge's role, they generally maintain that the law is substantially autonomous from politics. The modern legal view, broadly speaking, acknowledges that judges (especially at the appellate level) have a degree of discretion, but it maintains that they are constrained by precedent, the text of the constitution and the relevant statutes, and a host of long-held rules. Put simply, legal scholars argue that the law remains an important and independent factor in judicial decision making, even if it does not preordain the outcome of cases in the absolute fashion the pre-realist conception of legal theory may have once asserted.

This is not to say that all legal theorists hold homogenous views on what the law is and how judges ought to decide. The dominant perspective in both the United States and Canada is legal positivism, which conceives of the law as a system of rules that are generally distinct from politics or morality.[9] This view constitutes conventional wisdom within the law profession, legal academic community, and, of course, among most judges. In contrast to legal positivists, Ronald Dworkin argues that law consists of more than rules; it includes principles and so is unavoidably tied to morality.[10] He is perhaps the leading proponent of the idea that judges can obtain the "correct answers" to questions surrounding rights. Competing theories of constitutional interpretation try to prescribe judicial methods that limit the amount of discretion available to judges. So, for example, where variants of originalism maintain that the fixed meaning of the constitutional text or the intent of the framers should guide decisions,[11] the process-based approach put forward by John Hart Ely posits a representation-reinforcing brand of judicial review where judicial decision making avoids the substantive policy choices at hand.[12]

This book does not examine these or other theories of law or constitutional interpretation. As primarily normative treatises about how judges should conceive of law or interpret rights, these theories do not focus on describing and analyzing how judges behave in practice. Dworkin, for instance, is not concerned with how judges deal with specific social facts or how members of appellate courts make compromises to develop consensus, even though he acknowledges the importance of such matters.[13] The "Judge Hercules" that he describes to support his theory is a pre-eminent ideal-type whose interpretive abilities, Dworkin concedes, a real-world judge could never fully attain. Further, although some judges may subscribe to particular theories (US Supreme Court Justice Antonin Scalia is often described as an originalist, for example), many do not. As a result, the legal approach discussed in this chapter refers to the general descriptive account of judging based on legal factors such as precedent, the text of the relevant statutory and constitutional provisions, and rules (such as those that govern the admissibility of evidence).

Critics of the legal approach contend that legal rules provide little to no real constraint on judicial discretion. The harshest detractors have argued that there is no evidence to support the legal model's influence because factors such as precedent or textual analysis have not been (and could not be) subject to empirical falsification.[14] Since justices on both sides of a given decision can cite precedents in their favour, it is not possible to gauge the impact of precedent in any systematic or meaningful way. In making this assertion, these scholars discount important, albeit qualitative, case study research that purports to demonstrate the influence of legal variables – particularly the arguments put forward by the parties to cases – on decision making at the US Supreme Court.[15]

Relatively recent attempts by political scientists to examine the effect of *stare decisis* (precedent) on the US Supreme Court have failed to produce consensus on whether it successfully constrains judicial discretion. By examining a large set of judicial votes in the "progeny" cases of important precedents, Harold Spaeth and Jeffrey Segal find that US Supreme Court justices rarely adhere to precedents with which they previously disagreed.[16] Legal scholars are unlikely to be persuaded by this study, however, because the authors limit their analysis to the justices who voted in dissent in the precedent-setting case (that is, they include only justices voting in a later case who were on the Court when the precedent was established, and they do not include justices who voted in the majority in the precedent-setting case because that vote coincided with their "revealed preferences." In their view, counting such votes would not demonstrate that precedent was responsible for the subsequent vote).

Given that they operationalize their testing of precedent in such a narrow manner, it is unsurprising that Spaeth and Segal find little evidence of its effect. The modern legal model does not necessarily call for adherence to *stare decisis* in this rather mechanical manner. Unlike lower court judges, Supreme Court justices are not required to adhere to a precedent case in which they have already articulated a dissent. Legal scholars find it entirely unsurprising that justices would maintain opposition to a precedent when they have already articulated their opposition.[17] As Howard Gillman explains, this is not to say *stare decisis* is irrelevant, only that the narrow research design employed by Spaeth and Segal does not really capture it:

> We are left, then, with something of a paradox. Behavioralists want to force legalists into offering testable hypotheses, so that beliefs about law's influence can be verified by a kind of scientific knowledge that behavioralists consider more authoritative; however, legalists believe that doing such tests has the effect of changing the concept of legal influence so that it no longer represents what they believe.[18]

In some ways, then, Spaeth and Segal's testing of the legal model only re-inforces for legal scholars that political science perspectives treat the legal approach as a "straw man."[19]

The "jurisprudential regimes" approach examines the influence of legal factors in a way that is more consistent with the modern legal view of judg-ing. Mark Richards and Herbert Kritzer look for the influence of such regimes, which they define as the confluence of balancing rules and case factors that the Court establishes in precedent-setting cases and which structure later pertinent cases in the same area of law.[20] The authors note that legal scholars – unlike Segal and Spaeth – "do not talk about the Court creating precedents that define or predict outcomes of future Supreme Court cases. Rather [they] focus on how the decision structures created by the justices will affect future decisions."[21] Instead of *determining* future outcomes, the regimes established in precedent-setting cases *guide* future decision making by outlining cat-egories and rules for balancing, such as "compelling interest," "incitement of imminent illegal action," or "undue burden." Following these guidelines is not a mechanical process of obeying rules such as "if X, then decide Y." Instead, jurisprudential regimes involve reflecting on various factors and determining whether these factors exceed a particular threshold.[22]

Other political scientists, while acknowledging the potential of the juris-prudential regimes approach, remain unconvinced.[23] Nonetheless, the idea of jurisprudential regimes remains appealing, and scholars continue to apply more refined statistical approaches to show their effect. Yet, as useful as these innovations may be, the methodological rigidity exhibited by some critics of the legal approach in the American judicial politics literature is limiting because of their tendency to accept evidence of the impact of legal or other variables only in the form of quantitative proof. As is explored further in the context of the leading political science approaches to studying judicial behaviour, statistical modelling of decision making may not be capable of capturing fundamental variables that are not conducive to quantitative measurement. Even Kritzer and Richards point out that exclusive reliance on statistical tests may miss some of the nuance and complexity of jurispru-dential regime theory, particularly as it applies to the way judicial reasoning is framed in the Court's written decisions.[24]

Nevertheless, it does not help the credibility of the legalist approach that judges are usually less than forthright about the role that values and policy choices often play in their work. When Roberts US CJ talks about a judge as an umpire it simply rings untrue. Similarly, former Supreme Court of Canada Justice Claire L'Heureux-Dubé declared to a parliamentary committee exam-ining reform of the appointments process in 2004: "We talk about ideology, but very few of us have any. You may not perceive that, but we look at a case by first reading and knowing the facts and then reading the briefs, and then we make up our minds."[25] Statements such as these promote the belief among some political scientists that judicial reasoning serves only to mask political preferences and that, consciously or subconsciously, judges have constructed a smokescreen of legal verbiage to maintain authority and that they continue to exert policy influence.

The Attitudinal Model

Political scientists have studied judicial behaviour with respect to the US Supreme Court since the early twentieth century.[26] C. Herman Pritchett, who is credited as one of the first political scientists to draw on legal realism to examine Supreme Court decision making, examined dissents, concurrences, voting blocs, and the ideological configurations of the Court's non-unanimous decisions to conclude that judicial differences of opinion were a result of the conscious or unconscious preferences and prejudices of the justices.[27] Building on such work, and influenced by the "behavioural revolution" in political science, other scholars developed a full attitudinal model of judicial decision making.[28] With lifelong judicial tenure and significant control of the docket, attitudinalists see Supreme Court judges as particularly free to decide cases based on their ideological preferences. Segal and Spaeth, the leading proponents of the modern attitudinal model, write:

> The attitudinal model represents a melding together of key concepts from legal realism, political science, psychology, and economics. This model holds that the Supreme Court decides disputes in light of the facts of the case vis-à-vis the ideological attitudes and values of the justices. Simply put, Rehnquist votes the way he does because he is extremely conservative; Marshall voted the way he did because he was extremely liberal.[29]

They argue that legal explanations of judicial reasoning, such as the use of precedent, textual analysis of statutes or the Constitution, or framers' intent, "serve only to rationalize the Court's decisions and to cloak the reality of the Court's decision-making process."[30]

The attitudinal model uses measures of the justices' ideological positions and, controlling for other variables such as case facts, predicts judicial votes in a given set of cases. In the past, the justices' votes were themselves used as measures of ideology, which created obvious circularity problems – if votes are explained by ideology then using those votes to obtain the initial measure of ideology renders the findings of the model meaningless. Segal and Spaeth claim that one solution to this circularity issue was to use the justices' past votes to obtain the measure and then to predict a latter set of votes. They note, however, that this method "nevertheless begs the question as to what explains the justices' past votes."[31] To obtain "exogenous" measures of the justices' ideological positions, scholars have used the partisan affiliation of the appointing president or prime minister as a proxy. This measure is also fairly weak because judges do not always behave as the person appointing them expects. The most popular measures of attitudes employed by contemporary scholars are based on content analyses of newspaper editorials that label Supreme Court nominees prior to confirmation as liberal or conservative (at least as it pertains to civil rights and liberties issues). Attitudinalists claim that while this measure might be less precise than relying on votes, it prevents circularity issues.

Early efforts to apply the attitudinal approach to the Supreme Court of Canada were sparse, producing limited results.[32] One of the earliest *Charter*-era studies attributed to the attitudinal school of thought mirrors the work of attitudinal pioneers in the United States by examining the personal attributes of the Court's justices serving from 1949 to 1985.[33] Looking at variables such as the justices' region of origin, the party of the appointing prime minister, and judicial and political experience, the authors find that the "attributes model" is able to predict how the justices vote in civil rights and economics cases. Justices were found to be most "conservative" when they were non-Catholic, Québécois, politically inexperienced, and an appointee of a Conservative prime minister. They were most "liberal" when they were non-Québécois, Catholic, politically experienced, and appointed by a Liberal prime minister other than Mackenzie King. This study was recently found to be time bound. A study extending and revising the attribute model through the year 2000 finds that, in part due to the Court's heavier emphasis on civil liberties cases in the *Charter* era, gender and regional characteristics have come to be more important than partisan affiliations relating to appointment.[34] Donald Songer's 2008 book finds support for the importance of the party of appointing prime minister, the region, and religion.[35]

The full attitudinal model has only recently been applied to the Supreme Court of Canada by C.L. Ostberg and Matthew Wetstein.[36] Their 2007 book, which measures the justices' attitudes by performing a content analysis of newspaper editorials, finds that ideology plays a significant role in the justices' decisions. They explain that the role of these attitudes, however, is less definitive and more subtle than in the US context, and they acknowledge "that other factors, such as the cultural and historical legacy of parliamentary supremacy, the institutional norm of collegiality, and recent criticism of activist rulings, to name a few, help suppress attitudinal decision making by the post-Charter justices."[37] Finally, despite confirming the major premise of the attitudinal model, Ostberg and Wetstein note that not all judges can be labelled attitudinalists, strategists, or legal pragmatists, adding that more research is needed that sheds light on the inner workings of the Court.[38]

The most fundamental criticism of the attitudinal model is that it paints an extremely reductionist and instrumentalist portrait of decision making. For decades, this view prompted many legal scholars to ignore or dismiss the assertions of political scientists and their evidence. Attitudinal scholars espouse a narrow and simplistic conception of ideology. Despite the controls put in place to gauge the impact of attitudes relative to variables such as the justices' gender or relevant case facts, too much of the decision-making context is left out to provide a realistic portrayal of how judges make up their minds. Yet, for the proponents of the attitudinal model, its simplicity is a virtue. Modelling is not meant to provide a comprehensive depiction of the real world. Rather, by focusing on crucial aspects of reality, a model is said to "explain" a high percentage of behaviour through prediction.[39]

In both the leading American and Canadian applications of this model, however, scholars are able to predict, on average, fewer than three out of every four judicial votes. Even this statistic only applies to sets of cases in areas of law to which the attitudinal model is successful – in some areas, even those where one might expect political attitudes to be salient, the model fails.[40] This means that a significant portion of the justices' decisions are left unexplained by mere reference to attitudes. Segal and Spaeth suggest that potential errors in their model, such as incomplete specification of relevant case stimuli or the lack of precision in the newspaper ideology measures, mean that the attitudinal model is likely even stronger than their empirical evidence demonstrates.[41] This assertion seems unconvincing, given that any lack of precision in the ideological measures could just as easily make the results appear stronger than they actually are rather than weaker.

The thin conceptual understanding of ideology seriously reduces the attitudinal model's explanatory power. Proponents of the model do not provide an explanation of how the simple liberal-conservative dichotomy operates when applied to complex cases. James Johnson writes that progress in political science is made "not just to the extent that our theories survive empirical tests but also to the extent that our theories are 'well-founded' in the sense that we specify more clearly the mechanisms that animate them."[42] In a critique of the literature surrounding the study of political culture, Johnson contends that many of the leading scholars "define political culture in such a way that it is susceptible to analysis via survey methods," ignoring conceptual developments in other fields, such as anthropology.[43] Further, political culture scholars "offer no plausible account – causal, functional or otherwise – of how political culture 'works,' or how it motivates individual action or generates persistence or change in aggregate political or economic behavior."[44] This criticism applies equally, if not even more forcefully, to the problematic treatment that attitudinal scholars give the concept of ideology. The manner in which ideology is measured makes it impossible for scholars to specify the mechanisms at work between ideology and decisions. Judicial attitudes are treated simplistically, as one-to-one determinants of behaviour. Thus, even when the attitudinal model produces regularities that are statistically well established, the findings "do not so much *provide* an explanation as *stand in need* of one."[45]

However thin the attitudinal model is from a conceptual standpoint, and regardless of any arguments about the strength of the existing findings, the most damaging aspects of the approach stem from fatal methodological problems inherent in the way attitudinalists model judicial behaviour. First, problems pertaining to measuring judicial ideologies make the model inherently circular. Even ideological measures based on newspaper editorials about judicial nominees are not, contrary to the attitudinalists' claim, fully "exogenous" or independent, as they are no doubt often based on the judge's past voting records or views that journalists may label conservative or liberal but which could be premised on legal or other considerations of the nominee. As a result, the attitudinal model confirms its premise because the measures it derives for ideology are based on the very outcomes that it seeks to demonstrate are influenced by ideology in the first place.

Frank Cross argues that serious conceptual and methodological difficulties call into question exactly what the attitudinal model predicts:

> This taxonomical problem with the attitudinal model is a result of its methodology. The researchers take a legal issue, such as defendants' rights, and characterize prostate positions as politically conservative and the opposite as liberal. When the researchers find some judges consistently liberal or conservative in decisions on defendants' rights, they conclude that politics must explain the consistency of the outcomes. Typically, they ignore the possibility that some legal factor might explain the same consistency of result. In statistical terms, a legal issue might be highly collinear with a political issue. In such a circumstance, what may appear to be a statistically significant correlation with politics might actually be attributable to a legal variable.[46]

If a judge confronts a particular issue of law in a consistent way given his or her views about what some legal factor indicates is the proper way to decide, then it is entirely conceivable that such a judge's *legal* consistency could produce results that attitudinalists interpret as *political* consistency.

Another problem stems from the way attitudinalists classify certain case outcomes. In their examination of freedom of expression cases, Ostberg and Wetstein consider judicial votes supporting *Charter* claims to be liberal, while votes rejecting such claims are regarded as conservative. Yet, it is questionable whether the Supreme Court of Canada's decisions giving constitutional protection to tobacco advertising and other forms of commercial expression should be considered "liberal" decisions or whether rulings that uphold election campaign spending limits should be considered "conservative." Indeed, conservatives have been at the forefront of mobilization in opposition to campaign spending limits.[47] In some areas, it appears as though these classification problems actually undercut the theory Ostberg and Wetstein are testing.[48] Songer's finding that the party of the appointing prime minister is a significant factor in ideological cleavages on the Court might be questioned on a similar basis given that his analysis adopts the same type of classification system for judicial votes.

Measurement and classification issues are not the only reasons to question the usefulness of the attitudinal approach. Significantly, since the attitudinal model is predicated on ideological differences of the justices accounting for how they vote, it cannot account for unanimous cases.[49] Another criticism stems from the fact that the attitudinal model cannot account for instances when justices change their minds about the outcome of a particular case. This critique was introduced early on in the development of the attitudinal model by J. Woodford Howard, who asserted that evidence of voting "fluidity" – the fact that judges sometimes change their minds between their vote at the Court's conference and the final vote – presents a serious problem for an approach premised on the notion that ideology is the driving factor in judicial decisions. As he writes, "if a vote or an opinion has changed in response to a multiplicity of intra-court influences before its public exposure, how reliable is that vote or opinion as an indicator of attitude, ideology, or, if one pleases, predilection?"[50]

Empirical work on voting fluidity finds that judges on the "Vinson Court" (1946-53) voted the same way at the original conference votes and at the final decision stage in 88 percent of the cases.[51] Later work by Timothy Hagle and Spaeth interprets the pattern of vote shifts as consistent with the attitudinal model, showing a high proportion of instances in which the judge switched from the majority to the minority that is "ideologically closer" to one of the justices in dissent.[52] Both of these studies rely on a very narrow set of cases and thus do not substantially refute Howard's basic contention: group interaction is likely to have an effect on ideological decision making.[53] Further, because documentary evidence of the justices' vote intentions is only available for the conference stage, the incidence of vote fluidity is likely much higher, as justices are also likely to change their minds at the initial research and oral hearing stages. I explore vote fluidity on the Supreme Court of Canada more fully in Chapters 3 and 4.

Finally, the attitudinal perspective cannot explain the effort justices put into writing reasons, particularly dissents and concurrences. If adherence to precedent is so thin, it makes little sense that judges would spend so much time crafting the logic of a decision or collaborating over the wording of its provisions. Even if this is largely an exercise in masking ideological preferences, it cannot explain why a judge would bother writing a separate concurrence when she could just sign onto a majority opinion that already matches her favoured policy outcome. As Cross writes, "a concurrence is exclusively a legal model activity, because the ideologically favored result is reached, yet the judge expends her resources to write an additional opinion. The pure attitudinal model fails to explain why a judge would prefer any particular legal rationale for a given result."[54]

The attitudinal model has long been the leading conception of judicial decision making in American political science literature. Given its underlying intuitive appeal, this is not surprising. A careful reading of either the American or Canadian supreme court's most prominent decisions makes clear that judges do not rely solely on objective legal rules or standards. Political values play at least some part in judicial reasoning. It is understandable that behaviouralists would want to develop an approach that finds systematic evidence of the role ideology plays in decisions. Unfortunately, as the preceding discussion makes clear, the attitudinal model does not present a complete picture of how courts and judges operate. The theoretical and methodological difficulties I have explored have not gone unnoticed. Attitudinalism has been challenged by two "new institutionalist" perspectives.[55] New institutionalism, also referred to as neo-institutionalism, emerged as a response to the behavioural revolution in political science. Whereas behaviouralism generally envisions the study of politics as the objective, usually quantitative, analysis of observed individual behaviour to explain and predict this behaviour within a political system, new institutionalism re-emphasizes the relative autonomy and influence of institutions on political decision making. The following two sections explore two variants of new institutionalist thought: rational choice and historical institutionalism.

The Strategic Model

The strategic model is closely related to the attitudinal conception in that it also assumes that judges pursue their policy preferences, but it draws on rational choice theory to argue that in order to secure the majority decision on a multi-member court, judges must make strategic choices. Thus, judges may not vote according to their "sincere preferences" if they are not convinced the outcome of a case will be decided in their favour. In making decisions, they must consider the likely votes of their colleagues on the bench and the potential reaction of other actors in the system, including the legislative or executive branches of government, and modulate their choices accordingly. Walter F. Murphy is credited with bringing the strategic account of judicial decision making to prominence.[56] Through an analysis of US Supreme Court cases, congressional hearings, and interview data, Murphy shows that, as single-minded seekers of policy, judges care about the ultimate state of the law, broadly defined.

Attitudinalists are not insensitive to this early strategic work. Segal and Spaeth acknowledge that opinion writers have to move beyond their sincere preferences to convince colleagues and garner a majority decision, especially in closely divided cases.[57] They still expect that attitudes will play the crucial role in shaping decisions but recognize that they are not always the only factor. Thus, in more recent scholarship, they limit the attitudinal model in its pure form to the final decision on the merits. In their view, ideology is most likely to influence a justice's final vote, but it may not be as strong a factor, for example, in the justice's decision to grant or deny *certiorari* (known in Canada as leave to appeal) to hear a case.

One reason the strategic model was not initially as influential as the attitudinal model is that evidence of strategic behaviour was largely anecdotal. In 1979, journalists Bob Woodward and Scott Armstrong published *The Brethren,* which at the time was an unprecedented account of the internal workings of the US Supreme Court.[58] The book is based on confidential interviews with several justices, more than 170 former law clerks, and dozens of former US Supreme Court employees as well as internal memoranda, letters, notes taken at conferences, and other documents belonging to several justices. It provides a detailed description of how the interaction between justices – specifically, instances of behind-the-scenes lobbying for votes and negotiated compromises over the language of decisions – directly affected the outcome of cases. Several more "insider" accounts have since been published.[59] Assessed in relation to the standards of academic scholarship, the narratives presented in such works might be criticized as amounting to little more than storytelling. Indeed, conversations between justices and detailed accounts of their supposed motivations offered as fact in *The Brethren* and other historical or journalistic works are often based on one-sided accounts.[60] Yet, such studies are frequently cited as providing empirical support for the strategic conception of Supreme Court decision making.[61]

Ever since Murphy's original analysis, researchers examining strategic decision making have generally relied on case studies rather than systemic studies that thoroughly examine the patterns underlying interdependent behaviour.[62] According to Lee Epstein and Jack Knight, because work such as Murphy's early strategic analysis arose in the context of the behavioural revolution, with its emphasis on statistically derived evidence, it is little wonder that scholars ultimately spurned the approach.[63] Work such as Murphy's and others' relied on qualitative evidence from Court records and justices' private papers rather than on readily quantifiable data such as votes. With the new institutionalism prompting renewed attention to the importance that institutional context has for behaviour, scholars once again began taking advantage of such data.

Epstein and Knight's own qualitative analysis of US Supreme Court records and the justices' private papers uncovers systematic evidence of strategic behaviour on the court, including instances of bargaining among justices in more than two-thirds of cases, examples of "dispute avoidance" by the justices to steer clear of collisions with Congress or the president, and decisions to grant or deny *certiorari* based on whether the case outcome is likely to coincide with the justices' policy preferences.[64] In another leading study of the strategic model, Forrest Maltzman, James Spriggs, and Paul Wahlbeck use original data from the US Supreme Court's opinion assignment sheets, docket sheets, and circulation records to systematically test a multivariate model of strategic interaction and examine patterns of interdependent behaviour on the court.[65] Their analysis reveals how strategic decision making influences the choices the chief justice makes in assigning opinions when politically salient cases are under review. Further, while ideology plays a discernable role on an individual justice's decision to join a majority opinion, a variety of other factors have a statistically significant impact, including whether the opinion author has been unco-operative with a particular justice in the past, whether the majority coalition is smaller and therefore more likely to succumb to bargaining, whether the case has a higher degree of political salience, whether the particular judge has greater experience, and whether there is more time left in the court's term.[66]

Strategic scholars argue that their results show that the legal reasoning in written opinions, rather than just the votes on the case, is important and that justices prefer legal rules that reflect their policy preferences. The evidence, the authors contend, illustrates that rational actors rarely act solely on their preferences. For attitudinalists, the patterns of behaviour uncovered in these studies do not persuasively show that factors other than policy preferences serve as significant forces behind judicial behaviour. Segal and Spaeth contend that the strategic model fails as a "model" because no rational choice study of the US Supreme Court has taken advantage of an equilibrium analysis,[67] the tool they feel makes rational choice explanation powerful: "Similar to Murphy's work, the most prominent of the recent rational choice works on the Supreme Court do not derive or adapt equilibrium solutions, for example, they do not demonstrate that interactions among the justices constitute a best response to a best response."[68] For behaviouralists, the central problem with strategic studies is their lack of *predictive* value, something which Segal and Spaeth argue makes the attitudinal model so compelling. Further, the leading strategic works are generally consistent with, or at least not inconsistent with, earlier attitudinal works given that they find ideology plays a key role in decision making.[69]

Segal and Spaeth's critique belies the dominant view among rational choice theorists that in politics, unique equilibria can rarely be identified.[70] As Epstein and Knight point out, strategic bargaining by judges and other tactical decisions they make take place within a complex institutional framework.[71] A justice must consider her decisions in the context of the rules governing the relationship she has with her colleagues as well as the relationship between the court and other institutions of government. Various elements of uncertainty generated by the multiplicity of considerations at play make it impossible for actors to know what constitutes "a best response" or even that they would always make the same choices every time they are faced with similar circumstances. Without going down the path of engaging in a broader epistemological debate about Segal and Spaeth's questionable insistence that real explanation is only possible via prediction, this particular critique of the existing studies on strategic behaviour reflects the same scientific rigidity that impairs the usefulness of their attitudinal model: it assumes ideal situations and ignores institutional context.

More importantly, strategic scholars acknowledge that their approach is complementary to attitudinal theory but argue that their model is more complete because it takes a more comprehensive view by accounting for the various processes and structures beyond attitudes that shape decision behaviour. The strategic approach moves beyond a narrow focus on vote outcomes. According to its proponents,

> [w]hen institutional analysis is placed within the logic of rational choice, not only can theoretically sound hypotheses be generated, positing relationships which explain a significant amount of variance in judicial dissent behavior, but the rather disparate findings in the judicial literature on dissent behavior can be comprehensively integrated. Quite simply, the neo-institutional perspective bridges the gap between traditional institutional analysis and attitudinal theory.[72]

The strategic approach treats institutions as "players in their own right, and the primary unit of analysis is institutions that empower some actors and define sanctions."[73]

For this reason, the strategic model has forced even the most ardent attitudinalists to acknowledge that institutional constraints exist and influence judicial choices at multiple stages of the Court's decision-making process (if not at the final voting stage). As a result, some scholars assert that a strategic understanding "is now the closest thing to a conventional wisdom about judicial behavior."[74]

Despite this assertion, the strategic model remains susceptible to many of the same critiques as the attitudinal approach. Many of the strategic studies conceive of institutions in the narrow sense of seeing them as a set of rules within which the game of maximizing self-interest takes place.[75] Further, like the behaviouralist approach, the strategic model holds largely instrumentalist and reductionist assumptions about judicial decision making.

Critics suggest that rational choice models recognize "at best a narrow subset of possible human standards."[76] While any number of goals could conceivably be examined under a rational choice model, most strategic scholars see implementing policy preferences as the goal of judges. Noting that policy goals are not the only inspiration for judges' decisions, Richard Posner's economic analysis suggests that other factors might include seeking prestige or popularity or seeking more leisure time. Posner, himself a judge on the Seventh Circuit of the US Court of Appeals, maintains that "judges are rational, and they pursue instrumental and consumption goals of the same general kind and in the same general way that private persons do."[77] Without a more robust consideration of the ways in which the institutional environment helps to shape and even produce these different motivations, the strategic model cannot identify the circumstances under which the justices' strategic goals might change.

Insight into strategic behaviour on the Supreme Court of Canada is limited by a lack of available data. Only a handful of studies have examined strategic decision making, and those that have done so focus on particular aspects of the Court's work or on specific case examples. Scholars in Canada do not have access to docket sheets, internal memoranda, and private notes of the justices that have made the approach more comprehensive in the US context. Systematic analysis of any strategic behaviour at the Court may not be possible until researchers have access to such papers, which are currently restricted in the national archives.

Lori Hauseggar and Stacia Haynie examine panel assignments on the Supreme Court of Canada to see whether chief justices act strategically and assign particular justices with the aim of pursuing their own policy goals.[78] The authors find that for cases involving salient civil rights and liberties issues the chief justice is more likely to assign judges with close policy preferences. They suggest that institutional constraints, such as workload and the desire to have Quebec judges assigned to panels for cases coming out of that province, may inhibit some strategic behaviour. Roy Flemming provides the only systematic investigation into how the Supreme Court of Canada selects cases for judicial review.[79] He finds that the use of panels at the leave to appeal stage and the absence of an *en banc* tradition at the appeal stage complicates and adds uncertainty to justices' ability to act strategically. It is possible that if the Court's justices are being strategic in their decisions to grant leave, the institutional processes obscure the behaviour from study.

Christopher Manfredi uses strategic thinking to explain the Court's different remedial actions in two prominent cases, the abortion case *R. v Morgentaler* in 1988[80] and *Charter* protection for sexual orientation in *Vriend v Alberta* a decade later.[81] The Court's remedy in *Vriend* was to "read in" sexual orientation by effectively amending Alberta's *Individual Rights Protection Act,* which Manfredi describes as "a rarely used and relatively intrusive remedy that imposes specific policy choices on legislatures."[82] Manfredi views the remedy as particularly strong because the omission of sexual orientation was a conscious choice, rather than mere oversight, of the Alberta legislature. The strategic approach suggests that one explanation for different levels of remedial activism in the two cases "is the judicial assessment of the potential for successful legislative resistance to the Supreme Court's judgments."[83] Manfredi argues that the existence of a politically viable notwithstanding clause – which under section 33 of the *Charter* allows legislatures to temporarily suspend the effects of judicial decisions – during the *Morgentaler* deliberations meant the risk of legislative response was high. By the time the Court was deciding *Vriend,* the notwithstanding clause had fallen into political disrepute following Quebec's enactment of section 33 after the 1988 sign law case.[84] The lack of any systematic account of strategic interaction on the Court makes it difficult for Manfredi to draw on other sources for further evidence.

More recently, Wetstein and Ostberg have examined strategic leadership on the Court, finding that the voting behaviour of each of the three most recent chief justices changed significantly on becoming chief, leading them to write more majority opinions and fewer dissenting opinions.[85] They found that Chief Justices Brian Dickson and Antonio Lamer emerged as "task leaders" who were able to guide the Court through control of majority coalitions, whereas, in her first few years as chief justice, Beverley McLachlin has been a pre-eminent "social leader" through an effort to increase the level of consensus on the Court. The ability of the chief justice to strike panels and assign decisions is an important institutional feature in the Canadian context. The authors note that researchers "need to be sensitive to the possibility that other novel intra-Court characteristics might augment or hinder strategic choice behaviour on the part of justices."[86] The next section explores how such intra-Court characteristics might be identified.

Historical Institutionalism

Historical institutionalists consider the broader structural and institutional factors that shape judicial decisions. These scholars challenge the instrumentalist view of judicial decisions as merely the aggregate effect of individual behaviour. Historical institutionalism considers norms, values, and ideas to be an integral part of the analysis, going beyond the strategic model's consideration of institutional rules and the actions of other political actors. Central to the approach adopted here is a focus on judicial "role perceptions" – the institutional actors' sense of duty, obligation, or recognition that their actions are inherently meaningful – which inform the justices' behaviour in complex ways that intersect with ideological, strategic, and legal considerations. As Howard Gillman and Cornell Clayton write, institutional actors "come to believe that their position imposes upon them an obligation to act in accordance with particular expectations and responsibilities."[87] The choices and behaviour of actors in turn shape the institutional context in a reciprocal fashion.

The study of the judicial role is hardly new. Early in the development of the judicial politics field, Pritchett identified what he felt were the two principal factors in judicial decisions in civil liberties cases: a judge's ideology and his or her role obligations.[88] From the 1960s through the 1980s, various scholars examined a thin notion of the judicial role, often by using interview or questionnaire data to identify and analyze appellate or trial court judges' self-ascribed views of the propriety of their involvement in law making.[89] Most of these studies defined judicial role perception or orientation as a dichotomy between "activists" versus "restraintists" or "law interpreters" versus "law makers." One of the most compelling examples of this research, relying on questionnaires answered by twenty-six judges from the five Florida district courts of appeal, examines the interaction of the role variables with attitudinal measures to demonstrate that both liberal and conservative judges with more "activist" orientations permit their political attitudes more influence in their decisions than do their "restraintist" counterparts.[90]

This small body of research leads James Gibson to provide an oft-cited definition of how judges decide: "Judges' decisions are a function of what they prefer to do, tempered by what they think they ought to do, but constrained by what they perceive is feasible to do."[91] Nonetheless, the application of role theory using this particular approach seems to have fallen out of use. Attitudinalists dismiss the influence of such role concepts for two reasons. First, there is no data available to input the role concept as a variable into models at the Supreme Court level. Second, and more fundamentally, these scholars view notions of "restraint" as little more than rationalizations used by justices to further their substantive policy preferences.[92]

Yet, just as the historical institutionalists are guided by a much broader, more porous conception of institutions, I argue that judicial scholars should incorporate into theories of decision making a more expansive notion of the judicial role. While these earlier studies allow scholars to input narrow role orientations as simple variables into statistical models, an interpretivist, institutionally grounded vision of the judicial role would necessarily account for institutional culture, collegiality, and a judge's broader perspective on her – and her institution's – place in the rest of the political system and wider society. This sense of the primacy an actor's role perceptions can have on behaviour requires an historical institutionalist account. As Gillman and Clayton write,

[c]ounting votes and other positivist methodologies can describe a particular action or behavior, but not the motive, purpose, or meaning of that action or behavior. This is because the same action has different meanings in different contexts ... Thus, the assumption that similar votes in similar cases have similar motives and meanings cannot hold unless the cases are placed in similar historical and contextual space.[93]

What the attitudinal and strategic models appear to have difficultly accounting for is the simple fact that two judges taking the same action might have completely different motivations. It is unrealistic to assume strategic policy considerations for every instance in which a judge changes her vote, augments her views, or alters the language or reasoning of decisions. Such actions might be strategic or they may stem from a belief in institutional norms such as consensus or the need for clarity.[94] In other words, legal and institutional factors are sometimes at play, even when decisions appear to be predicated on a judge's policy preferences. Existing scholarship on judicial behaviour pays little attention to the distinction between motives and behaviour, at least to the extent that the methodology employed by the attitudinal studies explored in this chapter take the motives for granted. My analysis will demonstrate how other motivations can play a role at different stages of the process even if the behaviour itself appears consistent with behaviour driven by attitudes.

An historical institutional analysis would account not only for how formal structures and rules affect individual justices but also how informal norms influence, constrain, and shape their decision making as well as the very motivations for those decisions. This particular pattern of analysis is what distinguishes neo-institutionalism from traditional pre-behaviouralist political science (that is, it is what is said to put the "new" in "new institutionalism"). Rather than simply describing the institutional structure and the patterns of behaviour therein, the goal is to assess the reciprocal effects the institution and its actors have on each other. An historical institutional account can capture much more of the actual forces at play in judicial decision making because the approach explicitly seeks to accommodate as full a picture as realistically possible of the context, both in terms of the institution's internal environment and its external political setting. This approach does not discount attitudinal or strategic motives or behaviour but, rather, shifts the focus of analysis to the judicial role in a way that captures more of the intervening and interdependent factors that come into play.

Critics of historical institutionalism do not see it as providing sufficient analytic clarity or evidentiary rigor to accomplish these goals. Referring to the approach as post-positivist, Segal and Spaeth complain that by relying on justices' sense of obligation, post-positivist scholars reduce the legal approach to something that could never be proven because virtually any decision *can be* consistent with it if all that is required is for justices to convince themselves that their decisions are legally appropriate. The authors claim that "by accepted standards of scientific research" the post-positivist brand of neo-institutionalism simply cannot generate a valid explanation of judicial decision making because it is not falsifiable.[95]

On first glance, this complaint may seem compelling. As it seems so dependent on a contextualist understanding of the institution, historical institutionalism cannot lead to law-like explanations of behaviour. Yet, the critique becomes less of a concern when we take into account the pitfalls of the attitudinal model described earlier. The conclusions drawn by behaviouralists both about the concepts they attempt to operationalize and the results they draw from their modelling are themselves very much part of an interpretive process.[96] There is little reason to be persuaded that the manner in which attitudinalists conceptualize a variable such as ideology or assess the results of their statistical correlations are any more correct or legitimate than a careful, albeit qualitative, examination of the deeper institutional context.

Historical institutionalists are aware of the potential problems implicit in their approach, particularly the threat of raising a structure versus agency debate. If scholars blur the distinction between the institutional context and the actors' motives or ideas too far, then it becomes impossible to develop a reasonable picture of the influences on decision making. As Clayton writes, "if ideas and institutions are inseparable, if everything is connected to everything else, then it is unclear where new institutional analysis leads."[97] Historical institutionalism clearly stands as more of an "approach" than a full-fledged theory of judicial decision making. The utility of its premises, however, is that rather than attempting to explain decisions through prediction, the approach seeks to impart a more comprehensive understanding of the complex processes at play. As a result, historical institutionalists can take a diverse, cosmopolitan path to examining judicial behaviour, one that draws on, and builds bridges between, legal, attitudinal, and strategic theory.

The contemporary judicial politics literature offers many avenues through which these types of linkages are open for exploration. For example, recent work that has serious implications for the attitudinal model uncovers systematic evidence that justices' preferences change, even over short periods of time, after they are on the bench.[98] These studies, in which attitudinalist scholars Segal and Spaeth take part, are careful to note that nothing in attitudinal theory presumes attitudinal consistency, although they admit that this very assumption is embedded in empirical testing of the model, particularly because the "measures" of judicial ideologies are based on newspaper scores at the time of nomination and are treated as independent variables. The authors fail to elaborate on the potential implications for the attitudinal model or offer an explanation as to what causes such preference changes. Historical institutionalists would argue that the source of such change is obvious – the institutional rules and environment, in addition to the actors' role obligations, serve to shape and constrain the exogenous variables, such as ideology, that also comprise justices' preferences. On coming to the Court, judges may give more or less weight to their role perceptions in decision making. The approach would also envision preferences oscillating as a result of changes in the Court's external political environment.

The historical institutionalist account can also seek to accommodate a more realistic understanding of the justices' motivations. Lawrence Baum suggests that in many ways the strategic approach looks unrealistic, given that individual justices have little capacity to affect outcomes nor do they gain much in the way of tangible benefits from advancing favoured policies.[99] He argues that the evidence amassed by behaviouralists and rational choice scholars tells us very little about the motivations at play, as they really only demonstrate that the different outcomes judges reach accord to differences in policy preferences. By setting aside complexities – such as attempting to account for various motivations on the part of judges – and seeking prediction rather than "deep explanation," these models limit our understanding of judicial behaviour.[100] By examining judges' "audiences," Baum contends that we can understand the "motivational basis for patterns of judgments that are *incorporated into the dominant models*" as well as those patterns that go beyond them.[101] His basic point is that, like any professionals, judges care about what people think about them. For this reason, the esteem of their colleagues, the wider legal community, and even the media and the public at large matter. Attention to the reaction of these various audiences can consciously or subconsciously rein in attitudinal or strategic behaviour.

The new institutionalist literature developed in large part as a response to the dominance of behaviouralism in American political science. Behaviouralism failed to develop into the main paradigm of the Canadian discipline, where an emphasis on descriptive and normative work relating to institutions remained strong. So it should not be surprising to find that Canadian scholars draw from new institutionalism, as Gerald Baier does in his examination of the importance of judicial doctrine for federalism.[102] More common is to find elements consistent with new institutionalism *implicit* in scholarship. Indeed, scholars of the Supreme Court of Canada and the *Charter* are explicit about their underlying assumptions about judicial review and have taken account of factors fully consistent with the new institutionalism paradigm.

Christopher Manfredi shuns both traditional legal analysis and behavioural method in examining the importance of legal arguments by the Women's Legal Education and Action Fund's (LEAF) mobilization in the Supreme Court of Canada.[103] His work draws explicitly on strategic behaviour and interest group theories to help explain LEAF's success in effecting legal and political change through litigation. Janet Hiebert's analysis of judicial review and section 1 of the *Charter,* the general limitations clause, takes an institutional perspective to demonstrate how the very design of the *Charter* implicates the Court in policy evaluation and frames the very nature of this policy making from the outset.[104] Although Hiebert does not label her work as such, her analysis of the development of section 1 during the process of negotiation leading to entrenchment and subsequent examination of the clause's impact on the Court's jurisprudence is representative of historical institutional analysis. And as Miriam Smith points out, much of Alan Cairns's work is neo-institutional in every aspect but name.[105] His landmark article on the Judicial Committee of the Privy Council, in which he defends the committee's federalism jurisprudence against criticism by arguing that it was in fact "harmonious with the underlying pluralism of Canada," stands as a strong example of historical institutional analysis.[106] His later description of the *Charter* as a "citizens' constitution" and his analysis of its impact on civil society, political culture, and rights discourse serves as a further case in point.[107] As Smith argues, Cairns's body of work is representative of the idea that institutions have reciprocal effects on the society in which they are embedded.[108]

A Focus on the Judicial Role

By integrating judicial role perceptions into an historical institutional analysis of the Court, this book aims to capture how a myriad of factors shape or constitute the institution's work. In contrast to those methods that make justices' personal attributes or ideologies the focal point of analysis, this approach demonstrates that forces both endogenous and exogenous to the Court influence those perceptions in ways that micro-level behavioural analysis or theories based on single-variable assumptions about the justices' motivations cannot capture. The criticism laid out in this chapter of these dominant approaches should not be mistaken for a dismissal of their underlying premises. Just as many political scientists consider legal factors important to understanding how courts work, many legal scholars now acknowledge that judicial attitudes play at least some part in Supreme Court of Canada decisions. In fact, if legalists were to completely discount the role of judges' values in decision making, then they themselves risk adopting the straw man conception of the legal model that has been erected by some attitudinalists. Yet, a reliance on the attitudinal model leaves us with an impoverished view of judicial decision making, no matter how reasonable its foundation. It is notable that even with the rich history of academic attention devoted to American judicial behaviour by both political scientists and legal academics, scholars in the two disciplines have only recently begun to engage each other in the academic literature.[109] The same is true of Canada.[110] In this sense, and to a certain extent, this book also aims to integrate competing theories of judicial decision making.

Although politics is central to understanding the Supreme Court of Canada, I do not treat ideology as the primary means to explain judicial decision making. Rather, by treating the judges' role perceptions as the fulcrum to understanding how they arrive at decisions, one can develop a picture of the environment through which norms, rules, processes, and collegial interaction (strategic or otherwise) interrelate to inform behaviour. Ideology, values, or "policy preferences" become one part of the intricate mixture through which decisions are made. One can better understand the influence of these various factors not by generating questionable statistical correlations that rely on counting votes but, rather, through a contextualist understanding of the different stages of the institutional process juxtaposed against the broader political circumstances of particular issues or cases at hand. Different stages of the process or particular circumstances act as "sites of activity" through which particular motivations or actions become possible, such as strategic or attitudinally inspired behaviour.

The primary critique that scholars from the other traditions might make is that this perspective is insufficiently explanatory. Models of behaviour, susceptible to direct statistical testing, are presented as the keystone of credibility for present-day work in political science. Simplification through such models is necessary because human behaviour and the institutions in which actors operate are extraordinarily complex.[111] Given the preceding analysis of the behaviouralist approach, it should be apparent that I find such criticism unpersuasive. Paul Pierson and Theda Skocpol write that behaviouralists "are prepared to assume that very general variables operating independently of one another come together to account for the patterns of behaviour they are trying to explain. Historical institutionalists, by contrast, assume that operative variables may not be independent of each other at all ... [and] tend to suspect from the get-go that causal variables of interest will be strongly influenced by overarching cultural, institutional, or epochal contexts. *This is not a matter of getting mired in thick description.*"[112] In other words, the simplification demanded by scientific models comes at a cost, one that goes beyond the simple "explanation" versus "understanding" dichotomy frequently elaborated in epistemological debates: "If decontextualization is merely the removal of excess detail, then it's a fine thing, scientifically. If, on the other hand, it is the removal of defining locational information, it is a scientific disaster."[113]

Integrating judicial role conceptions into the analysis allows this study to extend beyond describing each of the important stages of the Court's decision-making process. It provides a consideration of the institutional forces at play that may be independent from, or otherwise constrain or shape, attitudinal, strategic, or legal motivations. As a result, this approach is also conducive to building bridges between the competing theories of judicial behaviour. There can be little doubt that a justice's background, ideology, personal values, or life and educational experiences influence her decision making. Some of the justices themselves have acknowledged as much in speeches or writing.[114] Yet, there can also be little doubt that different justices allow those values to come into play to varying degrees and in varying ways. Conceived of in this way, role perceptions might be broadly understood as the judge's "world view," overlapping with, but extending beyond, mere political ideology.

The remaining chapters illustrate that attention to judicial role perceptions can provide a more complete explanation of judicial behaviour. Many of the findings not only support the underlying theories of the attitudinal and strategic approaches but also demonstrate how judicial policy preferences become influential in certain stages of the Court's decision-making process and in particular contexts. The analysis also shows, however, that a myriad of other factors contribute to the work of this complex institution.

2
The Evolution of the Court and Its Justices

The Supreme Court of Canada has evolved from a relatively obscure institution to one of the country's most important governing bodies. In many ways, it has been subject to, and shaped by, external political forces. To a significant degree, the justices were thrust into their current position of prominence. Yet, decisions on their part have further consolidated the Court's power, including those that have loosened the rules governing justiciability (the set of legal doctrines that govern whether it is suitable to decide a matter in the courts), increased the role of third party interveners, and expanded the type of evidence and other considerations in adjudicating cases. After presenting a brief history of the Court, this chapter explores how some of these changes make judicial decision making at the Court a distinctly more political process.

The policy-driven nature of the modern Court has placed a substantial amount of attention on its legitimacy. Debate and criticism about the institution's appropriate role under the *Canadian Charter of Rights and Freedoms* has compelled some contemporary justices to state publicly their views on their role, the law, and the question of impartiality.[1] An analysis of these views reveals how judges' role perceptions might govern issues such as deference to the legislative or executive branches of government in a manner that the extant judicial behaviour literature often ignores. This chapter contrasts these judicial role conceptions with the political values often ascribed to them and explains how these views not only encapsulate but also extend beyond simple ideological labels such as "liberal" or "conservative."

Another integral component of the Supreme Court of Canada's evolution has been a concurrent change in the type of justice appointed to its bench. The *Charter*-era Court is relatively gender balanced and has a significant number of justices with backgrounds in academia as opposed to solely private legal practice. These characteristics are often said to have an important impact on the justices' style and general approach to decision making. The appointment of reform-minded justices, beginning in the 1970s and 1980s, has had a considerable impact on changes in the rules and policies noted earlier. This chapter begins to show how factors such as ideology, background, and other characteristics should not be treated simply as independent variables in assessing judicial behaviour but also as interdependent ones.

A Brief History of the Court

Given the prominence of the contemporary Supreme Court of Canada, it is easy to forget that for most of its history the institution has endured an inauspicious reputation. From its inception, the Court was mired in a position that afforded it little prestige or influence within the broader system of government. Where the Supreme Court of the United States was established as the head of one of the three branches of government under Article III of the US Constitution, the role of the judiciary at Canada's founding was viewed in light of the new country's colonial status. The Fathers of Confederation gave Parliament the power to establish a general court of appeal under section 101 of the *Constitution Act, 1867*.[2] The Supreme Court of Canada was thus created eight years later by ordinary statute.[3] Significantly, the Judicial Committee of the Privy Council (JCPC) in Britain remained Canada's court of last resort until 1949 (although criminal appeals to the JCPC were abolished in 1933). This context meant that the Supreme Court of Canada's justices adhered to a conservative formalism. In effect, they quickly recognized their "subservience to the Privy Council" and followed the lead set by the British law lords.[4] Worse still, *per saltum* ("by a leap") appeals allowed litigants to bypass the Supreme Court of Canada altogether – a course taken quite often – by appealing cases from the provincial appellate courts directly to the JCPC.[5] As James Snell and Frederick Vaughan explain,

> [t]he Court in Ottawa was thus in a weaker position than an intermediate appellate court; it was bound by decisions which inferior Canadian courts had helped to produce but which all too often lacked the influence of the justices of the Supreme Court of Canada. The ambiguity of this process, as seen from the point of view of the Ottawa justices, undermined their stature and reinforced the tendency to judicial strict construction.[6]

This practice, coupled with the justices' strict adherence to JCPC precedents, stifled any opportunity for the Court to create its own imprint on the formation of Canadian law. Writing in 1951, Justice Bora Laskin, who would later become the Court's chief justice, explains: "It has for too long been a captive court so that it is difficult, indeed, to ascribe any body of doctrine to it which is distinctively its own, save, perhaps, in the field of criminal law."[7]

Other practical difficulties only further contributed to the sense that the institution was of scant importance. In part because of the Court's poor reputation, the federal government had constant trouble appointing highly regarded judges to its bench. The justices of the pre-Second World War period were appointed almost solely on the basis of previous political service. Worse still, the Court apparently lacked an institutionalized decision-making process. An untitled article in a 1902 issue of the *Canada Law Journal* reports that "it is the practice for the judges to deliver their judgments without any previous consultation, or even without the members having any knowledge of what conclusions their brethren have come to."[8] As recently as the 1950s, the judges failed to hold regular conferences.[9]

Certain conditions were ameliorated over time. For the first several decades, the six-member Court would sit in panels of five justices. In 1927, the number of justices was increased to seven, and a mandatory retirement age of seventy-five was introduced. Better pay for the judges and a new building, which opened in 1946, helped improve conditions and attract quality jurists to the Court. The Court's membership was expanded to its current number of nine justices in 1949, when appeals to the JCPC were abolished entirely. Peter Russell writes that the *Statute of Westminster* (1931) was the key factor in facilitating the move to end appeals to the Privy Council, as it removed potential legal obstacles to the reform.[10] The major impetus for ending appeals, however, was a series of constitutional decisions by the Privy Council in the 1930s invalidating legislation enacted by the Canadian government to combat the Great Depression.[11]

Despite expectations, the abolition of appeals to the JCPC did not elevate the Court's status to one of prominence, either as a trailblazer in the law or in terms of garnering attention from the public or press. Having developed a substantial body of jurisprudence on Canadian constitutional issues, the Privy Council's decisions remained influential with justices who, for the most part, remained conservative and deferential in their approach to the law. Moreover, the judges were "aware of provincial anxieties that the Court might turn out to be dangerously centralist" and, thus, approached federalism cases with an abundance of caution.[12] There was some flirtation with judicial creativity in the 1950s, when the Court upheld challenges to Quebec laws that impaired the religious and expressive freedoms of minorities, relying in part on the notion of an "implied bill of rights" in the *British North America Act*.[13] This activism on the Court's part was short-lived, however, as the implied bill of rights never garnered the acceptance of a majority of the justices. More significantly, the Court's timid track record under the federal statutory *Canadian Bill of Rights*, enacted in 1960, contributed to strong criticism for its overall conservative nature.[14] Only once did the Court declare inoperative a federal statute that was in conflict with the Bill.[15] Russell explains that the judges were accused of demonstrating an excessive adherence to precedent and an overly narrow conception of legislative supremacy. Writing in 1969, he notes that the Court's actual procedures "have been found by some to reduce seriously the Court's capacity for providing Canada with effective judicial leadership," as the judges continued to lack meaning-ful consultative processes in arriving at decisions.[16]

The period leading up to the entrenchment of the *Charter* dramatically altered this reality. Two important developments occurred during this time. First, Pierre Trudeau, first as justice minister and then as prime minister, made a distinctive mark on the type of appointments made to the Supreme Court of Canada. Trudeau made the academic credentials of candidates to the Court important and placed a strong emphasis on selecting reform-minded justices who were more amenable to exercising stronger powers of judicial review.[17] The appointment of Justice Bora Laskin in 1970 was remark-able in several respects. Laskin J was the first non-Christian selected for the Court. After spending virtually his entire career in academia, Laskin J had not practised law. One historian of the Court writes that with Laskin J's ap-pointment, the institution "acquired a definite public image for the first time in its history; it would never be the same again."[18] Laskin J's elevation to chief justice just three years later caused considerable controversy within the legal profession, with some members describing him as an "academic lawyer."[19] The fact that Trudeau sidestepped the traditional convention of appointing the most senior justice to be chief only further illustrates his designs for the Court.

Second, through a series of amendments to the *Supreme Court Act,* which were finalized in 1975, the Court gained near complete control over its docket.[20] This development considerably reduced the number of private law cases and ensured that "public importance" was the primary criterion for case selection.[21] Even though appeals to the Privy Council had ended twenty-six years earlier, the justices lacked substantive influence over the cases and issues that came before them. The Court dealt with few cases each year that raised legal issues of any fundamental importance to the country. Through the 1950s and 1960s, no less than half of the Court's caseload dealt with automatic appeals (appeals by right) in civil cases involving more than $10,000.[22] Counting criminal appeals, 85 percent of cases prior to 1975 were appeals by right and 15 percent were by leave. After the reforms, these per-centages were almost completely reversed.[23] The new emphasis on cases specifically geared toward setting national standards in important areas of the law, coupled with the appointment of reform-minded judges, set the stage for a more visible and active Court. With the entrenchment of the *Charter* in 1982, the institution was provided an opportunity to delve into areas of social, moral, and political concern. In addition to the *Charter* itself, section 52(1) of the *Constitution Act, 1982* has been interpreted as enshrining the power of judicial review in Canadian constitutional law.[24] Aboriginal rights cases, established under section 35 of the Constitution, have also become an important part of the Court's docket, beginning with *R. v Sparrow* in 1990.[25]

Despite the fact that the Court's new mandate was to a large extent imposed on it by external political actors and new constitutional duties, the depth, style, and intensity with which the Court proceeded into this new era were very much dependent on choices made by the justices. The next section examines the Court's evolution as a policy-making institution as it pertains to three areas of concern: the relaxation of the rules governing justiciability; the liberalization of the policy governing third party or interest group intervention; and the acceptance of new kinds of evidence in the research process.

Toward a More Expansive Policy-Making Role

Justiciability

One of the most sweeping changes in the Supreme Court of Canada's evolving role is the nature and scope of issues in which it is now involved. Courts have traditionally limited themselves to taking cases only when the subject matter involved is "justiciable." Lorne Sossin defines justiciability as the "set of judge-made rules, norms and principles delineating the scope of judicial intervention in social, political and economic life."[26] Critics argue that the Court has altered the rules of justiciability in a manner that increases its policy-making power.[27] Justiciability is comprised of several components or doctrines. "Ripeness" mandates that courts will adjudicate a matter only when there is a live controversy, sufficient facts at hand, and other possible procedural avenues to settle an issue have been exhausted. "Mootness" occurs where a dispute no longer has a concrete effect on the parties bringing a case before a court because circumstances or the law itself has changed in the intervening time. The "political questions" doctrine suggests that there are issues that are "purely" political that should be resolved through a political process and are therefore non-justiciable.

Another legal concept, "standing," is related to, but distinct from, justiciability. As Sossin notes, while justiciability concerns *what* issues come before a court, standing pertains to *who* is entitled to bring proceedings forward.[28] He explains the important connection between these two concepts:

> Because justiciability so often is raised in public interest standing challenges, much of the case-law relating to justiciability has emerged from the case-law on standing. Furthermore, these analyses are related as both the doctrines of standing and justiciability call upon a court to consider, as Le Dain J. observed in *Finlay v Canada,* "the proper role of the courts and their constitutional relationship to the other branches of government." In this sense, both the law of standing and justiciability may be said to define the legal limits of judicial review.[29]

Rules of standing are typically justified on several important grounds, including the prevention of a flood of litigation and a desire to conserve judicial resources, limit judicial power, and ensure that only interested parties to constitutional disputes face off in the adversarial setting to present their arguments as forcefully as possible.[30]

Beginning in the 1970s, the Supreme Court of Canada changed its criteria for granting standing. In a series of cases known as the "standing trilogy,"[31] the Court mandated that to gain standing "a person need only to show that he is affected by [the legislation] directly or that he has a genuine interest as a citizen in the validity of the legislation and that there is no other reasonable and effective manner in which the issue may be brought before the Court."[32] Prior to the standing trilogy, potential litigants had to show that they were "exceptionally prejudiced" by legislation to challenge its constitutionality. According to Ian Brodie, the standing trilogy gave Canada one of the common law world's most lax laws of standing.[33] The Court acknowledged as much when it affirmed the standing trilogy in the 1992 case *Canadian Council of Churches v Canada (Minister of Employment and Immigration)*.[34] Justice Peter Cory, writing for a unanimous Court, began his analysis of the law of standing with a comparative examination of the United Kingdom, the United States, and Australia, finding that all three common law countries take a much more restrictive approach. In the period following the *Charter*'s enactment, the Court further relaxed the rules of standing.[35] Despite this approach, the Court will not allow any interested party to pursue a case in which it has no personal stake. In 2007, the Court issued rare written reasons denying leave to appeal to the Alliance for Marriage and Family, a third party that sought to appeal an Ontario Court of Appeal ruling permitting three-parent families.[36] Neither the parties to the case nor the Attorney General of Ontario sought to appeal the ruling. The alliance had been a third party intervener in the case. In denying leave to appeal to the Supreme Court of Canada, Justice Louis LeBel wrote that the alliance failed to establish that it had standing, noting that no third party has ever been permitted to "*revive* litigation in which it had no personal interest."[37]

The Court has also relaxed its approach to deciding issues that are moot. In the 1989 case *Borowski v Canada (Attorney General)*, the Court declined to decide the issue put forward by pro-life activist Joseph Borowski, whose action sought a declaration that the abortion provisions in the *Criminal Code* violated the fetus' right to life under section 7 of the *Charter* because the Court had already struck down the provisions the year prior in *R. v Morgentaler*.[38] In *Borowski*, Justice John Sopinka set out a framework for mootness that establishes three factors for exercising discretion to hear a moot case: whether the parties retain an adversarial stake in the issues; whether the issues are important enough to justify the judicial resources needed to hear the case; and whether the Court would be departing from its traditional adjudication role if it decided the case. However, despite these guidelines, the Court still routinely allows cases to proceed "notwithstanding that the issue is academic."[39] Sossin notes that "it remains surprisingly rare for a case *not* to be heard on the grounds of mootness," adding that "[t]he carefully laid out principles in *Borowski* serve most often as a cafeteria at which judges pick and choose the aspects which suit them without troubling about the rest."[40]

The other elements of justiciability have received less attention in the Canadian setting. Although no Canadian case has set out the criteria for determining "ripeness," Sossin argues that the *Charter* has "required that the Supreme Court address speculative issues with greater frequency and in unfamiliar circumstances."[41] The Court spent considerable attention on the "political questions" issue, and on justiciability more broadly, in the 1985 case *Operation Dismantle v The Queen.*[42] The case concerned whether the government of Canada's decision to allow the United States to test cruise missiles within Canadian territory violates the right to security of the person of Canadian citizens under section 7 of the *Charter*. Chief Justice Brian Dickson, writing for the majority, rested his reasoning in dismissing the appeal on one of causation. He wrote that the claims should be dismissed because they were speculative, hypothetical, and not capable of proof. While the majority judgment was not one based on justiciability, Dickson CJ endorsed the discussion of justiciability found in Justice Bertha Wilson's concurring judgment.[43] Wilson J's judgment explores the "political questions" doctrine as enunciated in the United States and concludes that the doctrine has not been particularly helpful in delineating which issues are appropriate for judicial review. Wilson J connects questions of justiciability to the proper role of the courts. She writes:

> I would conclude, therefore, that if we are to look at the Constitution for the answer to the question whether it is appropriate for the courts to "second guess" the executive on matters of defence, we would conclude that it is not appropriate. However, if what we are being asked to do is to decide whether any particular act of the executive violates the rights of the citizens, then it is not only appropriate that we answer the question; it is our obligation under the *Charter* to do so.[44]

In the context of *Charter* cases, Wilson J writes that the proper avenue for exploring this question is through the reasonable limits analysis under section 1 of the *Charter*:

> Section 1, in my opinion, is the uniquely Canadian mechanism through which the courts are to determine the justiciability of particular issues that come before it. It embodies through its reference to a free and democratic

society the essential features of our constitution including the separation of powers, responsible government and the rule of law. It obviates the need for a "political questions" doctrine and permits the Court to deal with what might be termed "prudential" considerations in a principled way without renouncing its constitutional and mandated responsibility for judicial review.[45]

Operation Dismantle is thus regarded as an explicit rejection of the "political questions" doctrine in Canada.

Sossin argues that this conclusion merits reconsideration. He contends that *Operation Dismantle* paradoxically rejects the "political questions" doctrine while acknowledging that certain types of political questions are not appropriate for judicial determination.[46] He also points out that in certain instances the Court has distinguished between legal and political aspects of questions. For example, in *Reference re Secession of Quebec*, the Court articulated "something approaching a political questions test" by noting that matters should be dismissed if there is no legal question posed or, if there is a significant extralegal component to the question, that the Court should sever it or refuse to answer the question.[47] Finally, Sossin is critical of the distinction Wilson J makes when she argues that section 1 of the *Charter* is about whether government action violates rights as opposed to the Court's questioning the wisdom of government legislation. He writes that the determination of governmental objectives and the impact of legislation that comprise the Court's section 1 analysis may not be identical to evaluating the wisdom of that legislation, but he argues "it would be inaccurate to describe such a judgment as other than 'political.'"[48]

Nevertheless, justices on the Court have more recently reiterated the rejection of the political questions concept in Canadian law. In the 2005 case *Chaoulli v Quebec (Attorney General)*, which involved the prohibition of private medical insurance, the Attorneys General of Canada and Quebec argued that the claims were not justiciable because they involved inherently political decisions.[49] Interestingly, while the justices in the majority who struck down the impugned provisions did not bother to address this argument, the minority did take the time to note that "[t]here is nothing in our constitutional arrangement to exclude 'political questions' from judicial review where the Constitution itself is alleged to be violated."[50]

The discussion thus far raises a fundamental question: what explains the Supreme Court of Canada's liberal stance toward the various doctrines relating to justiciability? As noted, some commentators assert that the justices' approach to the law of justiciability is but one part of a move over the last few decades to accumulate policy-making power. It is impossible to confirm whether this goal is the primary motivation. Nonetheless, if power is at least one plausible factor, there is no compelling rationale to explain why

Canadian judges would be more prone to a desire to increase their power than their counterparts in other common law countries.

There are, however, historical and structural reasons that account for the differences. Unlike its American counterpart, the Canadian Constitution does not provide for a formal separation of powers.[51] The American Constitution explicitly limits judicial power to dealing with "cases" and "controversies." As a result, American law has developed significantly more comprehensive doctrines of justiciability than Canadian law. The lack of a strict separation of powers in Canada also explains, at least in part, the historical acceptance of the Court's rendering advisory opinions, something that has been rejected in these other countries.[52] The reference cases themselves have helped to make the justices comfortable in dealing with issues that are more hypothetical and abstract than in regular disputes. Aside from the United States, the other countries referred to earlier – Australia and the United Kingdom – lack a constitutionally entrenched bill of rights.[53] Sossin's analysis suggests that much of the liberalization of justiciability rules occurred in the context of the *Charter*. Indeed, as former Justice Frank Iacobucci writes, "[o]ne of the most important consequences of the Charter is that the line of demarcation between justiciable and non-justiciable has shifted toward the political end of the decision-making process."[54]

The lack of a strict separation of powers and the existence of the *Charter* do not account for all of the changes, however. The law of standing does not hinge on the separation of powers doctrine, and the trilogy of cases that liberalized standing occurred before the *Charter*'s enactment. However, these cases did coincide with a change in the type of justices appointed to the Court. Pierre Trudeau's appointments reflected his vision for the country. As noted earlier, Trudeau made the academic credentials of candidates to the Court important and placed a strong emphasis on selecting reform-minded justices who were more amendable to exercising stronger powers of judicial review. This approach was exemplified by his appointment of Laskin J in 1970, who wrote the majority and unanimous judgments in the first two cases of the standing trilogy, respectively. Six of the justices who heard the third case, *Minister of Justice (Can.) v Borowski*, in 1981, were Trudeau appointees. This is not to suggest that appointments reflect a direct one-to-one explanation of how judicial votes are cast. In fact, Laskin J dissented in *Borowski*.[55] Yet, a disposition among the Trudeau appointees toward a more open stance on issues such as justiciability is one important element that should not be disregarded.

Sossin notes that two central principles underlie the law of justiciability: "First, that courts not adjudicate cases beyond their institutional capacity; and second, that courts not adjudicate cases beyond their legitimacy to resolve disputes."[56] His analysis makes clear that the justices of the Supreme

Court of Canada view the decision to adjudicate certain matters as having less to do with the various doctrines of justiciability and more to do with their conception of the Court's proper function. Iacobucci J contends that the shift in the law of justiciability "does not mean that courts are considering issues that are not justiciable, but rather, that issues that once were not justiciable are now properly cognizable by the court."[57]

The justices interviewed for this study view the Court's role to address political questions, particularly under the *Charter*, not just as a mandate but also as a duty. Further, they agree that questions of capacity and legitimacy are paramount when dealing with issues that have obvious political ramifications. The 1993 case *Rodriguez v British Columbia (Attorney General)* – in which a sharply divided Court upheld the criminal prohibition of assisted suicide – is illustrative.[58] All of the justices I interviewed who took part in the decision described the case as one of the most difficult they have faced, with a couple describing great personal anguish on their part. As one of these justices states, "I believe you're stressing the limits of the judicial function in that case to in effect say that a prohibition against assisted suicide was unconstitutional" (Interview). In part, this belief is based on the fact that the decision is not rooted solely in the law: "Is this just a legal question? What's the input coming [from] philosophers, medical science, care-givers, social workers?" Put simply, "[the Court] can't come to a legal resolution of this problem that ends up in unconstitutionality because [it is] not as well equipped to handle that" (Interview).

This statement has implications that go to the root of judging in the *Charter* era, far beyond the consideration of the doctrines of justiciability described here. Nevertheless, the liberalization of the law of justiciability and the blurring of the boundaries around judicial review – particularly those political questions that stress "the limits of the judicial function" – has contributed to critics' concerns about the Court's exceeding its role. I asked one justice whether, following such reasoning, a declaration that the law at issue in *Rodriguez* as it stood was constitutional was better than simply not accepting the case. Indeed, a majority of the justices on the British Columbia Court of Appeal felt the issue should have been left to Parliament. The justice's response was direct: "We should never start ducking cases."[59] The hope of this justice was that Parliament would attempt to address the issue and fashion some type of resolution. Further, former Justice Claire L'Heureux-Dubé, who was part of the minority in favour of striking down the law, has publicly stated she was glad in hindsight that the majority prevailed and that the matter was left to Parliament.[60] These expressions suggest that while the justices feel compelled to adjudicate such matters, certain issues may make them more deferential to Parliament in the course of rendering decisions.

As will be explored more fully in Chapter 6, the justices' respect for the respective roles of the legislatures and the courts are now most commonly understood as a "dialogue" between the institutions. This dialogue is said to be rooted principally in the structure of the *Charter* itself, with dialogue operating through the reasonable limits clause – which Wilson J identified as the site for justiciability analysis – and the notwithstanding clause, which allows legislatures to temporarily suspend judicial decisions on particular sections of the *Charter*. These structural features of the Constitution may be one more component of the array of factors that have influenced the Canadian justices in their approach to the issues of justiciability. Importantly, they may make them more confident in taking on issues that were once not justiciable because of a perception that legislatures retain wide latitude to act independently of the Court's determination.

Third Party Interveners

The Court has also liberalized its acceptance of third party interveners during the *Charter* era. The movement toward an American-style intervener mechanism was gradual, starting in the mid-1970s with two cases that Brodie writes "sent a signal to the legal community."[61] The current generous culture of granting intervener status did not begin until several years after the *Charter* was introduced, following significant public pressure from interest groups and an intense behind-the-scenes debate between the justices. Despite the "activist" stance that the Court took during the initial *Charter* years, it frequently refused to grant access to third parties. In 1983, the Court changed the rules on intervention for the first time since 1907. The new rules gave attorneys general the right to intervene in constitutional cases and interveners who had intervened at the lower court level the right to do so at the Supreme Court of Canada. The justices quickly reversed this latter policy.

The Court's reluctance to open up intervener access sparked what commentators suggest was an unprecedented public campaign by interest groups to pressure the justices to liberalize the policy.[62] The Canadian Civil Liberties Association (CCLA) was particularly active. In addition to an open letter from its general counsel, Alan Borovoy, Dickson CJ received a letter from his former clerk, Katherine Swinton, who sat on the CCLA's Board of Directors.[63] Swinton later wrote that the intervener policy seemed erratic and arbitrary during the early years of the *Charter*, as it was not clear why certain parties were granted or denied leave to intervene.[64] Brodie argues that the restrictive approach to intervention was because of how the justices perceived their proper role under the *Charter*.[65] Internal memoranda between the justices at that time reveal that some were wary of the notion of regularly opening up cases to interveners. According to Robert Sharpe and Kent Roach, these justices "insisted that cases had to be decided on strictly legal principles. Allowing non-parties to participate, particularly self-styled public-interest groups, could threaten this formal model of judging."[66] One justice circulated a memo complaining that the process threatened to become akin to "an ancient jousting contest, with each side gathering up as many spear bearers as they can," where the private litigant is "hopelessly lost in the suds frothed up by the intervention."[67] Justice Willard Estey was concerned the Court could become a "non-elected mini-legislature" and reportedly viewed interveners as "nothing more than publicity-seeking pressure groups."[68]

The justices who favoured granting leave to more interveners felt that the potential benefits outweighed the risks of politicization. Wilson J, writing in 1986, contends that liberalizing intervention would help diversify the points of view offered about cases and legitimize the Court's new role under the *Charter* by making the adjudication process more open and accessible.[69] Dickson CJ, who was concerned about the public criticism, circulated to his colleagues a *Globe and Mail* article critical of the Court's intervener policy in the hopes of pressing the issue.[70] Later that year, the Court asked the Canadian Bar Association's Supreme Court Liaison Committee to investigate the issue of interest group intervention and recommend a new policy.[71] Brodie writes that while such a consultation process was normal for government departments, agencies, and political parties, it was "an innovation for the Court, which was unaccustomed to having stakeholders."[72]

The Court released a new set of rules in 1987, and, although they appeared to be just as stringent as the old rules, the justices significantly changed the way they handled applications in practice, granting more than 90 percent of the applications for leave to intervene since the new rules were put in place.[73] The rules mandate that a would-be intervener must demonstrate an interest in the case in question and had to show that its position would be different from that of the parties in the case and would be useful to the Court. According to Brodie, a rare series of written reasons explaining decisions to grant or deny leave to intervene by Sopinka J shortly after the new rules came into effect accomplished two things. First, Sopinka J effectively eliminated the "interest" requirement by not placing any restrictions on the type of interest a potential intervener would have to demonstrate.[74] Second, by requiring that interveners demonstrate that they have a history of involvement in an issue, the Court automatically privileged "repeat players" – those groups that had been placing public pressure on the Court to liberalize its approach to intervention – in getting leave to intervene over private individuals and other groups.[75] A few years later, the Court allowed for the first time interveners to add new legal issues to a case.[76]

The movement toward an open intervener policy has not been completely without limits. One justice explains that the Court eventually became concerned about redundant interventions. In the first few years following the 1987 changes, the Court's decision to grant leave to interveners automatically meant they submitted a written factum and were given time for an oral presentation at the hearing. The Court eventually adopted a policy of dealing first with whether the intervener would be allowed to intervene via the factum and then at a later stage determining whether they would receive permission to address the Court and for how long. Sometimes this policy meant allowing the various interveners to sort out who would present at a hearing, but often the Court would just grant permission to specific applicants (Interview).

The Court has also moved to change the tenor of interventions. Throughout the 1980s and 1990s, interveners "strongly, indeed aggressively, supported one side or another in appeals."[77] Brodie contends that the Court treats certain interveners more favourably for reasons that "are hard to square" with Sopinka J's elaboration of the rules.[78] Some of the justices have been concerned with the potential perception that the Court plays favourites. Writing in 1999, Justice Jack Major states that interveners should be more objective in their approach:

> The value of an intervener's brief is in direct proportion to its objectivity. Those interventions that argue the merits of the appeal and align their argument to support one party or the other with respect to the specific outcome of the appeal are, on this basis, of no value. That approach is simply piling on, and incompatible with a proper intervention. The anticipation of the Court is that the intervener remains neutral in the result but introduces points different from the parties and helpful to the Court.[79]

A year later, Major, McLachlin, and Michel Bastarache JJ were quoted as saying that the door had been opened too widely to intervener groups and that it may be time to restrict access.[80]

There is no evidence that the Court has since tightened intervention. All of the justices I interviewed continue to find interveners very useful, and they connect this usefulness directly to the Court's distinctive function in the judicial hierarchy. As one justice explained,

> [intervention] alleviates, somewhat, a certain distance that exists between the basics of the trial and the role of the Court in pronouncing upon values, which may be very much at stake and at the heart of the case you're hearing, but in their application are of much broader effect. The reason to have interveners and for the Court to be fairly open in allowing interventions is to provide means of bringing into focus in the case aspects of which the parties perhaps were less aware or less interested in, but which were very pertinent to determining the values at stake and the achievement of a proper conciliation of these values. It's a way of allaying this discrepancy between the judicial function of a court of law, which is to decide a conflict between two parties, and what the Court is called upon to do, particularly under the Charter, and that is pronounce upon a better definition, both in concept and the application, of values. (Interview)

Iacobucci J states that the Court came to view interveners as necessary because of its increased policy-making role under the *Charter* and also because of the criticism of this role. In his view, interveners enhance both the quality and legitimacy of the Court in this regard.[81]

The evolution of the Court's policy on third party interveners has been shaped by the justices' understanding of the institution's role under the *Charter*. Simultaneously, the decision to give interveners generous access has indelibly affected that role, as it has made the decision-making process a less purely adjudicative or "legal" affair and a more political and explicitly policy-oriented one. This does not mean that interveners put forward arguments that are less legalistic or more political in nature. However, as some of the justices initially opposed to liberalizing the policy suggested, intervener involvement in the process opens the Court up to interest-based advocacy and threatens to make the justices look like they might privilege certain lobby groups over others. The changes in the intervener policy and the justices' explanations of the value of third party involvement demonstrate their concerns about the legitimacy of the Court's decision making under the *Charter*. The Court requires the acceptance and support of the general public as well as of particular interest groups and social movements in order to exercise its authority.[82] Further, the schism among the justices regarding interveners no longer exists. While on occasion the justices have acknowledged potential problems associated with third party involvement in cases, such as when Major J cautioned interveners to be more "objective" in their approach, the justices now appear to unanimously support intervener participation.

Evidence

Almost hand in hand with increased third party participation at the Supreme Court of Canada is an expansion of the type of evidence considered by the justices. Prior to the *Charter*, the Court was traditionally reluctant to consider anything beyond "adjudicative facts," which are facts specific to a given case. "Legislative facts," which might include social science data or parliamentary reports, were generally deemed inadmissible. This distinction was maintained for quite some time, despite the fact that the Supreme Court of the United States began to consider such extrinsic evidence early in the twentieth century.[83] The Court is widely held to have broken with this tradition in 1975, when it gave the parties leave to file extrinsic material on the seriousness of inflation levels in *Reference re Anti-Inflation Act*.[84] Yet, the use of extrinsic evidence did not become commonplace until after the *Charter*. As Iacobucci J explains, "the advent of the Charter has had an impact not only upon *who* may participate in a hearing, but also upon the factors that courts tend to take into consideration."[85] He notes: "As the attention that courts must pay to the operation and effect of broad social policies has increased, so too has the necessity of eliciting and paying attention to social science data that provide a greater understanding of the context in which legislation is enacted."[86] As is explored more fully in Chapter 4, this analysis usually occurs under section 1 of the *Charter*, the "reasonable limits" clause. In *R. v Oakes*, the Court indicated that governments would be required to present evidence that supports justifying infringements on rights.[87] As Sharpe and Roach explain, "[t]he result has been a significant expansion in the kind of materials coming before the courts. Historical, philosophical, and economic data, as well as government reports (both domestic and international), are presented, sometimes through expert witnesses, sometimes by way of judicial notice."[88]

In interviews, law clerks who served at the Supreme Court of Canada in the 1970s and 1980s note they were rarely confronted with such material during the research process. Clerks who served more recently, however, explained that the examination of journal articles and sociological data is a fairly regular practice. These more recent clerks differed, however, on the breadth of their research. While some emphasized that they never did research beyond the materials submitted by the parties, others state that they occasionally examined new issues because they could be addressed at oral hearings. The clerks' approach to this aspect of the research process depended on the preferences of their justice (Interview).

Scholarly writing, government reports, and research studies are often part of the parties' submissions in cases that pertain to public policy issues, particularly *Charter* cases. The Court's liberalization of its third party intervener policy only exacerbated this trend. Indeed, interveners have been granted regular access to the Court for the express purpose of shedding an "independent" light on the latest research in particular issue areas and on the impact of potential policies. Some justices have also taken to considering political and philosophical theory. Iacobucci J notes that such inquiry can be important because the *Charter* often involves abstract questions.[89] He writes that "the increased consideration of academic commentary enhances the quality of constitutional adjudication by ensuring that courts are aware of the various theoretical justifications for the protection of certain rights and freedoms."[90]

The level of attention paid and the weight given to extra-legal evidence varies from justice to justice. One former clerk suggested that older justices are less inclined to look at extrajudicial sources. The Court's decisions reflect some flexibility or, stated in more critical terms, a lack of consistency with respect to how strictly it demands supporting evidence. For example, Sharpe and Roach point to *RJR-MacDonald v Canada (Attorney General)*, a case in which the Court struck down as unconstitutional a ban on tobacco advertising, as an instance where the justices in the majority were quite strict with the requirements for evidence.[91] Alternatively, they note that in *R. v Edwards Books and Art* the Court relied on outdated and imprecise data to uphold Sunday-closing legislation.[92]

Most of the clerks agree that extrinsic evidence might be given less weight in analysis because it is less determinative than the adjudicative facts to which justices are more accustomed. One clerk expressed the difference in this way: "In cases where social policy is involved, the main question is often not what did the legislators mean by these words, for example, or did the court of appeal make an error in applying this law to this set of facts. It's more that there are two competing issues in society, such as expression versus religion" (Interview). According to this clerk, while non-judicial sources are not clear-cut in determining such issues, they are a legitimate tool to draw on because they can aid the Court in understanding the societal context. The clerk noted that statistical evidence on the impact of legislation on disadvantaged social groups, for example, might help the Court in a reasonable limits analysis under the *Charter*. Another clerk acknowledged that it was difficult to marshal extra-legal evidence in this way, particularly when an argument pertains to the systemic effect of legislation in *Charter* cases dealing with discrimination, for example. This clerk argues that such evidence was never a substitute for the finding of record at the trial level. A third clerk agreed with this sentiment but admitted that there is sometimes a temptation to ignore what the trial judge said three years earlier and draw one's own conclusions. This same clerk noted never feeling that the evidence was beyond the grasp of lawyers, justices, or clerks. Several other clerks, however, explained that dealing with such evidence was "difficult," "tricky," or "problematic" (Interviews). One clerk went further, noting: "I didn't always feel I was competent to do it. I don't think clerks had a lot of time to deal with such issues" (Interview). This clerk noted that experts in particular social science fields are often critical of the Court's judgments "and for good reason" (Interview).[93]

The capacity of the justices – or the judicial process itself – to evaluate the policy implications of complex legislative objectives is explored in Chapter 5. The policy-laden or "contextualist" sources now considered by the Court significantly lessen the force and constraint of legal rules and precedents in judicial decisions. For the present purposes, it is important to underscore the fact that the range of evidence considered by the Court has expanded, particularly under the *Charter*. The fact that several clerks serving within the last decade acknowledged the problematic nature of dealing with such evidence is a testament to the broader discretion inherent in cases that stress a focus on social context. Discussion of this idea in Chapter 5 reveals strong divisions within the Court about the weight that should be accorded to such evidence and that these differences stem from the justices' consideration of their proper role.

Diving into the Deep End?

With important changes giving it substantial control over its docket, followed by the introduction of the *Charter,* it is clear that the Supreme Court of Canada's responsibilities relating to judicial review were at least in part imposed on it as the direct result of political decisions by elected representatives. This is something about which justices often remind critics when defending their role as arbiters of the *Charter*.[94] Yet, if the justices were ordered to go swimming, they have made important choices along the way that have led them into the deep end of the policy-making pool. First and foremost among these decisions is the relaxation of the rules of justiciability. Restrictions pertaining to mootness, ripeness, and the law of standing are now considerably lenient. Perhaps most significantly, because section 1 of the *Charter* has become the *de facto* site for determining "political questions" – that is, whether an issue ought to be left to the legislatures – the Court has bound itself to explicit analysis and evaluation of policies and their effects. Since this approach calls into question the competence or capacity of the Court to perform such work, the justices have taken the presumably necessary step of liberalizing third party intervener access and the range of evidence they are willing to consider. These decisions were at least partially geared toward legitimating a more expansive policy-making role.

As explored in Chapter 5, cases involving complex social policy issues are generally more likely to increase judicial discretion. Despite their involvement in these questions, contemporary justices continue to assert their ability to remain impartial adjudicators. The next section explores the modern-day Supreme Court of Canada justice. First, it considers justices' views on the law, their role, and their impartiality and turns to an analysis of how ideology has thus far been conceptualized in the political science literature on judicial behaviour. This analysis suggests that current scholarship might do a better job of incorporating judicial role perceptions to generate a more sophisticated understanding of the part that ideology plays in decision making. It then turns to two other oft-discussed features relating to justices on the contemporary Court: the fact that the composition of the bench is more gender balanced than any other bench in the world and the fact that the justices are now more likely to have backgrounds in academia. The effects of each of these fairly new characteristics are briefly examined.

How Supreme Court of Canada Justices Have Evolved

Political scientists, journalists, and other commentators often ascribe differences between judges in terms of their personal characteristics, such as ideology or gender. By contrast, legal scholars often root these differences in the varying perceptions judges have of how the law should be developed or of the purposes of documents such the *Charter*. Thus, judges are often classified as "incrementalists" who see the law in narrow terms or "contextualists" who prefer to develop the law or particular *Charter* rights in broader terms. One interesting factor that marks the contemporary period is that the justices themselves are more likely to write or speak about their personal characteristics and values in the context of their role. In part, this new openness stems from a desire to defend the Court and themselves from criticism or allegations of politicization.

Somewhat surprisingly, the Court's justices readily acknowledge that certain characteristics – including background and gender – may influence their decision making, but they frequently articulate increasingly sophisticated arguments about how the influence of their individual ideologies can be pushed to the side. Despite the criticism presented in Chapter 1 regarding the particular methodologies some political scientists have used to "prove" the effect of ideology on the Court's decision making, I take the position that ideology has a significant impact on the justices' work. Since the claim here is that the justices' discretion to enact their personal policy preferences is structured by institutional role perceptions, it is important to understand the arguments and perspectives articulated by the judges when they confront claims about the influence of their ideology.

The Judicial Role, the Law, and Ideology

How the judges view their role can be seen as distinct from, albeit fundamentally connected to, their understanding of the law. The distinction is an important one because important assumptions about the supposedly principled nature of legal decision making are embedded in their view of the Court's proper function. Understanding how judges comprehend the law and their capacity to adjudicate issues in a sufficiently impartial manner can help us to understand their conception of their role, which, in turn, I argue, helps constrain or shape the actual decisions they ultimately make. For some time, judges and those in the legal profession have denied the fact that judicial decision making has had a significant policy component. In contrast to many of the judges who sat in the early 1970s, the Court's current justices do not deny their important policy role, although they continue to insist that their function is inherently legal, not political.[95] What is said to shield the Court from politics is the temperament of judicial decision making. The nature of appointment to the Court, secure tenure until age seventy-five, and a strong culture of judicial independence in the contemporary period are all said to prevent the corrupting influence of majoritarian politics from infecting judicial sensibilities.

Yet, many *Charter*-era justices have long abandoned the notion that they can make legal decisions in a wholly objective or seemingly scientific manner. In fact, many of them have made rather strong pronouncements on the value-laden elements of adjudication. Years prior to her appointment to the Supreme Court of Canada, Justice Rosalie Abella wrote:

What one really hopes for in a judge is a judicial polymath whose creative intelligence translates into practical judgments replete with empathetic objectivity. One hopes, but is it realistic? Every decision maker who walks into a courtroom to hear a case is armed not only with relevant legal texts, but with a set of values, experiences and assumptions that are thoroughly embedded.[96]

Bastarache J writes:

The days when judges and lawyers could credibly claim to be discovering an immutable truth in the law are now gone forever. The cataclysmic events of this century, combined with an onslaught in academic circles on the idea of "objective" truth have led judges and lawyers to the awareness that subjective views will always be a part of the adjudicative process.[97]

On retirement in 1988, Estey J noted in an interview that it worried him that Canadians still did not realize that the Court's decisions are dependent on the personality of each judge.[98] The fact that these statements apparently needed articulating after the *Charter*'s enactment, many decades after legal realism is said to have rendered them common sense, only illustrates the persistence of a traditional legal culture in Canada.

While modern-era justices acknowledge that truth and objectivity cannot be found through the law, most still cling to the arguably conflicting view that despite the presence of personal values, they are still capable of adjudicating issues in an impartial, apolitical manner. Bastarache J writes that acknowledging that subjective views are embedded in the process "does not mean that judges throw up their hands when faced with a difficult problem and go with their 'gut instinct.' Rather, it means that in the process of searching for the missing piece of the jurisprudential puzzle which any novel case represents, judges should and must be conscious of their own biases and moral inclinations."[99] Appearing before a parliamentary committee in 2004, L'Heureux-Dubé J states: "Judges, as I see it, don't have a philosophy, and make no mistake about that. They're not there for their own opinion. If you ask me what my position on abortion is, I might have an opinion, but it's not relevant to the case I'm dealing with." She adds: "[W]e may have an opinion, but we have sworn on the Bible – generally, at least – that we will rule in accordance with our mission, which is to render justice."[100]

One of the first Canadian justices to articulate this general position was Laskin J, who found the nineteenth-century understanding of law unsatisfactory and viewed the central tenet of "legal modernism" as meaning that the law must be responsive to society.[101] Despite this understanding, Laskin J was unwilling to follow some American thinkers, such as noted legal realist Jerome Franks, who felt that through the vagueness of constitutional language and the finding of fact judges, could make decisions primarily through their psychological makeup.[102] Laskin J believed judges could be made to "behave" even contrary to their personal inclinations.[103] So while Laskin J's general understanding of law and legal interpretation meant rethinking the Supreme Court of Canada's "traditional role as a simple forum for settling disputes and urging it to play a more important role in developing the law," it did not imply the Court could be viewed as a political institution.[104]

Yet, how can judges claim to set aside their personal values and preferences? Perhaps no Canadian justice has written or spoken more about law and impartiality than McLachlin CJ.[105] She too argues that "the true nature of judging seems to me to lie somewhere between the myths of the declaratory theory and the model of decision-making as the idiosyncratic application of personal preferences."[106] Over the course of her judicial career, McLachlin CJ has developed and articulated her conception of "conscious objectivity":

> The judge, by an act of imagination, places herself first in the shoes of one party, then in the shoes of the other. This practice enables the judge to see all the ramifications of complex conflicts and arrive at accurate and fair characterizations of the issues. The judge approaches the legal principles bearing on the question with the same objectivity. This process enables the judge to rise above personal views and acknowledged and unacknowledged prejudices and stereotypes to give a wise decision that takes into account (although not necessarily accepting) the parties' conflicting views on the fact, the law, and the interplay between them.[107]

In McLachlin CJ's view, a distinction between neutrality and impartiality is important. She states that "impartiality does not, like neutrality, require judges to rise above all values and perspectives. Rather, it requires judges to try, as far they can, to open themselves to *all* perspectives."[108] According to McLachlin CJ, "impartiality does not require that we adopt a 'view from nowhere.' On the contrary, it relies on the judge's close connection to the community in which she judges and its core values." A judge can accomplish this goal, she explains, by examining historical and current context and using recognized methods of logical reasoning. She states that "values and principles entrenched in our legal system, like equality or the presumption of innocence, do not prevent a judge from being impartial. A 'bias against bias,' for example, is not a judicial bane but a boon."[109]

Unfortunately, McLachlin CJ's explanation does little to help us understand how judges can accomplish this mental task in difficult or controversial cases. She presents easy examples of positive preconceptions such as "bias against bias" and negative ones such as racism or sexism. It is harder to identify and discard preconceptions that implicate complex policy issues, such as those relating to questions of redistribution. Yet, the contemporary Court is often confronted with such matters, particularly in the *Charter* era. McLachlin CJ's reliance on context – the notion that judges need simply to ascertain the core values embodied in Canadian society in order to render justice – thus suffers from a fatal flaw. With regard to the resolution of complex policy disputes or controversial moral issues, there is no single, hegemonic value system that can guide judges.[110] In other words, where society is fundamentally divided on such questions, judges are left with little to draw on. All that is left at that point is for judges to choose between competing principles or conceptions of justice.

Nevertheless, even those cases that present justices with the greatest amount of discretion in this regard are bound up by institutional factors such as rules, processes, and norms of collegiality. As the previous chapter makes clear, however, political scientists have tended to focus on the obvious role played by ideology and values, and most of the existing scholarship has done so to an extent that the individual justice's ideology has become the focal point for analysis of courts and judicial behaviour. This is true whether such an analysis comes from the behaviouralist perspective that treats it as the primary explanatory variable or from the rational choice perspective that understands it as the primary motivation for behaviour within the context of the rules of the game. I have argued that a shift in focus is required in order to better understand how the Supreme Court of Canada operates and how its justices arrive at decisions. By making judicial role perceptions the central focus of analysis, we can better gauge when and how particular factors have stronger or weaker influence in decision making. This approach does not discount the effect of ideology. In fact, given the relatively thin conception of ideology in the dominant approaches to the study of judicial behaviour, an emphasis on judicial role perceptions offers a more realistic and complex appraisal of the interplay between ideology and other significant variables. In order to elaborate, I will provide a brief examination of how the leading attitudinal scholarship conceptualizes ideology and the problems it confronts in doing so.

It is commonly asserted by attitudinal and other scholars that "justices are not forthright about their ideological tendencies."[111] Yet, many justices have spoken openly about their approach to the *Charter*, with some even using ideological labels to do so. In a 2001 interview, Bastarache J notes that "in criminal law, I am more conservative than the majority of the court of the last few years."[112] Former Justice William McIntyre, while disliking labels, would not reject descriptions of him as conservative, according to his biographer.[113] Former Chief Justice Antonio Lamer describes himself as a postmodernist in his approach to the *Charter*.[114] Nevertheless, it is more common for justices to describe decision making under the *Charter* as Major J does:

"You fall into one of two camps – or in between – incremental change or broader brush strokes."[115] L'Heureux-Dubé J puts it this way: "Some colleagues read the Charter as a civil liberties document, which is individual rights-predominant, whereas some others read it like a human rights document, which is a balance between the rights of society with the rights of the individual."[116]

All of the justices I interviewed responded to those attempts to label them in ideological terms in dismissive or amused tones. Generally, they said that they understood the rationale behind attempts to classify their voting records, but they saw ideological labels as being simplistic at best. In part, this reaction is because they tended to acknowledge that within certain areas of law they may render decisions that might be viewed as consistently "liberal" or "conservative" but that across different areas of law no single "worldview" along this unidimensional spectrum necessarily predominates (Interviews). As noted in the previous chapter, attitudinalists have traditionally spent little time elaborating on the concept of ideology. In their book, C.L. Ostberg and Matthew Wetstein's analysis of ideology's influence is examined with respect to three broad areas of law: criminal, civil rights and liberties, and economic cases.[117] In this respect, they acknowledge that the impact of ideology does not necessarily translate across all issues or areas of decision making. Only with respect to L'Heureux-Dubé J, however, do Ostberg and Wetstein code two separate ideological scores, depending on the area of law.[118] Thus, in the criminal context, L'Heureux-Dubé J is marked as a conservative and in regard to civil liberties cases as a liberal.

The case of L'Heureux-Dubé J is worth briefly commenting on because the attitudinal model is not conducive to explaining, in the first instance, why she might make such seemingly contradictory decisions across these two categories of cases. One explanation of her conservative decisions in criminal cases may be that in many instances they are perfectly consistent with the source of her liberal views in equality cases – her strong feminist sensibilities. This conclusion is particularly apparent when we consider the subject matter of some criminal cases, such as sexual assault cases, where L'Heureux-Dubé J's sympathies lie with the victims as opposed to the accused. In some respects, this explanation is not particularly sophisticated because feminism is just another ideological label. Giving consideration to L'Heureux-Dubé J's feminist outlook, however, avoids the limits inherent in a conception of values or ideology reduced to crude, dichotomous liberalism versus conservatism. It also highlights some of the measurement problems associated with Ostberg and Wetstein's approach explored in Chapter 1, where their model claims to explain votes within particular areas of law but, with respect to a justice such as L'Heureux-Dubé J, cannot explain differences across areas of law.

Similar variances also exist in other justices' voting behaviour – even within particular areas of law, such as equality cases – but the explanations are not necessarily rooted in ideological terms. Some of these differences pertain directly to a justice's conception of the Court's proper role or capacities. For example, McLachlin CJ writes that "the courts should show great deference to legislative determinations of where and how public money should be spent."[119] The position she articulates may help explain differences in her voting patterns across certain equality cases, such as her support for claimants in cases implicating gay rights[120] versus her opposition to equality claimants in cases implicating substantial government spending.[121]

A similar distinction articulated by Dickson CJ relates to the Court's approach when dealing with cases that involve claims between competing groups in society and when the decision may rest on assessments of conflicting social science research or demands on scarce resources. Dickson CJ states that "democratic institutions are meant to let us all share in the responsibility for these difficult choices. Thus, as courts review the results of the legislature's deliberations, particularly with respect to the protection of vulnerable groups, they must be mindful of the legislature's representative function." In other cases, however, "the government is best described as the singular antagonist of the individual whose right has been infringed."[122] In these instances, the Court is in a much better position to assess the reasonableness of the government's policy under section 1. The distinction Dickson CJ draws stems from two related concerns. The first regards the legitimacy of the Court's role. Dickson CJ has little problem with the Court's exerting its constitutional authority to protect the rights and freedoms of individuals or groups against government action, but it has difficulty from a normative perspective in leaving it entirely to the Court to balance the competing interests of different groups, particularly in instances where legislative choices concern the protection of vulnerable groups. The second issue pertains to the Court's capacity to make policy determinations where conflicting evidence exists. The Court lacks the time and resources to examine social science data, while the resources of the bureaucracy and legislative committees permit elected representatives to thoroughly debate and investigate policy proposals and their potential effects. As a result, in such instances, deference to legislative choices is appropriate.

A recent study by attitudinal scholars examines the notion of "ideological complexity" across different areas of law. Noting that it is typically assumed that judges from the Supreme Court of the United States have "a high level of consistency across a variety of issue domains," the authors investigate voting patterns on the Canadian and American supreme courts across three issues areas (economic cases, criminal cases, and civil rights and liberties cases).[123] Drawing on non-unanimous cases from a five-year period in which there was no personnel turnover in the Supreme Court of Canada (1992 to 1997), the authors use factor analysis to examine voting patterns and alignments as well as a detailed reading of those cases scoring most positively and negatively on each factor generated in order "to identify the underlying dimensions that fostered disagreement on the court."[124] In all three areas, the authors find that a liberal-conservative divide was the primary source of disagreement, while the second factors pertained to the question of deference to government agencies in economic and civil rights and liberties cases or to evidence in criminal cases. These findings prompt the authors to spell out their first conclusion: "Liberal-conservative tensions appear to be as strong a force for explaining conflict within the Canadian Supreme Court as in the US setting, thus lending credence to the attitudinal model."[125] It is worth revisiting critiques of this perspective explored in Chapter 1. What the results actually demonstrate is that voting patterns *reflect* simplistic liberal-conservative ideological divisions rather than being the *basis* for them. Indeed, unlike explicit testing of the attitudinal model, the factor analysis undertaken in this study does not rely on exogenous "measures" of the justice's attitudes. Rather, the focus is solely on voting patterns across specific sets of cases. As a result, despite the fact that the authors included an analysis of the written reasons, there is no way to be sure that the voting patterns are not the result of legal or other considerations.

Perhaps more significantly, the authors find that issues of deference are important, though secondary, factors in the voting patterns. In the criminal field, for example, the division stems from a debate over the degree of deference that should be accorded to the trial judge's finding with regard to evidence. The authors label conflict over deference as "ideological" but note that it is generally not driven by opposing liberal-conservative groups on the Court. This conclusion is left largely unexplained. Further, the authors find a "complex" pattern of ideological decision making on the Supreme Court of Canada. For example, the authors' findings suggest that justices who voted liberally in economic cases voted more conservatively in criminal cases and that voting patterns in civil rights cases do not align at all to the voting in the other two issue dimensions.[126] In contrast, voting patterns on the US Supreme Court were more consistent. The authors suggest that perhaps the less ideological appointments process, panel assignments, or broader Canadian political culture may explain these results. They conclude that their "conjecture suggests that the institutional and political dynamics of a court can have a direct influence on the levels of ideological consistency exhibited by justices in their votes."[127]

It is impossible to disagree with this conclusion. Their suggestion that "a more sophisticated, generalizable model needs to be developed in the judicial area to accurately capture decision-making patterns in high courts around the world" is an important conclusion as well.[128] Attitudinalists could conceivably integrate these institutional and cultural considerations, or the type of distinctions made by McLachlin CJ and Dickson CJ, as "case facts" or additional variables in their models. I would argue, however, that while such an approach would no doubt improve the efficacy of the attitudinal model, the fundamental problems of the approach as already explored would largely remain, especially the measurement difficulties inherent in the approach. Further, the centrality of ideology to the modelling of behaviour continues to leave too many of the broader structural and norm-related factors unattended, particularly those views that may resemble ideological consistency while, in fact, being premised on judicial role perceptions (for example, the specific factors that may call for deference, as noted earlier). This is an important distinction from a normative perspective because if the basis for decisions stems from a conception of the Court's proper role and capacities rather than from mere ideological considerations, then those decisions arguably have a greater air of legitimacy. Attending to this distinction by focusing on those role-related views may make it easier to identify those stages of the decision-making process or particular contexts under which personal values supersede the rules and norms that are generally thought to govern the Court's work.

This type of analysis is the guiding framework for the chapters that follow. The remainder of this chapter, however, briefly explores two other factors drawn from the justice's personal characteristics. Gender has been identified as a very important variable in several empirical studies of the Canadian Court, while less explicit attention has been paid to the justices' professional backgrounds.

Women on the Court

The first female justice, Bertha Wilson, was appointed to the Supreme Court of Canada in 1982. Since then, seven other women have been appointed. From 2004 to 2012, the bench had four women, making the Canadian Court the most gender-balanced court of its kind in the world. Wilson J herself made one of the leading analyses of the impact women judges might have on judicial decision making. Drawing on the psychological analysis of Carol Gilligan in a 1990 speech, she notes that there are entire areas of law in which there is no uniquely female perspective and that "in some areas of the law, however, a distinctly male perspective is discernable."[129] She states: "[I]f women lawyers and women judges through their differing perspectives on life can bring a new humanity to bear on the decision-making process, perhaps they *will* make a difference. Perhaps they will succeed in infusing the law with an understanding of what it means to be fully human."[130]

A couple of recent studies on Supreme Court of Canada voting appear to confirm Wilson J's views. Donald Songer finds that divisions on the Court are strongly structured by gender.[131] Female justices are 19 percent more likely to support the prosecution in criminal cases, 12 percent more likely to support rights claimants in civil liberties cases, and 12 percent more likely to support the underdog in economic cases. The differences are all statistically significant when controlling for a variety of other factors, including region, religion, and party of appointing prime minister. Ostberg and Wetstein's analysis suggests that in certain areas of law, female justices have exhibited distinct behaviour, "blazing their own legal trail in civil rights and liberties disputes, suggesting that female justices on the Canadian Supreme Court may approach fundamental freedoms and equality issues from a different perspective than their male colleagues."[132] All of the female justices are at the liberal end of the spectrum in these cases. According to Ostberg and Wetstein, female justices are 27 percent more likely than their male colleagues to rule in favour of discrimination claimants in equality cases and are 54 percent more likely to do so in non-unanimous cases.[133] However, the authors find no significant gender-based differences in expression cases or economic cases.[134]

These apparent gender disparities are consistent with Wilson J's perspective. A female justice's differing perspective and life experiences are more likely to come into play in areas of the law where those distinct viewpoints are more relevant. Important areas of jurisprudence have developed from an almost entirely male perspective. For example, the case of *R. v Lavallee* involved the acquittal of a woman who shot and killed her abusive husband in the back of the head as he left the room after an argument.[135] Drawing on expert evidence regarding the nature of the abuse, "battered women's syndrome," and the reasonable belief that her husband would kill her, the Court upheld the acquittal. Wilson J, writing for the Court, "recognized that the interpretation of s. 34 of the Criminal Code of Canada, dealing with self-defence, evolved from a male model, from the point of view of a one time bar room brawl encounter between strangers of equal size and ability."[136]

Gender differences are also significant in terms of the impact female justices have on the day-to-day operation of the Court. McLachlin CJ has been quoted as saying female justices could make for "happier courts."[137] It could be that women judges influence decision-making conventions, collegiality, norms pertaining to consensus, and the general tenor of deliberation within the institution. These important factors, which are often overlooked in studies of judicial behaviour, are the subject of Chapter 4. Rather than emphasizing only how gender influences ideological decision making, a focus on judicial role perceptions might allow some insight into how gender might interact with such factors.

Private Practice versus Academic Experience

One of the most overlooked potential factors of influence in the Canadian judicial behaviour literature are the career paths of the justices. While attention is devoted to ideology and gender, a consideration of the justices' post-law school, pre-Court experience has been limited to mostly impressionistic inferences, based largely on the controversy surrounding the initial appointments of judges with academic backgrounds by Trudeau in the 1970s. In their 1990 book on the country's judicial system, Peter McCormick and Ian Greene write:

> There has been a certain amount of friction on the Supreme Court between judges who have spent many years in private practice, and judges whose major background is in the academic world. The judges who come from private practice sometimes saw the academic judges as wasting time over trivial philosophical issues, while the academic judges saw the judges from private practice as not giving serious enough consideration to important legal and philosophical issues.[138]

Although he could not reach a definitive conclusion, Daved Muttart writes that it appears that the trend toward appointing judges with academic backgrounds coincided with the Court's increasing tendency to overrule past decisions.[139]

Interestingly, while most justices typically brush aside ideological labelling as either irrelevant or limited to academic interest, many of the judges I interviewed agreed that differences in career backgrounds are significant. One justice painted the differences as stark: "Academics tend to complicate the law. I always say for fun 'they know too much to be judges.' Academics on the bench who have never had any practice are a problem in many ways. Judge Beetz, who was probably one of the most brilliant judges on the Supreme Court of Canada, could not decide. He took two years, three years to write judgments, which is not acceptable ... The academics and the judges who have been picked up from the bar to the Supreme Court have been terrible" (Interview). Another justice pointed to other important differences but noted that, over time, experience on the Court can diminish certain tendencies:

> I think [academics] approach cases differently. They don't have the experience that you get with thirty years of practice. They have experience that they get from thirty years of writing and lecturing, and seeing a body of young people go through every year with their own ideas. So they have formed useful ideas, but they're not formed on the same background that the 'man on the street' has. And I think in some ways they may tend to be less practical or would not see as readily the 'unintended consequences.' I think if you come from practice you can see if you decide [a case] this way, the police are really going to grab hold of it and run, so you'd better put some kind of qualification on what you're saying, otherwise it's too broad

... On the other hand, after each has been a judge for say five years, that gap sort of closes ... The academic may have become over the years very conservative and vice versa, but at the beginning I think their life experience plays a part in their judgment, just as their life experience apart from their working life plays a part in the way they see things. You can't change who you are. (Interview)

A third justice argued that academics have a stereotypical "ivory tower experience," while an individual coming from practice deals with everyday life issues (Interview). A fourth justice noted that academics can be very practical as well but stressed that a majority of the Court should be people who have experience in practice. This justice also emphasized the need for the Court to have a diverse composition. A fifth justice, however, had difficulty with some of these conclusions, noting that many of the Court's justices have experience in both academics and private practice (Interviews).

With most of the justices seeing strong differences between the approaches of judges with particular backgrounds, it is surprising that this characteristic has not received much scholarly attention. If the experiential knowledge judges bring with them is important, it becomes all the more difficult to untangle socialization, education, ideology, and personal characteristics. Using Ostberg and Wetstein's newspaper scores for the Supreme Court of Canada justices' purported ideological positions, I compare the background of judges who served on the Court during the *Charter* era in Table 1.[140]

Although there are only five justices who have primarily academic backgrounds, all but one – Iacobucci J, who is scored as a moderate – are classified as liberal. The ideological classification of the justices who had mixed backgrounds (having had substantial experience in both private practice and academic settings) or were primarily practitioners is decidedly more diverse. The correlation between justices perceived as liberals and those with academic backgrounds is not necessarily surprising, but it should give some pause to a simplistic view of the relationship between ideology and decision making. It is impossible to say, for example, whether a judge's ideological leanings led them to academic pursuits or whether that career path fostered a more liberal outlook. It is also worth noting that six of the last seven appointments were individuals with a mix of both practice and academic experience.

Looking at the more specific career paths of individual justices might shed an even greater light on their behaviour while on the bench. For example, Lamer CJ's time as a criminal lawyer (he was even the founder of the Quebec Defence Attorneys' Association) makes his time leading the Court in expanding the *Charter* rights of the criminally accused unsurprising. Former Justice Gérard La Forest's stints working for the federal department of justice, including five years as assistant deputy attorney general, might explain his conservative voting record in criminal cases.[141] Again, these career choices

Table 1

Supreme Court Appointees by Professional Background, 1977-2008

	Judge	Year appointed	Ideological score
Academic	La Forest	1985	Liberal
	McLachlin	1989	Liberal
	Iacobucci	1991	Moderate
	Bastarache	1997	Liberal
	Arbour	1999	Liberal
Mixed	Chouinard	1979	Conservative
	Lamer	1980	Liberal
	Le Dain	1984	Liberal
	L'Heureux-Dubé	1987	Conservative (criminal) Liberal (civil)
	Sopinka	1988	Moderate
	Stevenson	1990	Moderate
	Fish	2003	Liberal
	Abella	2004	Liberal
	Charron	2004	Liberal
	Rothstein	2006	Moderate
	Cromwell	2008	Moderate
	Moldaver	2011	Moderate
Practice	Estey	1977	Liberal
	McIntyre	1979	Moderate
	Wilson	1982	Liberal
	Gonthier	1989	Moderate
	Cory	1989	Liberal
	Major	1992	Conservative
	Binnie	1998	Moderate
	LeBel	2000	Conservative
	Deschamps	2002	Moderate
	Karakatsanis	2011	Moderate

are themselves no doubt bound up by ideological considerations, but the justices' experiences also serve to shape their views and would unavoidably weaken or strengthen certain convictions. Disentangling the influence of experience, career path, and ideology is a difficult, if not impossible, proposition. Yet, it also highlights why simply labelling all of the intrinsic factors that judges bring with them to the Court as mere ideology is problematic.

Conclusion

This chapter provides the context for what follows. The Supreme Court of Canada evolved from its obscure, second-class status over a period of many decades. Even after becoming Canada's final court of appeal in 1949, it was not until the last thirty years that the Court emerged as one of the country's most important governing institutions. Two events, in particular, were responsible for this critical juncture in the Court's history. First, changes to the *Supreme Court Act* that came into effect in 1975 gave the justices wide discretion to choose which cases to hear on the basis of their national importance. The second change empowered the Court to determine the constitutionality of government action or legislation with regard to the broadly worded provisions in the newly entrenched *Charter*.

The fact that these significant developments thrust the Court into a new role is beyond question, but to assume that the external imposition of a new mandate and changes in particular processes are all that account for how the Court developed is far too simplistic. The Court's justices responded to the new incentives and pressures in a host of ways that were in no way preordained by external political actors. Changes in the institution's policies relating to justiciability, third party intervention, and evidence are connected in large part to the *Charter*, but there has been strong disagreement among the justices about how far to go in altering the Court's traditional approaches to each issue. Reform-minded judges clearly won out in regard to reshaping the law of justiciability to the extent that there are few issues the Court would now shy away from considering. Debate over third party intervention was particularly sharp among the justices during the 1980s. Ultimately, the deciding factor was a concern about the legitimacy of the Court's process. Among the contemporary justices, a strongly held consensus has existed about the propriety and necessity of the interveners in salient *Charter* cases. Varying more widely from judge to judge is the level of willingness to draw from extra-legal evidence in the course of deciding cases. The move toward a more liberal use of such extrinsic data runs parallel to these other reforms, all of which has meant that the Court has become a fundamentally more policy-oriented, and therefore political, institution.

This evolution, which has been both imposed and embraced by the justices, has brought with it the prominence, attention, and criticism to match the increase in policy-making power. It has forced the justices to speak out about their new role, respond to criticism, and articulate the distinctive nature of the Court's function. Although contemporary judges now acknowledge the potential influence of personal values and the fact that truly objective decision making is impossible, their assertions that full impartiality remains possible – such as through the psychological exercise of "conscious objectivity" and an appeal to widely held societal values – ring a bit hollow. Nevertheless, an appeal to the justices' consideration of their role suggests an awareness of the potential limitations of their institutional capacities and a recognition of the responsibilities of the other branches of government, all of which may curb tendencies to impose value-laden decisions about the balancing of particular interests or about government spending.

While the institution evolved, so too did the type of justice appointed to the Court. Where the importance of gender has been thoroughly analyzed, the intersection or overlap between background experience and ideology has received scant attention in the judicial behaviour literature. A brief examination of these characteristics further cautions against the attribution of simple labels such as "liberal" or "conservative" to explain complex psychological and cognitive decision-making processes. As the composition of the Court continues to grow more diverse, the relevance of such personal characteristics is only likely to grow in relation to the institution's decisions.

3
Setting the Stage: Exploring Court Processes Leading to Decisions

It is customary, when thinking of the Supreme Court of Canada, to picture only its nine justices, sitting behind the bench in the main courtroom. Yet, within the institution a small army of staff, including law clerks, administrators, staff lawyers, and librarians, work to serve the judges and the parties to cases, maintain resources and flows of information, and ensure efficiency. This hidden, but fundamentally important, administrative side of the Court's work has been largely neglected in the scholarly literature.[1] Following an overview of the role of the chief justice, court staff, and law clerks, this chapter explores how institutional efficiency is directly related to the integrity of the judicial process. Efficiency is an important constraint on the justices in terms of the number of cases they can hear in a given year and as a reflection of their concern for the quality of the Court's decisions.

A number of important stages comprise the "front end" of the Court's decision-making process. This chapter examines changes in rules and institutional procedure that govern the leave to appeal applications process as well as those that help to shape the inputs for the Court's decisions: written arguments put forward by the parties to the case (factums); the law clerks and the research and administrative support they offer; and the oral hearing. Placed in this institutional context, this chapter assesses how these various features and stages of the decision-making process might be susceptible to attitudinal or strategic behaviour on the part of the justices. As the analysis makes clear, many of the stages at the front end of the Court process – particularly at the leave to appeal stage – are dictated largely by norms of collegiality, consensus, and legal rules. The chapter concludes that legal rules and institutional norms do not eliminate opportunities for justices to engage in attitudinal or strategic behaviour, but it reveals how they can minimize such behaviour at specific stages of the decision-making process.

The Contemporary Court

The Chief Justice

The chief justice's role *vis-à-vis* the puisne judges is one of "first among equals" rather than hierarchical.[2] The chief justice has a number of powers that place her in a position of leadership on the Court, such as selecting panels to hear appeals and assigning writing duties, but, as will be explained, even these decisions are conditioned by conventions and norms of collegiality. For the most part, the other eight justices are completely autonomous in their decisions. The ability of a chief justice to exert leadership is accomplished through her ability to persuade her colleagues. This power is achieved in part as she takes the lead in writing. Every chief justice since John Cartwright (who became chief justice in 1967) has led the Court in the delivery of decisions.[3] The chief justice can also lead by example to increase consensus on the Court. As Peter McCormick writes, "[a] Chief Justice who frequently distances himself from the opinions of the majority encourages colleagues openly to express any doubts they may have about the decision, while a Chief Justice who frequently joins the majority despite some minor reservations about its details similarly encourages colleagues to close ranks."[4] Responsible for the day-to-day management of the Court, successive chief justices have introduced innovations designed to increase collegiality or improve institutional efficiency. For example, it was Cartwright CJ who entrenched the system of regular judicial conferences. Even relatively minor decisions, such as Chief Justice Bora Laskin's introduction of a judges' lunchroom to the Court building, can have a positive impact on collegiality.[5]

As the Court's figurehead, the chief justice also has enormous responsibilities that are external to her institutional duties. As the chief justice of Canada, she is also the deputy governor general of Canada, meaning she can fill in for the governor general to meet foreign dignitaries or give royal assent to bills of Parliament.[6] The chief justice chairs the Canadian Judicial Council (CJC), which has authority over all federally appointed judges in the country. The CJC has the power to investigate complaints against judges and hold inquiries that result in recommendations that, if necessary, may include removing a judge from office. The chief justice is also the chair of the Board of Governors of the National Judicial Institute, an independent body that promotes judicial education through seminars and various programs. She is also a member of the advisory board of the Order of Canada, which awards the country's highest civilian honour.

As the Supreme Court of Canada has grown in public stature, the chief justice's role as primary representative of the Court has also grown more prominent. Former Chief Justice Brian Dickson was the first chief to give regular public speeches and media interviews, something his successors Chief Justices Antonio Lamer and Beverley McLachlin have continued. Dickson CJ, with former Prime Minister Brian Mulroney, also regularized the convention of consultation that surrounds new appointments to the Court. The chief justice's external duties are so significant, it has been said that Dickson CJ, for example, spent no more than 50 percent of his time on law and cases.[7]

The various styles of the different chief justices can have a discernable impact on the efficiency and collegiality of the Court. According to his biographer, Laskin CJ (chief justice from 1973 to 1984) displayed a "top-down management" style with regard to the organization of the purely judicial work of the Court and with respect to important events, such as the Court's centenary. The other justices often felt his approach was disrespectful, particularly given the controversial nature of his promotion to chief justice. Laskin CJ was much less attentive or controlling with respect to the day-to-day management of the Court.[8] As described in this chapter, Dickson CJ's tenure as chief justice (1984-90) came at a time of considerable backlog and division on the Court. Despite implementing important procedural changes in response to the backlog, administrative work was secondary to Dickson CJ. Dickson CJ's former colleagues described him as congenial (Interviews). His efforts to achieve consensus on the Court's approach to the new *Canadian Charter of Rights and Freedoms*, though initially successful, ultimately did not produce a higher degree of unanimity.[9] Nevertheless, his style, personality, and willingness to listen to his colleagues instead of dictating the Court's jurisprudential direction were met with appreciation from the other justices. Lamer CJ (1990-2000) spent considerable time dealing with the Court's efficiency and administration (Interviews). His general approach was professional, but, as is detailed in Chapter 4, divisions on the Court during his time as chief justice occasionally resulted in near-animosity with particular colleagues. Finally, McLachlin CJ, the current chief justice, has generally sought to build consensus on the Court. She is described by colleagues as exceptionally amiable (according to my interviews), and, as explored in the next chapter, her approach has been quite successful.

The Court Staff

In the late 1970s, the Court had approximately fifty to sixty employees; they now number nearly 200. Integral to the operation of the institution and under the leadership of the Court registrar, staff members are responsible for both legal and administrative work. The Court's administrative procedures place practical boundaries on how many cases the justices can take on in a given year, something that, as is explored in the following discussion, has important implications for the quality of judgments and relations between justices.

The position of the executive legal officer (ELO) was created by Dickson CJ in 1985. The ELO was originally envisioned as another clerk for the chief justice, but Dickson CJ decided it was preferential to have someone with more experience and a broader job description. The position typically lasts three years and never more than five. The ELO serves as the chief of staff to the chief justice; sits as a member of the board of governors of the National Judicial Institute (which is chaired by the chief justice); and provides a support role for the chief justice's work with the CJC. The ELO is also responsible for the co-ordination of the law clerk program. A great deal of the ELO's work, however, involves acting as the Court's media relations officer. In this capacity, the ELO provides not-for-attribution briefings to the press on judgments of the Court.

Each judge has a judicial assistant, a court attendant, and three law clerks attached to their chambers. The law clerk program, which began in 1968, initially allowed the justices to each hire a single clerk for a one-year term.[10] The program was expanded to two clerks per judge in 1983 and to three clerks per judge in 1989. Law clerks are hired immediately out of law school. The program has grown increasingly competitive over the years. As shall be discussed, one of the clerks' main duties is to provide the justices with bench memoranda, which synthesize the facts of the case, the decisions of the lower courts, and the litigants' factums (legal arguments). Bench memos typically include the clerk's assessment of the case and an analysis of the arguments on both sides. The judges freely acknowledge that although they review all of the material relevant to each case, the clerks' research function is fundamental to their ability to perform their duties in a timely manner. The Court's overall caseload makes it impossible for them to check all of the counsel's citations or go to the Court's library to research all of the pertinent case law. Most of the justices also have their clerks work on the drafting or editing of written reasons. The writing practice and the clerks' influence on the overall decision-making process are explored in depth in the next chapter.

There is considerable variation among the justices with regard to how they select their clerks.[11] According to several former clerks, some justices hire clerks who appear to think very much like they do (or are "clones of themselves," as one clerk put it), some justices purposively select clerks who will challenge their way of thinking, while other justices end up with a mix of the two because they rely more heavily on the application material and select candidates based on transcripts, letters of recommendation, and resumes (Interviews). One justice acknowledged choosing clerks who have a "social conscience," suggesting that the social perceptions of their clerks can be important and, indeed, that such perceptions are important in decision making (Interview). The variation in the justices' selection of clerks is as wide as the variation in how they utilize their clerks. Some justices treat their clerks principally as research assistants, while others encourage active debate and deliberation with their clerks. Although it is impossible to correlate the method of selection to how clerks are used, there is some obvious overlap. Those justices who select clerks who will challenge them tend to be those who have the clerks more actively involved in all areas of the decision-making process.

Efficiency and Administration

Efficiency and effective administration are important to the justices and reflect their concern for quality and the Court's general reputation. Over time, this concern has mandated important changes in procedure. One major impetus of the 1975 changes to the Court's leave system was the overwhelming workload that hit the Court in the early 1970s. After appeals by right were severely restricted, the judges managed to reduce the number of cases heard between 1975 and 1980 by 30 percent. By the mid-1980s, however, the judges were struggling with "an alarming backlog of reserve judgments just when the Court was meeting the onslaught of difficult Charter cases."[12] One significant cause of the backlog was a sharp increase in the number of leave applications following the 1975 reforms – the number of applications grew from 101 in 1969[13] to 419 in 1982.[14] The public importance criterion also meant that the justices were dealing with harder or more complex cases. As former Justice Claire L'Heureux-Dubé writes, the judicial decision-making process compels the justices to elaborate on their reasoning in such cases: "When a particular case presents the Court with an opportunity to give definite direction on a particular point of law, the natural inclination is to explore each facet of the particular legal problem, recount history and account for each theory or precedent."[15] In particularly important cases, there is some degree of pressure on the justices to speak with one voice, a consensus-building process that further extends the length of time it takes to produce a decision.

With the bulk of cases suddenly carrying more weight, it is little wonder that the Court was confronted with a backlog not long after it gained substantial control of the docket. The influx of *Charter* cases that hit the Court beginning in 1984 only compounded this difficulty. With less case law to draw on, fewer legal rules, and a more "contextual" and policy-oriented approach to *Charter* rulings, *Charter* cases are often more difficult to decide than other types of cases, something confirmed by recent studies.[16] Expansion of the law clerk program through the 1980s seems to have been essential for the justices to cope with the intensified demands on the research and drafting that went into most cases. Yet, some commentators speculate that one effect of the clerks' involvement in the drafting phase since the 1970s has been to increase the use of citations to scholarly sources in the Court's decisions.[17] The clerks' involvement, then, has likely contributed to longer and more wide-ranging decisions. Nevertheless, the justices' ability to delegate so much of their research and writing responsibilities to a dedicated staff has been beneficial to the Court's efficiency. The clerks' influence and the implications of their involvement in decision making are explored more thoroughly in Chapter 4.

The escalating difficulty of the cases was not the only cause of the backlog and nor was increasing the number of law clerks the only means of addressing it. Diverging attitudes and work habits among the judges created tensions over the speed with which comments on drafts were returned to colleagues. Justices Jean Beetz and Gerald Le Dain, who were described by Dickson CJ's biographers rather generously as "perfectionists," took exceptionally long to complete their work during this time period. The differences produced such a strain that former Justice Bertha Wilson implicitly threatened in a memo to Dickson CJ that she might resign if the delays continued. Illnesses among some judges further worsened the problem.[18] Beyond careful attempts at persuasion, the chief justice has little authority over her colleagues in these matters. Justice Gérard La Forest worried that a push to expedite matters might lessen the quality of the Court's work. He suggested one remedy might be to take on fewer cases, but his colleagues rejected this idea.[19] Turnover among the judges helped alleviate some of the personnel issues that had played a part in the backlog. Nonetheless, Dickson CJ initiated several important procedural reforms to address the structural factors he felt also contributed to delays. The 1980s witnessed the computerization of the Court's scheduling procedures to facilitate docketing and case tracking. Computerization also allowed the Court to publish judgments and headnotes in both official languages at the same time.[20] The Court altered the rules for oral argument in 1987, going from holding fairly open-ended oral hearings to imposing time limits. Each side now normally receives one hour for arguments (fifteen to twenty minutes for interveners). These changes allowed the Court to transition from scheduling one case for argument each day to two cases each day.[21]

As a result of the turnover among judges and these other procedural changes, the backlog that the Court struggled with in the mid-1980s was eliminated by the end of 1990. In 1988, the average time it took a case to work its way through the Court – from the filing of an application for leave to the rendering of judgment on the appeal – was well over thirty-three months. In 1991, this average timeframe had been cut to almost twenty-two months. Table 2 provides the number of reported judgments and the average time each case took for the years 1987 to 2011.

Since the early 1990s, other efficiency problems have cropped up, but they have generally been less severe. In 2001, McLachlin CJ publicly declared that the Court's resources were "stretched to the limit," and she felt two changes could help prevent a newly developed backlog from worsening.[22]

Table 2

Average case lapse times, 1987-2011

Year[1]	Total number of judgments	Notices of appeals as of right	Total applications for leave submitted	Months for decision on leave application	Months between leave decision and hearing	Months from hearing to judgment	Total months from application to judgment
1987	90	na	na	na	21.0	7.1	–
1988	101	na	na	na	26.0	7.2	–
1989	133	na	na	3.6	18.5	6.4	28.5
1990	140	na	na	4.7	17.0	6.2	27.9
1991	112	60	480	3.5	15.0	3.6	22.1
1992	119	63	460	3.6	12.4	3.6	19.6
1993	150	47	513	4.0	13.1	4.1	21.2
1994	120	54	496	3.4	10.5	3.0	16.9
1995	103	57	445	3.8	9.9	3.8	17.5
1996	124	43	573	4.4	11.8	3.0	19.2
1997	107	34	615	3.5	10.9	2.8	17.2
1998	92	30	572	3.9	12.0	2.8	18.7
1999	73	15	458	5.2	11.1	5.4	21.7
2000	72	17	640	5.4	12.5	5.8	23.7
2001	91	21	668	4.3	11.4	5.6	21.3
2002	88	13	498	5.7	12.2	5.6	23.5
2003	81	12	609	3.9	10.5	5.1	19.5
2004	78	12	559	3.7	9.4	4.0	17.1
2005	89	16	575	3.7	9.1	5.2	18.0
2006	79	7	477	3.4	7.7	5.9	17.0
2007	58	16	629	3.5	9.0	6.6	19.1
2008	74	18	509	3.2	8.9	4.8	16.9
2009	70	14	518	3.2	7.6	7.4	18.2
2010	69	24	465	3.4	7.7	7.7	18.8
2011	70	12	541	4.1	8.7	6.2	19.0

Notes: Data was compiled using the Court's statistics documents. See Supreme Court of Canada, *Statistics 2001-2011* (Ottawa: Supreme Court of Canada, 2010).

First, she advocated the total abolishment of appeals by right. To date, the move to give the Court absolute control of its docket has not been made.[23] The second concern McLachlin CJ addressed pertains to severe space limitations at the Supreme Court of Canada building. This constraint makes it difficult to hire more editors and translators, contributing to delays in the rendering of decisions.[24] The Federal Court and Federal Court of Appeal still retain space at the Supreme Court of Canada building, as plans for a new federal court building – announced in 2003, named in honour of former Prime Minister Pierre Elliott Trudeau, and intended to house those courts as well as the Court Martial Appeal Court of Canada, the Tax Court of Canada, and the Courts Administration Service[25] – have been shelved.[26] One senior staff member at the Court noted that another difficulty relating to the space constraints is that few structural changes can be made to accommodate increases in staff, due to the Supreme Court of Canada building's status as a historical site and its management by the Department of Public Works (Interview).

With the effective cancellation of a new federal court building and no movement on the part of the federal government to eliminate the final category of appeals by right, these two issues are essentially out of the hands of the registrar or chief justice. Despite these setbacks, McLachlin CJ managed not only to eliminate the slight backlog that developed at the turn of the century but also to helm the Court to its fastest productivity level in a decade.[27] She is credited as having been "innovative" and "aggressive" in setting dates for appeals and for "cracking the whip" on counsel and stimulating the Court staff.[28]

The Court's output in the last decade has also seen a notable drop in the number of cases heard. For most of the 1990s, the Court heard well over 100 appeals per year. Since then, it typically hears only seventy to ninety cases each year. The fact that the Court made fifty-eight reported judgments in 2007 appears to be a short-term anomaly, largely due to a sharp drop in the number of applications for leave to appeal in 2006 (which rebounded the following year). However, the Court's 2007 performance report to the Treasury Board also asserts that "in general, cases have become more complex."[29] Given that case complexity is unlikely to diminish in the near future, it is probable that the Court's output will remain close to seventy judgments per year. Whether or not the Court made the decision consciously, La Forest J's preference in the 1980s for a reduction in caseload seems to have won out twenty years later.

Efficiency has an important impact on the substance of the Court's work. According to Wilson J, the tendency for judges struggling under a heavy caseload is for them to focus on the cases assigned to them and spend less time carefully scrutinizing cases being prepared by their colleagues. When backlogs develop, she argues, there becomes an institutional preference by judges to support the majority result. Wilson J writes: "[U]nder the pressure of a heavy caseload the delicate balance which should exist between judicial independence and collegiality may be displaced and collegiality may give way to expediency. This is an extremely serious matter for an appellate tribunal because the integrity of the process itself is threatened."[30] The initiatives made to ensure efficiency represent more than the pursuit of a simple bureaucratic virtue. Efficiency has a direct effect on the effectiveness of the institution and the quality of its judgments. To an extent, as Wilson J's comments imply, the legitimacy of the Court process is also at stake when significant backlogs develop. Efforts toward strong administration are left unconsidered in attitudinal and strategic conceptions of decision making. As an important component of the justices' responsibilities and given the critical effects on the Court's work, it is essential to reflect on this aspect of the judicial process.

Getting Cases to the Supreme Court of Canada

The Leave to Appeal Process

The bulk of the Court's annual caseload consists of those cases that have worked their way up through the court system and are appealed to the Supreme Court of Canada on the basis that the issues involved constitute matters of public importance.[31] Within this context, however, the Court has unfettered discretion to determine what constitutes public importance, and it rarely explains its decisions on leave. For critics who see the Court as beholden to particular interests, this discretion only serves to enhance the political nature of the institution.[32] Similarly, attitudinal and strategic scholars envision case selection as just another site for policy-motivated behaviour on the part of the justices. This section makes clear, however, that role-related norms have a powerful constraining effect on judicial choices regarding leave.

Until 1956, leave could be granted by a single judge in chambers. Even then, it took a rare public controversy that year for amendments to be made to the *Criminal Code* and the *Supreme Court Act,* mandating that hearings for leave be held in panels.[33] The Court now decides leave applications in panels of three. One of the most crucial changes pertaining to the leave application process was an amendment to the *Supreme Court Act* in 1987, which allowed the Court to consider leave applications through written submissions rather than oral hearings. Until then, bench applications were made before panels of three justices (three justices sat in the main courtroom and three sat in each of the two Federal Court rooms in the Supreme Court of Canada building). Lawyers had fifteen minutes per side. Oral hearings for leave applications are now rare. The contemporary Court routinely receives over 500 applications per year (sometimes over 600) and, in the last decade, usually grants leave to approximately eighty cases (with a yearly acceptance rate ranging from 10 to 15 percent).

Once submitted, applications for leave are certified by the process clerk of the Registrar's Office to ensure they conform to Court rules and are then forwarded to the Law Branch, where staff attorneys prepare "objective summaries" of each application. Since 1995, the staff attorneys also prepare recommendations on whether to grant leave (as will be discussed below, this task was previously done by the law clerks). While the summaries are part of the public record and available on request, the recommendations are not.[34] The Court also has a data retrieval program under which potentially related leave applications are cross-referenced. Appeals raising similar issues may be grouped by the Court. If an application urgently requires a timely decision, counsel are requested to inform the Court or make a motion to expedite the decision. Beyond such requests, leave applications in criminal and family law cases generally receive priority.[35]

The three-judge panels usually vote by written memorandum rather than by meeting face to face to make their decisions. The composition of the panels is relatively fluid, although applications from Quebec are normally sent to justices from Quebec, given their familiarity with the *Civil Code of Québec*.[36] Further, those raising special issues are sometimes forwarded to a justice with expertise in a particular area.[37] The list of cases granted is discussed at a conference of the full Court, giving the Court as a whole some control over the number and kind of cases that are heard from the set of applications granted at any one time.[38] Any justice may also bring any case rejected by a panel up for discussion. Despite this policy, the tradition has been for the panels of three to retain the final word on whether a case will be heard.

Applications for leave to appeal are distributed by the panels from a main list to three different lists (designated simply as the B, C, and D lists). In a 1997 speech, former Justice John Sopinka outlined the process as follows:

> If the panel or majority votes to grant, the application goes on the "B" list. If the majority votes to dismiss, the dissenting member may place the application on the "D" list. If there is no dissent, or the dissenting member does not place the application on the "D" list, the panel must advise the other members of the Court of their intention to dismiss unless any member of the Court wishes to place the application on the "D" list.
>
> As a result of this process, applications are either placed on the "B" or "D" list for discussion at the Conference. All others are dismissed. After discussion at the Conference, the panel makes its final decision. This discussion can get quite spirited.[39]

About thirty to forty applications per year are placed on the D list.[40]

Additions to the *Supreme Court Act* in 1994 gave the Court the power to remand cases to the trial court or relevant appellate court when those courts have been unable to address issues dealt with by the Supreme Court of Canada after the judgment in the court of appeal was made. Virtually all of these cases are first placed on the C list.[41] The C list was previously used for cases raising issues similar, or identical, to those in cases already before the Court. The cases remained on this "deferred" list until the outcome in the pending case was decided, and then the application was granted or dismissed. The C list rarely consists of more than a handful of cases per term.

In *Tournament of Appeals,* Roy Flemming provides the first comprehensive exploration of the Supreme Court of Canada's leave to appeal process.[42] Flemming draws on three major accounts developed in the American litera- ture relating to the granting of judicial review (referred to as the granting of *certiorari*) at the Supreme Court of the United States, each of which purports to explain how the justices determine leave. The "litigant-centred" account is the most developed. It suggests that the justices' behaviour in granting *certiorari* is influenced by the type of litigant: "upperdogs," or higher-status litigants, are more likely to gain access to the court than litigants with lesser status. Those parties backed by organized interest groups also have more success, as do those represented by lawyers who are "repeat players" with significant experience before the US Supreme Court.

The second account is the "jurisprudential" account, in which the justices' main consideration is to apply legal rules and standards to *certiorari* applica- tions. As Flemming notes, this does not necessarily mean a mechanical or rigid process: "Instead, legal factors prompt justices to give certiorari applica- tions a second look in a process otherwise strongly governed by the presump- tion that few requests for review warrant approval."[43] Finally, the "strategic" account envisions the justices as anticipating the outcome of a potential case and deciding to grant leave based on whether the likely outcome co- incides with their personal policy preferences.

Flemming draws on a dataset of judicial votes on leave applications from the first three years of the "longest natural court" of the *Charter* era – January 1993 to December 1995 (a "natural court" being a period of no turnover among the nine justices sitting on the Court). He finds that, as it pertains to the Supreme Court of Canada, the jurisprudential account is the most persuasive. The "litigant-centred" approach does not seem to apply in the Canadian context. With the exception of government litigants, particularly the federal government, asymmetries in the status of Canadian litigants or their resources do not appear to make a significant difference in the Court's decision to grant or deny leave.[44] This is in contrast to a number of studies that find that certain types of litigants or specific interest groups do have a comparative advantage over others at the actual merits stage.[45] One key distinction of the leave to appeal stage, as Flemming points out, is that the Court discourages third party interveners from participating.[46] Also unlike the United States, the experience of the lawyers appearing before the Court does not seem to matter. Where a small, elite group of lawyers in Washington funnel applications to the US Supreme Court, no similar group exists in Ottawa.[47]

Flemming also contends that the institutional context makes strategic behaviour less likely – or at least less evident – than in the United States. He contends that "the absence of an *en banc* tradition and the use of panels at both stages in Canada" complicates and adds uncertainty to the justices' ability to act strategically.[48] Since appeals can be heard in panels of five, seven, or nine, a strategically minded justice cannot be sure which justices will hear an appeal. More significantly, of the 3,600 individual votes on leave applications for the period of Flemming's study, there were only thirty dissenting votes – panel decisions on leave applications are virtually always unanimous.[49] This unanimity did not reflect a "homogenous preference on the panels" because the judges who sat together on leave to appeal panels did not vote together once the case was actually heard.[50] At least in the most direct sense, then, voting on leave applications at the Supreme Court of Canada does not reflect the type of strategic behaviour frequently documented in the United States.

The guidelines governing the Court's leave to appeal decisions were unknown until recently. The Court has traditionally refused to publish written reasons for grants or denials of leave. In 1995, Lamer CJ explained that this refusal has been "[i]n order to ensure that this Court enjoyed complete flexibility in allocating its scarce judicial resources toward cases of true public importance."[51] Two years later, Sopinka J elaborated on the "guidelines" and broad principles that the justices employ to identify cases that involve matters of public importance:

1 the presence of a constitutional issue in the form of a challenge to a statute, common law rule or a government practice is usually a strong indication of public importance;
2 a conflict between courts of appeal of different provinces on issues that should be dealt with uniformly as between provinces;
3 a novel point of law:
   Examples:
   reversing the burden of proof of causation;
   extending liability for economic loss;
   reconsidering the test for informed consent in medical malpractice;
4 interpretation of an important federal statute or provincial statute that exists in several provinces;
5 defining Aboriginal rights.[52]

Flemming's analysis reveals that several "jurisprudential" indicators have a significant influence in determining leave. Cases with issues reflecting conflicting lower court decisions are more likely to be granted leave, as are cases where there are dissenting votes in the lower appellate court decision; applications that urge the Court to revisit previous decisions; and arguments that demonstrate how lower court decisions affect the interests of the provincial governments or the federal government. On the other hand, arguments that are fact-specific or stress the need to correct procedural or interpretative errors without connecting them to larger questions of public importance are more likely to fail.[53]

The justices interviewed for this book acknowledged that there is an intuitive aspect to granting leave, although one justice preferred to view the discretionary element of deciding leave to appeal as an "internalized expertise," noting that "we know the law, and immediately when we see it we know if it's not for us" (Interview). Another justice explained that "the intuition is more at the level of balancing the various elements that come into play" (Interview). There tends to be a set of obviously worthy applications and a set of clearly frivolous ones. For those falling in the continuum between those two groups of applications, the threshold of worthiness is not set in stone. Generally speaking, this justice viewed the leave process as reflecting the Court's role "to state the law and give guidance to the other courts ... A case should lend itself to that" (Interview).

Most of the justices and law clerks stressed that the Court is not a court of error – the fact that a lower court reaches the wrong result in a case is not by itself sufficient for the Supreme Court of Canada to grant leave (Interview). This general rule holds even in instances where an appellate court misapplies or fails to follow a judgment of the Supreme Court of Canada. Where the Court has recently pronounced on an issue, the justices prefer to allow the lower courts to deal with subsidiary issues before agreeing to hear a similar case again. Only in instances where the lower courts' failure to properly apply a Supreme Court of Canada precedent becomes an "epidemic" do justices choose to set the record straight.[54] That said, the justices will sometimes grant leave to a case for the sole purpose of affirming the judgment of a lower appellate court in order to "nationalize" a precedent and give direction on the point of law to all of the courts in the country.[55]

Despite what most justices appear to understand as a cardinal rule – that the Court is not a court of error – on rare occasions a justice will push to have the Court rectify a perceived injustice (this occurrence is so rare that one justice described it as a once-in-a-year event) (Interview). Wilson J, writing in 1983, noted that after nine months on the Court she had still not come to understand how the Court exercises its discretion in a leave to appeal.[56] On the question of error correction, she wrote:

Leave cannot be granted to some and denied to others except on some rational basis of selection if people's respect for the institution is to be maintained. I have been struck since I went on the court by the absurdity of telling an unsuccessful litigant in person that the decision in the court below may well be wrong ... but his case raises no issue of public importance as to merit the further time and consideration of the court! There is no way the layman can be persuaded that doing justice in a particular case is not the proper function of the courts and that, if the courts are falling down in the performance of this function, it is not a matter of the utmost public importance![57]

More recently, although there has been a lot of disagreement about departing from the norm and accepting cases that only involve correcting an error of a lower court, one justice noted at times being insistent about taking such cases: "I said I would write it, I know [the case as decided] is wrong and we have to take it" (Interview). The fact that the other justices relent reflects a norm of collegiality and consensus that Flemming identifies in his speculation about how the leave to appeal process inhibits obvious forms of strategic behaviour and tends to result in unanimous voting, even on those applications that are more difficult to determine:

> If a norm of reciprocity infuses the relationship between the justices, it may explain why panel votes tend to be consensual in marginal cases that are neither obvious grants nor obvious denials. If a justice feels particularly strongly about a case, the other justices evidently accommodate the justice, which produces unanimous votes. At the same time, the uncertainty and costs of dissenting reinforce the attractiveness of this norm.[58]

One important consequence of this collegial norm is that some of the cases that fall into the "grey area" are granted leave by the Court when they would normally be rejected under different institutional arrangements or in a less consensual environment.[59]

This behaviour confirms Lawrence Baum's contention, explored in Chapter 1, which is that judges care about what their colleagues think. Indeed, with regard to granting leave to cases solely on the basis of error correction, the motivation of most of the justices appears to have been to keep their insistent colleague satisfied. However, as it pertains to "grey area" cases, could the decision to yield to a justice who "feels particularly strongly" itself be strategic? That is, could a norm of reciprocity be at work to create an understanding that judge x votes for judge y when judge y feels strongly and thus can expect the same in return later on? While this explanation seems plausible, it fails to amount to a regularized pattern of behaviour.

Based on the earlier analysis and Flemming's examination of the process, these instances are relatively infrequent.[60] The majority of leave to appeal decisions are fairly straightforward. Thus, most of the time, legal rules dominate the process. Further, even if it is the case that the majority of justices acquiesce to what amounts to purely policy-driven or "attitudinal" behaviour from a colleague in such instances, it only confirms that most of the time the majority of justices are responding to attitudinal behaviour as opposed to being motivated by their own attitudes. This distinction is an important one because it appears that even when attitudinal behaviour comes into play, collegial norms, rather than attitudes, can dictate the response among other justices.

Although Flemming's account of the leave to appeal process is persuasive, it is important to acknowledge that his study is temporally bound, relying on votes on leave applications from 1993 to 1995. Several important factors can influence the broader pattern of decisions to grant leave to appeal over relatively lengthy periods of time. The introduction of the *Charter* was one event that, not surprisingly, had a significant impact on selecting cases for leave. Several former law clerks who served in the early to mid-1980s noted that they feel that it was easy for *Charter* cases to get leave (Interviews). As one clerk explained, "the fact that it was a *Charter* case that had [made] its way up to the Supreme Court of Canada was itself a pretty good reason for granting leave" (Interview). While this sentiment appears not to have lasted very long, the impact on the Court's agenda should not be understated. According to several clerks who served just a few years later, it was evident that some litigants applying for leave would try to squeeze *Charter* arguments into their applications when they did not fit. One former clerk noted that it felt as though everyone was making a *Charter* argument (Interviews). The justices tried to look at all of these applications carefully, but they became more selective after the first few years of the *Charter*.

Another important consideration when assessing Flemming's analysis is that the end of his study corresponds to the time when the law clerks were, for the most part, removed from any involvement in the leave applications process. When the number of leave applications spiked after 1975, the judges came to rely heavily on the clerks for leave memoranda (summarizing the applications and supplying recommendations), where each justice would have a clerk provide a written opinion on each application. Even this process soon became unworkable, and out of necessity a "pooling system" developed in which each clerk was associated with one of the leave panels and was responsible for producing a leave memorandum for all nine justices.[61] This process is now completed by the Court's staff lawyers. In the United States, the justices have their own clerks provide memos for every case.[62] In Canada, most of the justices rely on the memo prepared by a single clerk. However, some justices required their own clerks to comment on leave memos prepared by clerks working for other judges.[63]

The switch from oral to written appeal applications in 1987 had unforeseen consequences for the Court's efficiency. Although the change helped alleviate a frustrating backlog that hit the Court around that time, the new emphasis on written submissions created its own problems. According to one senior staff member, the Court had the oral leave applications process "down pat," but after a while it became apparent that the written process would accumulate with the clerks. Unfortunately, the applications for leave were often placed on the back burner, as over-burdened clerks focused on bench memoranda and judgment work. One staff member explained that depending on how organized certain judges were, a significant backlog could ensue. By the mid-1990s, Lamer CJ, concerned about timeliness, decided that handing the job to staff lawyers would help streamline the process (Interview). One former justice explained that law clerks were not completely removed from the leave process – as the judges are always free to ask their clerk to review an application for more depth or to examine a particular aspect – but added that the change was conducive to better using the clerks, giving them more time to prepare cases for hearing and to research and work on judgments (Interview).

Thus, since 1995, staff lawyers have been responsible for preparing summaries and recommendations regarding leave to appeal applications. This change may have produced a stabilizing effect on the outcome of leave applications. Law clerks typically serve only one year on the Court. This turnover rate means that a substantial number of leave applications each year are prepared by individuals with little familiarity with them. Giving long-term staff attorneys at the Court responsibility for leave applications means the summaries and recommendations that come to the justices are prepared by people with substantially more experience. Mitchell McInnes, Janet Bolton, and Natalie Derzko contend that clerks at the Supreme Court of Canada are likely to have less "undue influence" over the outcome of the applications than has been reported about clerks in the US Supreme Court, in part because the leave memoranda prepared by Canadian clerks, which range anywhere from four to forty pages, are much more substantial than those prepared by their American counterparts.[64] This argument suggests that because Canadian clerks must provide extensive justifications for their reasoning they are less likely to get anything past their justice. Lorne Sossin contends that this view "does not make very much sense."[65] He writes that "[c]lerks rarely have an interest in intentionally misleading the Justices. Nonetheless, they do tend to favour granting leave to appeal more often than the Justices do."[66] One senior staff member at the Court concurred with Sossin on this point, noting that clerks tend to arrive at the Court eager about their role and might tend to see more cases as being "worthy" or, at least, more likely to conform to the criteria of public importance (Interview).

I explore the role of the law clerks more fully in the next chapter. For present purposes, however, it suffices to point out that the removal of clerks from regular involvement in the leave process may have reduced or stabilized the number of leave memoranda received by the justices that recommend granting leave. The drop in the number of cases accepted by the Court in Table 2 corresponds to the years when staff lawyers took responsibility for summarizing the applications. While a judge may still ask a law clerk to review a particular application in depth, most of the law clerks I interviewed who worked at the Court after 1996 suggest that such requests happen only occasionally. The impact the clerks may have had, or the staff attorneys have now, is of course mitigated by the fact that the judges retain the final say on the leave applications and will disagree with the recommendations of those screening the applications with some regularity (Interviews).

Other broad trends and decisions shape the pattern of the Court's choices in granting leave. *Charter* cases play a less prominent role than they once did in terms of their proportion of the Court's total caseload. The justices are acutely aware of what types of cases the Court takes, and many of them have strong opinions on the areas of law they think receive too much or too little attention. Flemming notes that Lamer CJ felt *Charter* appeals overshadowed commercial law cases. Shortly after becoming chief justice in 1990, Lamer CJ felt he had the support of some of the other justices to "reaffirm a national perspective in private law."[67] Flemming asserts, however, that Lamer CJ's efforts had little impact on the mix of cases granted leave by the Court. Indeed, one justice I interviewed who served at that time noted agreeing with Lamer CJ's sentiment – but only prior to coming to the Court. This justice initially felt the Court was not taking enough civil cases and was dealing with too many *Charter* claims and Aboriginal cases. Yet, once on the Court, the justice found that many commercial cases, even those involving many millions of dollars, had carefully followed trial processes and had seemingly correct appellate judgments: "I was surprised at how few civil cases came with important questions of law that were of national interest" (Interview).

Another justice complained that many of the other justices seemed to feel that every criminal case was important. The fact that the Court would take on such cases and often ended up dismissing the appeals immediately from the bench only added to this justice's frustration (Interview). The Court has recently moved to reduce the number of criminal as-of-right appeals on the docket. In 1997, the Court won the support of the Canadian Bar Association for changes to the *Supreme Court Act* that eliminated appeals as of right in criminal cases where acquittals were overturned on appeal. This change cut the number of automatic appeals by roughly half.[68] There is some indication that McLachlin CJ may agree with the view that many criminal appeals still fail to involve matters of national importance. Since she became chief justice, the Court has sought, but thus far not received, the abolition of the final category of automatic appeals (criminal cases involving dissenting votes at the appellate court level).[69] The primary impetus for the change, however, is said to be to further ameliorate the Court's workload.[70]

Workload problems may create an impetus for another broad change to the leave process – curtailing the total number of cases granted leave. In 1972, then Justice Laskin wrote that there was no support for "any conclusion that there is a policy of rejection according to the volume of work awaiting the court."[71] At least one account contends that since then the Court has purposely cut the number of cases heard in the face of the large backlog it faced in the early 1980s. Ellen Anderson writes: "Quietly and without announcement to the public or the profession that it was doing so, the Court clamped down pre-emptively through a more stringent exercise of the leave to appeal provision provided in the 1975 amendment."[72] Significantly, it appears the legal profession at the time failed to notice.[73]

Since the early 1980s, several justices have publicly voiced their opinion that the Court should cut back on the number of cases it agrees to hear. Several of the Court's former justices, including William McIntyre, Claire L'Heureux-Dubé, and Louise Arbour JJ, are on the record as saying a reduction in cases would result in judgments that are better crafted. L'Heureux-Dubé J argues: "I think we could ease it a little bit so that we could take more time for each case and not rush all the time ... There is no doubt the cases are not as clear-cut, they are much more difficult, we are refining the jurisprudence and we have a long way to go."[74] Interestingly, both L'Heureux-Dubé and Arbour JJ expressed these sentiments while still serving on the Court.[75] However, the chief justice recently refuted the suggestion that a drop in the number of appeals granted leave by the Court in 2006 (when it granted only fifty-five appeals) was an indication that the justices sought to reduce their workload by curtailing the number of cases granted. McLachlin CJ describes such assertions as "alarmist" and notes that the Court typically aims to take on eighty to eighty-five cases per year, but that this number fluctuates in any given year depending on the number of appeal applications and their complexity. The chief justice also notes that while the justices recognize that if they were overworked there could be negative repercussions for the quality of the Court's judgments, none of her colleagues have requested caseload reductions.[76]

Reference Cases

The preceding section examined broad trends and changes in the processes through which the vast majority of cases reach the Court: by right or through the leave process. The final category of cases with which the Court engages are questions referred to it by the federal government or reference questions from provincial governments that have been appealed from provincial courts of appeal.[77] References, or "advisory opinions," usually pertain to constitutional questions, but they can involve any area of law. Final appellate courts in other common law jurisdictions have refused to render advisory opinions on the basis that they are not a proper function of the judiciary.[78] The Supreme Court of Canada is compelled to consider references by the *Supreme Court Act*, but it has repeatedly asserted the discretion to refuse to answer a reference question, particularly if the issues raised are non-justiciable.[79] Nonetheless, it has rarely exercised such discretion.[80] Where it has refused to answer a question, aside from issues of justiciability, the decision is usually because the question is too ambiguous to allow a precise answer[81] or because the parties have not provided the Court with sufficient information to provide an answer.[82] John McEvoy argues persuasively that the Court does not enjoy the discretion to refuse to answer questions referred to it.[83] Indeed, the language of the relevant provisions of the *Supreme Court Act* suggest that it is in fact required to do so.

Although the Court's decisions in reference cases are not technically binding and are not thought to carry the same weight as legal precedents or opinions in regular cases, Peter Hogg notes that, in practice, advisory opinions are treated every bit as authoritatively by lower courts and other branches of government as any of the Court's decisions.[84] Interestingly, however, the Court's decision to refuse to answer one of the four questions referred to it in the 2004 *Reference re Same-Sex Marriage* was based in part on the fact that the non-binding nature of the reference opinion could result in confusion in the law.[85] The first three questions in the reference dealt with whether Parliament had exclusive authority over the definition of marriage, whether extending civil marriage to same-sex couples was consistent with the *Charter*, and whether the *Charter* protected religious officials from being forced to perform same-sex marriages. The fourth question concerned the constitutionality of the opposite-sex definition and was added by then Prime Minister Paul Martin after the initial three questions had already been posed to the Court. The final appellate courts in three provinces (British Columbia, Ontario, and Quebec) had already ruled that the traditional understanding of marriage lacked constitutionality under the *Charter*'s equality provisions, and the federal government had not appealed these decisions to the Supreme Court of Canada. As a result, in the reference, the Court expressed concern that an advisory opinion stating that an opposite-sex definition of marriage was constitutional would result in a lack of uniformity in the law because the provincial appeal courts' rulings would remain binding in those provinces.[86]

Without stating as much, the justices seem to have recognized the overtly political nature of Martin's decision to add the fourth question, noting in the opinion that "[t]here is no precedent for answering a reference question which mirrors issues already disposed of in lower courts where an appeal was available but not pursued."[87] Despite this example, there are many instances in which the Court has failed to show similar prudence. The reference procedure lends itself to use as a tool for politicians to pass off difficult decisions to the courts, regardless of whether those issues are almost entirely political. Hogg criticizes the Court for an "astonishingly liberal" approach to answering questions referred to it surrounding the constitutional battles of 1982, particularly on the meaning of constitutional conventions that raise "no legal issue and had only political consequences."[88] Writing just prior to *Reference re Same-Sex Marriage,* Hogg argues that the Court has not been cautious enough in its handling of reference questions:

> [T]he Court has not made sufficient use of its discretion not to answer a question posed on a reference. The reference procedure has often presented the Court with a relatively abstract question divorced from the factual setting which would be present in a concrete case. It has been a common and justified complaint that some of the opinions rendered in references have propounded doctrine that was too general and abstract to provide a satisfactory rule. A number of the most important Canadian cases are open to criticism on this ground.[89]

Grant Huscroft argues that any decision by the Court to refuse to answer such questions does not reflect prudence on its part but is inherently political.[90] Like McEvoy, Huscroft points out that the Court lacks the discretion Hogg encourages. In the context of *Reference re Same-Sex Marriage,* Huscroft notes that the Court's decision not to answer the fourth question posed to it effectively entrenched the political strategy of the Martin government to use the Court for political cover. He writes that it is inappropriate "for the Court to attempt to stave off political controversy for the government – especially when the government has engendered that controversy."[91] Some of the justices I interviewed acknowledged the political opportunism that arises in the context of the reference procedure, but they generally viewed advisory opinions as a serious component of the Court's role and an occasion to provide clarity to the other branches of government on matters of great importance (Interviews).

Written Submissions and Case Research

Once leave to appeal is granted, the Court sets a date for the oral hearing. The parties and interveners submit written legal arguments for the justices to review, which are called factums. Just over thirty years ago, these factums were said to have played a far less significant role than the equivalent legal "briefs" submitted by parties to the US Supreme Court. Up until the 1960s, oral argument was by far the most important stage of the decision-making process.[92] Several important developments have changed this situation. Since the public importance criterion for leave to appeal was introduced in 1975, the majority of the cases before the Court involve substantive issues of the law rather than merely the resolution of disputes between two parties. The public importance criterion, coupled with the entrenchment of the *Charter* in 1982, means that cases reaching the Court in the contemporary period have become increasingly complex. Thus, the justices must pay more attention to the written arguments, lower court decisions, and issues at hand prior to the oral hearing. Furthermore, the backlog that built up during the 1980s led the Court to introduce time limits for oral hearings in 1987.[93] Together, all of these factors have greatly increased the emphasis and importance of the written materials for the outcome of the cases.

One of the law clerks' most important tasks – and the one that occupies most of their time – is to synthesize and analyze factums and accompanying documents and prepare bench memoranda for their justice on each case. Justices generally need to receive the bench memos approximately one week before the hearing. Most justices appear to allow their three clerks to divide the cases evenly among themselves at the start of each term. Although some of the justices noted that their preference is that the clerks expose themselves to as many different areas of law as possible, they typically allow the clerks to pursue cases that are particularly interesting for them or that fall under their specialization (Interviews). Once assigned to a case, a clerk is responsible for that case throughout the process. If the clerk's justice is assigned to write the decision on that case, the clerk might assist in further research or drafting or editing the decision. Alternatively, if another justice is assigned, the clerk might be asked to produce a "comment memo" for the justice on the draft once it has been circulated. For some time, the clerks have also been required to attend the oral hearing for the cases to which they are assigned (Interviews).[94]

The substance and style of the bench memos vary from justice to justice and even from clerk to clerk. In the 1970s, when each justice had a single clerk, some preferred to have their clerks do in-depth research on a limited number of cases, while others wanted their clerks' impressions of each case via a bench memo prior to the hearing.[95] During this period, the bench memos were but a few handwritten pages in length.[96] As the law clerk program expanded, the norm became for the clerks to prepare a bench memorandum on each case. Bench memos are now typically twenty to forty typed pages and, in rare instances, may even exceed 100 pages in length (Interviews). Larger bench memos include an executive summary, a recitation of the facts and proceedings in the lower courts, summaries and analyses of the parties' arguments, and, depending on the justice, a recommendation on how to treat the appeal.

The importance or influence of the clerk's bench memo appears to vary, depending on the justice. All of the justices emphasized that they read the factums and the lower court decisions themselves. In one sense then, the bench memo is largely an aid. As several justices noted, the volume of cases and the sheer amount of written materials associated with each case makes it impossible for the justices to check all of the cases cited in the material or to go to the library to do further research themselves. The clerks' role in what one justice described as "the process of validation and verification" is extremely important (Interview). The justices might reasonably be placed along a continuum in regard to how they treat the bench memos. On one end, some justices aim to read as much of the material themselves and thus prefer short, concise bench memos that they use primarily as a reference tool. Further, these justices may not even solicit the clerks for their recommendations on how to handle the appeal. On the other end, some justices appear to rely more heavily on the bench memos as a primary aid in preparing for the hearing. Many of the justices will discuss the bench memo in person with their clerks prior to the hearing in order to flesh out particular issues or even to argue certain points. In this sense, then, the bench memo is both the start and end point on which the justice's first impressions of the case rests.[97] This is significant because, as discussed later in this chapter, the written material is usually determinative of the outcome of the case.

Panel Selection: Determining Which Justices Hear an Appeal

As noted earlier, unlike the US Supreme Court, where all of the justices sit in each case *(en banc),* the Supreme Court of Canada has traditionally heard cases in panels of five, seven, or nine. The chief justice determines both the size of the panels and which justices sit on which panels. This decision is thus a potential site for strategic behaviour, assuming that a chief justice might try to determine panel compositions based on her preferred outcome. Lori Hauseggar and Stacia Haynie examine the use of panels to see whether chief justices have taken advantage of the power to assign them for the strategic purpose of pursuing their own policy goals.[98] The authors gauge each justice's policy preference based on the percentage of votes he or she casts in favour of the accused in criminal cases, with the hypothesis that the closer a judge's score to that of the chief justice the more likely he or she will be assigned to a panel. They coded all of the published cases from 1986 to 1997, creating a variable for each judge sitting on the Court when the case was heard. The authors found that for the full range of cases, the chief justice was actually significantly more likely to select individuals for panel assignment who are ideologically further removed.[99] However, for cases involving "salient civil rights and liberties issues," the chief justice is more likely to assign judges with close policy preferences.[100] The authors suggest that institutional constraints, such as workload and the desire to have Quebec judges assigned to panels for cases coming out of that province, may inhibit some strategic behaviour. Nevertheless, the finding that the chief justice is more likely to assign judges with close policy preferences to more salient cases confirms their central premise.

However, even this qualified conclusion seems problematic. First, Hauseggar and Haynie extrapolate the justices' ideological position based on their votes in criminal cases and then apply that to all cases for the period under study. Yet, as explored in Chapter 1, justices do not necessarily vote with ideological consistency across different types of cases or areas of law. Second, even without this crucial measurement problem, a new emphasis by McLachlin CJ to assign panels with all nine justices appears to render Hauseggar and Haynie's time-bound study less applicable.

The convention that all nine justices sit in particularly important cases has strengthened over the period since the *Charter* was released. Panels of five are normally struck for appeals by right or in cases implicating the *Civil Code of Québec,* so that the justices from that province constitute a majority on the panel. On other occasions, illness, retirement, or recusal from new appointees to the Court in cases they have already heard require the creation of smaller panels. As Lamer CJ explains,

> [i]f there is a possibility that the outcome of a case might be different with fewer than nine judges, I'll do my best to strike a panel of nine judges. How do I know if there will be a division? First, my executive legal officer helps me to flag these cases. Also, I know my colleagues and I have a fairly good idea about what they are thinking on particular issues. I might ask what the other judges think about a particular issue, even if it is not of national general importance. I wouldn't like to see a minority in the court impose its views on the court, and even for the cases that are not of general importance I will strike the bench of nine if necessary.[101]

While Lamer CJ's comments about knowing what his colleagues are thinking about particular issues suggest that an opportunistic chief justice could conceivably use his or her power to strike panels in an ideological manner, the long-term trend toward larger panels in the *Charter*-era Court suggest that strengthening norms override such considerations. McLachlin CJ, the current chief justice, has an even stronger preference to strike panels with the full court. Donald Songer finds that the percentage of nine-judge panels went from 9.8 percent under Dickson CJ, to 30.4 percent under Lamer CJ, to 51.7 percent under McLachlin CJ.[102] This increase may be in part due to the reduction in appeals by right after 1997, which was the last year in Hauseggar and Haynie's study. Further, all of the justices interviewed for this study stated that they were satisfied with how the panels are selected, regardless of which chief justice they served with.

Oral Hearing

Historically, arguments by counsel during oral hearings have been given considerable weight compared to the written factums.[103] As noted earlier, a dramatic change in the type of cases heard by the Court since it gained control over its docket in 1975 has effectively reversed this reality. Oral hearings for leave applications were eliminated in 1987. In the same year, Dickson CJ established time limits for oral hearings of actual appeals, a move that allowed the Court to begin the practice of hearing two cases per day.[104] The Court holds three three-month terms beginning in January, April, and October, during which it alternates sitting for two weeks to hear appeals and two weeks off for research and judgment writing. New, stricter time limits that were established in the 1990s by Lamer CJ limit litigants on each side to one hour each, with those interveners that have been granted access to the oral hearing normally limited to twenty minutes. Lawyer's arguments are frequently interrupted by questions from the justices, which count toward the time limits. This format leaves a rather short period for litigants to convince the justices in the hearing. As a result, the oral hearing is only determinative of the outcome of a minority of cases (Interviews).

Such a process does not mean the hearing is inconsequential. Rather, by the time the justices have considered the written submissions of the parties and completed their preparatory work going into the hearings, they tend to at least lean toward a probable outcome. In most cases, the oral hearing serves largely to confirm these initial inclinations. Nevertheless, in a substantial number of cases – from 10 to 25 percent, according to the justices I interviewed – the hearing can change this line of thinking in a manner that either reverses a justice's support for an appeal or fundamentally alters the main line of reasoning they might have in mind going into the hearing (Interview).

Sopinka J has written that "[b]y the time a case reaches our court, counsel's performance contributes no more than 10 or 15 percent to the outcome."[105] Most of the justices I interviewed generally agreed with this sentiment. As one justice explained, "you have to realize when a case gets to the Supreme Court it has already been dealt with by two courts, a trial court and a court of appeal ... Things have been pretty well sifted through by that stage" (Interview). This justice noted that in rare instances the justices may have such a firm view that they need only to hear from one of the parties during the oral argument:

In some cases by that time the direction may be pretty obvious and the Court will decide, depending on which way things appear, either to hear the appellant and then not call on the respondent, because they feel that the appeal is obviously unfounded. Or, in the reverse, call upon the respondent, before calling on the appellant, and then rendering judgment without hearing the other side because the Court was already of the opinion that the other side was correct but still felt it should give the side that was arguing otherwise a full opportunity to be heard. To be able to do that before actually sitting you have to know the case very well. That's a minority of cases. Most cases the Court will hear both sides, but it may well stick to the initial impression it had and the impression may be different with different judges. (Interview)

Another justice noted being a bit leery of indicating in what percentage of cases the oral hearing impacts the thought process but stated that the effect hearings have can take different forms:

You may change your mind in respect of the outcome. And you may change your mind in respect of what are the relevant issues, on what basis the judgment should be prepared. Sometimes oral arguments in the Court will have an impact on the outcome. More often, on the way issues are defined and the reasons drafted by bringing sometimes more clarity to what are really relevant issues, what are the matters which are of grave concern to the parties, or often bringing out what the members of the Court think the issues are [and] which issues should be addressed. It may happen during the hearing and sometimes after, during the writing process. (Interview)

A third justice acknowledged that oral hearings can change the thinking on a case, usually if new or unexpected issues arise and "you decide to see it in a different light." However, this justice noted the percentage of cases in which this would happen is nowhere near 25 percent: "After you've read all [of the written material] it would be unusual for me not to have a pretty good idea of how I thought the case should go. And most times it went the way I thought it was going to go" (Interview). Another justice contended that the hearing becomes less important the further up the judicial hierarchy a case goes. Nevertheless, this justice noted that even if a judge only changes her mind 5 percent of the time that is very significant for the highest court in the land (Interview).

The fact that the oral hearing is not usually determinative of the outcome of a case does not render the hearings unimportant. This point is something all of the justices emphasize. As one justice stated,

[t]he oral hearing is a useful exercise in a significant number of cases – not the majority – but even if it doesn't change the Court's opinion about which way a case should go, it may enlighten the issues further and may bring a

better or different focus on the issues and sometimes that focus may be different from the focus that appeared from the factums. (Interview)

Another justice put it this way:

> There is a dynamic in the collegial process, in the discussion with the counsel for the parties, and you may suddenly acquire a different perspective on an aspect of the case. You may discover something that you may have missed in your analysis of the case or of the judgment, some fact you may have overlooked which is really critical to the case. (Interview)

While oral hearings have their part, both for the outcome and with respect to the reasoning in the decision, this justice did acknowledge that the Supreme Court of Canada is probably closer to the US Supreme Court, which places little emphasis on hearings, than to the British House of Lords, where hearings "are virtually unlimited" (Interview). Another justice noted that the Canadian Court puts more emphasis on the hearings than the US Supreme Court, which limits arguments to half an hour. The time limits that the Canadian Court imposes are important for the discipline of both the lawyers and the judges because "it helps efficiency and forces you to really focus on what's important for the case" (Interview). This justice also noted that the hearing is important because it can confirm a justice's view – something that is often neglected in academic literature that examines judicial voting behaviour.

The oral hearing is an opportunity for the justices to flesh out the ideas they have developed about the issues involved in a case. The usual effect is to solidify these ideas, but in a significant number of cases, the hearing has an important impact on the justices' perceptions of the written material. What does this say about the judicial motivations that are involved? As noted in Chapter 1, the attitudinal model has difficulty accounting for changes in judicial attitudes over time. What is even more problematic for the attitudinal model is explaining why justices would change their minds during the course of deciding particular cases. These changes in votes, referred to as "vote fluidity" in the American judicial behaviour literature, should not occur if justices are pursuing outcomes that are predicated on ideological policy preferences.

As examined in Chapter 1, limited studies exploring fluidity in the US Supreme Court have found instances of vote changes that are near 12 percent.[106] Attitudinal scholars have asserted in such studies that because judicial votes are consistent in the majority of cases, the existence of fluidity does little damage to their theory. Yet, because these studies rely on voting records accessible through the justices' private papers, they focus on changes in votes from the original conference votes to the final votes. Thus, they do not capture the justices' considerations before and during the oral hearing. It is therefore likely that the American studies capture only a fraction of the actual voting fluidity in the US Supreme Court. This conclusion is significant because it means judges might change their minds as a result of legal argument more often than thought. All of the Canadian justices I interviewed reported that they are considerably more likely to change their minds with respect to the outcome of a case before or during the hearing stage rather than later.

Voting fluidity and its possible sources are explored more fully in the next chapter. It is worth pointing out here, however, that although scholars of the Supreme Court of Canada lack access to the internal memoranda and voting records of the justices, the fluidity levels found in US studies approximate the self-reported rates of vote change by the Canadian justices. Patterns of when and how often justices change their minds were independently confirmed by most of the clerks interviewed for this study.[107] The justices' attention to the legal arguments of counsel at oral hearings and the frequency with which it changes the outcome shows that such considerations are at least one important factor in decisions. The even larger percentage of cases where oral hearings have an impact on the reasoning involved in a decision but not on the vote itself is also significant and is largely ignored by attitudinal scholars.[108]

One justice I interviewed acknowledged that, like everyone, judges are (at least in part) a product of their experiences. This justice spoke at length about how the hearing itself might help justices avoid value-based decision making:

> The challenge is to use that experience to enlighten, not to prejudge, issues. It's easy for me to say that, but it's difficult to be faithful to that. So why is this all relevant to the hearing? Well, until the hearing of the case, you might find when you read the case it looks like something you would [resolve] in a certain way because you've had familiarity with the issue or you've had experience with the issue. But you can quite often get a different perspective on that through the hearing. You might have missed it in the reading of the facta. You might get it from an intervener – because you grew up with a certain set of values and a certain set of experiences – that says "hey wait a minute, that's conventional thinking that I'm not sure is called for in this case." And there are a lot of areas, in the area of the *Charter* in particular, where you get a far better view of the issue through the hearing emphasizing certain points in a way that [may result in] a more enlightened way of looking at certain issues. We're all products of our experiences and we have to make sure that we're not just prematurely giving into those experience-based perceptions as opposed to the more logical and more objective analyses. (Interview)

The give and take in the hearing can provide different lenses of analysis for justices who might otherwise rely on their own perceptions and preferences to determine the appropriate outcome in certain cases. The justices' comments about the frequency with which their perceptions are changed by the oral hearing makes it clear that this process of elucidation does not occur in the majority of cases. Further, it would be naive to presume that this process always precludes the justices' ideological preferences or personal values from creeping in (consciously or subconsciously). Finally, the time limits and the reduced emphasis the Court has placed on the hearings over the past several decades means the parties have limited opportunity to impress these varied perspectives on the justices. Nevertheless, the fact that many clerks confirmed that on occasion their justice would return from an oral hearing with a different perspective on a case lends some independent credence to the preceding description of how the hearing can impact the justices' thinking (Interviews).

Voting fluidity is also cited as a central indicator of strategic behaviour.[109] Some justices have publicly commented on their expectations for the hearings. Former Justice Michel Bastarache states that the approach of different justices varies widely in oral hearing: "There are the 'get on with it' judges, the patient judges, the chatty judges and the quiet judges." The justices' sympathy to passionate advocacy varies as well, as "some will be upset by arguments based on simplistic morality, others not."[110] Bastarache J also points out that in many instances, if counsel does not move beyond the arguments already presented in the factums then they may not be successful in changing most of the justices' minds:

> It is all but impossible for us judges to come into a hearing without having a preliminary view of the matter to be heard. This does not mean that oral advocacy cannot make a difference, but it does mean that except in those cases where a judge still thinks there is a good chance of going either way, counsel will have to do a lot more than repeat what they have argued in their factum to persuade him or her.[111]

Sopinka J notes that counsel should be direct and should not regard questions as imposing on their time: "An effective answer will often persuade other judges even if it does not persuade the questioner."[112]

One of the only external indicators of the judges' possible train of thought in the oral hearing is the type of questions they pose to counsel.[113] The questions and the justices' reaction to the responses given by the lawyers might suggest which way they are leaning.[114] However, the justices' questions may be misleading for several reasons. Most of the justices note that they will occasionally play "devil's advocate" by asking questions that challenge counsel, even if the justice is already sympathetic to the arguments. At times, this approach may be used because justices want to emphasize a point for their colleagues (Interviews). Alternatively, such questions may help a justice consider the implications of coming down on one side. One justice noted that good lawyers make the justices reflect on issues they had not considered that may result from a decision. This justice cited *R. v Askov* as an example of a case in which questions during the oral hearing may have presented controversial repercussions (Interview).[115] In *Askov*, the Court ruled that a two-year delay in trial proceedings, the product of an overburdened system, violated section 11(b) of the *Charter*, the right to be tried within a reasonable time. The decision resulted in thousands of criminal charges being dropped or stayed by the lower courts and was subject to intense media scrutiny and criticism. This justice argued that government counsel failed at the oral hearing to sufficiently highlight the possible effects such a ruling would have had at the lower court system. The justice stated: "I think [the decision in] *Askov* was perfectly right, but we may have been more precise in avoiding that onslaught" (Interview).

Finally, a justice may be leaning in favour of a counsel's case but still have difficult questions relating to subsidiary issues of concern to that justice. The justices generally agree that lawyers are usually (or should be) thankful for such questions, as they allow counsel to focus specifically on what is troubling the justice and give them the opportunity to resolve it. Several justices argued that, as a result, it would be futile for an observer to attempt to draw conclusions about where the justices might be leaning with respect to a case based on the questions posed at the hearing. It was for this very reason, according to one justice, that the Court decided there would be no questions from the bench during arguments at the hearing for *Reference re Secession of Quebec* (Interview).[116] All of the questions the judges had were given to the chief justice and were put to the lawyers by the chief justice after argument. As one justice explained, "the Court wanted to avoid as much as possible the hearing being relayed in the form of little bits, extracts, which would be presented out of context" (Interview). The justices agreed that given the intense media coverage of the reference this measure would help avoid misperceptions that would not be helpful for the public (Interview).

Nevertheless, the justices do often ask questions or otherwise give some indication at the hearing that reveals their sincere sentiments about the disposition of the case or the issues at hand. Some justices may pose questions that, in effect, dispute or damage a counsel's point. Alternatively, a justice might come to the aid of a counsel. As Wilson J states, "a lot of ink has been spilled on the subject of whether or not it is appropriate for judges to compensate for unevenly matched counsel by putting forward arguments themselves. I have never had much doubt about that. I think we have to – in the interests of justice."[117] This advocacy rarely comes in the form of a speech or statement from the bench. The convention among the justices is to frame their sentiments in the form of a question to counsel. In the course of posing questions, however, the justices might refer to precedents or evidence that answers another justice's question for counsel. Coming to counsel's aid in this sense can be interpreted as a strategic move on the part of some justices to highlight certain issues or to frame the debate before the justices meet in the post-hearing conference.

The emphasis on written material in the contemporary period is regarded as having diminished the importance of the oral hearing stage. Nevertheless, it is clear that in a significant percentage of cases the hearing can be determinative as to outcome or the rationale supporting the outcome. The fact that vote fluidity exists illustrates the need for attention on aspects of judicial decision making that do not pertain to the justices' ideological policy preferences. Nonetheless, the hearing can certainly be said to act as a site for strategic behaviour on the part of the justices, at least on occasion. The questions posed to counsel in the hearing are unlikely to yield reliable predictions about vote intentions or the justices' motivations because information gathering, attempts to sway colleagues, and sincere questions are all part of the mix that reflects judicial incentives.

Conclusion

This chapter identifies how a number of important institutional factors outside of policy preferences influence decision making at the Supreme Court of Canada. Continuous procedural reforms enacted throughout the modern period reflect a concern for the administrative effectiveness of the Court. Imbued in this attention to efficiency is a consideration of the institution's reputation and the quality of its work. The evidence in this chapter also demonstrates that a variety of factors come into play when justices make decisions. At the leave to appeal stage, strong norms of consensual decision making, or collegiality, tend to predominate. Legal rules governing the process dictate how cases are selected for hearing. In rare instances where they do not, it is often the case that justices relent to the preferences of an individual colleague to have a particular case heard. Even occasions such as these seem to be a result of collegial, rather than attitudinal or strategic, concern. There appears to be little room for strategic manoeuvring due to the institutional design of the process. When a conference of the full Court considers a particular case, the panel of three justices to which it was originally assigned retain the final say. Nor have changes made to the process over the years made case selection any more susceptible to attitudinal or strategic behaviour. Rather, changes like the removal of the clerks from the process have generally been made to ensure institutional efficiency. Finally, a number of justices in recent years have advocated reducing the number of cases accepted by the Court, something that makes little sense from an attitudinal perspective given that it would reduce the number of opportunities available to justices to influence policy. The concern for quality evidenced by such a preference suggests that many of the justices care about the work of the Court for its own sake.

Moreover, stages of the Court's process that might make for obvious sites of activity for strategic behaviour, such as the selection of panels to hear appeals, are not clearly representative of such activity. Contrary to the findings of other studies, the analysis presented here suggests that norms and conventions dictate the composition of such panels. Under successive chief justices in the contemporary period, full panels of nine judges are becoming more and more the norm. Further, in none of the interviews that I conducted with justices or former law clerks was there any suggestion that a justice was unhappy with not being assigned to a panel.

The oral hearing provides room for all types of behaviour. The justices acknowledge sincere and strategic approaches to questioning counsel. Court observers must be careful, however, because of the difficulties associated with correctly identifying such behaviour. The fact that the justices acknowledge sometimes changing their minds around the oral hearing stage suggests two important things. First, the law is often indeterminate as a resource for coming to the correct conclusion about issues confronting the Court. Second, there are a significant number of cases left unexplained by the attitudinal model, as it cannot account for why justices would change their minds.

The approach undertaken in this chapter is not limited to demonstrating that a multitude of factors influence judicial decisions. It is also well suited to identifying when and under what conditions particular factors are most prominent. Attention to changes over time also shed light on how specific procedures and rules act to constrain or dictate motivating factors. Changes in the rules governing appeals by right have allowed the Court to focus on cases of national importance, but these changes have had repercussions on the efficiency of the Court, which has instigated further reforms. In addition, the shift in emphasis to written materials and away from oral hearings reflects the Court's transformation to a more full-fledged policy-making institution. The consequences of this evolution are explored more fully in the next two chapters.

4
The Decision: Collegiality, Conflict, and Consensus

Many studies of court decision making focus on the voting patterns of individual justices. At a basic level, this emphasis makes sense: judges on multi-member courts are independent and free to decide cases as they see fit. Yet, the Supreme Court of Canada is a highly collaborative institution, and a true understanding of the development of its decisions requires an account of group interaction. Judicial role conceptions regarding collegiality – the extent to which a justice should come to conclusions on his or her own or in collaboration with colleagues, how to utilize law clerks, what the proper limits of deliberation and negotiation are – vary significantly among individual justices. The drafting of the Court's written reasons and the compromises the justices make along the way are driven by these individual perspectives. This chapter explores how these differences affect consensus on the Court, how consensus can vary over time, and how they account for the different degrees to which individual justices might pursue attitudinally inspired or strategic behaviour. A focus on the various stages in the development of written reasons illustrates how potential "sites of activity" for these kinds of behaviour can develop under particular circumstances. During the Court's recent history, interpersonal divisions and incidents of informal lobbying among certain justices have created tension. During other periods, particularly on the current Court, an effort to achieve more consensus has informed the collaborative process.

Preparation and revision of drafts are the most time-consuming components of the justices' work, in part because written reasons are viewed as the institution's primary legitimating and accountability function. The relative lack of attention in much of the judicial behaviour literature to the development of the Court's actual written reasons, as opposed to merely judicial votes, is highly problematic. As the analysis in this chapter demonstrates, understanding this component of the Court's work is central to explaining what motivates judges and how judicial processes, norms, and values impact outcomes. One central feature of this process is the consensual nature of the

Court's decision making, including a marked tendency for unanimous decisions. Although discussion in this chapter will show that the extent of unanimous decisions should not be overstated (especially since cases under the *Canadian Charter of Rights and Freedoms* involve more judicial disagreement than other types of cases), the collegial nature of the Canadian Court (especially relative to the Supreme Court of the United States) is a particular aspect of group interaction that warrants attention.[1] This chapter will show that only on rare occasions do the justices make unanimity an explicit goal but that it does occur in especially important cases. Importantly, an analysis of those cases where unanimity is an explicit objective of the Court suggests that the result is to actually reduce the depth and breadth of consensus in terms of the concrete legal or policy outcomes manifest in the written reasons.

Conference

Following the oral hearing of each case, the justices retire to the conference room, where each indicates where he or she stands on the case and the primary rationale in support of this position. The conference is often the only time that the full panel of justices will discuss the case together at the same time. The general tenor of the conference varies over time, something influenced by the approach taken by the chief justice. Within this broader context, the length and depth of deliberation that takes place also varies from case to case. Conferences were not regular practice at the Supreme Court of Canada until the late 1960s, when John Cartwright became chief justice and standardized the meetings. Although little is known about the Court's internal practices prior to that time, decision making was a much more individualized process. In the Court's first few decades, *seriatim* opinions (where each justice writes individual reasons) were the standard practice, and most of the time there was little to no communication between justices prior to the delivery of decisions.[2] Through these early decades, conferences were occasionally held in the chief justice's chambers, but the frequency of these meetings and the benefits that they brought is unknown.[3] At least one justice of this era reportedly refused to participate in discussions with his colleagues altogether.[4]

The lack of regularized internal procedures arguably contributed to the Court's slow progress toward becoming a true leader in the development of Canadian law. It has been suggested that without a conference, Court decisions gave "fuller rein to the idiosyncratic legal views of individual judges."[5] In effect, more debate, compromise, and collaboration result not only in more authoritative pronouncements on the law for the lower courts to follow but also in judgments of better quality. Peter McCormick notes, however, that while the move to a regular system of conferences helps make for more coherent leadership (and innovation), the *seriatim* court is well suited to applying long-standing principles of law. If multiple judges reach the same conclusion in *seriatim* decision making, then it is evidence that previously established doctrine directs a given outcome.[6]

The timing of conferences has not changed since they became regular practice. As one justice explained, conferencing immediately after hearing "leaves you the freshest" (Interview). There has been some discussion of changing this process, perhaps moving to weekly conferences where groups of cases are discussed, but no such reform has taken place. If a consensus is immediately reached and the jurisprudence does not require substantive elaboration, the justices may decide to dispose of the case with an oral pronouncement in the courtroom. The vast majority of cases disposed of in this manner are appeals by right, and often the Court will simply signal agreement with the reasons of the court below. The majority of cases are reserved, and the Court releases written decisions some months later.

At conference, the justices have long expressed their views on the case in reverse order of seniority, which is a convention designed to ensure that junior justices are not unduly influenced by, or deferential to, their more experienced colleagues – something former Justice Bertha Wilson notes is of little risk because judges on the Court are "fiercely independent."[7] (Interestingly, the justices of the US Supreme Court speak in order of seniority). Two of the justices interviewed for this study acknowledged being nervous the first time they spoke at conference. The added burden of speaking first contributed to their apprehension (Interview). In the past few years, this conventional speaking order has given way to a somewhat less formal discussion around the table.

The tone, duration, and comprehensiveness of the conference appear to ebb and flow, something that is usually dictated by the style of the chief justice. Whereas some justices would prefer more opportunity for comprehensive, free-flowing group discussions of the cases, in reality, the conferences can be as short as five minutes long (Interviews). Under Chief Justice Bora Laskin, they were quite brief. In the early years of the *Charter*, under Chief Justice Brian Dickson, however, longer discussions would take place. Dickson CJ believed the new issues the Court was facing required more collaborative attention. According to McCormick and Ian Greene, "because of the tendency of the judges on the Dickson court to debate issues with each other directly, comments were sometimes not made according to the usual junior-senior order, but ricocheted around the room in a more random and variable manner."[8] In his biography, Dickson CJ's "collegial" approach has been contrasted with Laskin CJ's "more austere and professorial style." Whereas Laskin CJ was reportedly "inclined to try to influence the result," Dickson CJ "was less interested in imposing his own views than in achieving broad consensus; he was looking for clear and practical solutions that would attract the widest possible support from his colleagues and the community at large."[9] The drawback to this approach, according to former Justice Gérard La Forest, was that "the discussions were sometimes like faculty meetings – need I say more.'"[10]

The tone at conference is almost always cordial. The behaviour of Supreme Court of Canada judges has been described as less vigorous than what has been reported of the US Supreme Court's conferences.[11] Nevertheless, some justices are more forceful than others.[12] The personalities and the circumstances of the Court play a role with regard to the congeniality of the conferences. Laskin CJ's blunt management style occasionally cropped up at conference. For example, his biography recounts his scolding Justice Jean Beetz in front of the others for the slow production of decisions.[13]

On the contemporary Court, the majority of conferences are typically twenty minutes in duration or less, although they can exceed that when consensus does not develop or the case is particularly complex or controversial. One justice interviewed for this book complained that conference discussions are limited, sometimes even as short as "two to five minutes" (Interviews). Another justice noted, however, that the conference is not meant to be a drafting process. Discussion is usually meant to formulate where each justice stands, the outcome of the case and the main reasons or basis for it. Sometimes it will take considerable discussion to accomplish this goal, but where a consensus is reached quickly it would be inefficient to prolong the conversation: "There is an effort that when the first people speak, you try to build on what they say. You don't repeat what they say, you simply say 'I agree with that point or that point.'" The discussion will take longer if certain judges are uncertain or if there is disagreement on "how far to go in our reasoning" (Interviews).

Despite this effort, conferences on the current "McLachlin Court" tend to be more comprehensive than they were under her predecessor, Chief Justice Antonio Lamer (Interviews). Former Justice Michel Bastarache noted not long after Beverley McLachlin became chief that she "rejuvenated" the process, seeking from the outset of a case to reduce the number of written reasons.[14] This goal tends to require more thorough conference meetings, something that occurred with less frequency on the Lamer Court, where, in particular areas of law, such as *Charter* cases involving due process issues, deep divisions were evident.[15]

Once the justices have aired their views as to the disposition of the case, the remaining task is usually to assign an opinion writer. Justices will typically volunteer to write because they specialize in the particular area of law or because the case interests them. According to the justices, case assignment tends to be a collegial process. C.L. Ostberg and Matthew Wetstein's analysis suggests justices will defer to colleagues with expertise in a particular area of law, as this is a strong factor in determining the authorship of reasons.[16] Nonetheless, on occasion, a justice will push strongly to write the majority reasons, particularly if the case is one of high visibility or constitutional importance (Interviews). Competition between the justices in the period immediately following the creation of the *Charter* was especially strong, "with judges jostling to write majority judgments and make legal history."[17] Donald Songer's findings suggest that under some chief justices, the primary determinant in these instances was seniority, although under McLachlin CJ this factor is not necessarily automatic.[18]

In instances where no volunteers are forthcoming, the chief justice will assign the case, with careful attention paid to the workload of each judge.[19] One account suggests that on occasion the judges have demonstrated avoidance techniques:

> [Bertha] Wilson soon discovered that her new colleagues were fully capable of looking down at the table (or even bending under it to attend to a propitiously untied shoelace) in order to avoid catching the chief justice's eye when he was seeking a volunteer to prepare the first draft. Such evasive techniques were understandable in dry technical cases where the decision seemed relatively uncontroversial.[20]

While this account is an amusing anecdote, the justices asserted in interviews that writing assignments is almost always made with little "jostling" or attempts at avoidance. Under McLachlin CJ, in particular, workload considerations and legal specialization tend to dominate assigning priorities (Interviews). In addition, one study finds that a transitional effect exists, such that junior members write significantly fewer decisions in their first five or so years on the Court.[21]

The generally collegial and professional approach to writing assignments does not mean there is no room for strategically minded behaviour. For example, at conference following hearings for the "labour trilogy," all of the justices except for Dickson CJ and Wilson J spoke strongly against protecting the right to strike under the *Charter*.[22] According to Robert Sharpe and Kent Roach, Dickson CJ refrained from expressing his view, thereby "preserving his prerogative as chief justice and leading exponent of the Charter to write first reasons, a task he could not have assumed had he taken a strong position at odds with the majority of the Court."[23] Such behaviour is reminiscent of the political machinations revealed in accounts of the US Supreme Court under former Chief Justice Warren Burger, who would routinely abstain from voting or would even switch his vote at conference to retain decision assignment power.[24] Where the controversial practice appears to have been representative of a pattern of behaviour on Burger CJ's part, the same cannot be said of Dickson CJ. Nevertheless, the story reveals one avenue for outright strategic manoeuvring by the chief justice when particularly important or controversial cases arise.

Preparation of Reasons

There is no uniform approach among the justices with regard to how they prepare drafts of written reasons. Some of the Court's members will prepare a simple outline of the reasoning explored in conference, while others will go through the case materials and begin work on a substantial rough draft. Regardless of the starting point, most judgments go through several drafts before they are circulated to the rest of the Court, and they are then subjected to even more revisions (Interviews). Each justice also varies in the extent to which she relies on her law clerks, and the extent of this reliance can vary from case to case. One thing is especially clear: the law clerks' involvement in the preparation of reasons is substantial, ranging from assisting in editing and additional research to writing full drafts of the reasons themselves (Interviews). Typically, the clerk that prepares the bench memoranda for a particular case will be the clerk assigned to work on the judgment.

One justice suggested that the two primary aspects of the clerks' relationship with the judge are professional and educational (Interview). The professional relationship ensures the justice understands all aspects of the case through the clerk's research and assistance. In the educational aspect of the relationship, the judge tries to give the clerks as much exposure as possible to the judicial process and all areas of the law during their year of service. With this view in mind, this particular justice allowed the clerks to participate in all aspects of handling a case, including working on the drafting of the reasons. When assigned writing responsibilities for a case, the justice prepared an outline following the conference discussion for the clerk to follow when the clerk was working on the reasons (Interview).

Another justice followed every conference by writing a memo of a page or two in length, describing what was discussed, what the consensus was and why, and the key issues or problems of the case. This justice noted that "through these years, I've written the majority of the first drafts of my own reasons. If I'm assigned to write the reasons, I have habits going back to college – I write an outline of the reasons, I almost never start cold." Occasionally this justice would have clerks prepare a first draft. In these instances, the clerk "has this outline that I discuss with him. If I do it myself, I start writing after doing my research, asking sometimes my clerk for a summation of research" (Interview).

A third justice noted relying "a great deal" on the clerks: "My philosophy was that the essential role of the judge, for which he can't be replaced or substituted, is judging. The rest, he can get assistance." Such assistance includes both research and writing: "Our clerks are the cream of the crop from the law faculties across the country. They have good minds, therefore, they research intelligently and understand [how] the judge is thinking." The real substantive thinking remains the purview of the justice. One of the key reasons for including the clerks so thoroughly in the process is efficiency: "You have to be mindful that each judge has three clerks, and he's dealing with cases that were worked on by each one of the three law clerks" (Interview).

A fourth justice was even more effusive about the importance of the clerks' work: "You can have a wonderful exchange with these young people." In some respects, the clerks are "much more knowledgeable" than justices, because they are just out of law school and have received training on constitutional issues and the *Charter*. Describing the clerks as a "great resource," this justice noted initially avoiding having clerks write drafts, but over time deciding it could be fruitful: "I thought it was good for them to be able to sit in 'my chair,'" the justice explained, adding that the clerks' writing can produce interesting things for discussion and contemplation (Interview).

Some commentators suggest that the law clerks' activity is important, not only because their research and intellectual contributions reflect the fact that the Court has evolved into a more full-fledged policy-making institution but also because they have a high degree of influence on case outcomes. F.L. Morton and Rainer Knopff write, for example: "[I]n effect, the clerks function as a filter between what comes into the court (factums) and what goes out (written judgments). Lawyers can no longer assume that the judges have actually read their factums, as opposed to selective summaries prepared by the clerks."[25] The justices and law clerks interviewed for this study asserted that the justices look at all of the relevant material for each case. Yet, Morton and Knopff's assertion that the "rapid growth in the number of functions of the clerks has effected a devolution of power from the top (judges) to the middle (clerks) of the bureaucratic pyramid" is worth examining.[26] While it is obvious that the justices retain the final say in the outcome of a case, the process of research and writing undertaken by the clerks may help shape the judgments in a fundamental way. By choosing to frame issues in a particular manner in the course of writing the first draft, or by introducing or emphasizing particular research on a given issue, the clerks wield tremendous power. Most of the clerks are modest about the extent of their influence, although a couple of the clerks I interviewed say they were surprised at how much power they had. One clerk noted that there were justices who would give surprisingly little instruction, telling their clerks: "I want to find for the appellant, go write the first draft." This clerk noted: "[T]hat's an extraordinary amount of power to give somebody who just graduated from law school" (Interview).

Most of the justices also acknowledge that clerks do have significant influence. This influence extends from bringing better wording to reasons or strengthening the research – and therefore the justifications – of a given decision to developing arguments or bringing new ideas to the logic of a decision. The strength of the clerks' influence, however, no doubt depends on which justice they work with. Dickson CJ worked very closely with his clerks. His biographers describe in detail the impact they had on important cases, including the development of what would become the Court's approach to the *Charter*'s reasonable limits clause in *R. v Oakes*.[27] Dickson CJ had in-depth discussions with his clerks, using them as sounding boards for ideas and encouraging them to challenge his ideas. He also gave his clerks great leeway in advocating for particular outcomes. His private papers relating to the labour trilogy show that "his drafts and memoranda to and from his law clerks suggest that the matter was one of lively debate in his chambers and the issue remained unresolved in his mind for some time."[28] As a result, his biographers conclude that in important, groundbreaking judgments he was more influenced by his clerks than by the arguments of counsel.[29]

For Wilson J, similar participation of her clerks was indispensable. She told the clerks: "We want your views ... Don't be shy. Don't be modest. If you disagree with us, say so. If you think we've missed the point, say so. This is one of your most important functions – to be a critic and a sounding board for your judge. Through argument and discussion and debate our thinking is refined and our insights sharpened. *We try to do this with our colleagues but it's not always possible.* So we rely on you."[30]

This is not the case with some of the other justices. One justice I interviewed specifically tells the clerks at the start of each year that they "are not there to be advocates" (Interview). As noted earlier, the experiences of the clerks vary quite widely. Some of the clerks described their function primarily as that of research assistants, and a couple of them stated that they had relatively little face-to-face contact with their judge. Even some of those clerks who regularly drafted decisions would not challenge their justice's reasoning in the way Wilson J encouraged. One explained: "I guess I wouldn't have seen it as appropriate for clerks to be seeking to influence their judge, I always saw my role to respond to what my judge wanted. But there would be other clerks who have different perspectives on that and may have been more ready to try to convince a judge to their point of view" (Interview). Simply put, some justices do not foster a type of relationship with their clerks that permits the clerks significant input on case decisions. Finally, it is worth recalling that there is no question as to who has the final say. One clerk summed it up nicely by remarking that "there were several cases where clerks were researching reasons, and the nine clerks who worked on the case came to one conclusion and the nine justices on that case came to an opposite conclusion" (Interview).

Circulation of Drafts: The Process of Deliberation and Negotiation

The Supreme Court of Canada has developed a culture of substantial collaboration. Once a judge has completed a draft of reasons, it is circulated among colleagues for comment. If a justice finds the draft satisfactory, she signs on to the reasons as written. Normally, justices will send out comments on the draft, either asking for clarification about certain points or proposing a different way to frame or word particular sections of the judgment. Some of the justices will update their clerks on the proceedings at conference, not giving them specifics or a verbatim report but, rather, an explanation of what the main positions were. These clerks will thus have an idea of what to look for when the draft is finally circulated, and the clerks themselves will sometimes produce a comment memorandum on the draft for their justice. Other justices do not involve their clerks at all in commenting on colleagues' drafts. Sometimes these comment memos are intended as suggestions for improvement, and a justice's support is not contingent on the changes being adopted by the author. At times, however, a judge will make their support conditional on the author's making particular modifications.

The level of collaboration can at times be much more comprehensive. One justice noted: "I know that there are judgments that are under my name that could really reflect other members of the court's names. And I could point to judgments that are not under my name that could have reflected my name. And there are judgments under one judge's name that could basically be a judgment of 'The Court'" (Interview).

An opinion's author will routinely accommodate changes if the comments or requests are not significant points, in that they do not fundamentally alter the rationale or structure of a decision. In this context, adopting such changes – particularly when the majority of judges agree with them – is part of the collegiality of the contemporary Court. Consensus and unanimity are common features of the Court's decision making, and thus many decisions end up being the by-product of a collaborative writing process. One justice explained: "In this Court a first draft is only that, a first draft. It usually attracts comments, objections and discussion. This process of exchange, review, modifying reasons, removing things, adding some, I think is a fairly regular process" (Interview). A second justice described how minor changes might commonly occur: "I read his reasons, and there's a paragraph that to me could be interpreted to mean something that I can't agree with or that I didn't think he intended to say. I would go to him and say, 'you know that paragraph in particular, you can read that two ways ... if you want to say what I think you want to say you're going to have to take out that sentence or this sentence, or write it in the affirmative rather than negative, or something like that'" (Interview). This justice noted that more major differences are often about the scope of the reasons:

> You might [vote to] allow the appeal, and then you see the reasons, and the reasons for allowing the appeal might turn on a particular section of the

Criminal Code or the *Charter,* and the interpretation given by the judge might be far broader than he needs to give for the reasons in that particular case. [Or] you might see a judgment where the appeal is allowed because of a particular section of the Constitution or the *Criminal Code* or some other Act, [and] you say "you can allow the appeal, but you don't have to give the section that broad an interpretation in this case. Why don't you restrict it, and we'll wait for the next case that might require the extra interpretation." It gives us time to think about it ... But at the end of the day, if the judge says "well, I feel more comfortable with the reasons as they are" you can either agree or you can write a concurrence that says "I agree with the results but I don't agree that section 17 necessarily means x, y, z." (Interview)

It is with these more significant differences that a judge may accommodate minor or even major changes to ensure a colleague will sign on to his or her decision. These types of choices are a major focus of the strategic model in the judicial behaviour literature.

Lamer CJ has made what is likely the most explicit public explanation of the give and take involved in the process of garnering votes in favour of a particular set of reasons. He explains that if his draft contains elements that his colleagues do not like, but that they indicate they would join his reasons if he removed them, he would do so, so long as the removal of the offensive components of the judgment did not do damage to the primary rationale for the result. Lamer CJ argues that if a justice does not get colleagues to sign on to his reasons, "the rest of it is literature. And so I horse-trade. I don't compromise on principle, though. I would never do that. But if I can't get something through as it is, I'll get half of it through, and see to the rest of it the next time around."[31] For example, Lamer CJ describes not being able to move his colleagues to support a particular approach in the 1987 case *R. v Vaillancourt,* which involved a *Charter* challenge of a provision of the *Criminal Code* that allowed the charge of murder for a death caused in the commission of an armed robbery.[32] Lamer CJ, writing for the majority, struck down the section of the *Criminal Code* as unconstitutional, but he could not get his colleagues to agree on a "subjective test" of foreseeability, instead relying in this case on a minimum standard of objective foresight (that is, a reasonable expectation that death could occur in the eyes of a "reasonable person" as opposed to in the eyes of the accused). Three years later, however, he was able to swing the Court to favour his approach: "In *Vaillancourt,* the felony murder, I wasn't getting a majority for the subjective test. Well I got at least the objective test, and said we need not decide in the case whether it has to be subjective ... But you'll notice that in *Martineau [R. v Martineau]*[33] I went up the further step with different judges. The court had changed."[34] Of the seven judges deciding *Martineau,* only three – Dickson J, Wilson J, and Lamer CJ – were involved in the *Vaillancourt* decision.

Lamer CJ's description of his conduct in these cases epitomizes the strategic considerations some scholars view as being central to judicial behaviour. He presents a frank account of his willingness to forgo or alter his sincere preferences in order to avoid an outcome that runs contrary to his preferences. The willingness to settle one issue in his favour and leave others out of a judgment in the hope of dealing favourably with them later is consistent with the bargaining depicted in strategic accounts of judicial decision making.[35]

Without access to the private papers of the justices, it is impossible to definitively document how common such strategic behaviour is at the Supreme Court of Canada. How often a justice writes narrower reasons with the express intent of pushing the Court further at a later opportunity is thus unknown. Nevertheless, strategic behaviour on a much broader level appears quite common. Based on my interviews with the justices, during the initial writing stage two approaches seem to predominate. On one hand, some judges acknowledge writing reasons – even first drafts – with the explicit consideration of whether their colleagues will be willing to sign on. From the outset, these justices modulate their views and make strategic choices about how forcefully the reasons are worded or how broadly the decision applies *before* circulating the first draft to the other judges. Other judges take a different approach, choosing instead to write the reasons they personally believe are best (in other words, writing their sincere preferences) and then allowing their colleagues to respond and later deciding based on that feedback whether or not to incorporate changes. Both approaches might be said to fall under the rubric of strategic behaviour because all of the justices at some point in the drafting process may be willing to modulate their views to accommodate colleagues and secure votes.

To characterize the overall process as strategic is problematic for two reasons, however. First, norms of collegiality and collaboration infuse the process to the point that, as noted earlier, reasons are sometimes attributed to a particular justice in name only. In instances where a judge works hard with colleagues to produce the "best" possible reasons, where changes are made not to secure votes but, rather, to improve the quality of the decisions, then such choices are not strategic in the instrumentalist sense that is predominant in the political science literature. Second, because half, if not more, of the initial votes at the conference stage are unanimous, there are invariably many occasions where strategic behaviour on the part of the justice assigned to write the reasons is simply unnecessary. This scenario is especially true of instances where the justices are unanimous not only on the outcome of the case but also on the reasoning for the outcome from the outset, something that is fairly common at the Court.

Some of the justices described their thinking when deciding to write a concurring or dissenting opinion. One justice stated:

Law is a very rigorous intellectual enterprise, but it isn't mathematical. It's not science. It's not *scientific*. It is argument and persuasion and deciding cases according to principle, precedent, policy, and when you put those things together you're going to get different views of an outcome in a particular case and a reason that supports that outcome. (Interview)

This justice continued: "I would ask myself the basic question: can I go along with the majority on this particular case? I didn't say 'I must go with the majority on this case' but 'can I?' If I can't, then I have to think about dissenting if I'm in strong disagreement, or concurring if I agree with the result but not the reasoning. Those are the legitimate reasons for taking a different view. But my first question was always 'can there be a consensus opinion on this?'" (Interview). Another justice noted that, particularly with dissents, separate reasons should only be written on matters of substance: "You won't just write for the pleasure of writing." That said, this justice noted that dissents and concurring opinions can be important for the future of the law, even on an aspect that is not a central issue in the given case (Interview).

Bastarache J has commented on the emotions that can arise during this process: "It's obviously very frustrating when you consider that the majority in a decision is going to adopt a decision that you think is wrong or that you think is going to pose problems for the application of the law ... There are also frustrations in difficult cases when you find it difficult to make your views understood by colleagues or when it's difficult to reach consensus when you think it's essential ... But overall, this is not a frustrating job. It's a very cordial atmosphere. We can discuss, and we do discuss, our cases intensely and we all understand that people have strong views on various subjects and that we will not convince colleagues easily on any given point, and this is all part of the process."[36]

In Chapter 3, I explored vote fluidity with respect to the impact of the oral hearing on the outcome of a case. The justices generally agree with former Justice John Sopinka's statement that the hearings are determinative in approximately 10 to 15 percent of cases.[37] They also concur that while they are less likely to change their minds after the oral hearing, a certain degree of fluidity exists at the latter stages of the decision-making process. All of the judges at some point arrive at conference unable to make a firm decision on the merits of an appeal. In such instances, that justice typically needs to see the first draft of reasons before deciding how to vote. While cases where a justice votes one way at conference and switches to the other side during the writing stage are less common, they do occur. Explanations of judicial behaviour premised solely on ideologically based policy preferences cannot account for this type of vote fluidity.

One justice's approach was to study a case, "give it your best, and you issue your reasons. You put the case to rest in your mind and you're on to something else" (Interview). Another justice noted that it was not uncommon to change one's mind on whether or not to dissent (Interview). A judge who thought she would dissent can end up joining the majority on the strength of their arguments and vice versa. Although rare, it is not unheard of for a justice assigned to write the reasons to have a change of heart. In one very rare instance, confirmed by two justices, the entire Court changed sides after the justice who was assigned what everyone thought to be unanimous reasons to dismiss an appeal could not get to the originally desired result and ended up writing reasons that held the appeal (Interview). Quite obviously, such an occurrence does not fit with either the attitudinal or strategic conceptions of decision making.

One justice stated: "I don't think I ever changed my mind after I started writing a judgment. Now I know some judges have. One in particular said he was going to write for a unanimous Court, and he changed his mind writing. He didn't tell anybody, and I'm reading the judgment, and I'm thinking 'this doesn't make sense, I thought we were going the other way.' And I called him and he said 'oh, well I changed my mind as I was writing it.' And I said 'well, you might have told me, it would have saved me a lot of guessing.' He said, 'yes, I suppose I should have'" (Interview). Former Justice Claire L'Heureux-Dubé also confirms that the Court has had "a few cases where we unanimously said [at conference] we would reject an appeal, and then eventually we unanimously allowed it."[38]

The extent to which justices change their minds is verified in interviews with the law clerks. My impression was that some of the justices actually downplayed the extent to which they change their minds, perhaps because they interpreted the question as implying, or vote fluidity as demonstrating, that the law is often indeterminate. Further, drawing on rare access to internal court documents, Dickson CJ's biographers point to several instances of vote fluidity at later stages of the decision-making process.[39] The 1989 case *Borowski v Canada (Attorney General)* involved a challenge to the *Criminal Code* provisions concerning abortion on the grounds they contravened the life, security, and equality rights of the fetus.[40] According to conference notes accessed by Sharpe and Roach, Wilson and L'Heureux-Dubé JJ favoured deciding the case on the merits and holding that the fetus was not protected under the *Charter*.[41] The other justices, determined to avoid the abortion issue, ultimately convinced the two to sign on to a unanimous opinion declaring the issue moot, as the impugned provisions had already been struck down in *R. v Morgentaler* a year earlier.[42] In *R. v Edwards Books and Art*, which focused on the constitutional validity of a Sunday-closing law, all of the judges at conference voted to uphold the law because it had a secular purpose.[43] The actual decision, however, reveals sharp divisions on both the question of whether the law infringed religious freedom and on whether it could be upheld under section 1. In a case involving the assault by a caregiver on a twenty-one-year-old patient with mental disabilities, Dickson CJ was in the minority at conference but wrote reasons that became the Court's unanimous judgment upholding the conviction.[44] And in *R. v Lavallee*, Dickson CJ voted at conference to overturn the acquittal of a battered woman who shot her husband but ultimately joined his colleagues in upholding the acquittal.[45]

These examples lend credence to the argument that vote fluidity runs counter to attitudinal conceptions of judicial behaviour. Of course, these examples may conform to expected behaviour under the strategic model. For example, it is possible that Wilson and L'Heureux-Dubé JJ's colleagues convinced them to join the judgment in *Borowski* in the strategic interests of protecting the Court from undue controversy. By contrast, if the breakdown in *Edwards Books* was the result of attitudinal differences, the initial consensus at conference remains unexplained. Moreover, it is difficult to characterize Dickson CJ's vote changes in the other two cases as representative of policy considerations. Without access to judicial papers, it is impossible to know the extent of this type of behaviour or of vote fluidity more broadly. Yet, it is clear that the institutionalized give and take often has an important impact on the Court's decisions. The collaborative nature of decision making on the Court is viewed as a fundamental component of the justices' role. A focus by scholars on the justices' final votes has resulted in insufficient attention to this aspect of judicial behaviour.

Formal versus Informal Deliberation: "Lobbying" within the Court?

Discussion of draft judgments does not take place solely through written memoranda. The justices will also discuss cases on an informal, face-to-face basis. There appears to be strong disagreement among previous studies of the Court about the extent to which deliberation takes place via written memoranda or in-person meetings. One 1998 study suggests that face-to-face discussions are "rare."[46] In their biography of Dickson CJ, however, Sharpe and Roach suggest that "post-conference discussion between judges appear, for the most part, to have been oral and informal."[47] All of the justices I interviewed confirm that informal discussions are common.

The very human nature of this process has occasionally caused friction or frosty relations on the Court. "Insider" accounts suggest outright lobbying between the justices.[48] In her biography, Wilson J describes being left out of informal deliberations:

> The concept of lobbying your colleagues to support you became an important part of the process. So people would spend quite long periods in each other's rooms, arguing about changes and amendments and so on and so forth. You might not know anything about this, of course, and that person wouldn't come and speak to you, because they were going to speak to the

person that they thought, well, this is the judgment I am going to be supporting. So there never was any kind of opportunity to explain why you didn't think that was a sound addition, or a sound subtraction. The first thing you knew was the group had now formed.[49]

In the same book, L'Heureux-Dubé J recalls numerous occasions when she, Wilson J and, later, McLachlin J, were left out of some deliberations.[50]

The interviews confirmed that some members of the Court are significantly more likely than others to engage their colleagues in informal deliberations about drafts of reasons. In part, this tendency depends on personality. Some justices are more gregarious than others and feel more comfortable "walking the halls" and having discussions in each other's offices. On occasion, however, this process suffers from political manoeuvring or, at least, the perception that such strategic machinations are occurring. One former clerk recalled an instance in which Wilson J distributed dissenting reasons and a couple of her colleagues came to her to say that while they agreed with her, they had already promised the judge writing the initial draft that they would sign on to his reasons (Interview). Such an example would confirm a type of strategic behaviour, but one predicated less on policy preferences and more on concern about good relations with colleagues (although they risked poor relations with Wilson J as a result). It is important to emphasize that this type of incident may be exceptional, but the broader issue of what Wilson J refers to as "lobbying" between justices is precisely the type of activity strategic scholars contend is at the core of judicial decision making. Indeed, one of the troubling aspects for Wilson J was that "once a particular group knew it had 'won,' there was little incentive for it to consider any diverging or opposing opinions."[51]

Again, without access to the Court's records or justices' private papers, a systematic study of this type of behaviour is not possible. Lamer CJ disputed Wilson J's contention, arguing that "there was no little clique, no little gang. Like-minded people tend to congregate."[52] In an interview with the *Globe and Mail*, Lamer CJ states that "there was no point in going to Bertha's office and saying: 'Bertha, if you were to change this or that, I could go along with it.' Because she was stubborn as a mule."[53]

The justices I interviewed differed on the extent to which informal discussions prevented others from fully participating and on whether they were as problematic as Wilson and L'Heureux-Dubé JJ describe. One justice expressly denied that there was any attempt to "lobby" or change minds. "The majority would write the first opinion, probably in the hope that they would write an opinion that the dissenters would find answers their dissent. But there was never any arm-twisting ... you were from the beginning and all through the process completely independent [without] any pressure from anybody" (Interview).

Another justice pointed out that personality does make a difference: "Some are more outgoing, more extroverted by personality, easier to approach or deal with ... You can't take human nature away from the judges. They've got their own personalities. But there was no antagonism. There's too much going on – you may disagree on one case, but how long are you going to want to talk about it when you've got two or three more that should get done?" (Interview). This justice continued: "[E]verybody's very polite about this, but some [colleagues] you know from past history are just reluctant to change anything. Sometimes you don't bother trying, you just simply write your concurrence or your dissent" (Interview). A third justice stated: "I think the principle is that if something is important enough to warrant changes, normally other colleagues should be added to the discussion. But it's not that formal. There is still a lot of face-to-face interaction" (Interview). A fourth justice explained: "[W]e do some walking around the halls, but you can't do it in an unprincipled way. By that I mean you've got to be transparent eventually about it." For example, "there's one paragraph of a judgment that you say, 'look, I could send a memo on this if you want, but here's something, would you consider this.' And it does see the light of day, because if the judge does accept it, then he or she [reports on] why they made the changes" (Interview). This justice acknowledged, however, that there is on occasion the potential for harm to the Court's collegial relations:

> There's a danger when you have informal discussions that somebody will not be involved. That's something that one has to be sensitive to. And sometimes that will happen. But it doesn't detract, in my view, from having both formal and informal contact. And if you know that that's going to happen, then you can be more sensitive to it. But I never felt that – maybe others did – but I didn't feel that there was a sort of deliberate cabal or factionalizing. Sometimes it came together that five judges were all seeing a problem in a particular way, and four were not.

In other instances, "you may have a question that you're not sure about. You don't want to waste everybody's time exploring something by sending a formal memorandum around when it's something that you want to raise and have a discussion with a colleague about" (Interview).

Wilson J viewed the "lobbying" process as being too dependent on personalities and as reflecting ideological considerations.[54] Further, the lobbying described in her biography suggests that these informal discussions were about far more substantive issues than changes in wording to a particular paragraph or minor changes that might amount to a waste of everyone's time. Part of the problem, in Wilson J's view, was that it manifested as a "boy's club," where some of the justices would often lunch together or play squash, but Wilson and later L'Heureux-Dubé JJ were never invited. The problem was that these activities could carry over to discussions of decisions and that, in Wilson J's words, "those who weren't part of that didn't have the benefit of that private intimate discussion and exchange of views."[55] It bothered Wilson J enough that, according to one justice, she broached the topic at conference: "Dickson was furious. He didn't accept that because he didn't do that. It was not him at all. He couldn't imagine that others would do that. But that was what [was] going on" (Interview).

Wilson J felt that the Court required a clear protocol on decision making, such as ensuring justices did not sign onto opinions until all dissenting or concurring drafts had been circulated.[56] Her understanding was that once a justice notifies her colleagues that she proposes to dissent, the process of concurring to the original reasons stops, as it is "bad form" to concur with the first set of reasons until the dissenting reasons are circulated.[57] Such a protocol never materialized because the justices did not agree on the best approach.

Within this dynamic, different avenues emerge through which strategic decision making becomes possible. Lorne Sossin writes that "[i]f, at a conference meeting, one or more Justices remain undecided, then persuading the 'swing' Justice(s) becomes the subject of intense lobbying by others who have already voted on one side or the other."[58] Separately, lobbying among the law clerks occurred as well, with clerks "attempting to persuade a 'swing' Justice's clerks to agree with their Justice's position."[59]

The clerks I interviewed were sharply divided on whether this type of behaviour occurred. Some noted that there was often very "active" debate between clerks, which on occasion would border on "heated." Other former clerks suggested that such discussions normally arose out of purely analytical interest as opposed to strategic efforts to change each other's minds. As one clerk put it, "I don't think that, to the extent that there were discussions among the clerks, aspirations of trying to lobby the other clerks to adopt their judges' perspective, I don't think that ever happened" (Interview). Further, several clerks noted that certain justices did not want their clerks speaking to other justices' clerks, evidently to preserve independence.

For the most part, however, regular deliberation occurred between the various clerks. For many clerks, this activity entailed acting as an advocate for their judge's position, particularly if their judge was writing the opinion. As one clerk described, "I'm there to defend [my judge] in front of other clerks when we're writing the decision, but at the same time I'm still talking to him and expressing a different point of view if I don't completely agree with his position. And sometimes I think it did have a significant impact on the outcome ... For example, if I'm talking to a clerk about what my judge thinks, and [this clerk says] 'my judge is thinking the same thing,' I would sometimes tell that clerk, 'well don't you think this' and I would sometimes talk to that person about my own opinion, so that he or she can also raise the issue with their judge" (Interview).

A crucial component of the strategic model is that justices have knowledge of the preferences of their colleagues. The law clerks can prove to be useful in gaining information about informal deliberations between other judges. The clerks have much more opportunity to engage each other in discussion and debate about issues surrounding cases than the justices do. As a result, justices can occasionally ascertain where their colleagues are positioning themselves through their clerks. Wilson J's biography notes that, in instances where for whatever reason she was left out of private discussions among her colleagues, she often depended on her clerks in this manner.[60] Conversely, Lamer CJ made it clear to his clerks that he was not keen on them having discussions with other clerks about cases (Interview). Any suggestion that such restrictions were intended to prevent other justices from gaining information about coalitions forming between the other justices, however, would be purely speculative.

While the clerks' discussions often take the form of debates and attempts to sway each other, only occasionally does this behaviour include attempts to influence the justices. Yet, because, in the words of one former clerk, "there was often communication between clerks where there wasn't necessarily between those judges," the clerks often served, to an extent, as an information network for some justices (Interview). This feature of the Court's environment suggests at least the potential and capacity for the justices to pursue strategic behaviour, but it is an element of the process for which direct evidence is unlikely to be captured even if scholars had access to Court records and the justices' private papers.

The debate over lobbying and when a judge should sign on to a set of reasons stems from competing conceptions of the Court as a collaborative decision-making collegium versus one composed of nine individual decision makers. While the pursuit of particular outcomes manifested in these patterns of decision making reflects both attitudinal and strategic behaviour, the differing approaches of the various justices and their willingness to engage in certain methods of conduct are dependent on their views of their role in this regard. A host of factors can influence the degree to which justices are motivated to engage in such lobbying. There is little doubt that, as noted earlier, like-minded justices will deliberate and collaborate more often with each other. Over the Court's history, "voting blocs" of justices have been identified. In the 1970s, Laskin, Wishart Spence, and Dickson JJ came to be known as the "L-S-D Connection" for their frequent joint dissents.[61] Through much of the 1990s, a bloc consisting of Lamer, Sopinka, Peter Cory, Frank Iacobucci, and Jack Major JJ, also known as the "gang of five," was instrumental in consistent rulings strengthening legal rights under the *Charter* for the accused in criminal cases. The Court often sharply divided on these issues, with other justices, McLachlin and L'Heureux-Dubé JJ especially, frequently in dissent.[62]

It is clear that, depending on the issue, certain justices are inclined to speak to those colleagues they believe are predisposed to agree with them. Lamer CJ's comments that "there was no point in going to Bertha [Wilson's] office" provide further confirmation of this point.[63] Several former law clerks confirmed that their respective justices would have obvious choices among their colleagues regarding who to approach, and who not to approach, about a particular case (Interviews). One clerk explained: "[M]y judge tended to take the opinions of certain judges with more seriousness than some of the other judges. I think that's normal in any institution ... that the closer your opinions lie to somebody the more likely you are to consider their input and take them seriously." Just as significantly, "when he was considering whether to concur on judgment x, it mattered to him if it was coming from judge x or judge y, judge x being someone he had a lot of respect for, judge y less so" (Interview).

This observation, of course, depends largely on the issues at stake, although personality conflicts could at times infect and deepen the patterns of division on the Court. Recent studies make clear that the *Charter* itself has been a major source of jurisprudential division on the Court. *Charter* cases are twice as likely to generate disagreement as non-*Charter* cases.[64] Even throughout the *Charter* era, the collegiality on the Court has ebbed and flowed. Despite the consensus-driven approach that Dickson CJ strived for in the first couple of years after the *Charter* was released, sharp divisions quickly became evident. Between the tensions involved in dealing with a large backlog of cases and strong disagreement among the justices over how expansively to interpret the *Charter*, the Court of the mid-to-late 1980s has been described as an unhappy place. As L'Heureux-Dubé J explains, "there is a little joke that says marriage is like a tower which is under siege: 'Everybody that's in wants to get out, and everybody that's out wants to get in.' When I arrived here [in 1987], the Supreme Court was exactly that ... There will always be divisions between nine people of different backgrounds, nine people of different visions ... Sometimes it will become more personal, more bitter."[65]

Levels of disagreement on the Court peaked in the middle of the 1990s, also the middle of Lamer CJ's tenure as chief justice. Under McLachlin CJ, as noted earlier, consensus has increased, particularly as it pertains to reducing the number of separate reasons. McCormick speculates on why patterns of disagreement seem to coincide with the tenure of different chief justices: "Perhaps it is a question of a forceful personality in the centre chair to whom the others defer; perhaps it is a successful attempt to persuade the members of the Court to a certain style or tone of disagreement; or perhaps it is leadership by example."[66] With regard to the latter, McCormick notes that McLachlin CJ and Dickson CJ wrote or signed onto minority opinions with less frequency after they became chief justice, suggesting a "moderating effect" on the behaviour of their colleagues, while Lamer CJ's behaviour did not change. Ostberg and Wetstein also suggest that McLachlin CJ "is more interested in consolidating the Court by letting others shoulder the majority opinion workload, and in casting few dissenting votes and writing few dissenting opinions as chief."[67]

By the mid-1990s, the major backlog problems of the 1980s had largely been alleviated, but divisions and a certain degree of interpersonal tension remained significant (Interviews). On retiring in 1997, La Forest J described the Court as having a "closed style" under Lamer CJ, reflecting some of the concerns Wilson J had about the Court's collegiality a decade earlier. A few years later, after his own retirement, Lamer CJ was dismissive of such concerns:

> [La Forest J] was never one of the boys [who], after an important judgment, would say: 'Let's go up to the dining room at the end of the day and have a beer or a scotch ... To me, it's just sour grapes. La Forest sulked because he didn't get a couple of majorities. He wasn't getting the majorities he thought he should be getting ... He thought it was a clique, but it wasn't. We just didn't agree with him. If you go to a collegial court, you've got to take the knocks and the bumps and accept that people are going to disagree with you.[68]

Several justices, without commenting negatively on Lamer CJ's approach to collegiality, agreed that under McLachlin CJ, the level of deliberation and congeniality has increased. One former clerk described Lamer CJ as "arrogant" and contended that the less than friendly relationship he had with certain justices would have prevented consensus (Interviews).

The implication of this discussion is clear: the influence certain justices have on each other is a combination of good personal relations and past records of agreement. Similar ideologies matter, of course, but mutual respect plays a role as well. Collegiality (in terms of how the justices work together) and the interpersonal relationships on the Court (in terms of how well the various personalities mesh) are connected and mutually reinforcing.[69] It should not be surprising that jurisprudential divisions and personality conflicts might, on occasion, come together in a manner that impacts the Court's decisions and working environment. Despite the fact that identifiable voting blocs develop from time to time, these divisions are far from permanently entrenched on the Canadian Court in the way they seem to be on its American counterpart. The justices acknowledge these tensions but maintain that, for the most part, the Court has been a very collegial place, even during the more tumultuous periods of its modern history. Comments throughout the interview process that the McLachlin Court is a particularly happy and collegial place are important, not only for what they say about the current environment but also because they reflect how it can improve or deteriorate over time.

Re-Conferencing

On occasion, the Court, usually at the behest of the chief justice, will re-convene for a second conference about a particular case. One justice noted that there is a general acceptance among members of the Court if one of their colleagues wants to reconvene. The practice was relatively common in the first few years of the *Charter*, when the Court was first developing approaches to its various provisions (Interviews). Dickson CJ's biographers confirm this practice, noting that at the time "ongoing, seminar-type discussion of broad legal issues was virtually unheard of, but ... the judges were conscious that their early Charter pronouncements would set the tone for the future, and they wanted to sound as clear, confident, and unanimous as possible."[70] While reconvening was quite rare under Lamer CJ, it has increased again under McLachlin CJ (Interviews). This practice comports with her stated intention to increase consensus on the Court.

Re-conferencing usually occurs in particularly difficult or divisive cases. For example, many conferences were convened with respect to the case *Reference re Secession of Quebec*.[71] More generally, one justice described why a second conference might be called: "Sometimes, for example, there would be two main streams of reasoning after the circulation of drafts. Or quite often a reason would be complicated so you'd have three sets of reasons, and there would be consideration of whether you can combine two sets of reasons in some way" (Interview). Often the second conference would help smooth over divisions or help to get the justices to reach some type of consensus. Nonetheless, they are not always successful. Another justice noted that "you can never be sure how helpful the [second] conference will be until after the fact" (Interview). McLachlin CJ has publicly stated that re-conferencing also helps to prevent unnecessary friction between majority and minority factions. She notes that they are intended "to make sure that anything which could develop into a more major issue gets defused at an early level ... Occasionally you just have a chat on something that you think might blow up, even if it's just a [single] case."[72]

The practice of reconvening, from the perspective of a clerk on the McLachlin Court, can help reduce confusion as well: "You'd sometimes see a flurry of memos and comments going around, and then there'd be a pause, and then [the justices] would actually have a discussion following from that [in the conference room]. And then you'd hear the results of that discussion ... Once the judges can get together and talk again about what their points of disagreement [were] they'd realize they weren't that far apart" (Interview).

Norms of Consensus

As the preceding discussion makes clear, the Court is driven by norms of consensus and collegiality. These norms so infuse the process of decision making at the Court that in any given year, a majority of the cases are resolved on a unanimous basis. This is something that the predominant political science models of judicial behaviour are at pains to explain. The attitudinal model cannot account for the high degree of collegiality on the Court, unless we presume ideological consistency among all of the justices or cases extreme enough to compel agreement among an ideologically diverse panel.[73] One recent study confirms that the attitudinal model fails to explain the Court's unanimous cases.[74] The strategic model explains how judges with competing policy preferences might sometimes reach consensus, but studies of the Supreme Court of Canada have thus far not examined in any comprehensive manner judicial views on consensus or unanimity or why rates of consensus or unanimity might vary over time.

In a wide-ranging lecture on the Court's decision-making processes delivered in 1985, Wilson J emphasizes the collegial nature of a court. She notes that "if there is, indeed, an obligation on a collegial court to strive for a consensus, or at least submerge individuality in the interests of a few sets of reasons, then the dynamics of the Court's process would seem to be extremely important."[75] Her alert that "very little has been said or written" about this aspect of judicial decision making on multi-member courts of appeal remains true to this day.

One aspect that Wilson J identifies as being important is the tension between the judge as an individual member of the Court and the Court as an institution.[76] This feature of decision making relates directly to collegiality and raises two important questions. To what extent should justices make decisions autonomously and how important is consensus or, more specifically, unanimity? The justices interviewed for this book had a variety of views on these questions. Some justices saw unanimity as an ideal, as it is said to add clarity to the law, provide unambiguous direction for lower courts, and potentially give the decision more legitimacy in the eyes of the public. These justices viewed strong dissents as inevitable on occasion, but they contended that keeping the number of separately written reasons to a minimum is a good principle, both for the development of the law and to avoid confusion on the part of other political actors and the legal community (Interviews). Indeed, on becoming chief justice, one of McLachlin CJ's key goals was to increase consensus on the Court.[77]

The traditionally high rate of unanimity on the Court is worth noting. The Court's statistics categorize as unanimous those cases that do not produce a dissenting opinion.[78] Since concurring opinions are not considered, "unanimous" judgments may have more than one set of written reasons. In his recent book, Songer adopts this understanding as well. Thus, he finds that from 1970 to 2003, unanimous judgments represent nearly three-quarters (74.4 percent) of all cases.[79] This finding is in sharp contrast to the US Supreme Court, which over a similar period (1975 to 2005), had a unanimity rate of only 28.4 percent.[80]

This measure of unanimity is problematic, particularly if the future legal and policy effect of a given case matters more than the simple dichotomous outcome of the case itself. The justices' reasoning is what ought to be given the most weight in examining rates of unanimity. A preferable measure of unanimity would thus exclude from consideration those cases that include concurring opinions. As noted in previous chapters, some scholars dismiss written reasons as "mere rationalizations" for particular outcomes. These scholars simultaneously view judicial policy preferences as the most import-ant factor in decisions. Since the rationale for a judgment can result in wider or narrower implications for the policy issues at stake in a case, written reasons are arguably a more precise representation of those policy preferences than the simple yes or no vote represented by majority and dissenting opin-ions. McCormick draws on this latter understanding of unanimity in previous studies. In contrast to Songer's reporting of 74.4 percent unanimity for 1970 to 2003, McCormick finds that for the slightly shorter period of 1970 to 2002 there was a unanimity rate of 63.7 percent.[81]

Unanimity rates are only one measure of how successful McLachlin CJ has been in increasing consensus on the Court, but they provide some indication. Following the last few years of the Laskin Court, which saw unanimity rates of well over 80 percent, the Court entered the age of the *Charter*. Unanimity rates under Dickson CJ (1984-90) were 64.7 percent,[82] falling to 58.4 percent under Lamer CJ (1990-99).[83] The Court's unanimity rate under McLachlin CJ from 2000 through to 12 July 2009 was 62.8 percent.[84]

At first glance, it might seem that McLachlin CJ has only been marginally successful at achieving her goal of increasing consensus on the Court. This conclusion can be placed into further perspective, however, by recalling that McLachlin CJ is much more likely than her predecessors to assign full panels of nine justices.[85] Larger panel sizes decrease the opportunity for unanimous judgments because it is harder to achieve unanimity when there are more justices involved in a decision. The increase in unanimous judgments under McLachlin CJ is thus more impressive than the simple statistics indicate. Further, earlier data reported by McCormick suggests that in her first few years as chief justice, McLachlin CJ was especially good at reducing the number of extra written reasons that were produced when the Court did split.[86] In other words, the chief justice worked with her colleagues to con-solidate disagreement as much as possible. Comments by Bastarache J confirm this effort. He notes that "there are a lot more things that are being reconsidered. There is more place for discussion and dialogue in the sense that we strive more to discover each other's reasons and opinions, and try to determine ways in which we can reduce the number of dissents, or reduce the number of published reasons in a case. I don't mean to say that there wasn't discussion before. There was always a conference and a meaningful discussion. But I think we've tried different approaches to reduce the number of written reasons and try to produce decisions that are more useful to the courts of appeal."[87]

Regardless of whether McLachlin CJ has been successful, not all justices think striving for consensus should be an overarching goal of the Court. One justice viewed attempts by the chief justice to push for it as interference, noting that because justices are totally independent, compromise cannot be forced (Interview). Another justice explained: "I think that chief justices would like to think that they could have a court marching to the same tune, but it just doesn't happen" (Interview). This justice noted that with all chief justices, the degree of unanimity achieved on the Court varies year to year. Neither Lamer CJ nor McLachlin CJ are said to have ever attempted to persuade the judges for unanimity just for its own sake, although there have been important cases where the justices have agreed that a unanimous judgment would be ideal. Where there is disagreement, the degree of division on a panel makes a difference with respect to the ability of the majority to persuade those in the minority: "I don't remember seeing a case where there's been four judges dissenting where the majority was able to persuade all four that their dissent was not well founded. If it's eight people see it one way, and one dissenter, I think the one might spend some time reflecting on whether or not all eight others could be wrong and he could be right" (Interview).

A third justice, however, suggested that the chief justice is capable of at least some influence in this regard:

There is such a thing as collegiality and people influencing each other. For some people influence is a nasty word, but in reality you're subject to all sorts of influences. The answer is that you should remain impartial and independently minded, and be able to properly integrate or refuse to integrate these influences. And the chief justice can have influence. She may be persuasive in her arguments. She may bring certain elements, aspects home for better understanding, or find ways of reconciling divergent views because, of course, these really difficult issues are usually issues on which reasonable people can reasonably differ. There's no absolute answer that is evident to everybody. And that's why they're before the Court. But someone has to decide them. (Interview)

A fourth justice concurred with this assessment, noting that "in an ideal world a Supreme Court would speak with one voice." This justice explained the role of the chief justice in this regard: "One of the functions of the chief is in fact to try to bring people together, [and] make sure that if there are disagreements those are what I would call 'real,' 'true' disagreements, but not matters of what I would call pure drafting or style of judgments. I think the chief justice normally will, if there are disagreements, try to probe the depth of the disagreements and see if there are ways to bring people together. This is part of the process of most collegial courts" (Interview).

A fifth justice stated that "there is no doubt that the whole environment of decision making is influenced at an important level on the Court by the chief justice." Nevertheless, "the other eight judges have to play an important role in what might be called 'creating the collegial environment' at the Court ... it's a collegium, it's not individuals. It has an institutional, or collegial, role. The institution is ongoing, we just occupy those seats for a period of time. The work of the Court continues as we leave it." This final justice felt that McLachlin CJ has been successful at improving consensus, but does not want to give the impression that her predecessor, Lamer CJ, was somehow unconcerned with collegiality: "The preferential outcome for a collegial court, especially a Supreme Court, is a unanimous judgment," because it provides the most clarity and guidance for lower courts, lawyers, and, most importantly, the public who are affected by the decision (Interview). Any success McLachlin CJ has had, this justice noted, depends on the attitude and approach of the other eight justices.

Unanimity as a Goal and Its Effects

The chief justice, like her eight colleagues, has no authority to ensure a particular level of consensus on the Court. Instead, she must rely on the art of persuasion. Further, there is some question about whether unanimity actually produces better results. Bastarache J agrees that consensus can occasionally "muddy the legal waters":

> We have had a few experiences that I think were meant to be helpful, but didn't produce very good results because I guess too much compromise [by the judges], or too much wording to try and meet the minimum requirements of everybody on what should be said, produces [decisions] that are difficult to read and too long and not helpful with regard to the use that can be made of them, in the courts of appeal especially. So, thinking about it now I think there are some cases where we might have been better to produce a few sets of reasons instead of one.[88]

Wilson J felt the informal negotiations between justices were too often justified on the basis that they produced clear majorities instead of split decisions, even if the result was increased ambiguity in the reasons: "Calculated ambiguity, as one colleague described it, was anathema for her; far better to have a range of judgments offering options, including a dissent and a diverging concurrence if necessary, as long as each judgment was written with crystal clarity."[89]

Wilson J's sentiment raises the question of what effect a goal of unanimity might have for the Court's decisions. Before exploring this question, it is worth noting that the Supreme Court of Canada's high general rate of unanimity is a natural outgrowth of the collegial atmosphere of the institution. In other words, according to several of the justices, while unanimity is desirable, it is not an overarching goal in a strict sense. There are, however, exceptional circumstances under which the justices have made unanimity a goal in particularly important cases. This is especially interesting given that scholars have found that within the Court's more visible cases, particularly *Charter* cases, the Court's unanimity rate is generally lower.[90] Thus, it appears that where unanimity becomes an explicit goal of the justices, it is often in those cases where it is generally harder to achieve.[91] Further complicating the matter is the fact that no one outside the Court knows when unanimity is an express objective of the justices. There are a couple of instances, however, where the justices have expressly sought unanimity, and these have been identified as a goal by them in public or in the interviews conducted for this study.

Unanimity has the effect of both narrowing and broadening the Court's written reasons. On the one hand, decisions become narrow because the compromise required among the justices necessitates focusing only on those issues to which all of the justices on a panel can agree. Otherwise important issues about which agreement cannot be reached are deemed tangential to the main problem at hand and are left out of the decision. Dickson CJ has stated that "it might be necessary to pass up the benefits to be had from discussion about fine points of difference between various colleagues" in order to achieve unanimity around an issue that requires a "clear and firm statement of principle from the Court."[92] One recent study confirms that narrow opinions, measured by the number of separate legal issues raised by a case, are more likely to be unanimous.[93] On the other hand, decisions become broader or more ambiguous when the justices agree on particular concepts but leave them underspecified to avoid conflict. It is likely that this development is what Wilson J suggests when she notes that the pursuit of unanimity might result in "watered down" decisions[94] and what Bastarache J means when he concurs that the result might be to "muddy" the legal waters.[95]

Perhaps the most important decision the Court has rendered is its opinion in *Reference re Secession of Quebec*. The justices put considerable effort into producing a unanimous judgment and signed it with no lead author, choosing instead to write as "the Court." Following the narrow victory of the federalist side in the 1995 referendum on Quebec sovereignty, the federal government tossed the Court a political hand grenade, asking it to rule on whether the provincial government of Quebec could effect secession unilaterally. The stakes for the Court's legitimacy, across Canada but also specifically within Quebec, were clear. Throughout much of Quebec, a decision limited to a declaration that the province had no constitutional right to secede unilaterally would only confirm suspicions that the Court was firmly in the hands of federalist Ottawa. Indeed, separatists initially claimed that the Court would prove itself politicized if it chose to even render a decision.[96] Rather than limiting the decision in this manner, however, the Court balanced its reasons by ruling that in the event of a "clear majority" on a "clear question" in favour of sovereignty, the rest of Canada has a duty to negotiate.

The Court has generally received high praise for the political acumen the justices demonstrated in fashioning a decision from which both federalists and sovereigntists could claim some victory. Commentators have described the decision as "masterful"[97] and "ingenious."[98] Lacking legal precedent or explicit guidance in the Constitution's text, the Court's decision refers to four "basic constitutional principles" – federalism, democracy, rule of law and constitutionalism, and the protection of minority rights – and from those principles developed an opinion that "reads more like an essay than a legal decision."[99]

Yet, the decision is also remarkable for what it left unanswered. The Court leaves "for the political actors to determine what constitutes 'a clear majority on a clear question.'"[100] The justices provide no guidance on a host of other issues: what amending formula should be used to achieve secession; the rights of Aboriginals or other minorities; and the content of negotiations between Quebec and the rest of Canada. Peter Leslie writes that the "*Secession* case actually resolved almost nothing, in the sense of removing any critical questions from the realm of political controversy. Even the 'obligation to negotiate,' highlighted by so many commentators (certainly by the *indépendentistes*), left in place almost all the existing ambiguities and uncertainties surrounding the process that could lead to secession."[101]

The explanation for this decision is almost universally ascribed to the Court's concern for protecting its institutional legitimacy.[102] Put simply, the Court left these questions to the "political" sphere so as preserve its role as guardian of the Constitution in the eyes of all Canadians. In the judgment, the Court notes that "judicial intervention, even in relation to the *law* of the Constitution, is subject to the Court's appreciation of its proper role in the constitutional scheme."[103] Writing further, the Court explained:

> The role of the Court in this Reference is limited to the identification of the relevant aspects of the Constitution in their broadest sense. We have interpreted the questions as relating to the constitutional framework within

which political decisions may ultimately be made. Within that framework, the workings of the political process are complex and can only be resolved by means of political judgments and evaluations. The Court has no supervisory role over the political aspects of constitutional negotiations.[104]

There is little reason to disagree with the consensus view that part of the reason for the Court's restraint was to avoid breaking the balance the justices fought so hard to achieve. Having given something for both federalists and sovereigntists to cling to following the ruling (and with which to claim victory), spelling out the requirements for a potential negotiated secession or the meaning of "clear majority" or "clear question" risked disaffecting one side and raising the spectre of attacks on the Court's legitimacy.

Seemingly ignored in extant analyses of the reference decision is a consideration of the written judgment as a product of a collegial process where, in this instance, unanimity was an important goal of the justices. Under this condition, the tendency is for justices to coalesce around the major issues of agreement. Where disagreement arises over specific issues, if the desire for unanimity is strong enough, the effect of a collegial decision-making process is to leave those issues out. This depiction is not intended as an alternative explanation to the legitimacy-centred account of the issue avoidance the Court demonstrates in the reference. Rather, the point is that a consideration of unanimity as a goal in the justices' decision may add another layer to understanding how the Court formulated the decision.

A second case in which the goal of unanimity effectively narrowed the Court's final decision was in *Tremblay v Daigle*.[105] The appellant, Chantal Daigle, sought to overturn an injunction obtained in a Quebec Superior Court by her former boyfriend that prevented her from terminating her eighteen-week pregnancy. A memorandum circulated by Dickson CJ indicated his intention to write reasons declaring that a fetus had no legal status under section 7 of the *Charter*. La Forest J responded by saying he would write separate reasons dealing only with Quebec's *Charter of Human Rights and Freedoms,* as it was unnecessary, in his opinion, to deal with the issue under the Canadian *Charter*.[106] According to Sharpe and Roach, "this prompted Dickson to pull back. He did not want a divided opinion. Although it seems possible that he might have attracted a majority of the Court on his more broadly based draft, he preferred an immediate and unanimous decision on narrower grounds."[107]

It is important not to understate the significance of Dickson CJ's preference for unanimity in this case. It was not surprising that the justices sought unanimity in a case such as *Reference re Secession of Quebec*. For one thing, the notion that federalist judges in a case involving Quebec secession would have ideological differences premised on simple liberal versus conservative considerations is highly questionable. However, in a case dealing with abortion rights, most observers – attitudinal scholars, in particular – would not expect an institutionally derived preference for unanimity to override the philosophical or ideological predilections of any of the justices involved. Indeed, if Sharpe and Roach's supposition based on their reading of the Court documents is correct, the decision was not a strategic move to ensure compromise but, rather, a decision to ensure a quick and unanimous judgment for its own sake.

Where the decision to seek unanimity in *Daigle* resulted in a decidedly more narrow set of reasons, other instances in which the justices have aimed to achieve unanimity have resulted in judgments that hinge on vague concepts or ambiguous wording. One prominent 1999 case, *Law v Canada (Minister of Employment and Immigration)*, established a new approach to the *Charter*'s equality provisions.[108] In so doing, a finding that a law impaired the "human dignity" of the claimant became a crucial component of the Court's approach to section 15. This concept proved to be so vague that its application in later cases created sharp disagreement among the justices. Ten years prior to *Law,* in *Andrews v Law Society of British Columbia* – the Court's first equality case – the justices agreed to an approach that promoted a substantive understanding of equality as opposed to a more restrictive, formal understanding of it as identical treatment under the law.[109] A finding of discrimination, however, would be limited to the grounds enumerated in section 15(1) of the *Charter* as well as to any "analogous" grounds.[110] In subsequent equality cases, the justices soon split into three camps on the proper way to identify discrimination.[111] In *Law,* the justices decided to develop a unanimous approach that resolved these divisions (Interview).

The new interpretation of section 15 incorporated a novel element to discrimination beyond a distinction based on an enumerated or analogous ground – the impairment of "human dignity." Iacobucci J, writing for the Court, defines human dignity as follows:

> Human dignity means that an individual or group feels self-respect and self-worth. It is concerned with physical and psychological integrity and empowerment. Human dignity is harmed by unfair treatment premised upon personal traits or circumstances which do not relate to individual needs, capacities, or merits. It is enhanced by laws which are sensitive to the needs, capacities, and merits of different individuals, taking into account the context underlying their differences. Human dignity is harmed when individuals and groups are marginalized, ignored, or devalued, and is enhanced when laws recognize the full place of all individuals and groups within Canadian society. Human dignity within the meaning of the equality guarantee does not relate to the status or position of an individual in society per se, but

rather concerns the manner in which a person legitimately feels when confronted with a particular law. Does the law treat him or her unfairly, taking into account all of the circumstances regarding the individuals affected and excluded by the law?[112]

Iacobucci J writes further that the "equality guarantee in s. 15(1) of the *Charter* must be understood and applied in light of the above understanding of its purpose. The overriding concern with protecting and promoting human dignity in the sense just described infuses all elements of the discrimination analysis."[113] Although not setting up a strict legal "test" per se, Iacobucci J outlines four "contextual factors" to help guide analysis: whether there is pre-existing disadvantage experienced by the individual or group at issue; whether there is a correspondence between the distinction made in the impugned law and the claimant's characteristics or circumstances; the ameliorative purpose or effects of the law with respect to other, potentially more disadvantaged groups; and the nature of the particular interest affected by the impugned law.[114]

Although the justices aimed to reconcile diverging equality approaches into a single framework, the decision has been widely criticized for its complexity, for being confusing, and for increasing burdens on *Charter* claimants to prove violations of human dignity.[115] The latter criticism makes the unsupported normative assumption that subsequent cases should have been decided differently. Yet, critics are correct to point out that the decision failed to add clarity to the Court's overall approach to equality issues under the *Charter*. Indeed, the justices fell rather quickly into the pattern of disagreement that marked equality jurisprudence prior to *Law*. The 2002 case *Lavoie v Canada*, which concerned the constitutionality of the Public Service Commission's hiring preference for citizens, had four sets of written reasons.[116] As Sonia Lawrence writes, "[a]ll of the reasons purport to apply the *Law* test, which confirms the criticism that the test is too vague and open-ended and cannot be the basis for consistent decision-making."[117] Similar disagreement appears in a number of important equality cases decided after *Law*.[118]

The justices sought and achieved unanimity in *Law*, but the vague nature of the central element of the new approach – human dignity – and the subsequent disagreement among the justices over its meaning reveals that the level of consensus achieved was quite thin. Moreover, since most equality cases failed under the *Law* regime, it is clear that judicial readiness to push for more consensus-based decision making can have important repercussions not only for statements of the law but also for the outcomes of subsequent cases.[119] Criticism of the Court's post-*Law* equality jurisprudence has been so significant that the Court addressed it in 2008, when the justices unanimously backtracked on the human dignity standard and re-enunciated the original approach to equality found in *Andrews*.[120] McLachlin CJ and

Justice Rosalie Abella write: "[A]s critics have pointed out, human dignity is an abstract and subjective notion that, even with the guidance of the four contextual factors, cannot only become confusing and difficult to apply; it has also proven to be an *additional* burden on equality claimants, rather than the philosophical enhancement it was intended to be."[121] It remains to be seen whether the divisions that have plagued the Court with regard to the proper approach to section 15 are solved by this restated position.

Consensus and unanimity are important elements of the Court's decision-making process that are obscured by other approaches to the study of judicial behaviour. It is difficult to view a justice's orientation toward independent versus group decision making as reflecting simple ideological concerns. Ideological motivations play part of the role in determining whether unanimity is likely in a given situation, yet the general view a justice holds regarding the desirability of achieving unanimous decisions has as much to do with normative principles about the clarity of the law and a broader culture of collaboration and collegiality. This is not to say ideology has no effect in these cases. Judicial policy preferences modulate the outcomes of cases where unanimity is desired by introducing ambiguity into the reasons or by narrowing the scope of the reasons, sometimes by removing issues of contention altogether. Significantly, it is possible that the impact of ambiguous wording is to make ideologically based decision making easier for judges in subsequent cases, as the Court's equality jurisprudence suggests. Nor should we ignore the importance of strategic considerations, particularly those that pertain to a desire among the justices to safeguard the institution's legitimacy. There is evidence in other areas, such as cases dealing with security policy in the post-9/11 period, that a concern for unanimity has had a similar effect on the Court's reasons.[122]

The behaviouralist attitudinal model overlooks written reasons and instead focuses on mere votes, providing little explanation of how and when ideological considerations are tempered or intensified. And while the process of achieving unanimity is infused with the type of bargaining considered central to the strategic model, the ultimate motivation is often fundamentally different. Instead of negotiating and making compromises to achieve a minimum winning coalition, the justices seek consensus. In this respect, straightforward liberal versus conservative policy preferences are not at play in the manner in which the strategic model is normally operationalized. Rather, institutional norms shed light on this important aspect of judicial behaviour.

Conclusion

The exploration of the various processes and factors that come into play in generating the Court's primary product – its written judgments – make three things clear. First, the energy and time exerted in crafting written reasons and the tenor, style, and general attitude through which the justices approach this task render false any assertion that written reasons are mere post hoc rationalizations of votes. This is not to say that the process uncovers the "correct" answers to difficult questions. The task at hand has not been to assess whether the justices find the right answers. Rather, it is to describe and analyze how they go about resolving the questions before them. Indeed, the fact that critics and commentators have for decades pursued the former without addressing the latter is one of the primary impetuses for this study.

Second, judicial role perceptions are central to understanding both case outcomes and the process by which judgments are produced. The various stages of decision making and the rules that govern them restrict certain choices or forms of behaviour, while giving wide latitude to others. Ideology does not appear to play a large role in assigning authorship, for example, but the chief's prerogative to decide who will write permits strategic decision making. The justices' individual approaches to how they use their clerks or the extent to which they view consensus as a favourable goal add to the complexity of interaction between these many variables by making certain types of behaviour more or less likely. For example, a justice who is more willing to achieve consensus is more likely to engage in the type of bargaining that characterizes strategic behaviour, but the motivation behind such bargaining may not represent the most commonly asserted goal of implementing personal policy preferences or rational choice theory's basic assumption that the desire is to achieve a minimum winning coalition. The fact that personal relations can reinforce divisions on the Court and can play a role in the extent to which justices have informal deliberations about judgments is another facet of the institutional environment that is often obscured from study. Further, changes in both rules and institutional culture over the contemporary period have had a significant impact on the Court's operation. Important factors such as the chief justice's leadership style can increase or diminish the degree of consensus over time.

Finally, the analysis in this chapter also makes clear that norms such as those governing consensus can have a clear impact on policy outcomes. In instances where unanimity is an express goal, for example, the result is that the degree of consensus can actually be quite shallow. Reaching compromise in these instances necessitates issue-avoidance and can reduce the clarity of the judgment. For those advocating the strong judicial enforcement of *Charter* rights, the moderation and ambiguity that can result is problematic. Moreover, while in these particular cases it seems that any ideologically based preferences are stifled, abstract wording or concepts used in the reasons can open the way to increased value-based decision making in subsequent cases.

5
A Question of Competence: Examining Judicial Policy Making

As the Supreme Court of Canada evolved into a more prominent governing body over the last three decades, the normative debates surrounding its proper role have intensified. Fundamental to this debate is the question of whether courts and judges are equipped to deal with the moral and policy-laden issues entailed in the judicial review of constitutionally enshrined rights. In part, this question arises from the contested nature of rights, both in terms of defining what constitutes rights and in determining their limits.[1] Cases involving moral and social policy issues are said to allow judges far more discretion than cases viewed as falling within the more traditionally legal domain. Concern about the Court's involvement with policy issues is linked to the broader themes explored in this book in two distinct ways. First, the justices' considerations of their appropriate role in relation to the elected branches of government become especially pertinent when they must consider the Court's capacity or competence to deal with complex questions of policy. Many justices have themselves expressed apprehension at judicial involvement in the resolution of competing values or complex policy choices. How these views have evolved and how they have implicated actual case outcomes is thus significant. Second, if social policy cases provide a particular context for attitudinal behaviour, understanding how judicial role perceptions may constrain, or fail to constrain, such discretion is important.

The Court has often made a distinction between cases implicating social policy issues and other cases that are traditionally viewed as being more consonant with the judicial process, with the understanding that legislatures are better suited to determine the effects of policy choices. This distinction has often meant deference to legislative policy choices in those cases where the evidence necessary for the analysis of impugned policies is unclear or controversial. Interviews reveal that whether individual justices believe this distinction is appropriate depends on their views about the relative indeterminacy of the rights – and especially the "reasonable limits" of those rights

– implicated in cases that involve matters of social or moral concern. I examine the Court's *Canadian Charter of Rights and Freedoms* cases involving health policy and find that in practice the justices give surprisingly little attention to the issue of whether they have the capacity or legitimacy to resolve contentious social policy issues.[2] This attitude gives them wide discretion to decide such cases according to their personal policy preferences. Moreover, it limits the clarity and consistency of such rulings by producing a jurisprudence that offers the other branches of government little indication of their obligations under the *Charter*.

Institutional Boundaries and Questions of Capacity

In Chapter 2, I examined the Court's development of the law of justiciability, concerning which cases, controversies, or issues courts ought to decide. A related and important constraint on the Court's decision making pertains to what the justices feel they are *capable* of deciding. This aspect of the justices' role perceptions has become of heightened significance under the *Charter*, particularly as the justices have determined that nearly any issue may legitimately fall under their purview. As discussed in Chapter 2, the open approach to issues of justiciability and standing is one important part of the reason the Court ultimately decided to liberalize its stance on allowing third party interveners and the type of evidence it examines when determining complex moral or social policy matters. The justices came to realize they required external assistance in synthesizing the new policy issues they would now confront. These developments are significant given the sharp concern many of the justices have expressed over the years about the institutional capacity and general appropriateness of the Court's dealing with social policy questions.

Just six years prior to the *Charter*'s enactment, in a case involving whether peaceful picketing at a shopping centre was considered trespassing on private property, then Justice Brian Dickson described his unease with the idea that the Court should weigh competing social values:

> The submission that this court should weigh and determine the respective values of society of the right to property and the right to picket raises important and difficult political and socio-economic issues, the resolution of which must, by their very nature, be arbitrary and embody personal economic and social beliefs.[3]

Similar concerns continue to be expressed by some judges during the *Charter* era. In *R. v Morgentaler*, the 1988 abortion case, Justice William McIntyre acknowledged that the *Charter* imposed on the Court new responsibilities to ensure that legislative initiatives "conform to the democratic values expressed" within its guarantees. Nevertheless, he argued that "it is still fair to say that courts are not the appropriate forum for articulating complex and controversial programmes of public policy."[4] McIntyre J noted that nothing in the *Charter* makes clear that there exists an inherent right to abortion and that without an obvious basis for such a right, it was not for the Court to interfere with Parliament's balancing of the societal values at stake in the case.

More recently, the Court divided sharply on the issue of prisoner's voting rights. Justice Charles Gonthier, writing for the minority, emphasized the competing social values underpinning the issue:

> This case rests on philosophical, political and social considerations which are not capable of "scientific proof." It involves justifications for and against the limitation of the right to vote which are based upon axiomatic arguments of principle or value statements. I am of the view that when faced with such justifications, this Court ought to turn to the text of s. 1 of the *Charter* and to the basic principles which undergird both s. 1 and the relationship that provision has with the rights and freedoms protected within the *Charter*. Particularly, s. 1 of the *Charter* requires that this Court look to the fact that there may be different social or political philosophies upon which justifications for or against the limitations of rights may be based. In such a context, where this Court is presented with competing social or political philosophies relating to the right to vote, it is not by merely approving or preferring one that the other is necessarily disproved or shown not to survive *Charter* scrutiny. If the social or political philosophy advanced by Parliament reasonably justifies a limitation of the right in the context of a free and democratic society, then it ought to be upheld as constitutional.[5]

The problem articulated by Gonthier J strikes at the core of normative arguments about the role of the courts under the *Charter*. In 1983, Peter Russell noted that "excessive reliance on litigation and the judicial process for settling contentious policy issues can weaken the sinews of our democracy. The danger here is not so much that non-elected judges will impose their will on a democratic majority, but that questions of social and political justice will be transformed into technical legal questions."[6]

For both conservative and liberal critics of the judicial role under the *Charter,* the concern is not just about the supposed anti-democratic or counter-majoritarian nature of judicial review. Rather, the more fundamental concern with the Supreme Court of Canada's handling of social policy issues under the *Charter* is that the truly "principled" form of adjudication that would justify the counter-majoritarian nature by which the Court resolves them is ultimately impossible.[7] In other words, because there are competing answers to what constitutes a reasonable resolution to complex moral or social questions that implicate rights, many consider courts ill-suited to resolving such issues. Jeremy Waldron, a leading critic of courts' resolving such matters, notes that even where there is apparent consensus over rights (strong, universal support for guarantees such as freedom of expression or the right to equality), disagreement over their application remains.[8] In such instances, legal expertise provides no substantive guidance and judges are left with nothing to rely on but their personal conceptions of justice.

Reasonable Limits and the Social Policy Distinction

Gonthier J's statement in *Sauvé v Canada (Attorney General)* underlines the notion that the principal site of activity for the judicial consideration of institutional roles under the *Charter* is in its reasonable limits analysis.[9] Under section 1 of the *Charter*, rights are guaranteed "subject only to such reasonable limits prescribed by law as can be demonstrably justified in a free and democratic society." Ultimately, it is under section 1 that governments can defend policy objectives and the means by which they are achieved. Section 1 analysis is thus where these capacity or competence issues are paramount.[10] The Court's two-stage approach to *Charter* review conditions this process. First, the Court identifies whether rights have been infringed, while the second stage involves assessing the reasonableness of the impugned policy objective. The Court consciously decided from the outset of its *Charter* jurisprudence to avoid narrow definitional limits on the rights themselves. As a result, the justices are more likely to have to evaluate policies under section 1. If rights were interpreted more narrowly, the necessity of complex policy assessment would be reduced. In *R. v Oakes*, the Court established a two-prong test to determine the reasonableness of a law.[11] First, the objective of the measure must be important enough to warrant overriding a *Charter* right. The second stage is a "proportionality test," of which there are three steps: first, the measure must be rationally connected to the objective; second, the means by which the objective is achieved should impair the *Charter* right as little as possible; and, finally, there must be proportionality between the effects of the means and the objective.

Since the *Oakes* test was first established, two trends are worth noting. First, the minimal impairment step of the proportionality stage has become the most pivotal component of the test. The Court rarely strikes down legislation on the basis of the objective or the rational connection between the objective and the measure used to meet it.[12] A 1998 study found that in every instance in which the minimal impairment step was passed, the proportional effects step also passed, giving the final step of the *Oakes* test "a wholly vestigial role within section 1 decisionmaking."[13] Second, over time, the Court has relaxed or made "flexible" the standard of scrutiny applied.[14] Critics have argued that the test is insufficiently objective or predictable, with some complaining that it encourages deference on the part of the Court[15] and others expressing concern that it involves the Court too deeply in evaluating the merits of particular policies.[16] Janet Hiebert writes that there was a realization among many of the justices "that a large and liberal interpretation of protected rights in the initial stage of review, if accompanied by a strict application of the proportionality criteria, will result in the frequent invalidation of government objectives. It has quickly become apparent that a majority of the Court is not comfortable with this possibility."[17] She describes the crux of the problem as follows:

> The complexity of policy development makes it difficult to undertake careful and prudent policy analysis by judges (or others) who are external to the policy process or who lack the resources, relevant information, and analytical skills to evaluate conflicting social science evidence. It is therefore not surprising that the Court found the *Oakes* criteria of limited guidance when assessing the reasonableness of impugned policies. The difficulty of analysing the merits of policy encouraged individual justices to read into the standard their particular normative perspectives of liberty or democracy or institutional assumptions about the appropriate role of courts in a representative democracy.[18]

This difficulty is especially apparent in the context of social policy cases. However, the Court has been less reticent about applying a stricter level of scrutiny to criminal matters.[19]

The general capacity of courts to deal with social policy questions and the evidence surrounding them has long been called into doubt in the political science literature.[20] As explored in Chapter 2, the role of social or legislative facts has become prominent under the *Charter*. The judicial process does not lend itself to the collection and analysis of legislative facts necessary to formulate policy. Judges may take "judicial notice" of facts that are generally well known and may rely on expert witnesses at the trial level, government reports, legislative history, and published studies submitted by the parties. However, courts, particularly appellate courts, cannot conduct extensive hearings to gather additional information or commission new studies and reports as those in the legislative process can. Nor do courts have the entrenched resources of governmental bureaucracy from which to draw. Further, the adjudicative process is focused on particular litigants instead of whole categories of people, it is piecemeal and incremental, and it is passive, in that judges can only act when parties come before them.[21] These features make judicial investigation into historical facts surrounding particular cases relatively straightforward, but they make the process of synthesizing broader social facts extremely difficult.

Studies of the Court's application of legislative or social facts suggest its track record is fairly weak. Mahmud Jamal's exploration of how the Court's treatment of legislative facts has evolved reveals a discretionary and *ad hoc* approach. Jamal suggests that the Court's approach "will ultimately depend on whether the Court is in a mood to think creatively and reach out beyond the party-prepared record of evidence."[22] Danielle Pinard writes that "the reliance on a language of fact and evidence creates an illusion of certainty."[23] Her analysis of several Court decisions leads her to conclude that the justices routinely refer to evidence or facts for their rhetorical appeal, but these facts do not play a very important role in the ultimate decisions rendered. For example, in *Figueroa v Canada (Attorney General)*, the Court ruled that there were unconstitutional provisions in the *Canada Elections Act* mandating that political parties must nominate candidates in at least fifty ridings to qualify for certain benefits.[24] The majority decision lamented the lack of evidence on the rule's practical effect on the costs to government, on majority building or majority government, or even on whether minority governments are "less democratic" than majority governments. In effect, the justices were asking for evidence to answer questions for which, in some instances, there are no single correct answers. Pinard writes that in using their latitude to invoke such evidence (or the lack thereof), the justices in *Figueroa* adopted "a 'not our fault' type of reasoning" in which they "reasoned the facts necessary to come to a conclusion of violation of rights. And [they] regretted the lack of factual justification for such a limitation."[25]

Several of the Court's justices have spoken publicly about the problems associated with scientific or social scientific evidence. In 2003, Justice Ian Binnie commented on the "scientific illiteracy" of the judiciary. He noted that judges are "generalist decision makers" and made the somewhat shocking statement that they find they have to "sail into the Internet" to try to further understand scientific evidence, acknowledging they can encounter "all sorts of misinformation" as they do so. Binnie J stated that this problem is not insurmountable because the courts are not "unteachable," and reforms, such as having court-appointed, "neutral" experts at the trial level, could make scientific material more "digestable."[26] His former colleague, Justice Frank Iacobucci, places the onus on governments to improve the extent and quality of evidence provided to the courts:

Owing to the fact that judicial decision-making in the context of an adversarial trial is a far less sophisticated process for addressing social welfare concerns than the research, drafting and debate that accompanies legislative development, the quality of the dialogue between government and the judiciary is compromised where the government does not make a concerted effort to engage in that dialogue. It is more difficult for the judiciary to assess the constitutionality of legislation, or to provide suggestions as to alternative means to achieve the same objective in a less intrusive means, if it has little basis upon which to verify a government's claim that the effects of the legislation are reasonable.[27]

Although identifying problems associated with social facts and the judicial process, Binnie and Iacobucci JJ suggest the solution lies in reforms to improve the delivery of the evidence as opposed to more carefully proscribing the use of such evidence in a court setting. Their suggestion reflects a confidence on their part in the ability of courts to delve into the intricacies of policy making despite the institutional limitations they identify.

Other justices are even less concerned about the competency of courts to deal with such matters. According to Justice Claire L'Heureux-Dubé, the Court merely needs to be more explicit about the underlying policy assumptions with which it approaches cases implicating social science evidence. She writes that "the more courts acknowledge their active contribution to lawmaking, the greater becomes both their duty and their need to lay bare the policy assumptions upon which their decisions are based." She argues that courts must not impose overly strict rules on the taking of judicial notice so as not to discourage courts from admitting they use it, a consequence of which is that "underlying questions of policy are obfuscated by a mask of legal 'principles.' Principles formulated on such a basis, in turn, may lead to illogical applications in subsequent cases. Judicial notice must not be a convenient means by which courts can escape examination of their underlying policy assumptions."[28] Former Justice Louise Arbour argues passionately in favour of enforcing social and economic rights under the *Charter* and contends that reviewing such claims is "no quantum leap from those associated with ordinary review."[29]

The question of social and economic rights has become central to the Court's jurisprudence under section 7 of the *Charter*, which states that "[e]veryone has the right to life, liberty and security of the person and the right not to be deprived thereof except in accordance with the principles of fundamental justice." The evolution of the Court's approach to section 7 illustrates uncertainty and disagreement among the justices about their role in dealing with substantive policy issues. Falling under the "legal rights" section of the *Charter*, section 7 was originally understood to apply to matters relating to the administration of justice, as opposed to substantive issues. In other words, at the time of the *Charter*'s adoption, it was generally understood that the phrase "principles of fundamental justice" was restricted to issues of procedural fairness.[30] In the Court's first section 7 case, *Re B.C. Motor Vehicle Act*, the justices unanimously decided to ignore the intention of the framers and allow for a substantive interpretation of the clause.[31]

Justice Antonio Lamer, writing for the Court, saw the distinction between procedural and substantive content as importing an American debate into the Canadian system. This distinction is inappropriate, he argued, because that debate pertains to the nature and legitimacy of the US Constitution, which is structured very differently than the Canadian one (the latter of which includes section 1 and 33 of the *Charter* and section 52 of the *Constitution Act, 1982,* of which there are no equivalent American provisions).[32]

At least some of the justices were concerned that opening section 7 to substantive interpretation risked placing the Court in the position of dealing with pure policy matters. Lamer J acknowledged that such an approach would raise "the spectre of a judicial 'super-legislature.'"[33] In the decision, he restricted the scope of the guarantee to matters pertaining to the administration of justice, which he described as "the inherent domain of the judiciary."[34] This explicit articulation of the distinction between criminal cases and those relating to social and economic policy corresponds with the tendency of the Court to defer to legislatures in decisions involving the latter.[35] In a later section 7 case, Lamer J writes that "[t]he courts must not, because of the nature of the institution, be involved in the realm of pure public policy."[36] As Jamie Cameron notes, this institutionally grounded distinction between matters of justice and those of public policy has slowly dissolved over time, as the Court has delved more deeply into more pure policy matters in its section 7 jurisprudence.[37]

Arbour J's position that the life, liberty, and security of the person guarantees outlined in section 7 should be interpreted as having a positive dimension was clearly articulated in the 2002 case *Gosselin v Québec (Attorney General).*[38] *Gosselin* was the first case in which the Court faced squarely the question of whether the *Charter* imposed positive welfare obligations on government. The case demonstrated sharp divisions among the justices on the issue. Arbour J's minority opinion stated forcefully that the Court should take an expansive approach to section 7 that included the right to basic needs. Writing the other dissent, Justice Michel Bastarache acknowledged that in "certain exceptional circumstances," section 7 rights might include those outside of the traditional criminal context, but he maintained that there must be some link between the right and the administration of justice.[39] Chief Justice Beverley McLachlin's majority opinion refused to settle the matter conclusively, however. Citing the "living tree" metaphor, McLachlin CJ left open the possibility that section 7 jurisprudence may grow to include basic welfare and social rights.[40]

Cameron argues that the Court failed to acknowledge "the boundary which separates judicial and democratic functions."[41] She contends that "*Gosselin* demonstrates how easy it is for the judges to ignore or dismiss institutional questions which might require them to recognize limits on the scope of Charter rights, as well as on their own powers of review."[42] A decade after *Gosselin,* the future status of positive welfare rights in the *Charter* remains uncertain. Nevertheless, as discussed later in this chapter in relation to the health care case *Chaoulli v Quebec (Attorney General),* the decision in *Gosselin* to leave the door open to positive welfare rights has had a significant impact.[43]

Dealing with Social Policy: The Justices' Views

Lamer J's description of cases pertaining to the administration of justice as the "inherent domain of the judiciary" relates in part to the fact that there is a relative lack of determinacy with respect to evidence in social policy cases.[44] In interviews, the justices provided a range of responses on their views about the potential for uncertain or conflicting evidence surrounding policy issues. Some justices supported the distinction between social policy cases and criminal cases, while others dismissed it as generally unhelpful (Interviews). A major implication of this distinction in the Court's jurisprudence has meant that the Court has been more deferential to legislative choices when social policy issues are implicated.[45] The justices' views or concern about the use of social science evidence seem to correlate with their perspective on this distinction. Those justices concerned about the indeterminacy of evidence or the Court's capacity to deal with legislative facts are more likely to see a distinction between social policy cases and other cases and, thus, the need for deference in the former.

One justice noted never being concerned about difficulties in evaluating evidence in social policy cases. For this justice, relying on such evidence is crucial to understanding the context surrounding the issues that come before the Court. This justice did state, however, that the Court generally relies on such evidence only when it is clear. Asked about the distinction between social policy cases and criminal cases, this justice stated that it is relatively meaningless, noting that many criminal cases involve social issues as well (Interview).

A second justice stated that "the social sciences are less certain than the physical sciences ... let us say that perhaps they're another element that feeds into the decision-making, but they aren't as determinative as some law of physics might be." This justice saw the distinction between social policy cases and others as a "fact of life," noting that it pertains to the proper roles of the courts and Parliament in terms of their institutional capabilities and vocation. This justice noted that it is very important – but also very difficult – to draw the line (Interview).

Another justice expressed an even more reserved or guarded approach to the consideration of evidence:

I think [research] articles have to be taken, I shouldn't say with a grain of salt, but you have to consider exactly what they are. Depending on the article, suppose it's written by a psychiatrist on mental illness, you have to remember that he's a doctor, and that he's writing it from a medical perspective. And he's writing it with the hope that the Court can change something that will make his job easier or better, that you'll get better results on, say, forcing medication on a person. But they're just opinions. Some judges quote them; L'Heureux-Dubé used to quote a lot of them. I never relied on them very much. I never relied on them without hearing what the lawyers on both sides had to say about the article. I can't think of an article that was decisive on a judgment. (Interview)

This justice thus viewed the distinction between cases involving social policy and other ones as necessary: "In spite of what you read about 'the nine most powerful people, the unelected group that run the country,' I think the Court is very conscious of the fact that Parliament runs the country and that on social policies they have budgetary restraints, they have a number of factors that go into running the government and how they spend their money. The Court's pretty reluctant to tell the government how they should be spending their money. That came up a couple of years ago on treatment for autistic children."[46] He continued: "As I recall, we took the position that we couldn't interfere with the way the government chose to spend their money, in the absence of a clear violation of the *Charter*. Even with a clear violation, on money matters you point out where you think the violation is and you give them a year or a certain amount of time to correct it" (Interview).

A fourth justice acknowledged that judges place a degree of faith in scientists or social scientists, and they hope that the data has been rigorously tested, that it's not shoddy, anecdotal, or speculative. The justice noted that "this is where interveners come in, who have experience in the social science areas and can provide a helpful perspective" for the Court. This justice saw it as simply a reality of the *Charter* era that these other disciplines are "incredibly important" to the Court. The justice noted that some issues may stress "the limits of the judicial function" because by their very nature scientific or social scientific evidence is not clear, pointing to *Rodriguez v British Columbia (Attorney General),* which dealt with the prohibition against assisted suicide, as an example (Interview).[47] Implicit in this response is the notion that deference is warranted in social policy cases where evidence is unclear or a lack of consensus exists.

A fifth justice explained that "we're quite aware of some of the difficulties and limitations of the material, and I believe that some recent judgments of the Court have raised some caveats about the use of some of the evidence and of the need to build and test proper evidentiary record ... Over the years I think we have perhaps become a little more cautious than the Court was at first, in the first years after the *Charter* about the use of that material, and about the need to put it through a more rigorous and analytical process."

The justice noted that the line between criminal cases and social policy cases is becoming blurred. Criminal cases raise more than just the common law. This justice suspected that in both the Court's jurisprudence and in the academic literature more broadly it will be difficult in the long run to bother speaking of such a distinction (Interview).

Most of the justices acknowledged that the distinction between criminal cases and those involving social policy is not always cut and dry. Several cited as an example the Court's ruling in *R. v Askov,* which involved the right of defendants to a trial in a reasonable time (Interviews).[48] The decision stated that six to eight months would be the "outside limit" of a reasonable delay. This ruling resulted in tens of thousands of cases being dismissed, mainly in Ontario (where *Askov* originated).[49] The case is noteworthy because it clearly demonstrates that criminal cases have important policy effects. *Askov* also stands as one of the early *Charter* cases to illustrate the "fallibility of judicial decision making," particularly when it involves policy making.[50] According to Carl Baar, the Court in *Askov* made social science data "more central to its judgment than in any previous constitutional case."[51] Baar notes that the Court arrived at the six-to-eight-month standard by doubling the amount of time it took an average case to proceed in Montreal, a jurisdiction for which no evidence was presented in the case (the justices gathered the data on their own initiative). More significantly, there was no empirical basis for the conclusion that multiplying the average time in Montreal would yield good results or constitute reasonable delays in a standard case in other jurisdictions.[52] Just over a year later, the Court, reacting at least in part to the public outcry, used two cases to declare that its decision in *Askov* should be interpreted flexibly.[53]

Despite the fact that *Askov* shows that criminal cases have significant policy implications, the distinction made with regard to social policy cases is clearly reflected in the Court's jurisprudence. A recent study of the Court's reasonable limits analysis examines the distinction and finds that the Court divides on the outcome of section 1 analysis nearly twice as often in social policy cases (typically involving challenges under sections 2, 7, or 15) than in criminal cases (those challenges brought under sections 8-14 and occasionally section 7).[54] This significant difference highlights the lack of legal certainty in adjudicating matters of social policy. The justices have not settled on an approach that allows them to evaluate social policy matters in a more unified way. In effect, the value-laden issues at stake in such cases permit a more discretionary form of decision making.

The Court's Approach to Social Policy Cases: Health Policy and the Use of Evidence

In what follows, I examine the Court's *Charter* cases involving health policy. These cases have garnered considerable attention in the scholarly literature, reflecting their importance both for the substantive outcomes of the cases themselves and for debates over judicial review more generally. Moreover, health policy cases tend to be limited to two distinct strands of *Charter* law: the right to life, liberty, and security of the person under section 7 and equality rights under section 15.[55] The weighing of values in each of these areas of the *Charter* is an exercise fraught with difficulty. As the discussion in Chapter 4 demonstrates, section 15 concerns one of the most contested concepts in equality. Further, as noted earlier, section 7 jurisprudence has direct implications for judicial perceptions of institutional roles. An exploration of the health policy cases exposes a piecemeal and discretionary approach to the primary issues at stake. The analysis reveals that the justices have not been overly concerned about deference to Parliament or respecting earlier judicial concerns about what constitutes an appropriate institutional division of labour for contested social policies. The Court delves primarily into a discussion of the particular policy issues at stake, often emphasizing an analysis of whether the impugned policy constitutes a reasonable limit of the right in question.

Two primary considerations come into play in the Court's dealing with health policy. In the first two cases explored in this discussion, which involved the constitutionality of abortion and assisted suicide, the justices dealt with diverging philosophical conceptions of justice.[56] The justices generally failed to address whether or under what conditions the Court is the suitable venue for addressing competing values. The next two cases involved the delivery of particular services, sign language interpreters for deaf patients in public hospitals and a form of intensive behavioural therapy for autistic children.[57] These cases required a consideration of under what conditions the *Charter* imposes positive obligations on governments. They show that the justices have not provided a framework of analysis for the conditions under which the Court should require legislative policy choices that necessitate direct distribution of scarce resources. The final two health care cases – *Chaoulli*, which brought the Court into the heart of the debate over the delivery of private medical insurance, and *Canada (Attorney General) v PHS Community Services Society*, which examined whether the federal government's decision to try to shut down a safe injection site in Vancouver violated the right to life, liberty, and security of the person, involved both types of considerations.[58] As will be shown, the nature of the decision making in these cases reflects a piecemeal approach.

The 1988 *Morgentaler* case on abortion was arguably the first *Charter* case that involved the Court in a highly visible, controversial moral question. It is certainly among the most prominent examples of judicial involvement in an issue that sharply divides society and over which there are no obviously correct answers. The four opinions reflect not just a split over the abortion issue itself but also uncertainty among the justices about how to approach a case that rests principally on the balancing of fundamental values. At stake was a provision in the *Criminal Code* that required women seeking an abortion to obtain a certificate from the therapeutic abortion committee of an accredited or approved hospital. The seven justices hearing the case split into four camps in the decision, with five voting to strike down the provision. Justice Jean Beetz's reasons struck down the law on the narrowest grounds, finding that the law violated women's right to security of the person because the committee system was arbitrary and applied in an uneven fashion. Dickson CJ cited testimony and reports that made clear the committee system produced significant (and potentially dangerous) delays in care and that these delays violated the right to security of the person because they were manifestly unfair. Only Justice Bertha Wilson directly tackled the substantive issue of whether women had the right to abortion. She argued that "the right to liberty contained in s. 7 guarantees to every individual a degree of personal autonomy over important decisions intimately affecting their private lives" and concluded that "the decision of a woman to terminate her pregnancy falls within this class of protected decisions."[59]

The four justices in the plurality wrote decisions that rest, on the surface at least, on procedural grounds, avoiding the substantive issue of whether women have the right to an abortion. As Cameron points out, however, "it is difficult to see how delay can be a constitutional violation if there is no right of access to the procedure in the first place."[60] Indeed, in his dissenting reasons, McIntyre J noted that Dickson CJ's judgment "has not said in specific terms that the pregnant woman has the right to an abortion, whether therapeutic or otherwise. In my view, however, his whole position depends for its validity upon that proposition."[61] Thus, where the other opinions on the majority side paid lip-service to the Court's position in *Re B.C. Motor Vehicle Act* that section 7 only applied to matters related to the administration of justice and not pure policy concerns, Wilson J's opinion explicitly rejected it.

McIntyre J's dissent also reflects a concern about the values at stake and the basis for the rights in question. He argued that there was no textual or historical basis for the right to abortion, writing that "the *Charter* should not be regarded as an empty vessel to be filled with whatever meaning we might wish from time to time." This understanding, in McIntyre J's view, "does not mean that judges may not make some policy choices when confronted with competing conceptions of the extent of rights or freedoms. Difficult choices must be made and the personal views of judges will unavoidably be engaged from time to time. The decisions made by judges, however, and the interpretations that they advance or accept must be plausibly inferable from something in the *Charter*. It is not for the courts to manufacture a constitutional right out of whole cloth."[62]

The Court's reliance on extrinsic evidence in the case is also significant. Although there appears to be little doubt as to the veracity of the facts relied on in the case that demonstrate significant delays and unequal access across the country, the Court's reliance on such data is not without controversy. Just over a decade earlier in the 1976 *Morgentaler* case, Chief Justice Bora Laskin rejected the use of similar evidence, noting: "It would mean that the Court would have to come to ... decide how large or small an area must be within which an acceptable distribution of physicians and hospitals must be found."[63] Further, the 1988 case relied heavily on the *Report of the Committee on the Operation of the Abortion Law (Badgley Report)*, which was commissioned by the Trudeau government in response to the 1976 case.[64] As Thomas Bateman et al. note, "[the *Badgley Report*] was intended to serve as the basis for possible legislative reform to the abortion law, but Parliament never acted on it. Now, 10 years later, the Badgley Report was being used by judges to strike down the same abortion law."[65]

Morgentaler made clear that under the *Charter* some judges would not shy away from the most contentious of topics or from dealing directly with policy issues. Just as significantly, the division among the justices over their approach to the abortion issue and, more broadly, to section 7 reflects that their conceptions of the appropriate institutional roles pertaining to judicial review were very much in flux. Further, the policy impact of the *Morgentaler* decision has been immense. Christopher Manfredi documents a sharp rise in the number of abortions following the case (after one year, the rate of abortions per thousand women increased by 15.9 percent; after ten years, it had increased by 35.3 percent).[66] He writes that this increase "is primarily a function of an increase in the number of abortions performed in clinics rather than hospitals, a development directly traceable to *Morgentaler*."[67]

A few years later, the Court grappled with the constitutionality of a provision of the *Criminal Code* prohibiting assisted suicide in *Rodriguez*, which involved a forty-two-year-old woman suffering from a degenerative disease that would eventually leave her unable to move, eat, or breathe on her own. The case raised many of the same section 7 issues as *Morgentaler*, but this time a narrow five-to-four majority voted to uphold the law. Justice John Sopinka, writing for the majority, acknowledged the discretionary nature of the values at stake in the case:

> On the one hand, the Court must be conscious of its proper role in the constitutional make-up of our form of democratic government and not seek to make fundamental changes to long-standing policy on the basis of general constitutional principles and its own view of the wisdom of legislation. On the other hand, the Court has not only the power but the duty to deal with this question if it appears that the *Charter* has been violated. The power to review legislation to determine whether it conforms to the *Charter* extends to

not only procedural matters but also substantive issues. The principles of fundamental justice leave a great deal of scope for personal judgment and the Court must be careful that they do not become principles which are of fundamental justice in the eye of the beholder *only*.

Sopinka J went on to explain that the principles of fundamental justice are concerned not only with the rights of the individual claimant but also with the protection of society as a whole. Additionally, he noted the lack of consensus over the issue of assisted suicide, adding: "To the extent that there is a consensus, it is that human life must be respected and we must be careful not to undermine the institutions that protect it."[68]

McLachlin J's dissenting opinion argued that the law was not in accordance with the principles of fundamental justice because it was arbitrary (it made a distinction between passive euthanasia and suicide on the one hand, which are not prohibited, and assisted suicide on the other).[69] Arbitrariness as a concept for appraising laws under section 7 would arise again in the plurality judgment in *Chaoulli* (discussed later in this chapter). This point is significant, Cameron argues, because like the "manifest unfairness" principle articulated by Dickson CJ in *Morgentaler*, the arbitrariness concept "collapsed the distinction between justice and policy, and in doing so, ignored [Re B.C. Motor Vehicle Act] logic and its search for principled limits on review. Each lacked criteria and both presented an unlimited potential for review as a result."[70]

Rodriguez, as much as any other case, highlighted for the justices the question of the appropriate institutional roles in resolving such matters and the issue of the capacity of courts to do so. As noted in Chapter 2, one justice interviewed for this book said of *Rodriguez*: "I believe you're stressing the limits of the judicial function in that case to, in effect, say that a prohibition against assisted suicide was unconstitutional." The justice explained: "Is this just a legal question? What's the input coming from philosophers, medical science, care givers, social workers ... It's a poly-centric kind of issue, not left only to judges to decide on the basis of evidence and input that might be incomplete. So there are questions you always have" (Interview). Implicit in this response is the notion that deference is warranted in social policy cases where evidence is unclear or where a lack of consensus exists. The fact that not all justices agree with such logic reflects the large degree of uncertainty and haphazardness in the Court's jurisprudence on social policy questions. More specifically, the Court has not addressed or developed in any systemic way an underlying logic or approach to dealing with such matters.

Morgentaler and *Rodriguez* highlight sharp disagreement among the justices regarding the appropriate institutional roles when the matters before the Court involve contentious moral or philosophical concern. The justices who resisted deference to Parliament's choices in these cases gave little explicit attention to the idea that there might be "institutional boundaries" surrounding judicial review.[71] In other words, less than a decade after the *Charter,* some justices appear to have abandoned the idea expressed by the Court in *Re B.C. Motor Vehicle Act* that under section 7, the Court ought to leave pure policy issues to the legislatures.

The relative inattention to the appropriate institutional roles applies not only to cases involving moral controversy but also to those extending positive rights, as the next two health policy cases demonstrate. In *Eldridge v British Columbia (Attorney General),* the Court unanimously ruled that the Medical Services Commission in British Columbia acted unconstitutionally under section 15 of the *Charter* when it failed to provide sign language interpreters to deaf patients in hospitals.[72] In *Auton v British Columbia (Attorney General),* the Court unanimously rejected the claim that the *Charter*'s equality provisions required the provincial government to fund a particular intensive behavioural treatment for children with autism. If critics are generally concerned about the supposed anti-democratic nature of judicial review, they are especially skeptical of the enforcement of positive rights under the *Charter* given their belief that decisions involving the distribution of scarce resources are the proper domain of elected representatives.[73] It is perhaps for this reason that the Court has generally shied away from decisions that inflict direct costs on governments. A prominent example of this logic is the unanimous judgment in the 2004 case *Newfoundland (Treasury Board) v N.A.P.E.,* which upheld as reasonable the government of Newfoundland and Labrador's decision to cut pay equity payments owed to female hospital employees because the province was in severe financial distress.[74]

In holding that the failure to provide sign language interpretation violated the equality rights of deaf patients in *Eldridge,* Justice Gerard La Forest, writing for the Court, moved immediately to the minimum impairment stage of the *Oakes* test in his section 1 analysis to deal with the question of cost:

> In the present case, the government has manifestly failed to demonstrate that it had a reasonable basis for concluding that a total denial of medical interpretation services for the deaf constituted a minimum impairment of their rights. As previously noted, the estimated cost of providing sign language interpretation for the whole of British Columbia was only $150,000, or approximately 0.0025 percent of the provincial health care budget at the time ... In these circumstances, the refusal to expend such a relatively insignificant sum to continue and extend the service cannot possibly constitute a minimum impairment of the appellants' constitutional rights.[75]

La Forest J further remarked: "The respondents have presented no evidence that this type of accommodation, if extended to other government services, will unduly strain the fiscal resources of the state."[76]

Manfredi points to significant problems with how the Court handled the question of costs. Noting that the Court's estimate of $150,000 was extrapolated from a private, volunteer-based institute in Victoria and the lower mainland of British Columbia, he points out that "there was no serious analysis at any stage of the proceedings of whether this would be an adequate basis for supplying the more extensive services implicit in the appellants' claim."[77] Further, no consideration was given to whether the costs of the service in more remote or rural regions of the province would be higher.[78] Manfredi is also critical of the fact that the Court's judgment brushes aside concerns of the province that the broader implication of the decision is to invite similar claims from other disadvantaged groups. This latter concern is shared by Cameron in the sense of the decision's implications for the Court's jurisprudence. In her view, *Eldridge* implies that

> decisions affecting the allocation of resources are subject to the Charter, except when the fiscal integrity of the state is at stake. This line of reasoning is problematic, though, because it treats the consequences of imposing positive obligations as an isolated phenomenon, which is limited in significance to the circumstances of a particular case. An approach that assumes the consequences are discrete allows the Court to minimize their importance. As a result, the cumulative or systemic impact of such obligations can be avoided, and might never be addressed.[79]

The lack of consistency in such an approach became evident in *Auton*, where the Court refused to require the province to provide an intensive treatment for children with autism. In her judgment for the Court, McLachlin CJ distinguished the case from *Eldridge* by noting that the province "was obliged to provide translators to the deaf so that they could have equal access to core benefits accorded to everyone." In *Eldridge*, she wrote, the province was denying in a discriminatory fashion benefits that were prescribed by law. The particular form of autism treatment at issue in *Auton*, however, involves "access to a benefit that the law has not conferred."[80] Despite this determination, McLachlin CJ nevertheless proceeded to consider whether failure to fund the treatment constituted discrimination under section 15. She wrote that "the appropriate comparator for the petitioners is a nondisabled person or a person suffering a disability other than a mental disability (here autism) seeking or receiving funding for a non-core therapy important for his or her present and future health, which is emergent and only recently becoming recognized as medically required."[81] In drawing these conclusions, McLachlin CJ noted the controversial and "emergent" nature of the treatment in question. She also pointed out that at the time of the trial, the government funded "a number of programs for autistic children."[82]

McLachlin CJ's logic in distinguishing the cases is arguably narrow and unconvincing. As Manfredi and Antonia Maioni write, "[b]y focusing on these facts – rather than on the tragic impact of autism, bureaucratic intransigence, personal economic sacrifice, or individual progress under [the treatment in question] – the Chief Justice provided a relatively benign picture of the pre-*Auton* status quo."[83] Just as significantly, in framing the facts in this way, McLachlin CJ reinterpreted their application in sharp contrast to the trial judge, who rebuked government attempts to question the scientific validity of two existing studies on the treatment.[84] The Supreme Court of Canada's judgment also overturned the unanimous holding of the British Columbia Court of Appeal, which held that the province's failure "to consider the individual needs of the infant complainants by funding treatment is a statement that their mental disability is less worthy of assistance than the transitory medical problems of others."[85] Finally, in her narrow definition of the appropriate comparator group, McLachlin CJ made it "virtually impossible" for a finding of discrimination.[86] This latter determination allowed McLachlin CJ to avoid a section 1 analysis, which would have required the government to justify the funding decision (something it failed to do at the trial or appeal court levels) and the Court to more deeply consider the evidence surrounding whether the treatment was medically necessary.

Taken together, the decisions in *Eldridge* and *Auton* provide no indication of how the Court might determine whether a government is obligated to provide particular policy programs. How relatively inexpensive must a particular program be for the Court to feel comfortable enforcing and imposing the cost of an impugned *Charter* right? How established or scientifically proven must a particular medical treatment be for it to become mandatory under the *Charter*? *Eldridge* and *Auton* do not address these issues. More importantly, the cases do not provide any framework for which the Court might determine the answers to such questions or provide governments any clues that might aid them in identifying their obligations.

Like *Morgentaler* and *Rodriguez* before them, *Eldridge* and *Auton* reflect reasoning focused squarely on the particular policy issues at hand. Little attention is paid to the broader bases for determining when and under what circumstances the Court ought to mandate positive obligations on governments. Without an explicit consideration of the respective institutional responsibilities and capacities involved in the design of complex policies, the legitimacy, coherence, and principled nature of the Court's decision making is put at risk. There is no better example of this than *Chaoulli*.[87]

In *Chaoulli*, the Court was essentially tasked with determining the validity of one of the founding principles of the country's health care system. Under challenge was the Quebec government's prohibition of private health insurance. The case exemplifies the type of issue that concerned those who were critical of the Court's liberalization of its approach to justiciability. As noted in Chapter 2, the justices even took the time to once again repudiate the notion that there ought to be a "political questions" doctrine that restricts the scope of *Charter* review.[88] *Chaoulli* also forcefully highlights the continued division among the justices about the fate of section 7 as a vehicle for the resolution of policy disputes that do not involve matters of the administration of justice. In the decision, the Court split four to three in finding the provisions unconstitutional under the Quebec *Charter of Human Rights and Freedoms* and three to three (with Justice Marie Deschamps abstaining) on whether the prohibition was constitutional under the Canadian *Charter*.[89] On the majority side, McLachlin CJ and Justice Jack Major wrote that the prohibition of private health insurance subjects Canadians to physical and psychological harm stemming from the long delays under the existing system and, thus, violates the right to life, liberty, and security of the person under section 7. In determining whether this violation was in accordance with the principles of fundamental justice, McLachlin and Major JJ invoked a standard of arbitrariness, first raised by McLachlin J in *Rodriguez*. Relying on the evidence presented at trial and drawing heavily from a 2002 report by the Canadian Senate's Standing Committee on Social Affairs, Science and Technology (the *Kirby Report*), the justices purport to refute the government's contention that the prohibition on private health care maintains and protects the integrity and quality of the public system.[90] Their analysis and treatment of the evidence in this part of the decision has been roundly criticized, with one commentator arguing that the justices "violated almost every scholarly standard for competent policy analysis."[91]

The majority judgment misrepresented some evidence and ignored other evidence surrounding the question of whether expanding private insurance would improve care. First, it misrepresented the evidence by giving one solitary expert witness who claimed that allowing private insurance would not harm the public system equal weight to six others who said it would.[92] As David Schneiderman contends, "the *Chaoulli* expert's rogue opinion was elevated to a status equivalent to that of all the other experts. [Then], all of the expert opinion then was demoted to the realm of mere common sense."[93] Second, the majority attributed the waiting lists in Canada to the public system, something that comparative evidence demonstrated was "clearly wrong."[94] In fact, the justices drew on comparative evidence to demonstrate that other Western nations allow a substantial degree of private care, but they ignored the fact that waiting lists are just as much of a concern in those countries.[95]

Binnie J and Justice Louis LeBel's dissenting opinion cautioned that the Court might be unable to address the complex, fact-laden policy issues at stake in the case. Their judgment highlights the judicial debate over the Court's role in resolving complex policy issues. In doing so, they appealed to the deferential approach the Court adopted in *Auton*:

> The Court recently held in *Auton* ... that the government was not required to fund the treatment of autistic children. It did not on that occasion address in constitutional terms the scope and nature of "reasonable" health services. Courts will now have to make that determination. What, then, are constitutionally required "reasonable health services"? What is treatment "within a reasonable time"? What are the benchmarks? How short a waiting list is short enough? How many MRIs does the Constitution require? The majority does not tell us. The majority lays down no manageable constitutional standard. The public cannot know, nor can judges or governments know, how much health care is "reasonable" enough to satisfy s. 7 of the *Canadian Charter* ... It is to be hoped that we will know it when we see it.[96]

Most significantly, the dissenting justices criticized the majority for wading deep into the realm of policy analysis and ignoring the appropriate limits of institutional boundaries: "The evidence certainly established that the public health care system put in place to implement this policy has serious and persistent problems. This does not mean that the courts are well placed to perform the required surgery. The resolution of such a complex fact-laden policy debate does not fit easily within the institutional competence or procedures of courts of law."[97]

The Binnie-LeBel judgment also serves to underscore the concern some critics have with the Court's handling of the social facts at stake in the case. The minority criticized McLachlin and Major JJ for their characterization of the expert witnesses as providing little more than "common sense" appraisals of the policy. They wrote: "The respondent's experts testified and were cross-examined. The trial judge found them to be credible and reliable. We owe deference to her findings in this respect."[98] Further, they identified as problematic the majority's reliance on the *Kirby Report* to substantiate the problems with the Canadians system and to make note of private delivery in other countries, while ignoring the fact that the *Kirby Report* itself recommends continued support for the single-tier system of delivery in Canada.

The *Chaoulli* judgment also highlights the underlying values at stake in the case. The minority decision suggests that the majority erred in drawing their own conclusions about the facts on the case without considering that the legislative choices constitute a reflection on societal values. They wrote that the snippets the majority drew from the *Kirby Report* "do not displace the conclusion of the trial judge, let alone the conclusion of the Kirby Report itself. Apart from everything else, it leaves out of consideration the commitment in principle in *this* country to health care based on *need*, not wealth or status."[99] Taken together with the other statements in the Binnie-LeBel judgment, it is clear that the minority was uncomfortable with judicial resolution of policy matters, especially when those policy choices reflect a balancing of competing interests and values.

The two sides in *Chaoulli* came to divergent conclusions based on substantially different premises regarding institutional roles and responsibilities. The minority viewed the central question of the case as one that pertained to social values rather than constitutional law.[100] The majority, by contrast, asserted that "[t]he mere fact that this question may have policy ramifications does not permit us to avoid answering it."[101] In her solo opinion in favour of striking down the law, Deschamps J presented an impassioned argument on why the Court should not defer to the legislative policy choice in question:

> Governments have promised on numerous occasions to find a solution to the problem of waiting lists. Given the tendency to focus the debate on a sociopolitical philosophy, it seems that governments have lost sight of the urgency of taking concrete action. The courts are therefore the last line of defence for citizens.
>
> ... While the government has the power to decide what measures to adopt, it cannot choose to do nothing in the face of the violation of Quebeckers' right to security. The government has not given reasons for its failure to act. Inertia cannot be used as an argument to justify deference.[102]

Deschamps J's portrayal of government inaction notwithstanding, the fact remains that the *Chaoulli* majority imposed a policy constraint on the Quebec government for its failure to resolve a particular policy problem (waiting lists) in part on the basis that other jurisdictions – other countries and four Canadian provinces – do not prohibit private insurance. As already noted, many of these jurisdictions face similar waiting lists. Following Deschamps J's logic, had a section 7 claim originated from a province that had not prohibited private insurance, the Court could have imposed on that province the requirement that it do so. There appears no basis on which the majority relied, except on their personal policy preference to allow the delivery of private health insurance.

In part, this judicial discretion stems from the problematic treatment the majority gave the evidence at hand in the case. Indeed, critics of the decision contend that the evidence strongly supports the opposite conclusion – that the introduction of private health care is likely to increase costs and exacerbate the problems in the system rather than alleviate them. Even if the justices had determined that the evidence was inconclusive, more restraint would have been appropriate. As Robert Charney notes, "the Supreme Court has held that in justifying legislation under Charter section 1 the legislature is not to be held to a standard of 'scientific proof based on concrete evidence' but to a standard of 'reasoned apprehension of harm.' When confronted with competing experts in disciplines such as economics, the courts must accept that there is no one 'right answer' to many policy questions, and legislative

deference is appropriate."[103] The McLachlin-Major judgment's characterization of the law as "arbitrary," however, essentially pre-determined the outcome of their reasonable limits analysis. As the justices themselves noted,
it is unlikely that any arbitrary law could ever be considered rationally
connected to the objective and thus pass that stage of the *Oakes* test.[104]

The Court's collective record in dealing with health policy issues, cul-
minating in *Chaoulli*, makes it difficult to agree with Arbour J's argument
that review of social and economic rights claims is "no quantum leap from
those associated with ordinary judicial review."[105] The justices' treatment
of the evidence in *Chaoulli* stands as the foremost confirmation of Donald
Horowitz's contention that certain policy problems "are beyond the capabilities of even the most able judges to handle well."[106] For Manfredi, the case
"is the entirely predictable consequence of a process in which the Court
has progressively liberated itself from the ideas that there are fixed limits
to its decision making capacity and that the Charter has any meaning independent of what judges give it."[107]

Chaoulli may stand as the paradigmatic example of how the Court is not
well suited to evaluating social science evidence, but the health policy cases
leading up to *Chaoulli* set the stage for that decision by not explicitly addressing what the appropriate institutional roles ought to be in the determination of policies under the *Charter*. At the start of the first chapter, I
argued that the leading explanations of judicial behaviour could not, in
isolation, fully account for the different outcomes in cases such as *Auton*
and *Chaoulli*. The justices reached unanimous agreement on two fundamental considerations in the autism case. First, in distinguishing between the
nature of discrimination in *Auton* versus the provision of sign language interpreters in *Eldridge*, they agreed on the principal legal issue at stake. Second,
the *Auton* decision notes the relatively emergent nature of the autism treatment in question and repeatedly emphasizes the province's discretion to
fund non-core medical services. Two justices interviewed for this book cited
Auton as an example of how the Court should show restraint in decisions
implicating government spending. These considerations show that the
justices deciding the case agreed on their understanding of the Court's institutional limits – those issues that embody constraints on its capacity or
legitimacy to determine the policy questions at stake (Interview).

By contrast, the *Chaoulli* case shows that when agreement concerning the
Court's institutional role breaks down, the decision becomes ripe for the
manifestation of the justices' personal policy preferences. As has been demonstrated, the justices have a wide range of views on the Court's capacity
for evaluating social policy evidence and on whether such issues call for
more deference to legislative choices. And although strong norms of consensus infuse the Court's collaborative environment, the previous chapter

revealed that individual justices each have their own perspectives on the best approach to collegiality, deliberation, and compromise. Thus, while unanimity is desired, it is rarely an explicit goal. When the justices fail to agree about these role-related considerations, particular cases can become sites of activity for attitudinal and strategic behaviour.

Two important, and perhaps obvious, qualifications are warranted. First, nothing in this analysis suggests that because the legal and institutional considerations were paramount in *Auton* that the decision was somehow the objectively "correct" one (although an argument might be made that a unanimous decision carries more weight and legitimacy than a sharply divided one such as *Chaoulli*). Indeed, future provincial governments may decide that the *Charter* does impose an onus on them to provide funding for medical services such as the intensive behavioural treatment for autism. Second, this account does not imply that ideological considerations played no role in *Auton* or that legal and role-related variables were not present in *Chaoulli*.

Chaoulli stands in many ways as a culmination of the Court's evolving section 7 jurisprudence and its adjudication of previous health care cases more specifically. In addition to drawing on the "arbitrariness" standard from *Rodriguez*, the McLachlin-Major plurality also invoked *Morgentaler* as an important precedent establishing that delays in medical treatment violate security of the person.[108] The minority judgment criticizes the majority for "extending too far the strands of interpretation" in *Morgentaler*, noting: "We cannot find in the constitutional law of Canada a 'principle of fundamental justice' dispositive of the problems of waiting lists in the Quebec health system. In our view, the appellants' case does not rest on constitutional law but on their disagreement with the Quebec government on aspects of its social policy. The proper forum to determine the social policy of Quebec in this matter is the National Assembly."[109]

Extending the logic of *Morgentaler* and adopting the arbitrariness standard in *Rodriguez* effectively gave the *Chaoulli* justices free rein to determine the acceptability of the policy at stake in the case. As Cameron writes, the application of the arbitrariness standard "allows the Court to invalidate laws which are seen as fundamentally unjust."[110] In effect, it provides no obvious standard by which the justices would determine whether the law is in accordance with the principles of fundamental justice. Taken together with the problematic manner in which the McLachlin-Major plurality judgment treats the evidence in *Chaoulli*, it is clear that the decision rests on little more than their personal conception of what is just.

The impact of the Court's earlier decision in *Gosselin* also played a significant role in *Chaoulli*. As noted earlier, the majority in *Gosselin* refused to determine whether section 7 included positive rights or imposed positive obligations on governments, but it explicitly left the door open to the possibility. Despite their obvious concern that it was inappropriate for the Court to involve itself in the resolution of fact-laden policy debate in *Chaoulli*, the Binnie-LeBel minority judgment cited *Gosselin* in rejecting the argument of Quebec's attorney general that section 7 was limited to matters relating to the administration of justice.[111] This opinion arguably severed the final string that may have attached the Court to the institutional logic it articulated in *Re B.C. Motor Vehicle Act*. Although they articulated concern about the values and policy choices at stake in *Chaoulli*, the justices in the minority still abandoned the notion of limiting section 7's reach. This decision suggests that the current Court's justices are much more comfortable with the notion that there are no boundaries surrounding their powers of judicial review than their predecessors had been just two decades earlier. Moreover, the decision of Deschamps J to abstain from deciding the matter on the Canadian *Charter* may have been a deliberate strategy to leave open the section 7 issue for the future, something other scholars have viewed with suspicion.[112]

The arbitrariness standard re-emerged in 2011 when the Court rendered its decision in *PHS Community Services Society* (the Insite case). Established as the first supervised injection facility in North America, "Insite" was a pilot project developed in 2003 in response to the rampant drug use that marked the downtown eastside neighbourhood of Vancouver. It was the result of an agreement between local health authorities, the province of British Columbia, and the federal government. Insite was initially granted an exemption from the federal *Controlled Drugs and Substances Act (CDSA)* by the Liberal government in 2003, and although the Conservative government decided to end federal funding of the facility after coming to power in 2006, it extended the exemption that year and again in 2007 to allow for further research before minister of health Tony Clement decided to deny a third extension and shut the facility down in 2008.[113]

The case dealt with two primary constitutional issues. The first pertained to the constitutional division of powers. The provinces, local health authority, and Insite clients asserted that the safe injection site was fundamentally a provincial health concern rather than a matter for the federal criminal law power. The Court determined that the *CDSA* was a valid federal power. The second issue the justices were faced with was whether the minister's decision to deny a further exemption (therefore forcing Insite's closure) contravened section 7 of the *Charter*. Significantly, McLachlin CJ's unanimous decision crafted the *Charter* ruling in quite narrow terms, upholding the *CDSA* itself by noting that the impugned provisions do not violate the principles of fundamental justice because the provision granting the minister discretion to make exemptions to the prohibitions acts as a safety valve. Instead, the Court ruled that the minister used his discretion in this particular instance in an arbitrary manner and that the decision's effects were "grossly disproportionate" to any benefit that might result from enforcing the *CDSA* in the context of Insite.

In contrast with *Chaoulli*, the justices gave due consideration to the overwhelming evidence presented at the trial level in the Insite case that the facility helped reduce the spread of disease and the risk of death from overdosing. The minimalist nature of the ruling – leaving the legislative regime intact and ruling that only the decision in this instance was a violation – is reflective of a cautious but unified Court dealing with a highly publicized case. In these respects, the decision avoids the overtly political nature of *Chaoulli*.

Yet, like the *Eldridge* and *Auton* decisions, the Insite case provides little indication about exactly what the arbitrariness standard means for similar future cases. In fact, it is unclear whether the Court's decision paves the way for other safe injection sites across Canada. In her judgment, McLachlin CJ cautioned that the section 7 finding as it relates to Insite is not "an invitation for anyone who so chooses to open a facility for drug use under the banner of a 'safe injection facility.'"[114] This warning might suggest that the federal government is by no means obligated under the Charter to provide exemptions for similarly supervised injection facilities in other provinces or other contexts. The near-epidemic status of Vancouver's downtown eastside and the sheer concentration of drug addicts in the immediate vicinity factored into not only the Court's decision but also the evidence used to support it. It is conceivable that the federal health minister might have refused to grant an exemption if the circumstances were different. On the other hand, it is difficult to see how a decision to deny another province or city an exemption to open a supervised injection facility does not infringe the Charter rights of individuals addicted to drugs in those localities.

A major problematic feature of the Court's logic in this case is that it creates a positive obligation on the government to keep this site open but avoids placing an obligation on other provinces and localities to open their own facilities. This standard creates an inherent internal tension in the Court's application of the Charter in this case. By opening the site in the first place, the various governments have, according to the Court, created legitimate rights claims, which suggests that the unique nature of the downtown eastside and of the pilot project itself contributes to the application – indeed, the existence – of the rights in question. However, even if the circumstances of the downtown eastside are what make closing Insite "grossly disproportionate" in effect, then given that Insite runs at full capacity and only serves up to 5 percent of the drug users in its vicinity, why is the province not obligated to open more facilities there? And why should governments risk developing new projects or social programs in other contexts if doing so might create permanent rights obligations? Unfortunately, like the *Eldridge* and *Auton* cases, the Insite decision provides no standards by which to answer these various questions. The Court left it to the various governments to deal with future situations and to consider their obligations under the Charter when making decisions. This respect for inter-institutional relationships is laudable (and, as noted, has not been something that the Court has always been consistent with). Yet, Insite continues the Court's trend of applying section 7 in a very piecemeal manner.

I have argued that a more explicit consideration of institutional roles in social policy cases may lead to more principled decision making. This argument corresponds to the broader contention made throughout this book that judicial role perceptions can and do constrain attitudinal decisions on the part of the justices. In the context of the health policy cases examined in this section, a consideration of the Court's proper role in social policy cases is likely to lead to deference in instances where the policy effects are unclear, the evidence is not determinative, or the balancing of competing values is at stake. Yet, it is not a normative argument in favour of deference for its own sake. As Aileen Kavanagh writes, judicial deference is not about courts submitting blindly to the choices of the elected branches or about judges approaching their role uncritically.[115] Indeed, development of a clear, role-based framework for approaching social policy issues (either within the confines of section 7 or, as it pertains to section 15 cases, within section 1), will provide legitimacy for those occasions when the Court can justify incursions into the social policy realm. The lack of attention paid to institutional roles and whether there ought to be boundaries around the Court's powers of judicial review has made social policy cases clear sites of activity for the imposition of the justices' personal policy preferences.

In Chapter 2, it was noted that the Court has determined that section 1 is the appropriate site for the development of a quasi "political questions" doctrine. The analysis in this chapter suggests that, instead, the Court's approach to a reasonable limits analysis (within section 1 or in the internal limits provided by section 7) has in fact shielded the justices from a consideration of the division between judicial questions and political questions altogether. In part, this development is because the Court's two-stage approach to *Charter* review, specifically its broad and generous interpretation of the rights themselves, encourages recourse to policy evaluation under the guise of its reasonable limits analysis. More importantly, the justices have tended to deal only with the particular policy issues at hand in each case instead of developing a framework by which to determine when the Court ought to make incursions into substantive policy or value-laden issues, when it ought to impose costs on governments, or even when deference is warranted given the limitations of the judicial process to properly resolve such matters.

Conclusion

This chapter's discussion of the institutional relationships surrounding judicial review of the *Charter* suggests two important things about judges' understanding of the institution's role. First, judicial consideration of the Court's capacity to deal with complex social policy issues and the relatively indeterminate evidence often involved in evaluating them is directly related to whether justices see the distinction between such cases and those cases of more traditional judicial import as being useful. In turn, this aspect of justices' role perceptions tells us whether they see as appropriate some measure of deference with regard to particular policy matters or whether they see the boundaries surrounding the Court's role in judicial review as essentially limitless.

Second, analyses of cases involving health care policy illustrate that where explicit consideration is not given to the question of whether courts are well equipped to address complex social policy problems that permit a range of reasonable prescriptions, judicial decisions can more easily reflect judicial policy or ideological preferences. In this respect, the conclusions drawn in this chapter reinforce the arguments made by attitudinal scholars that ideological factors influence outcomes. Yet, this approach demonstrates not just that attitudinal behaviour occurs but also how it is permitted to come about in the context of social policy cases. Unlike the attitudinal model, the role-centric approach advanced here suggests that the effect of these individual preferences is consciously or subconsciously made possible because of a lack of explicit attention to institutional roles or a coherent framework that dictates when deference to legislative policy choices is appropriate. The justices have not settled on a framework that would force them to pay heed to what specific conditions might make the Court an appropriate venue for the settlement of value-laden or policy-intensive issues. Rather, they have determined each case with exclusive attention to the particular issues at hand on a piecemeal basis. The lack of guidelines dictating such factors as when the Court should impose direct costs on government resources or when deference to legislative choices is fitting in the event of conflicting or unclear evidence leave open a site of activity for attitudinal behaviour. This problem is related to the Court's liberal approach to the law of justiciability explored in Chapter 2 and is why some contend that the Court ought to reconsider adopting a "political questions" doctrine. Just as significantly, the examination of health care cases confirms the concern of critics and some judges that social policy cases are inherently problematic for the judicial arena.

6
The Court in Government and Society: Dialogue, Public Opinion, and the Media

Defenders of the Supreme Court of Canada's role in determining social policy issues argue that the policy impact of judicial decisions is limited. The most prominent expression of this claim is through the notion that judicial review of the *Canadian Charter of Rights and Freedoms* constitutes a "dialogue" between the courts and legislatures.[1] This chapter explores the theoretical and empirical basis for understanding the institutional relationships in this way. This exploration is important not only because of the debate over the Court's role in social policy matters but also because the justices themselves have invoked the dialogue metaphor on several occasions in case decisions. Understanding judicial perceptions of the institutional relationships surrounding *Charter* review is thus important for several reasons. First, consistent with the approach adopted throughout this book, a focus on judicial role perceptions allows for a deeper understanding of how and why the justices arrive at decisions. Second, if the dialogue metaphor is a useful indicator of how *Charter* review operates in practice, it may temper the normative concerns of critics of the Court's role. Finally, it is worth examining whether a dialogic understanding of judicial review on the part of the justices constrains the degree to which their policy preferences influence decisions.

The dialogue metaphor views legislatures as generally able to respond to court decisions either by amending impugned legislation or by temporarily suspending judicial decisions by using the *Charter*'s notwithstanding clause. Proponents of the metaphor contend that dialogue, conceived of in this manner, eliminates or seriously lessens concerns about the policy impact of the Court or its institutional competence to make decisions regarding social policy. The analysis that follows explores the intense normative and empirical debate surrounding this conception of inter-institutional activity. Bringing the justices' conceptions of dialogue to bear on these debates reinforces the concerns critics raise about conceiving of the institutional relationships in dialogic terms.

The final part of this chapter examines the justices' considerations of public opinion and the Court's evolving relationship with the media. These relationships are of considerable importance to the justices in an era when the Court's decisions often garner substantial scrutiny. While it is difficult to gauge the specific impact public opinion may have on judicial decision making, judicial perceptions of popular opinion act as a meaningful constraint in terms of the frequency with which they might otherwise be willing to make decisions that divert significantly from public attitudes. The justices' concern regarding public opinion, particularly their interest in ensuring their institution's continued legitimacy in the eyes of the public, has also meant increased accessibility and transparency in the Court's relationship with the media.

Institutional Relationships and the Notion of Dialogue

The dominant understanding of inter-institutional dialogue was first articulated in a 1997 article by Peter Hogg and Allison Bushell.[2] The article was originally envisioned as a response to democratic objections to judicial review (specifically the "counter-majoritarian difficulty"). More importantly, and relevant to the preceding analysis, the dialogue metaphor stands as a particular defence of court involvement in social policy matters. The authors state that judicial review should be viewed as "the beginning of a dialogue as to how best to reconcile the individualistic values of the Charter with the accomplishment of social and economic policies for the benefit of the community as a whole."[3] All *Charter* rights are subject to the reasonable limits clause in section 1, which is viewed as the primary avenue through which legislatures can respond to judicial decisions.

Hogg and Bushell state that dialogue "consists of those cases in which a judicial decision striking down a law on Charter grounds is followed by some action by the competent legislative body."[4] Not surprisingly, given this broad definition, they find that dialogue occurs in a substantial majority of cases. Hogg and Bushell also claim that in most cases only minor amendments are required to respect *Charter* decisions and that the legislation's original intent is thus rarely compromised.[5] This account of the relationship between the Court and the legislatures has produced a voluminous response from critics.[6] One of the principal claims shared by many of these commentators is that dialogue fails in practice because legislatures routinely treat the Supreme Court of Canada's decisions as the final word. Thus, the dialogue is really a judicial "monologue" about what policy prescriptions the *Charter* requires.[7]

One major problem that the concept of inter-institutional dialogue suffers from is the metaphor itself. Dialogue connotes two-way communication in which the parties involved listen to each other, but the dialogue metaphor "maintains judicial supremacy as far as interpretive authority is concerned."[8] It is for this reason that some scholars advocate abandoning the judicial-centric understanding of dialogue in favour of alternative approaches. For example, Janet Hiebert's relational approach envisions Parliament and the Supreme Court of Canada as each having distinct but complementary roles in ensuring that *Charter* values inform the legislative process.[9] A key component of the relational approach is that each governing institution starts from a perspective that accounts for, and reflects on, the other's judgment and that neither institution considers its position on *Charter* values as the last word. Dialogue, therefore, does not necessarily begin with judicial invalidation of a legislative initiative. Dennis Baker's support for co-ordinate interpretation goes even further.[10] Under co-ordinate constitutionalism, elected and appointed officials are required to interpret the *Charter,* and legislative interpretations are viewed as being as legitimate and authoritative as the Court's.

Hogg has written that he and Bushell "went too far" when they originally claimed that the dialogue metaphor successfully answered the counter-majoritarian objection to judicial review. Nevertheless, he states that "we were surely right to say that our finding that the decisions of the Court were not usually the last word should at least transform the debate about the legitimacy of judicial review."[11] More recently, the authors argue that while critics have attacked an "idealized" conception of dialogue, they "never made the ridiculous suggestion that courts and legislatures were actually 'talking' to each other." Instead, their claim is that "Canada has only a weak form of judicial review, because Charter decisions usually leave room for a legislative response and usually received legislative response."[12]

The dialogue metaphor, then, is a descriptive statement on *Charter* review as opposed to a normative theory. Although underlying the debates about dialogue are the normative questions surrounding judicial review, the dispute over dialogue's veracity is fundamentally an empirical question. Proponents and critics differ on what counts as dialogue and what tools are or should be available to the legislatures in responding to Court decisions. One major critique of Hogg and Bushell's original study is that the focus on instances of judicial nullification of legislation ignores other exercises of judicial power, especially particularly intrusive remedies such as "reading in," in which the Court explicitly adds new words to a statute in order to render it constitutional.[13] The response to this concern is that legislatures are free to override such decisions by using the notwithstanding clause.[14] Yet, the reasonableness of this option is itself in dispute. The notwithstanding clause is only available in cases involving sections 2 and 7 through 15 of the *Charter* (sexual equality rights are also exempt because of the language of section 28). More significantly, use of the clause is generally viewed as politically unfeasible since the decision by Quebec premier Robert Bourassa to invoke it to protect the province's language laws in 1988 amid intense debate over the Meech Lake Accord.[15]

Tsvi Kahana examines the use of the notwithstanding mechanism and finds that it has been used more often than thought. However, it has almost always been used to pre-empt judicial review rather than to express disagreement with judicial rulings on the *Charter*. Further, in most cases, public reaction was virtually non-existent because "these uses were both invisible and inaccessible."[16] Any attempt to use the clause in more visible cases is practically impossible from a political perspective because it is usually viewed as an "override" of the *Charter* rather than an expression of disagreement with a Court ruling.[17] It has never been used at the federal level and has only been used three times by a province other than Quebec. The idea of "overriding" rights so dominates general perceptions about the notwithstanding clause that Prime Minister Paul Martin attempted to salvage a faltering 2006 election campaign by promising to abolish Parliament's capacity to use it.[18] Mark Tushnet writes that the "limited use of section 33 itself suggests that there is little difference between the Canadian system and one in which the Constitutional Court's decisions are final."[19] Even former Justice Frank Iacobucci has publicly stated that the clause's "legality can't be questioned, but one could question [its] legitimacy."[20] Dialogue proponents argue it is unfair to blame the Court for the failure of the legislatures to invoke the clause.[21] This sentiment is fair enough, but it does not alter the political reality that as an "instrument" of dialogue, the notwithstanding clause is more pipe dream than pipe organ. If section 33 is not viewed as an option, then it cannot be considered an avenue through which legislatures take part in dialogue.

Another major disagreement concerns whether all forms of legislative amendment constitute legitimate dialogue. Critics argue that instances where legislatures simply enact the Court's policy prescriptions should not be counted as dialogue. Manfredi and James Kelly write that elected officials who are simply repealing offending sections or replacing entire acts is tantamount to "Charter ventriloquism."[22] Proponents do not accept that cases in which a "constitutional defect" was "properly corrected" by the legislature should be discounted. They contend that precluding instances where legislatures have followed the prescription laid out by the courts invites too narrow a definition of dialogue: "After all, it is always possible that the outcome of dialogue will be an agreement between the participants!"[23]

This response to Manfredi and Kelly's contention seriously underestimates the powerful effect of the Court's declarations on rights. Elected representatives face a tremendous rhetorical disadvantage in responding to rulings that claim the *Charter* has been infringed. Public debate surrounding the notwithstanding clause, for instance, illustrates that Court rulings are viewed as authoritative and that, rather than being viewed as signalling disagreement over interpretation of the *Charter,* the mere mention of section 33 implies that legislatures are seeking to "override" rights.[24] Legislators face the same rhetorical challenges in attempts to enact amendments that differ from the dictates of judicial decisions. As Matthew Hennigar points out, "the government's Charter review process does not occur within a legal vacuum, but typically involves bureaucratic actors attempting to gauge the courts' likely response to legislation, based on existing case law. To this extent, there is usually, if not always, an external judicial influence on internal legislative-executive discussions of constitutional rights."[25] The impetus is thus for amendments to reflect Court rulings.

This reality does not mean genuine agreement is impossible but, rather, as Hennigar correctly points out, "genuine agreement and grudging compliance 'look' identical."[26] The implications that this argument has for how dialogue is defined and operationalized is clear: "Dialogue requires a legislative response which dissents, to some degree, from the court's ruling; that is, it must entail a creative element."[27] Thus, it is difficult to classify as dialogue one of the Court's most recent references to the metaphor – in a case in which it upheld Parliament's response to an earlier decision striking down restrictions on tobacco advertising[28] – because, as Grant Huscroft writes, "Parliament simply legislated in accordance with the parameters that the Court's majority decision allowed. The Court did not just *influence* the democratic process; it dictated the content of constitutionally permissible legislation."[29] The empirical assessment of the extent of dialogue has varied widely, with Hogg and Bushell's original article claiming that two-thirds of cases result in dialogue.[30] By contrast, Manfredi and Kelly's follow-up study found that only one-third of cases are followed up by the type of legislative response that constitutes legitimate dialogue.[31] My own study goes further and, following Hennigar's logic, assesses the substantive content of legislative responses at the federal, provincial, and municipal level to all Court invalidations through 2009. I found that fewer than one-in-five cases resulted in genuine dialogue.[32]

Dialogue proponents also understate the actual policy impact of legislative amendments. Tushnet writes that in instances where legislatures enact reply legislation "the new legislation *cannot* accomplish precisely what the earlier one did, because the enhanced protection of constitutional values necessarily reduces the statute's policy-effectiveness relative to the original."[33] Huscroft points out that a judicial decision "creates powerful incentives and disincentives to political action that dialogue theory ignores."[34] He points to the inability of Parliament to pass new legislation regulating abortion after the Court's decision in *R. v Morgentaler* as a classic example in this regard.[35] Finally, Hennigar's study of government responses to lower court

Charter decisions contradicts Hogg and Bushell's suggestion that legislative sequels usually involve only minor changes.[36]

Just as significantly, the amount of legislative room available to governments is uncertain because in those "second-look" cases that have reached the Supreme Court of Canada, the justices have become strongly divided on how much deference to award amendments. The first reference to the dialogue metaphor by the Court was introduced by Iacobucci J in *Vriend v Alberta*, where the Court ruled that the omission of sexual orientation from the province of Alberta's human rights legislation was unconstitutional.[37] Manfredi notes a certain irony in that the metaphor was first cited in *Vriend*.[38] First, because the legislation failed to meet the requirement that legislative objectives be pressing and substantial, dialogue was precluded.[39] Second, the Court's remedy was to read sexual orientation into the legislation, leaving little possibility of a response from the legislature. Manfredi suggests that "the utility of the metaphor was its rhetorical value as a defense against democratic unaccountability rather than as a serious theory of judicial-legislative relations."[40]

R. v Mills was the first second-look case in which dialogue was invoked by the Court.[41] In *R. v O'Connor*, the Court ruled that defendants in sexual assault trials had a fair trial right to third party medical and therapeutic records.[42] The justices divided five to four over the rules governing the production of such records, with the minority emphasizing issues of privacy and equality to establish a much tougher test to determine the relevance of records prior to their admittance. When the federal government responded to *O'Connor* with Bill C-46, it developed guidelines that closely mirrored the position of the minority.[43] When the new provisions were challenged in *Mills*, the Court was faced with a parliamentary response that clearly contradicted its own majority judgment. In upholding Bill C-46's constitutionality, Justices Beverley McLachlin and Iacobucci note that "Courts do not hold a monopoly on the protection and promotion of rights and freedoms; Parliament also plays a role in this regard and is often able to act as a significant ally for vulnerable groups."[44]

On first glance, if any case was going to confirm Hogg and Bushell's original argument that a democratic dialogue often informs the *Charter* review process, it would be this one. Interestingly, however, neither critics nor proponents of dialogue view the *O'Connor-Mills* sequence as a healthy reflection of how dialogue ought to occur. Manfredi and Kelly write:

> If any dialogue occurred in *Mills*, it was an internal one among the justices about which *O'Connor* regime should prevail. The Court did not defer to legislative judgment in *Mills*, but merely affirmed a policy that four of its own members had constructed in 1995. Indeed, the "privacy shield"

amendments were not the product of an independent legislative assessment of what might constitute optimal public policy, but of the government's best guess about what policy might withstand judicial scrutiny.[45]

On the other side, Kent Roach describes *Mills* as an "in-your-face reply" and argues that the more legitimate response by Parliament would have been to invoke the notwithstanding clause.[46]

The combined effect of these views makes clear that the debate over dialogue is irreconcilable. Rather than viewing the justices' reference to dialogue as a signal of respect for Parliament's judgment, critics see the justices' invocation of the metaphor as a convenient rhetorical tool around which they "could rally in the face of external criticism that they had usurped or unduly deferred to legislative power."[47] Proponents, meanwhile, hold steadfastly to a conception of dialogue that leaves little room for substantive disagreement from the legislative side, especially as it applies to the interpretation of particular *Charter* provisions. To admit otherwise, they say, would invite "interpretative anarchy."[48] For critics, then, dialogue describes deference or restraint.[49] For proponents, dialogue describes any legislative response except those that would undermine judicial supremacy in interpretation. Under both conceptions, the metaphor is rendered meaningless.

Further exemplifying the barren nature of the dialogue metaphor are a series of cases that reveal strong disagreement among the justices about the extent to which dialogue should encourage deference toward legislative choices. *R. v Hall* involved a challenge to bail provisions in the *Criminal Code* that were enacted in response to an earlier case in which the Court declared unconstitutional a provision authorizing pre-trial detention in the "public interest."[50] In a five-to-four ruling, the Court upheld the new provisions. McLachlin CJ, writing for the majority, called the case "an excellent example" of constitutional dialogue, noting that Parliament considered the Court's earlier decision when it drafted language this time around.[51] Iacobucci J, by contrast, viewed Parliament's response as an example of "how this constitutional dialogue can break down."[52] Iacobucci J argued that the new provisions were crafted without due regard for the standards set out by the Court by simply introducing vague wording that effectively reintroduced the same unconstitutional element. Using particularly strong language, Iacobucci J accused McLachlin CJ of having "transformed dialogue into abdication."[53]

A similar split is evident in a second-look case on prisoner voting rights. This time, McLachlin CJ took the view that Parliament's response to the first case, *Sauvé v Canada (Attorney General) (Sauvé I)*, should not be accorded deference.[54] In this case, the Court struck down a provision of the *Canada Elections Act* that disfranchised inmates in a short, unanimous decision that simply stated that the law was drawn too broadly.[55] Parliament redrafted the legislation to prohibit from voting those prisoners serving sentences of two years or more. In her majority judgment in *Sauvé v Canada (Chief Electoral Officer) (Sauvé II)*, McLachlin CJ wrote that constitutional dialogue "should not be debased to a rule of 'if at first you don't succeed, try, try again.'"[56]

Writing for the minority, Justice Charles Gonthier argued that dialogue and deference to Parliament's competing, but equally legitimate, conception of the values at stake in the policy was warranted:

> I am of the view that since this case is about evaluating choices regarding social or political philosophies and about shaping, giving expression, and giving practical application to values, especially values that may lie outside the *Charter* but are of fundamental importance to Canadians, "dialogue" is of particular importance. In my view, especially in the context of the case at bar, the heart of the dialogue metaphor is that neither the courts nor Parliament hold a monopoly on the determination of values. Importantly, the dialogue metaphor *does not signal a lowering of the s. 1 justification standard*. It simply suggests that when, after a full and rigorous s. 1 analysis, Parliament has satisfied the court that it has established a reasonable limit to a right that is demonstrably justified in a free and democratic society, the dialogue ends; the court lets Parliament have the last word and does not substitute Parliament's reasonable choices with its own.[57]

Sauvé II is significant in undercutting the dialogue metaphor in another respect, in that McLachlin CJ's majority judgment uses the unavailability of the notwithstanding clause (which does not apply to the voting rights under section 3) as a reason for stricter scrutiny by the Court.[58] Manfredi notes that "McLachlin could just as easily have interpreted the non-applicability of section 33 as a reason for judicial caution. Indeed, the dialogue metaphor would seem to support the view that judicial deference should *increase* as the potential for dialogue decreases."[59] A strategic conception of judicial decision making might suggest that a policy-oriented justice would want to avoid legislative "override" of a judgment and so might be more deferential in cases where it applies. Manfredi has persuasively argued elsewhere that there is evidence that the Court has been willing to act more assertively after it became clear the notwithstanding clause was no longer a viable political choice.[60]

Division among the justices over deference and dialogue persisted in *Harper v Canada (Attorney General)*, where the Court voted six to three to uphold limits on third party spending in election campaigns.[61] The legislation was the federal government's response to the Court's decision to strike down spending limits in *Libman v Quebec (Attorney General)*.[62] The majority in *Harper* found that "broadly speaking, the third party election advertising regime is consistent with an egalitarian conception of elections and the principles endorsed by this Court in *Libman*."[63] The justices in the minority agreed that Parliament went to considerable lengths to adopt non-intrusive means to pursue its objectives. However, they stated that good faith, "said to be evidenced by the ongoing dialogue with the courts as to where the limits should be set," was insufficient: "Good faith cannot remedy an impairment of the right to freedom of expression."[64]

Not all of the cases in which the justices cited dialogue have resulted in disagreement, although even in some of these cases the metaphor is linked to the idea of deference.[65] Some of the justices have clearly come to view this development as problematic. In *Doucet-Boudreau v Nova Scotia (Minister of Education)*, the Court was faced with the question of what remedies are available under section 24 of the *Charter* in the context of minority language education rights.[66] Iacobucci and Arbour JJ, writing for the majority in favour of a lower court judge's ability to retain jurisdiction over a case to ensure compliance with his order, cautioned that "judicial restraint and metaphors such as 'dialogue' must not be elevated to the level of strict constitutional rules to which the words of s. 24 can be subordinated."[67] Most recently, McLachlin CJ's unanimous judgment in the second-look case involving tobacco advertising restrictions stated that "[t]he mere fact that the legislation represents Parliament's response to a decision of this Court does not militate for or against deference."[68]

Disagreement among the justices about the use of dialogue and its conflation with deference is pronounced enough that even the metaphor's original proponents have acknowledged that it may be best if judges did not refer to it in decisions.[69] This argument is made most forcefully by Richard Haigh and Michael Sobkin, who argue that judges "can remain neutral observers if they only describe the metaphor, but they can also unintentionally change a simple metaphor into an analytical tool by being interfering observers and using the metaphor prescriptively."[70] The preceding analysis confirms the substance of their argument. Nevertheless, Haigh and Sobkin's assumption that judges are, or should be, "neutral observers" in the purported dialogue makes little sense. The dialogue metaphor may be a descriptive statement about the relationship between courts and legislatures, but the justices' views on the relationship are certainly pertinent to their decisions, regardless of whether or not they cite the metaphor.

Despite the extraordinary amount of attention devoted to the question of dialogue over the past fifteen years, one facet that has not been explored outside of Court decisions is the justices' views on the metaphor. Perhaps not surprisingly, some of the justices in the interviews were themselves highly skeptical about how the dialogue metaphor has been invoked or used by their colleagues. One justice stated it was a fine theory but that it did not work well in practice because it had been used to justify undue deference:

"There are cases where the law is wrong and the government has to face it and change it ... Dialogue yes, as a goal, but not necessarily dialogue" (Interview). This justice described *O'Connor* as the best example of dialogue and *Morgentaler* as an example of the impossibility of dialogue, noting that "one should not sacrifice to dialogue his principles." One of the key problems of the dialogue metaphor, this justice argued, is that it promotes the idea of restraint: "I don't see why at the start of a decision you would say 'oh, I have to be restrained.'" Such an attitude is not a proper component of a judge's role: "Restraint to me is not something that a judge should start with. It may be that in the course of things deference should be shown for one reason or the other. We [do] that regularly. But it shouldn't be a principle that you start with" (Interview).

Other justices described the metaphor as largely symbolizing the respect the Court should have for the respective roles of the legislative or executive branches. One justice stated: "[W]hen you're telling the legislature or the executive through a judicial outcome [or] decision, that they're offside of the Constitution, you want to lower the temperature. You don't want to get into adversarial kinds of relationships that have happened in other countries. There's going to be tension, but I don't think it helps anybody's role – legislature, executive or judiciary – to say that somehow there is this adversarial nature to the functioning of each of the branches of government." This justice argued that it is a mistake to take the dialogue metaphor literally:

> One of my former colleagues [said] "what do you mean 'dialogue'? We're not talking to anybody." That's just such an impoverished view of what I think dialogue is all about. It's about trying to have a proper amount of respect for each other's roles. That doesn't mean going crazy deferentially or going crazy in an activist way. Because you get into all these debates about labels and I think that takes you away from what the proper role of the judiciary is and what the proper role of the legislature is. And there's where political science is very important. This is not just about lawyers monopolizing this conversation. (Interview)

A third justice argued that the metaphor is "useful in the sense that it points out that the *Charter* is everybody's business." This justice said of *Mills* that the Court decided that Parliament chose an alternative to the Court's majority decision in *O'Connor*, noting that "in that sense, there was a dialogue. They weren't speaking to each other, but each had a view of what the other had said and what the other was thinking about." Despite this example, for this justice there are clear limits to a dialogic understanding of review under the *Charter*: "Where there isn't a dialogue is in the final resort, as regards the Charter framework. The Court's decision is final. If the Court says such a provision is contrary to the *Charter,* meaning contrary to the Constitution, it becomes inoperable under the Constitution. And there's no going against that, unless eventually you get the Court to change its mind, which is highly unlikely" (Interview).

Another justice stated: "I really wonder how much has changed with that notion of a dialogue. What I always understood from that was that the Court should make an effort to understand what Parliament was trying to do rather than substituting your own view ... All it really meant to me was that you had to carefully consider what it is that the government was trying to say" (Interview). A fifth justice stated:

> I think the term was perhaps overused over the years. I think it's sending a message that courts would unduly defer. I think the real meaning of that is whether we like it or not the simple fact that we make decisions on legal issues impacts on the work of Parliament, of government sometimes, and triggers responses, changes in the law, changes in administrative process. Those responses sometimes generate other issues, other exchanges, in this ongoing process of interaction between courts and legislatures. (Interview)

In this sense, dialogue is a useful concept, but it has practical limits: "It's a way to reflect the fact that in the Canadian state there is an interaction and interplay between the courts and the other branches of government. They will influence one another, sometimes through their own responses. And sometimes the dialogue falls flat" (Interview).

The distinction many justices make between "deference" to the other branches, on the one hand, and "respect" for them, on the other, may strike critics as thin. For those critics who support the idea of a legislature having an equal say in constitutional interpretation, the view among the justices that the Court's judgment is final with respect to the meaning of the *Charter* renders meaningless any talk of respect. Yet, respect for the legislative process on the part of the justices might prove useful in terms of the inter-institutional relationship in two ways. First, the justices I interviewed generally acknowledged that legislative preambles can sometimes be useful – though not determinative – in the Court's reasonable limits analysis. Hiebert points out that a preamble can be used as an "education device" for courts as well as a "statement of parliamentary intent" in the event that legislation is challenged.[71] She notes that preambles are "a more honest and forthright way of attempting to justify a legislative objective than relying on government lawyers to speculate, after the fact, about the reasons behind a legislative decision."[72] Another signal of judicial respect for the legislative process is the remedy of a suspended declaration of invalidity, where the Court strikes down unconstitutional legislation but suspends the effect of its ruling for a period of time (usually six to eighteen months) in order to give the legislature time to respond or to avoid potentially serious consequences from a vacuum in the law. First used in the 1985 case *Re Manitoba Language Rights*, the remedy was originally intended for exceptional circumstances, but it has become quite common under the *Charter*.[73]

The extent to which the justices have demonstrated sensitivity to the role of the legislatures in this manner may reflect strategic considerations. Suspended declarations of invalidity are a useful legitimating function, in that they reduce the immediate impact of the Court's incursion into policy making. In this respect, such remedies, coupled with a cursory acknowledgement of items such as legislative preambles, might simply be new weapons recently added to the justices' strategic arsenal to avoid more direct conflict or potential acrimony with the other branches. If the Court were too confrontational, it might risk damage to its reputation or authority. This is a somewhat cynical interpretation, particularly because remedies such as suspended declarations have real effects. For example, the Court granted the Quebec government a one-year suspension of its decision in *Chaoulli v Quebec (Attorney General)*, allowing the province time to craft new legislation.[74] This action is something Roach argues demonstrates that "legislative paralysis is not the necessary Canadian response to judicial activism."[75] Further, my previous study on dialogue shows that the Court's use of suspended declarations of invalidity makes dialogic responses from the relevant legislature more than twice as likely than in instances where it is not used.[76]

The expression of respect for the legislative role that justices find at the heart of the dialogue metaphor also serves to once again emphasize that the cornerstone for the inter-institutional relationship as it relates to the *Charter* is section 1. It is within the reasonable limits analysis that the Court is most likely to give strong consideration to the objectives of, and justification for, legislative initiatives. As the analysis in the previous chapter demonstrates, however, a crucial component of the consideration justices give to the appropriate institutional boundaries at stake pertains to their competence or capacity to deal with complex policy issues and the evidence necessary to determine the effects of those policies. Considering the state of the Court's jurisprudence in dealing with social policy matters, the rhetoric surrounding the dialogue metaphor is largely a facade. While more empirical work is necessary to evaluate the extent and nature of the legislative responses to judicial decisions, the way in which the justices conceive of dialogue fails to correspond to the descriptive account put forward by its advocates.

Until the Court develops a more robust and explicit framework for addressing the institutional boundaries at stake in social policy cases, the fundamental concerns of critics of *Charter* review remain pressing and substantial. In many ways, despite these important concerns, the justices likely feel little pressure to develop an approach with more explicit attention paid to the legitimacy issues surrounding review. This is in large part due to the broad support they receive from the public. The analysis thus far suggests that judicial consideration of legislative roles, particularly in a context in which the notwithstanding clause is viewed as irrelevant, fails to place significant constraints on discretionary decision making on the Court. The next section explores whether, and to what extent, public opinion might influence judicial decisions.

Public Perception

The tethers of any public institution's legitimacy are ultimately tied to society. In this respect, the justices may make strategic decisions designed to ensure the Court's continued legitimacy. Opinion surveys routinely show that the public has highly favourable opinions of the Court when compared to elected politicians.[77] Few studies in the Canadian context attempt to explain what drives public support for the Supreme Court of Canada. Lori Hausegger and Troy Riddell's 2004 study suggests that public opinion of the Court became more closely tied to its specific decisions after it began to issue rulings on controversial issues such as abortion.[78] A more recent study by Elizabeth Goodyear-Grant, Janet Hiebert, and J. Scott Matthews, focuses on public attitudes toward the courts versus elected legislatures.[79] It shows a somewhat complicated picture, with evidence that gender, partisanship, and language may influence favourable opinions of the courts (women, Liberals, and New Democrats were more likely to defer to courts rather than legislatures, while Quebecers tend to be more suspicious of courts). However, the authors find that a general lack of knowledge about how our governing institutions operate might mean that for many people these are malleable, as opposed to deeply held, attitudes.

Although more research needs to be conducted to explain public support for the Court, there is ample evidence that the justices are sensitive to public perceptions of the Court and to the media or academic criticism that might affect these perceptions. As recently as 1998, scholars of the Court noted that the "judges themselves have played very little role in the debate about judges and democracy; to do so would, from the perspective of most of them, draw them into the political arena in violation of the principle of judicial independence."[80] This picture has changed considerably. In the late 1990s, former Chief Justice Antonio Lamer was outspoken about the potentially deleterious effects of "judge-bashing" on the "fragility of the judiciary."[81] In 1999, Lamer CJ wrote a letter to the editor of the *National Post* following an article that was highly critical of the Court to say he had been misquoted.[82] McLachlin CJ and some of her colleagues routinely speak or write on the subject of the Court's place in democracy.[83] The contemporary justices are also much more likely to grant interviews to the media.

This relatively new engagement with the public is a response to the significant amount of attention, criticism, and commentary to which the Court is subjected. Some of these forays into public dialogue can be risky, as the justices are occasionally accused of being biased or ignoring judicial independence. As Iacobucci J states, "[n]owadays, when a judge, especially one of our court, gets up to give a public talk, he or she is poised between a cliché and a complaint to the Canadian Judicial Council."[84] Justices Bertha Wilson, Claire L'Heureux-Dubé, and McLachlin have all been the subjects of complaints of feminist bias to the Canadian Judicial Council (CJC) by the conservative group REAL Women after making public statements.[85] Former Justice Michel Bastarache was subject to CJC complaints by criminal lawyers and Aboriginal chiefs after a controversial interview in which he criticized the Court's record on Aboriginal rights.[86] Although such complaints are usually dismissed, they raise the question of the extent to which judges must restrain their public statements.[87] Contemporary justices obviously feel compelled to engage in the debate about their role and the legitimacy of judicial review. At times, the legitimacy of the institution is at stake in this discourse in the eyes of the broader public. As a result, public perception of the Court might be viewed as having an accountability function or, to some extent, as being a factor in the decision making.

The justices interviewed for this book were unanimous in their view that public opinion does not directly influence their decision making. Yet, they also acknowledged that public opinion can sometimes be important because it provides an indication of societal values. Bastarache J states that public opinion matters "because the Court's legitimacy can at some point be questioned if it's consistently seen by a majority of people as going too far, as extending rights, as having sort of an agenda ... The rule of law reflects a certain understanding of society's concerns, and the Constitution is also a political document. And in that sense I think it's still a question of line drawing."[88] Former Justice Gerard La Forest writes that "[t]he opinion of the public generally can sometimes afford us considerable assistance. This is not to say that judges should be swayed by public opinion from applying long term community values, and particularly Charter values, in unpopular circumstances ... Yet there are cases where even a generally wise court may be seduced by the attractiveness of its own logic to adopt a course that is not in the long term benefit of society."[89]

It is ultimately concern about public perception that might make the justices react to criticism from the media or academic circles. Roach writes that "there is some evidence that the Court has not ignored the critique of judicial activism that has swirled around it for the last twenty years."[90] He notes, for example, that the Court "appeared to back away" from its unpopular decision regarding the private records of sexual assault complainants in the *O'Connor-Mills* sequence.[91] Chief Justice Brian Dickson's biographers note that "he was always sensitive to public criticism of the Court" and reveal, for example, that it influenced his push to change the Court's policy regarding interveners, as explored in Chapter 2.[92] F.L. Morton and Rainer Knopff contend that Lamer CJ hinted at his true reasoning in *Morgentaler* when he referenced public opinion on abortion in saying: "[Y]ou should not make a crime out of something that does not have the large support of the community ... Who am I to tell 50 percent of the population that they are criminals?"[93]

Sensitivity to public, media, and academic attention may influence particular cases and policy decisions, but such awareness has also been attributed to broader patterns in the Court's decision making. Former Justice William McIntyre criticized his colleagues' approach to the *Charter* during its first decade, arguing that Dickson CJ and others had responded to "the pressure of all the propaganda in the newspapers and the academic world, all the professors were writing articles and there was a certain amount of hysteria about it."[94] More recently, critics have claimed that the Court's more deferential approach under McLachlin CJ is the result of attacks on the institution for perceived activism.[95] L'Heureux-Dubé J spoke out against this charge, but her answer implicitly confirms the effect of considerations given to broader societal context: "I don't think we are bending to criticism. We are just taking the pulse of reality. We cannot ignore what happens in a society. We cannot ignore that there is a war against terrorism ... it's inevitable that the Court will be in sync with society. It would be totally unhealthy if the Court were [here] and society was there."[96]

Asked about the oft-stated axiom that the Court should not be too far ahead nor too far behind society, the justices interviewed for this book generally agreed with the sentiment but cautioned that they cannot be held captive to the passions of public opinion. One justice stated: "I think someone once said to me many years ago that the United States Supreme Court could not come out with a *Brown v Board of Education* every month," referring to that court's famous school desegregation decision (Interview).[97] The Court's legitimacy is rooted in public acceptance of its decisions, even when those decisions are controversial in nature. According to this justice, "there are what I call 'badges of legitimacy' to the judicial process." These badges include competent appointments, independence and impartiality, a fair process in open court, transparency, and reasons supporting every decision for everyone to see and to criticize. For this reason, this justice argued, some of the criticism the Court faces misses the mark: "The current debates about the judiciary have been very unfortunate. I think there is an assumption that the judiciary comes with one background, with agendas, etcetera." The Supreme Court of Canada has to live up to its mandate to apply the law:

There are many areas where the legislatures refrain from taking action. That is a legitimate legislative decision. But courts cannot walk away from their responsibility to decide a case, to apply the law. [For example], in the same-sex area of cases, legislatures were not acting to provide sexual orientation as a ground for equal treatment. Courts felt compelled, and I think rightly so, to move in on that. Was that controversial? Yes it was controversial. And you do take risks in making unpopular decisions. (Interview)

Returning to the example of *Brown v Board of Education*:

There's a fragile relationship between the people and the Court. The Court gains the acceptance of the people through its role. The people say they want to have a court that is the arbiter of disputes. It's a civilized way of dealing with it. But if every decision the Court comes out with is going to be controversial, then you're going to test that fragility of acceptance ... You hope that your reasons will not just attract support from the wider public over time, but if they don't support it, enlightened people, informed people, will stand up [for the *role* of the Court]. (Interview)

A second justice concurred with this sentiment: "I do not say that courts should seek controversy, but they should not shy away from the decisions that they think should be made because they would be controversial." That said, this justice explained that the Court does not set its own agenda: "We keep in tune with society because society determines what comes before us." Issues have had time to mature and develop in the "surrounding social milieu" before reaching the Supreme Court of Canada (Interview). A third justice noted, however, that "courts that are too distant from reality are not credible. It's very important that the people believe in the institutions" (Interview).

A fourth justice framed the issue of the Court's position *vis-à-vis* society in terms of values: "Where you have well-established values, they generally will be expressed in the first place in the most authoritative manner, in the law itself." Controversy arises where values change or are changed in certain people: "My own view, generally, because [there are] exceptions, is that the Court should not recognize what we might call 'emerging values' until they have really emerged. In the sense that the proper function of the Court is not to make law, but to apply the law that is being pronounced by the elected authorities." In other words, this justice argued, "there is a rule of prudence, or precaution, that you don't change the basic rules of a country or a society unless it's clear that they *have* changed. But reasonable people can differ on whether that's the case or not" (Interview).

For the most part, the judges stated that they can identify which cases will generate the most attention or criticism. As one justice said, "generally speaking, with some experience, you can pretty well foresee what's going to make waves or be controversial. Sometimes you get surprised. But there is a certain degree of foreseeability. Sometimes you think that a judgement is important and there will be barely a ripple. Other times more minor issues will be taken up" (Interview). Another justice stated that "we live in the community. It's clear that we know that there might be some reaction" (Interview).

Whether judicial perceptions of public opinion necessarily influence outcomes in particular cases remains unclear. Certainly, the justices' comments suggest that public opinion serves as a broad restraint on the Court as a whole, preventing it from moving too far "ahead" or too far "behind" society in general terms. Further complicating this balance, however, is the fact that some judges, such as Justice Rosalie Abella, point to popular opinion of the Court itself in support of a more robust role:

> We spent the last decade listening to a chorus of moaning over the fate of a majority whose legislatively endorsed wishes could theoretically be superceded by those of judges, only to learn in poll after poll that an overwhelming majority of that majority is happy, proud and grateful to live in a country that puts its views in perspective rather than in cruise control; who prefers to see judicial rights protection as a reflection of judicial integrity or independence rather than of judicial trespass or activism; and who understands that the plea for judicial deference may be nothing more than a prescription for judicial rigor mortis.[98]

Notwithstanding this sentiment, it is clear that judicial engagement in public debates is in part premised on ensuring the continued popular support of the institution. From this perspective, it seems obvious that on a broad level – if not in particular cases – public opinion acts as a constraint on the Court.

Engaging the Media

The *Charter* era bestowed a new prominence on the Court, and the judges and other personnel at the Court have not been oblivious to this new scrutiny. The three chief justices who have sat during the *Charter* era have each recognized the virtue of enriching public knowledge about the Court, its role, and the judges themselves.[99] Thus, the Court has increasingly opened itself to the public, particularly through the media. Chief Justice Bora Laskin gave the first media interview in the mid-1970s and created the Court-Media Liaison Committee in 1981, which consists of three judges and meets several times a year to discuss ideas and complaints from media representatives.[100] Since the committee's inception, the Court has persistently deepened its rapport with the press through various initiatives, the most significant of which may have been the creation of an executive legal officer (ELO) by Dickson CJ in 1985. As noted in Chapter 3, a great deal of the ELO's work is to function as the Court's media relations officer. In this capacity, the ELO provides not-for-attribution briefings to the press on judgments of the Court. Such briefings had been "categorically rejected" by Laskin CJ in the 1970s and were viewed with some suspicion by several of the other judges when Dickson CJ instituted them.[101]

Dickson CJ's openness stemmed from his concern that the Court not be accused of inaccessibility or, worse, threatened with lawsuits for better media access, even though some justices distrusted the media. According to his biographers, "it was inevitable that the media would shape public opinion about the Court and its work. In these circumstances, Dickson concluded that the Court should be open and as helpful as possible with the media."[102] In practising what he preached, Dickson CJ was the first chief justice to grant regular media interviews, to release advance text of all of his speeches, and to debate on a public stage with his British and American counterparts.[103] He even permitted cameras into the Court's conference room, judges' chambers, and private dining room in 1985 for a documentary by the Canadian Television Network's current affairs show *W5*.

While Dickson CJ's successor Lamer CJ opened up oral hearings to broadcasts on the Cable Public Affairs Channel in the 1990s, he was reluctant to go much further in the expansion of media access. When the parliamentary press gallery first proposed in 1995 that the Court hold lockups to brief the media in advance of the release of a judgment, Lamer CJ rejected the idea.[104] On being named chief justice in 1999, McLachlin CJ took another look at the concept. She held a wide-ranging press conference on 5 November 1999, which was itself an "unprecedented" event, at which she stated that improved communication would be one of her key priorities for the Court.[105]

When the press gallery reiterated its request for lockups, some judges still had significant concerns about the process. They generally felt that no one should know the outcome of a case before the litigants. In response, the gallery argued in letters to McLachlin CJ that "inaccuracies that result from the media reporting on judgments within seconds or minutes, without having the opportunity to read or understand the court's lengthy and complex reasons, can hurt both litigants and the public and can be minimized by a lockup procedure."[106] McLachlin CJ was apparently convinced. A memorandum of understanding was negotiated with the gallery, and a format for the lockups was created that roughly matched those that occur prior to the release of the federal budget. Since some of the justices were still resistant to the idea, the process was first initiated as a pilot project to show that it could be executed in a manner that would prevent leaks. Further, the parties to the case must give consent and be given access to the judgment at the same time as the press in a separate lockup. On 30 January 2004, twenty-three reporters from Canadian and international media outlets were participants in the first media lockup by a high court in the world.[107] The process has now become entrenched, and lockups are typically held for controversial or widely covered cases, assuming the parties provide consent.

The extent of the ELO's briefings with the media has also evolved. Initially, there were only post-decision briefings, but they are now commonly held before the start of a Court session, the day before a judgment is released, and the day before important hearings.[108] Several of the former law clerks I interviewed who served prior to the establishment of lockups said they felt the media typically performed poorly in its coverage of the Court and its decisions, but they believed the institution of lockups appears to have improved matters significantly. Clerks who have served since contended that the role of the ELO has been extremely important in helping the media "get it right" (Interviews). Yet, in their book on media and the Court, Florian Sauvageau, David Schneiderman, and David Taras point out that some critics believe the institutionalized relationship with the media can be problematic:

> The trust that most journalists place in the ELO gives the [C]ourt enormous leverage. First, the executive legal officer reinforces the image of professional detachment that the court wishes to present to the public. Just as the [C]ourt wishes to be seen as being above the rancour and partisanship of the political world, the ELO is above the blatant spin doctoring that is found elsewhere in Ottawa. Second, the ELO's main job is to point journalists to what the judges have written. The message that underlies all the ELO's briefings is that the "reasons" behind a judgment, the arguments and the logic of the judges, are the story. Lastly, some would contend that by directing journalists to one part of a judgment and not another, the ELO has the capacity to set the media agenda.[109]

One former clerk felt that the media was at least partially guided by this process. Several other clerks argued that while the ELO's briefings have aided accuracy in reporting, they have not been able to counteract a tendency among the press toward sensationalistic coverage (Interviews).

The justices receive daily press clippings (now in electronic format) of media coverage of the Court (Interviews). This procedure indicates a concern with how their reasons are received by the media and public and also an interest in external perceptions of the institution more broadly. Many of the justices I interviewed were critical of the overall quality of the coverage. One justice noted the repetitive nature of much of the coverage, pointing out that news stories are typically run from the flagship paper of a particular organization, in which its smaller, regional papers later pick them up: "You get a sense that press coverage of the Court, and I believe of other matters, is essentially press coverage for perhaps four or five media organizations" (Interview).

Several justices argued that the complexity of the decisions make it preferable to have journalists with legal training covering the Court, but they noted that news organizations have told them they do not have the resources to do this. One justice stated that the media are fairly accurate in describing the outcome of a case but that coverage is problematic in explaining the reasons. Two justices lamented that Canada lacks a Linda Greenhouse – the former *New York Times* journalist responsible for covering the Supreme Court of the United States – noting her knowledge of the case law and ability to place decisions in context makes her analysis superior to that of any comparable Canadian journalists. Further, the justices found that the news media rarely explores dissenting opinions, even in five-to-four decisions (Interviews). These issues are confirmed, to an extent, by a previous study I conducted examining media coverage of several of the Court's *Charter* decisions. The findings in this study suggest that reporters often fail to do a good job of conveying the complexities of the justices' reasons, which is particularly apparent with respect to explaining the Court's reasonable limits analysis under section 1.[110]

One justice also complained of exaggerated or sensationalistic coverage, noting that it likely stems from the profit-oriented nature of the news media. Another justice said that at times, over-the-top critical media coverage may threaten the Court's reputation and legitimacy: "I have been concerned that that is possible where the media chooses to be mischievous about what they report, and the harping for quite a while – I think it's abated somewhat – on judges being unanswerable, being the final word, being unelected, running the country, overruling the government. That constant barrage could have a bad effect on people's perception of the Court. On the other hand, you know the average person doesn't pay a lot of attention to what courts generally do" (Interviews).

For an institution rarely in the public spotlight before the 1970s, the Court's ascent to prominence during the *Charter* era has no doubt had many of its judges trepidatious at the thought of facilitating more exposure to the media and the broader public. Concerns for their independence, worries about politicization of the Court, and a distrust of the media among some judges have all contributed to a generally cautious attitude toward reforms. It is clear, however, that one of the sources of the considerable growth of the Court's staff is the initiatives that have been implemented to open the Court to public scrutiny. The Supreme Court of Canada has become a world leader in terms of the procedures it has established for exhibiting oral hearings and for dealing with the media.

Any caution that the Court has exhibited in expanding its relationship with the media stems from a concern for judicial independence. The desire to correct the public record when judges feel that the press has erred in its coverage must be tremendous. Yet, if the Court were to publicly respond to every criticism or error in the media, or if the judges were to hold regular press conferences, its ability to remain genuinely neutral or to at least appear above the political fray would be lost. The Court's legitimacy and authority rest on its reputation as an independent body whose decisions are based in law and reason. Nonetheless, as described earlier, the institution has developed formal mechanisms to facilitate an open dialogue with members of the press so that new initiatives, such as media lockups, can be discussed and considered. This relationship, in turn, has significant implications for public discourse surrounding the important issues confronted by the Court, given the media's role in facilitating such debate.

Conclusion

This book has advanced an approach to the study of judicial behaviour that emphasizes the importance of the justices' perceptions of their appropriate role and that of their institution. This chapter has shed light on how these perceptions influence our understanding of the Court in light of the broader governmental and societal context. First, the justices generally consign the notion of inter-institutional dialogue to the thin status of "respect" for the legislatures. In crucial ways, this respect aids the justices in ascertaining legislative intent (through the reading of preambles, for example) and provides a certain degree of leeway for legislative responses to judicial decisions (through remedies such as the suspended declaration of invalidity). However, where conflation of dialogue with deference to legislative judgment is problematic, in the sense that it threatens to dilute the Court's role in enforcing the *Charter,* reducing the metaphor to the simple concept of respect leaves it empty of any substantial content that might inform us of the distinct institutional relationship that governs judicial review. Further, as a descriptive statement on the nature of judicial review that stands as a defence of the Court's involvement in complex or controversial matters of social policy, the dialogue metaphor does not withstand scrutiny. Both of these conclusions are crucial in the context of the broader arguments in this book to the extent that they imply that judicial invocations of the dialogue metaphor are strategic.

This chapter also explored the justices' consideration of public opinion and the Court's relationship with the media. The prominence of the Court in the contemporary period, particularly following the introduction of the *Charter,* placed pressure on the justices to open up the institution and themselves to increased scrutiny. Public debate about the institution's new role has compelled some justices to engage the public, journalists, and critics in debate and defend the exercise of their policy-making power. In this respect, public opinion is regarded as a measure of the Court's legitimacy and is something to be fought for. In another respect, public opinion is an important constraint on the general direction or posture the Court takes over time. The justices are generally unanimous that the Court's legitimacy would be at stake if a string of important decisions were grossly inconsistent with broad public sentiment.

Public opinion might be considered a constraint in several different ways. The justices may gain personal satisfaction from the knowledge that the public supports the institution or particular decisions they have made. Second, they may have a normative desire to protect the institution's legitimacy or a belief that the law ought to conform to widely held social values. Finally, from a strategic perspective, the justices may not want any decision to engender such a negative reaction from the public as to justify the legislative use of the notwithstanding clause. If the clause were to ever gain political viability in this manner, it could considerably reduce the Court's policy-making power. As it stands, there is some indication that public opinion serves as a constraint in all three ways.

Conclusion

As the final arbiter of all areas of Canadian law, the Supreme Court of Canada's status as the country's most important legal institution is unquestionable. In the last few decades, significant changes – from the ability to choose cases based on their national importance to the entrenchment of the *Canadian Charter of Rights and Freedoms* – have also served to make the Court one of Canada's most important governing institutions.[1] While the institution has always had the power to influence policy, such as when it adjudicates federalism disputes, its role as a policy maker is considerably more prominent in the contemporary period. Through its *Charter* jurisprudence, the Court is involved in the resolution of deeply controversial and complex social and moral issues as well as those relating to the most important government policies in Canadian public life, including health care, criminal justice, education, and welfare. Legislative and executive decision-making processes are influenced not only by the Court's decisions but also by how political actors in those branches anticipate what the Court might say about the constitutionality of policies from their inception. Further, the Court's decisions help to shape media and public discourse about the *Charter* and rights in general. Despite its significant influence within the Canadian political system and wider society, the inner workings of the Court and the day-to-day practices of its justices and their law clerks have remained largely obscured from public knowledge.

This book has sought to remedy this lack of understanding. It has shown that the Court is a complex institution whose decisions are dependent on a combination of the individual approaches of its nine justices and the group interaction produced by them. In examining judicial behaviour on the Court, this study offers a shift in focus from political science approaches that emphasize the justices' individual voting patterns and decisions premised on ideological policy preferences. Instead, by emphasizing the collegial nature of the Court, the role-centred analysis in this book shows that certain variables have come to predominate in particular contexts. By explaining how the various stages of the Court's decision-making process act as sites of activity for certain types of behaviour, my analysis helps to integrate other approaches as well as to contextualize behaviour within a complex institutional environment. Although I have criticized the attitudinal and strategic approaches for their methodological limitations, nothing in this book denies that the justices' backgrounds, personal values, and ideological predilections play a significant part in decision making. Individual judges may feel especially passionate about specific issues or cases, while in others they may not hold any strong feelings. Some judges are more ideological than others and some may have ideological perspectives that change over time or are dependent on the type of issue or area of law at stake. Further, institutional processes, norms, and conventions that govern the various stages of decision making at the Court help shape and constrain ideological or strategic behaviour on the part of the justices.

Why Judicial Role Perceptions Matter

Attention to judicial role perceptions helps to place the various factors – legal, institutional, attitudinal, and strategic – into a context that recognizes the multifaceted, intricate nature of both the Court's internal environment and its place within government and society. This approach demonstrates why understanding judicial behaviour cannot be reduced to considering only the justices' votes. The broad conception of the judicial role developed throughout this book has three components. The first relates to the justices' views of the proper role of the institution itself. A common refrain among judges defending themselves against the charge of undue "activism" has been that the responsibilities they bear were thrust on them, particularly through the advent of the *Charter*.[2] It is certainly important to recognize that the elected representatives have put in place the means by which the judiciary could strike down laws and government actions that contravene the principles enshrined in the *Constitution Act, 1982*.[3] Further, Parliament enacted statutory changes prior to and after the *Charter* that dramatically altered the manner and overall importance of the issues that come before the Court. For example, the justices were given broad discretion in choosing which cases to hear.

Within this context, however, the justices themselves have made a series of choices that helped transform the Court from a primarily adjudicative body to a full-fledged political institution. As Chapter 2 explored, the justices dramatically liberalized the law of justiciability, the admittance of third party interveners into the process, and the type of evidence they are willing to consider in the course of making decisions. These decisions sent signals to the legal community and to interest groups that the Court was an open venue in which they could pursue their political goals. Additionally, the Court's expansion of the law clerk program and the manner in which many justices now use their clerks has been compared to the policy-making process and structure of the Prime Minister's Office and the Privy Council's Office.[4] In short, the Court's transformation has been the result of reciprocal forces that are both external and internal to the Court. The avenue for this transition was paved in large part by the constitutional initiatives of the federal government. Yet, it is the justices who ultimately determined the scope, depth, and tenor of the Court's handling of issues under the *Charter*. The very fact that there were sharp divisions among the justices with regard to issues such as justiciability and third party interveners demonstrates that the Court's current approach and process was not wholly imposed on the Court by outside forces or otherwise preordained.

The second component of the judicial role pertains to how the justices view their individual role within the institution. This focus extends far beyond the simple perspective of whether the judges consider themselves "law-interpreters" or "law-makers" or even how much they may allow their personal values to intrude on decision making. As explored in Chapter 4, a host of considerations play into their individual role when making decisions. These include, for example, the extent to which they strive to achieve consensus (or unanimity) with their colleagues. As examined in relation to the Court's equality jurisprudence, the extent to which compromise and unanimity is sought has deep repercussions for subsequent cases. Also important is the individual style or approach judges take to collaboration, such as a propensity to have informal, face-to-face discussions with peers or a preference to maintain primarily formal communication by way of written memoranda. Depending on the mix of personalities on the Court at a given time, congeniality (the degree to which the justices get along personally) can have a considerable impact on collegiality (how the justices work together). While "like minds" tend to congregate within the working environment, the extent to which they come to represent visible and entrenched divisions on the Court depends deeply on the approach taken by individual justices and on the leadership style of the chief justice.

As already noted, role theory is also useful for identifying which stages of the decision-making process and under what conditions sites of activity for attitudinal or strategic behaviour are likely to emerge. The process of deliberation and negotiation on the Court is closely intertwined with norms of collegiality and rules of convention. For example, the chief justice's ability to select panels for cases is largely dictated by widely shared views on when it is proper to compose a panel of fewer than the full nine members of the Court. Where attitudinal or strategic behaviour materializes, it usually coincides with those areas where consensus regarding such norms or conventions breaks down. This is especially apparent, for example, in the debate over the degree of "lobbying" that takes place between the justices.

The third component of the judicial role involves a consideration of both the Court and the individual justice in relation to broader government and society. The strategic literature emphasizes the degree to which justices must consider the preferences and actions of the other branches of government. Stressing the strategic element of these considerations too much, however, can overlook the variety of motivations at play when judges contemplate the different roles of other governmental institutions. Judicial motivations extend beyond policy considerations and include concern for the quality of the jurisprudence, media and public criticism, the legitimacy of the Court itself, personal reputation, and esteem from the legal and wider community. Further, the justices' decisions may reflect genuine, rather than strategic, regard for other factors. For example, they have normative understandings of the appropriate place of legislatures in making policy choices. This understanding shapes not only the degree of deference they give to those institutional roles but also the reasons for, and type of, action they choose to take.

In relation to the Court's external context, the question of institutional capacity is one that most judges do consider but that is rarely explicitly addressed in the Court's jurisprudence. Judicial conceptions of the Court's capacity for dealing with complex social policy matters correlate to the idea of a distinction between those cases and others that are viewed as belonging to a more traditionally "legal" domain. This has generally resulted in deference to legislative choices implicating issues of redistribution or program design. The investigation in Chapter 5 of the Court's jurisprudence in health policy cases suggests that the justices do not explicitly ground their decisions in a framework that considers institutional roles or the question of whether there are boundaries to their power to review matters under the *Charter*. This has resulted in a piecemeal and uncertain approach, opening a site of activity for the justices to impose their personal conceptions of the just outcome on an issue-by-issue basis.

The justices' differing views thus have implications for decisions and how they in turn conceive of the Court's relationship with the other branches of government. As Chapter 6 explored, where some scholars view the dialogue metaphor as the dominant theoretical understanding of *Charter* review, the justices tend to view it as little more than an elaboration of respect for these institutional roles. The fact that dialogic review in their eyes does not resemble a process with the communicative significance its proponents suggest has important ramifications for how scholars should evaluate the Court's policy decisions. Moreover, this point also suggests that dialogue fails as a defence against critics' arguments that judicial involvement in social policy matters is normatively problematic.

Implications

The role-centric, historical institutionalist approach undertaken in this book allows for a deeper description and analysis of what is, and what should be regarded as, a complex institutional context. It sheds a new and important light on the justices' perceptions of their roles and responsibilities in the contemporary period. More importantly, the empirical evidence makes clear that judicial role perceptions help to explain decision making on the Court. The findings in this book also illustrate that it is possible to build bridges between the dominant theories in the scholarly literature. The institutional norms at the centre of this analysis allow for the identification of when and under what contexts attitudinal or strategic motivations are likely to emerge on the Court. Rather than emphasizing a single factor in judicial decision making, this approach fosters a more ecumenical framework from which to explain the work of multi-member appellate courts.

Beyond this scholarly contribution, the analysis presented in this book has several practical implications. The first concerns the appointments process. The ability of the federal executive to select judges is the most significant power any of the elected branches of government have to influence the Court's work. Attention to the institution's policy-making role has in recent years generated demands for reform to the appointments process, which up until now has been conducted entirely behind the scenes and left to the discretion of the prime minister. The only statutory limitations are that an appointee must be a member of the bar of a province for at least ten years and that at least three of the judges on the Court at any time must be from Quebec. The March 2006 appointment of Justice Marshall Rothstein by Prime Minister Stephen Harper was the first in Canadian history to include a public hearing in which an appointee faced questions from representatives of the four political parties in the House of Commons. The hearing was moderated by constitutional expert Peter Hogg, who informed the committee that Rothstein J would not answer questions about controversial issues or hypothetical cases. The 2006 process has been lauded for making the selection procedure more transparent, for its relatively non-partisan feel (in sharp contrast to US nomination hearings), and for its potential to educate the Canadian public about the nominee and the Court itself.[5] Nevertheless, significant problems have cropped up since that event. The Harper government failed to follow a similar process when it appointed Justice Thomas Cromwell in 2008, leaving the status of reform to the appointments procedure in doubt. Then, in 2011, the appointments of Justices Andromache Karakatsanis and Michael Moldaver saw a return to the public interviews. Unfortunately, any chance to edify the public about the two new justices' views on their roles or on judicial decision making in general was overshadowed by the less-than-polite questioning by Joe Comartin, the New Democratic Party's member of parliament, who used the opportunity to focus on Moldaver J's lack of fluency in French. Although the question of whether the Supreme Court of Canada's justices ought to be bilingual is a legitimate one, Comartin's line of questioning bordered on rude. Furthermore, many of the other questions asked of the appointees failed to touch on topics that would illustrate to Canadians how each of these judges envisioned their role or that of the Courts'.

Opening up the appointments process to more public scrutiny is a controversial prospect, particularly in legal circles. Many of the Court's justices have spoken out against any reform that would risk "politicizing" the Court or emulating the partisan American process.[6] It is important to point out, however, that just because the long-standing process of appointments has not been subject to public scrutiny does not mean it has somehow escaped politics. The very lack of transparency in the process prevents the public from knowing what factors are significant when appointments are made, including perceptions of a potential justice's ideological leanings. More importantly, this book provides ample evidence that there exists a host of questions that might be posed to nominees regarding how they conceive of their role without treading into the more controversial waters of asking about their policy preferences or about hypothetical cases. Posing questions to nominees about how they balance the tension between individual and collective decision making, what emphasis they might place on unanimity, or how they believe they ought to treat conflicting social scientific evidence in cases is unlikely to risk damage to the nominee's reputation or a descent into partisanship surrounding the appointment. Such questions would, however, shed further light on how the Court operates and how individual justices approach their work.

By revealing how judges approach particular aspects of the decision-making process, the findings in this book may also benefit individuals or groups that come before the Court. Particularly pertinent in this regard, for example, is the discussion in Chapter 3 concerning what factors the justices consider important when deciding whether to grant leave to an appeal, how the justices approach the oral hearing, what type of questions they pose to counsel, and the best way litigants can have an impact. Chapter 6 also confirms for individuals and interest groups the intuitively obvious idea that public opinion and media coverage can be important to the justices. While the analysis does not suggest that waging a media campaign could in any way convince the Court to decide a specific case in a particular way, it does make clear that the Court is in no way isolated from its broader political environment or completely immune to the overarching effects of popular opinion.

Knowledge of how the justices conceive of the institutional roles relating to *Charter* review and a better understanding of how they view the dialogue metaphor might also prove useful to governments seeking to defend legislative initiatives before the Court. Studies by James Kelly and Janet Hiebert make clear that *Charter* considerations play a significant role in the legislative process.[7] Since some judges are hesitant to make incursions into policy areas that implicate competing values, governments may want to be even more explicit about the underlying values dictating their policy choices when passing legislation and when defending the reasonableness of those policies if they are challenged on *Charter* grounds. The fact that the Court's *Charter* jurisprudence has evolved in a manner that has made the justices less apprehensive about adjudicating social policy issues might also encourage governments to consider under what circumstances it might be plausible to revisit use of the notwithstanding clause. Rulings as controversial as the one in *Chaoulli v Quebec (Attorney General)* might make it feasible to invoke section 33 without sparking a public backlash.[8]

Finally, the findings explored in this book have implications for normative debates about judicial review in Canada. One of the starting premises for this study has been that arguments about judicial "activism" and the impact of the *Charter* have occurred without a sufficient understanding of how the Supreme Court of Canada actually operates. The analysis presented here is unlikely to change the minds of those engaged in debates over whether judicial review is sufficiently democratic or whether courts are the proper fora for the resolution of social policy issues. Nevertheless, this study confirms two of the central arguments put forward by both sides of these debates. First, as critics of the Court's role under the *Charter* contend, the Court's decision making is fundamentally political, not only because it is enmeshed in substantive policy issues but also because the justices have substantial discretion in settling the issues that come before them. Second, and on the other side, decision making on the Court is distinct in form and substance because the justices are bound by a host of procedural and legal rules and by a set of role-related norms and conventions that constrain and shape the extent to which their decisions are merely representations of their personal policy preferences. These two basic points are neither surprising nor novel. What this account of the institution offers, however, are specifics about the various motivations justices carry and under what contexts different factors become particularly influential. Normative or prescriptive scholarship might be able to draw on the empirical findings in this study to develop more specific arguments about how to better reconcile the institutional relationships and tensions inherent in judicial review.

The Court will continue to be involved in the resolution of complex and controversial political and policy issues, ranging from Aboriginal rights, to federalism disputes, to *Charter* claims concerning the regulation of hate speech, prostitution, and drugs. Nor should it come as any surprise if, in the not-too-distant future, the Court is confronted with issues it has already faced under the *Charter* – such as assisted suicide or abortion – as the jurisprudence of particular areas, such as section 7's right to life, liberty, and security of the person, have evolved significantly since *R. v Morgentaler* and *Rodriguez v British Columbia (Attorney General)*, which were explored in Chapter 5.[9] The recent Insite case, *Canada (Attorney General) v PHS Community Services Society*, which concerns a supervised injection site in Vancouver, demonstrates the tension created by the Court's approach to section 7.[10] The justices have thus far refrained from interpreting section 7 to create positive rights. Yet, the logic of the Insite decision, which prevented the federal government from denying a further exemption under the *Controlled Drugs and Substances Act* and closing the site, on the basis that it saves lives, is no far cry from suggesting that the *Charter* might also compel other provinces to open such sites.[11] As the Court continues to deal with substantive policy matters under the *Charter*, the debate over its role in doing so will remain vigorous. This study suggests that the justices are not always attentive to the institutional boundaries implicated by such cases. Yet, at the same time, the findings in this book suggest that many features of the Court's decision making cannot be reduced to mere ideological politics. Proponents and critics alike need to address this empirical reality when engaging in debates about the Court's proper role in Canadian governance.

Many of the issues and themes explored in this study are ripe for further investigation. As access to the justices' private papers opens up over the course of the next decade, more investigation into the extent of attitudinal or strategic behaviour on the Court will no doubt prove fruitful. Different elements of the justices' role perceptions should also be placed under further scrutiny. For example, in-depth case study research exploring the effect unanimity has on the depth and scope of judicial decisions is important, given the high rate of consensus on the Court. Additionally, scholars might examine more deeply the relationship between public opinion and judicial decisions. More empirical work into the policy impact of the Court's decisions is particularly warranted, given that the influence judicial decisions have on policy matters is bound up in the question of the institution's competence to resolve them. Despite the fact that the analysis in Chapter 6 suggests that the dialogue metaphor is devoid of substantive meaning from the judicial perspective, the basic notion that legislatures have ample opportunity to respond to the Court's rulings warrants further empirical investigation. In-depth case study research on specific policy areas to evaluate more carefully the effect that judicial interpretations of the *Charter* have on particular policies is also worthwhile.

Despite increased transparency during the *Charter* era, the Supreme Court of Canada remains a secretive place. Until or unless the Court reassesses questions of access, this book represents the first and last comprehensive examination of the internal workings of the Court that takes advantage of a substantial number of interviews of former law clerks. Contrary to the assertions of one former clerk who publicly claimed that information about case assignments and the clerks' work "is trivia of no scholarly value," the analysis presented in this book reveals how the various processes imbedded in the Court's decision making can serve to constrain or shape certain types of behaviour.[12] Further, given the importance of the Court's work, the extent of the law clerks' influence over substantive case outcomes is worthy of study.

The approach taken here encourages explicit attention to the development of theory and the consequences of particular methodologies in the study of judicial behaviour. Although one basis for the book has been to develop a critique of the dominant methodological approaches in the literature, I have sought to build bridges between the underlying theories implicit in each of the main approaches in political science scholarship. As noted in Chapter 1, James Gibson has provided an oft-cited definition of how judges decide: "Judges' decisions are a function of what they prefer to do, tempered by what they think they ought to do, but constrained by what they perceive is feasible to do."[13] The attitudinal model has emphasized what judges prefer to do and the strategic model has incorporated what judges perceive is feasible to do. The aim in this study has been to incorporate what judges think they ought to do, without discounting the other two factors. Attitudinal, strategic, and legal scholars will all benefit from attention to the competing theories and will in turn continue to refine their own approaches. The main conclusion to be drawn from this book is that a consideration of judicial role perceptions can greatly aid the development of such theory building in the broader judicial politics literature.

Notes

Introduction

1 *Canadian Charter of Rights and Freedoms,* Part 1 of the *Constitution Act, 1982,* being Schedule B to the *Canada Act 1982* (U.K.), 1982, c. 11 *[Charter].*

2 F.L. Morton and Rainer Knopff, *The Charter Revolution and the Court Party* (Peterborough, ON: Broadview Press, 2000); Rory Leishman, *Against Judicial Activism: The Decline of Freedom and Democracy in Canada* (Montreal and Kingston: McGill-Queen's University Press, 2006).

3 Michael Mandel, *The Charter of Rights and the Legalization of Politics in Canada* (Toronto: Wall and Thompson, 1989); Allan C. Hutchinson, *Waiting for CORAF: A Critique of Law and Rights* (Toronto: University of Toronto Press, 1995); Andrew Petter, *The Politics of the Charter: The Illusive Promise of Constitutional Rights* (Toronto: University of Toronto Press, 2010).

4 Alexander Bickel, *The Least Dangerous Branch: The Supreme Court at the Bar of Politics* (New York: Bobbs-Merrill, 1962).

5 Section 52(1) of the *Constitution Act, 1982,* being Schedule B to the *Canada Act 1982* (U.K.), 1982, reads: "The Constitution of Canada is the supreme law of Canada, and any law that is inconsistent with the provisions of the Constitution is, to the extent of the inconsistency, of no force or effect." The enforcement provision is located in section 24(1) of the *Charter*: "Anyone whose rights or freedoms, as guaranteed by this Charter, have been infringed or denied may apply to a court of competent jurisdiction to obtain such remedy as the court considers appropriate and just in the circumstances."

6 According to Christopher Manfredi, the shift from constitutional to judicial supremacy constitutes "the paradox of liberal constitutionalism." Christopher Manfredi, *Judicial Power and the Charter: Canada and the Paradox of Liberal Constitutionalism* (Don Mills, ON: Oxford University Press, 2001).

7 See, for example, Kent Roach, *The Supreme Court on Trial: Judicial Activism or Democratic Dialogue* (Toronto: Irwin Law, 2001), 116.

8 Peter Hogg and Allison Bushell, "The *Charter* Dialogue between Courts and Legislatures: (Or Perhaps the *Charter of Rights* Isn't Such a Bad Thing after All)," *Osgoode Hall Law Journal* 35(1) (1997), 75; Roach, *The Supreme Court on Trial.*

9 Janet Hiebert, *Charter Conflicts: What Is Parliament's Role?* (Montreal and Kingston: McGill-Queen's University Press, 2002); James B. Kelly, *Governing with the Charter: Legislative and Judicial Activism and Framers' Intent* (Vancouver: UBC Press, 2005); Dennis Baker, *Not Quite Supreme: The Courts and Coordinate Constitutional Interpretation* (Montreal and Kingston: McGill-Queen's University Press, 2010).

10 The judicialization of politics has two core meanings: "1. The process by which courts and judges come to make or increasingly to dominate the making of public policies that had previously been made (or, it is widely believed, ought to be made) by other governmental agencies, especially legislatures and executives, and 2. the process by which nonjudicial negotiating and decision-making forums come to be dominated by quasi-judicial (legalistic) rules and procedures." C. Neal Tate, "Why the Expansion of Judicial Power?" in *The Global*

Expansion of Judicial Power, edited by C. Neal Tate and Torbjorn Vallinder (New York: New York University Press, 1995), 28.

11 Peter H. Russell, "Canadian Constraints on Judicialization from Without," in Tate and Vallinder, *The Global Expansion of Judicial Power,* 138.

12 Ran Hirschl, *Towards Juristocracy: The Origins and Consequences of the New Constitutionalism* (Cambridge, MA: Harvard University Press, 2004), 186-87.

13 Hiebert, *Charter Conflicts;* Kelly, *Governing with the Charter.*

14 Hiebert, *Charter Conflicts,* 55.

15 Alan Cairns, *Charter versus Federalism: The Dilemmas of Constitutional Reform* (Montreal and Kingston: McGill-Queen's University Press, 1992), 4; Michael Ignatieff, *The Rights Revolution* (Toronto: House of Anansi Press, 2000), 86.

16 Mary Ann Glendon, *Rights Talk: The Impoverishment of Political Discourse* (New York: Free Press, 1991).

17 Morton and Knopff, *The Charter Revolution and the Court Party,* 156; Anthony A. Peacock, "Strange Brew: Tocqueville, Rights, and the Technology of Equality," in *Rethinking the Constitution: Perspectives on Canadian Constitutional Reform, Interpretation, and Theory,* edited by Anthony A. Peacock (Don Mills, ON: Oxford University Press, 1996), 124; Jeffrey Simpson, "Rights Talk: The Effect of the Charter on Canadian Political Discourse," in *Protecting Rights and Freedoms: Essays on the Charter's Place in Canada's Political, Legal, and Intellectual Life,* edited by Philip Bryden, Steven Davis, and Peter Russell (Toronto: University of Toronto Press, 1994), 57.

18 Emmett Macfarlane, "Terms of Entitlement: Is There a Distinctly Canadian 'Rights Talk'?" *Canadian Journal of Political Science* 41(2) (2008), 303.

19 Peter H. Russell, *The Judiciary in Canada: The Third Branch of Government* (Toronto: McGraw-Hill Ryerson, 1987), 3.

20 See Russell, *The Judiciary in Canada;* Peter McCormick and Ian Greene, *Judges and Judging: Inside the Canadian Judicial System* (Toronto: James Lorimer, 1990); Peter McCormick, *Canada's Courts* (Toronto: James Lorimer, 1994); Ian Greene et al., *Final Appeal: Decision-Making in Canadian Courts of Appeal* (Toronto: James Lorimer, 1998).

21 Peter McCormick, *Supreme at Last: The Evolution of the Supreme Court of Canada* (Toronto: James Lorimer, 2000); Daved Muttart, *The Empirical Gap in Jurisprudence: A Comprehensive Study of the Supreme Court of Canada* (Toronto: University of Toronto Press, 2007).

22 Roy B. Flemming, *Tournament of Appeals: Granting Judicial Review in Canada* (Vancouver: UBC Press, 2004); C.L. Ostberg and Matthew E. Wetstein, *Attitudinal Decision Making in the Supreme Court of Canada* (Vancouver: UBC Press, 2007); Donald R. Songer, *The Transformation of the Supreme Court of Canada: An Empirical Examination* (Toronto: University of Toronto Press, 2008).

23 Linda White et al., eds., *The Comparative Turn in Canadian Political Science* (Vancouver: UBC Press, 2008).

24 Christopher P. Manfredi, *Feminist Activism in the Supreme Court: Legal Mobilization and the Women's Legal Education and Action Fund* (Vancouver: UBC Press, 2004), 196.

25 Paul Pierson and Theda Skocpol, "Historical Institutionalism in Contemporary Political Science," in *Political Science: State of the Discipline,* edited by Ira Katznelson and George R. Milner (New York: W.W. Norton, 2002), 693.

26 Miriam Smith, *Political Institutions and Lesbian and Gay Rights in the United States and Canada* (New York: Routledge, 2008), 7.

27 Ibid, 10.

28 Paul Weiler, *In the Last Resort: A Critical Study of the Supreme Court of Canada* (Toronto: Carswell, 1974), 4-5 [emphasis in original].

29 Heather MacIvor, *Canadian Politics and Government in the Charter Era* (Toronto: Thomson Nelson, 2006), 92.

30 Muttart, *The Empirical Gap in Jurisprudence,* 7.

31 See Emmett Macfarlane, "Administration at the Supreme Court of Canada: Challenges and Change in the Charter Era," *Canadian Public Administration* 52(1) (2009), 1.

32 Bob Woodward and Scott Armstrong, *The Brethren: Inside the Supreme Court* (New York: Avon Books, 1979); Bernard Schwartz, *Decision: How the Supreme Court Decides Cases* (New York:

Oxford University Press, 1996); Edward Lazarus, *Closed Chambers: The Rise, Fall, and Future of the Modern Supreme Court* (New York: Penguin Books, 1998); Jeffrey Toobin, *The Nine: Inside the Secret World of the Supreme Court* (New York: Random House, 2007).

33 Indeed, the first book of this sort was only released in 2011, although even it was not completely devoted to what goes on inside the institution. See Philip Slayton, *Mighty Judgment: How the Supreme Court of Canada Runs Your Life* (Toronto: Penguin Group, 2011).

34 Brian Dickson and DeLloyd J. Guth, "Securing Canada's Judicial Heritage," in *Brian Dickson at the Supreme Court of Canada: 1973-1990*, edited by DeLloyed J. Guth (Winnipeg, MB: Supreme Court of Canada Historical Society, 1998), 323.

35 Put another way, dividing the Court into "eras" by chief justice, I interviewed two Laskin-era clerks (Laskin served as chief justice until 1984); four Dickson-era clerks (1984-90); six Lamer-era clerks (1990-99), and nine McLachlin-era clerks (2000-present).

36 Beppi Crosariol, "The Clerk's Tale Is a Supreme Story," *Globe and Mail* (17 August 2005), B7.

37 Kirk Makin, "Top Court Orders Clerks to Keep Quiet: U.S. Scholar Asking 'Inappropriate' Questions about Judges and Their Cases," *Globe and Mail* (19 June 2009), A4.

38 Many of the former clerks I interviewed declined to answer questions if they felt that doing so would break confidentiality. Several former law clerks I contacted to request interviews declined on this very basis. I left it to those who accepted my request for an interview to determine what information they were prohibited from sharing.

39 See Greene et al., *Final Appeal;* Florian Sauvageau, David Schneiderman, and David Taras, *The Last Word: Media Coverage of the Supreme Court of Canada* (Vancouver: UBC Press, 2006).

40 Songer, *The Transformation of the Supreme Court of Canada.*

41 Ostberg and Wetstein, *Attitudinal Decision Making in the Supreme Court of Canada.*

42 Ellen Anderson, *Judging Bertha Wilson: Law as Large as Life* (Toronto: University of Toronto Press, 2001); Robert J. Sharpe and Kent Roach, *Brian Dickson: A Judge's Journey* (Toronto: Osgoode Society for Canadian Legal History, 2003); Philip Girard, *Bora Laskin: Bringing Law to Life* (Toronto: Osgoode Society for Canadian Legal History, 2005).

43 See R.W. Kostal, "Shilling for Judges: Brian Dickson and His Biographers," *McGill Law Journal* 51 (2006), 199-208.

44 Sara C. Benesh, "Harold J. Spaeth: The Supreme Court Computer," in *The Pioneers of Judicial Behavior*, edited by Nancy Maveety (Ann Arbor, MI: University of Michigan Press, 2003), 123.

45 Russell, *The Judiciary in Canada*, 26.

46 F.L. Morton, *Law, Politics and the Judicial Process in Canada*, 3rd edition (Calgary, AB: University of Calgary Press, 2002), 533.

47 Peter McCormick finds that *Charter* cases are routinely cited as precedents not just in the context of *Charter* claims and challenges but also in non-*Charter* cases as well. He concludes that "Charter cases have become very much the centre of gravity of Supreme Court jurisprudence, to an extent that far exceeds their relative share of caseload." The *Charter* has become central to the broader "interpretive strategies and role-definitions of the Court." See Peter McCormick, "What Supreme Court Cases Does the Supreme Court Cite? Follow-up Citations on the Supreme Court of Canada, 1989-1993," *Supreme Court Law Review* 7 (1996), 464.

48 See, for example, Morton and Knopff, *The Charter Revolution and the Court Party;* Ignatieff, *The Rights Revolution.* See also Cairns, *Charter versus Federalism,* 4.

49 Hutchinson, *Waiting for CORAF,* 24.

50 Claire Bernstein, "How Top Judges Came to Grips with Charter," *Toronto Star* (20 May 1990), B1.

51 Beverley McLachlin, "The Charter of Rights and Freedoms: A Judicial Perspective," *University of British Columbia Law Review* 23 (1989), 579.

52 This conservative outlook within the Canadian legal profession was not without its critics. Paul Weiler criticized judges for their "outmoded and unduly narrow conception of the role of law in courts." Paul Weiler, *In the Last Resort,* 4.

53 Robert J. Sharpe and Kent Roach, *The Charter of Rights and Freedoms,* 3rd edition (Toronto: Irwin Law, 2005), 25.

54 Ibid, 11. *Canadian Bill of Rights*, S.C. 1960, c. 44.

Chapter 1: Studying Judicial Behaviour

1 *Canadian Charter of Rights and Freedoms,* Part 1 of the *Constitution Act, 1982,* being Schedule B to the *Canada Act 1982* (U.K.), 1982, c. 11 *[Charter].*

2 *Auton (Guardian ad litem of) v British Columbia (Attorney General),* 2004 SCC 78, [2004] 3 S.C.R. 657.

3 *Chaoulli v Quebec (Attorney General),* [2005] SCC 35, [2005] 1 S.C.R. 791.

4 *Charter of Human Rights and Freedoms,* R.S.Q., c. C-12, s. 10.

5 *Eldridge v British Columbia (Attorney General),* [1997] 3 S.C.R. 624.

6 Reaction to the *Chaoulli* decision ranged from strong support to condemnation. The editorial board of the *Globe and Mail* criticized the decision as the most "blatantly political" one since the enactment of the *Charter.* "The Court's Arrogant Judgment on Medicare," *Globe and Mail* (18 June 2005), A16. One poll following the ruling showed that a majority of respondents would favour their province's invoking the notwithstanding clause to negate the Court ruling. Mark Kennedy, "Canadians Rue Medicare's Decline, but Eager for Private System: Poll," *Ottawa Citizen* (18 June 2005), A3. Academic commentary is largely critical. See, for example, most of the contributions in Colleen M. Flood, Kent Roach, and Lorne Sossin, eds., *Access to Care, Access to Justice: The Legal Debate over Private Health Insurance in Canada* (Toronto: University of Toronto Press, 2005).
   The Court's deference in the autism case was itself not without criticism. See Margaret Philp, "Angry Parents Threaten to Leave Country," *Globe and Mail* (20 November 2004), A11.

7 Although legal formalism has its modern defenders, Brian Tamanaha writes persuasively that the formalist-realist distinction is at best a gross exaggeration and at worst a fabrication perpetuated by both legal theorists and political scientists. See Brian Z. Tamanaha, *Beyond the Formalist-Realist Divide: The Role of Politics in Judging* (Princeton, NJ: Princeton University Press, 2010).

8 Neil A. Lewis, "Senate Panel Endorses Sotomayor on a Partisan Vote," *New York Times* (29 July 2009), 12.

9 The leading advocate of positivism is H.L.A. Hart, *The Concept of Law* (New York: Oxford University Press, 1961).

10 Ronald Dworkin, *Taking Rights Seriously* (Cambridge, MA: Harvard University Press, 1978); Ronald Dworkin, *Law's Empire* (Cambridge, MA: Harvard University Press, 1986).

11 Steven G. Calabresi, ed., *Originalism: A Quarter-Century of Debate* (Washington, DC: Regnery Publishing, 2007); Randy E. Barnett, *Restoring the Lost Constitution: The Presumption of Liberty* (Princeton, NJ: Princeton University Press, 2003).

12 John Hart Ely, *Democracy and Distrust: A Theory of Judicial Review* (Cambridge, MA: Harvard University Press, 1980).

13 Dworkin, *Law's Empire,* 11-12.

14 Jeffrey A. Segal and Harold J. Spaeth, *The Supreme Court and the Attitudinal Model* (New York: Cambridge University Press, 1993), 33.

15 For a prominent example, see Lee Epstein and Joseph F. Kobylka, *The Supreme Court and Legal Change: Abortion and the Death Penalty* (Chapel Hill, NC: University of North Carolina Press, 1992).

16 Harold J. Spaeth and Jeffrey A. Segal, *Majority Rule or Minority Will: Adherence to Precedent on the U.S. Supreme Court* (New York: Cambridge University Press, 1999).

17 Keith E. Whittington, "Once More unto the Breach: PostBehavioralist Approaches to Judicial Politics," *Law and Social Inquiry* 25 (2000), 601-34, 607, n. 4.

18 Howard Gillman, "What's Law Got to Do with It? Judicial Behavioralists Test the 'Legal Model' of Judicial Decision Making," *Law and Social Inquiry* 26(2) (2001), 465-504, 482.

19 Sara C. Benesh, "Harold J. Spaeth: The Supreme Court Computer," in *The Pioneers of Judicial Behavior,* edited by Nancy Maveety (Ann Arbor, MI: University of Michigan Press, 2003), 122.

20 Mark J. Richards and Herbert M. Kritzer, "Jurisprudential Regimes in Supreme Court Decision Making," *American Political Science Review* 96(2) (2002), 305-20; Herbert M. Kritzer and Mark J. Richards, "Jurisprudential Regimes and Supreme Court Decisionmaking: The *Lemon* Regime and Establishment Clause Cases," *Law and Society Review* 37(4) (2003), 827-40.

21 Richards and Kritzer, "Jurisprudential Regimes in Supreme Court Decision Making," 306.

22 Ibid, 307.

23 Jeffrey R. Lax and Kelly T. Rader, "Legal Constraints on Supreme Court Decision Making: Do Jurisprudential Regimes Exist?" *Journal of Politics* 72(2) (2010), 273-84; Jeffrey A. Segal, "Judicial Behavior," in *The Oxford Handbook of Law and Politics,* edited by Keith Whittington, R. Daniel Keleman, and Gregory A. Caldeira (New York: Oxford University Press, 2008), 23.

24 Herbert M. Kritzer and Mark J. Richards, "Taking and Testing Jurisprudential Regimes Seriously: A Response to Lax and Rader," *Journal of Politics* 72(2) (2010), 288.

25 Parliament of Canada, Standing Committee on Justice, Human Rights, Public Safety and Emergency Preparedness, *Evidence,* Meeting No. 8, 37th Parliament, 3rd Session (30 March 2004) at 1545, http://www.parl.gc.ca/committee/CommitteePublication.aspx?SourceId =76982.

26 Nancy Maveety, ed., *The Pioneers of Judicial Behavior* (Ann Arbor, MI: University of Michigan Press, 2003), 2.

27 C. Herman Pritchett, "Divisions of Opinions among Justices of the U.S. Supreme Court, 1939-1941," *American Political Science Review* 35 (1941), 890.

28 See Glendon Schubert, *The Judicial Mind* (Evanston, IL: Northwestern University Press, 1965).

29 Segal and Spaeth, *The Supreme Court and the Attitudinal Model;* Jeffrey A. Segal and Harold J. Spaeth, *The Supreme Court and the Attitudinal Model Revisited* (New York: Cambridge University Press, 2002), 86.

30 Ibid, 53.

31 Ibid, 320-21.

32 See Donald E. Fouts, "Policy-Making in the Supreme Court of Canada, 1950-1960," in *Comparative Judicial Behavior: Cross-Cultural Studies of Decision-Making in the East and West,* edited by Glendon Schubert and David Danelski (New York: Oxford University Press, 1969), 257-91; Sidney Peck, "A Scalogram Analysis of the Supreme Court of Canada, 1958-1967," in *Comparative Judicial Behavior: Cross-Cultural Studies of Decision-Making in the East and West,* edited by Glendon Schubert and David Danelski (New York: Oxford University Press, 1969), 293-324.

33 C. Neal Tate and Panu Sittiwong, "Decision Making in the Canadian Supreme Court: Extending the Personal Attributes Model across Nations," *Journal of Politics* 51(4) (1989), 900-16.

34 Donald R. Songer and Susan W. Johnson, "Judicial Decision Making in the Supreme Court of Canada: Updating the Personal Attribute Model," *Canadian Journal of Political Science* 40(4) (2007), 911-34.

35 Donald R. Songer, *The Transformation of the Supreme Court of Canada* (Toronto: University of Toronto Press, 2008).

36 C.L. Ostberg and Matthew Wetstein, "Dimensions of Attitudes Underlying Search and Seizure Decisions of the Supreme Court of Canada," *Canadian Journal of Political Science* 31 (1998), 767-87; Matthew E. Wetstein and C.L. Ostberg, "Search and Seizure Cases in the Supreme Court of Canada: Extending an American Model of Judicial Decision Making across Countries," *Social Science Quarterly* 80(4) (1999), 757-74; C.L. Ostberg, Matthew E. Wetstein, and Craig R. Ducat, "Attitudinal Dimensions of Supreme Court Decision Making in Canada: The Lamer Court, 1991-1995," *Political Research Quarterly* 55(1) (2002), 235-56.

37 C.L. Ostberg and Matthew Wetstein, *Attitudinal Decision-Making in the Supreme Court of Canada* (Vancouver: UBC Press, 2007), 14.

38 Ibid, 209.

39 Segal and Spaeth, *The Supreme Court and the Attitudinal Model,* 32.

40 One example is judicial review of government agency actions, where Segal and Spaeth's model predicted thirteen cases correctly and twenty-seven incorrectly. Frank B. Cross, "Political Science and the New Legal Realism: A Case of Unfortunate Interdisciplinary Ignorance," *Northwestern University Law Review* 92(1) (1997), 303-4, citing Segal and Spaeth, *The Supreme Court and the Attitudinal Model,* 259.

41 Segal and Spaeth, *The Supreme Court and the Attitudinal Model Revisited,* 326, n. 44.

42 James Johnson, "Conceptual Problems as Obstacles to Progress in Political Science: Four Decades of Political Culture Research," *Journal of Theoretical Politics* 15(1) (2003), 91-92.

43 Ibid, 97.

44 Ibid, 103.

45 James Johnson, "Consequences of Positivism: A Pragmatist Assessment," *Comparative Political Studies* 39(2) (2006), 241 [emphasis in original].

46 Cross, "Political Science and the New Legal Realism," 291.

47 For example, then-president of the National Citizens Coalition, a conservative lobby group, current Prime Minister Stephen Harper challenged the constitutionality of federal campaign-spending legislation. The case reached the Supreme Court of Canada in 2004. See *Harper v Canada (Attorney General)*, [2004] 1 S.C.R. 827.

48 As I have argued elsewhere. See Emmett Macfarlane, "Attitudinal Decision-Making in the Supreme Court of Canada," *Queen's Law Journal* 33(1) 2007, 255-56. See *RJR-Macdonald v Canada (A.G.)*, [1995] 3 S.C.R. 199; *Irwin Toy v Quebec (A.G.)*, [1989] 1 S.C.R. 927; *Libman v Quebec (A.G.)*, [1997] 3 S.C.R. 569.

49 Benesh, "Harold J. Spaeth," 124.

50 J. Woodford Howard Jr., "On the Fluidity of Judicial Choice," *American Political Science Review* 62(1) (1968), 44.

51 Saul Brenner, "Fluidity on the United States Supreme Court: A Re-Examination," *American Journal of Political Science* 24 (1980), 380-86.

52 Timothy M. Hagle and Harold J. Spaeth, "Voting Fluidity and the Attitudinal Model of Supreme Court Decision Making," *Western Political Quarterly* 44 (1) (1991), 119-28.

53 Howard, "On the Fluidity of Judicial Choice," 49.

54 Cross, "Political Science and the New Legal Realism," 307. The importance of the concurrence at the Supreme Court of Canada should not be understated. See Peter McCormick, "Standing Apart: Separate Concurrence and the Modern Supreme Court of Canada, 1984-2006," *McGill Law Journal* 53 (2008), 137-66.

55 See James G. March and Johan P. Olsen, "The New Institutionalism: Organizational Factors in Political Life," *American Political Science Review* 78(3) (1984), 734-49.

56 Walter F. Murphy, *Elements of Judicial Strategy* (Chicago: University of Chicago Press, 1964).

57 Segal and Spaeth, *The Supreme Court and the Attitudinal Model Revisited*, 97.

58 Bob Woodward and Scott Armstrong, *The Brethren: Inside the Supreme Court* (New York: Avon Books, 1979).

59 Bernard Schwartz, *Decision: How the Supreme Court Decides Cases* (New York: Oxford University Press, 1996); Edward Lazarus, *Closed Chambers: The Rise, Fall, and Future of the Modern Supreme Court* (New York: Penguin Books, 1998); Jeffrey Toobin, *The Nine: Inside the Secret World of the Supreme Court* (New York: Random House, 2007).

60 Woodward and Armstrong readily admit to having received no co-operation from Chief Justice Warren Burger during the course of their research. See Woodward and Armstrong, *The Brethren*, xiv. Nevertheless, his actions, alleged conversations in conference and behind-the-scenes lobbying are central to the book's account of the Court's work.

61 See Lawrence Baum, *The Puzzle of Judicial Behavior* (Ann Arbor, MI: University of Michigan Press, 1997), 26-27; Forrest Maltzman, James F. Spriggs II, and Paul J. Wahlbeck, *Crafting Law on the Supreme Court: The Collegial Game* (New York: Cambridge University Press, 2000), 25.

62 Ibid.

63 Lee Epstein and Jack Knight, "Toward a Strategic Revolution in Judicial Politics: A Look Back, A Look Ahead," *Political Research Quarterly* 53(3) (2000), 634.

64 Lee Epstein and Jack Knight, *The Choices Justices Make* (Washington, DC: Congressional Quarterly, 1998).

65 Maltzman, Spriggs and Wahlbeck, *Crafting Law on the Supreme Court*.

66 Ibid, 80-84.

67 In rational choice theory, the search for equilibria allows for the development of predictive, law-like statements. The term is borrowed from the natural sciences, where physical equilibria occur when forces balance each other out so that a process repeats itself (such as orbits) or comes to rest (as in completed reactions). In politics, equilibria are the result of

the purposive behaviour of individuals, and they occur when each actor adopts a strategy that constitutes the *best reply* given the circumstances. In such an instance, an equilibrium point is reached. If a single equilibrium point exists under a given configuration of actors' preferences and set of institutional rules, then it becomes possible to derive predictive hypotheses. The search for equilibria in rational choice theory is intended to replace journalistic interpretations of events or the search for statistical correlations between independent and dependent variables. See Donald Green and Ian Shapiro, *Pathologies of Rational Choice Theory: A Critique of Applications in Political Science* (New Haven, CT: Yale University Press, 1994), 24-26.

68 Segal and Spaeth, *The Supreme Court and the Attitudinal Model Revisited,* 102.
69 Ibid, 103.
70 Green and Shapiro, *Pathologies of Rational Choice Theory,* 24-26.
71 Epstein and Knight, *The Choices Justices Make,* 112.
72 Melinda Gann Hall and Paul Brace, "Order in the Courts: A Neo-Institutional Approach to Judicial Consensus," *Western Political Quarterly* 42(3) (1989), 392.
73 Whittington, "Once More unto the Breach," 612.
74 Lawrence Baum, *Judges and Their Audiences: A Perspective on Judicial Behavior* (Princeton, NJ: Princeton University Press, 2006), 7.
75 Cornell Clayton and David A. May, "A Political Regimes Approach to the Analysis of Legal Decisions," *Polity* 32(2) (1999), 239.
76 Rogers M. Smith, "Political Jurisprudence, the 'New Institutionalism,' and the Future of Public Law," *American Political Science Review* 82(1) (1988), 93.
77 Richard A. Posner, "What Do Judges and Justices Maximize? (The Same Thing as Everybody Else Does)," *Supreme Court Economic Review* 3 (1993), 1-41.
78 Lori Hausegger and Stacia Haynie, "Judicial Decisionmaking and the Use of Panels in the Canadian Supreme Court and the South African Appellate Division," *Law and Society Review* 37(3) (2003), 635-57.
79 Roy B. Flemming, *Tournament of Appeals: Granting Judicial Review in Canada* (Vancouver: UBC Press, 2004).
80 *R. v Morgentaler,* [1988] 1 S.C.R. 30.
81 *Vriend v Alberta,* [1998] 1 S.C.R. 493.
82 Christopher Manfredi, "Strategic Behavior and the Canadian Charter of Rights and Freedoms," in *The Myth of the Sacred: The Charter, the Courts and the Politics of the Constitution in Canada,* edited by Patrick James, Donald E. Abelson, and Michael Lusztig (Montreal and Kingston: McGill-Queen's University Press, 2002), 148. *Individual Rights Protection Act,* S.A. 1972, c. 2.
83 Manfredi, "Strategic Behavior and the Canadian Charter of Rights and Freedoms," 150.
84 *Ford v Quebec,* [1988] 2 S.C.R. 712.
85 Matthew E. Wetstein and C.L. Ostberg, "Strategic Leadership and Political Change on the Canadian Supreme Court: Analyzing the Transition to Chief Justice," *Canadian Journal of Political Science* 38(3) (2005), 653-73.
86 Ibid, 670.
87 Howard Gillman and Cornell W. Clayton, "Beyond Judicial Attitudes: Institutional Approaches to Supreme Court Decision-Making," in *Supreme Court Decision-Making: New Institutionalist Approaches,* edited by Cornell W. Clayton and Howard Gillman (Chicago: University of Chicago Press, 1999), 4-5.
88 C. Herman Pritchett, *Civil Liberties and the Vinson Court* (Chicago: University of Chicago Press, 1954) 191.
89 Theodore L. Becker, *Political Behavioralism and Modern Jurisprudence: A Working Theory and Study in Judicial Decision-Making* (Chicago: Rand McNally, 1964); Theodore L. Becker, *Comparative Judicial Politics: The Political Functionings of Courts* (Chicago: Rand McNally, 1970); John T. Wold, "Political Orientations, Social Backgrounds, and Role Perceptions of State Supreme Court Judges," *Western Political Quarterly* 27(2) (1974), 239-48; J. Woodford Howard Jr., "Role Perceptions and Behavior in Three U.S. Courts of Appeals," *Journal of Politics* 39(4) (1977), 916-38; James L. Gibson, "Judges' Role Orientations, Attitudes, and Decisions: An Interactive Model," *American Political Science Review* 72(3) (1978), 911-24;

James L. Gibson, "From Simplicity to Complexity: The Development of Theory in the Study of Judicial Behavior," *Political Behavior* 5(1) (1983), 7-49; John M. Scheb, II, Thomas D. Ungs, and Allison L. Hayes, "Judicial Role Orientations, Attitudes and Decision Making: A Research Note," *Western Political Quarterly* 42(3) (1989), 427-35.

90 Scheb et al., "Judicial Role Orientations, Attitudes and Decision Making," 434.
91 Gibson, "From Simplicity to Complexity," 9.
92 Segal and Spaeth, *The Supreme Court and the Attitudinal Model,* 235-36.
93 Gillman and Clayton, "Beyond Judicial Attitudes," 27.
94 Harry T. Edwards, "The Effects of Collegiality on Judicial Decision-Making," *University of Pennsylvania Law Review* 151(5) (2003), 1660.
95 Segal and Spaeth, *The Supreme Court and the Attitudinal Model Revisited,* 432-33.
96 Gillman, "What's Law Got to Do with It?" 491-92.
97 Cornell W. Clayton, "The Supreme Court and Political Jurisprudence: New and Old Institutionalism," in *Supreme Court Decision-Making: New Institutionalist Approaches,* edited by Cornell W. Clayton and Howard Gillman (Chicago: University of Chicago Press, 1999) 34.
98 Lee Epstein et al., "Do Political Preferences Change? A Longitudinal Study of U.S. Supreme Court Justices," *Journal of Politics* 60(3) (1998), 801-18; Andrew D. Martin and Kevin M. Quinn, "Assessing Preference Change on the U.S. Supreme Court," *Journal of Law, Economics and Organization* 23(2) (2007), 365-85; Lee Epstein et al., "Ideological Drift among Supreme Court Justices: Who, When, and How Important," *Northwestern University Law Review* 101(4) (2007), 1483-1541.
99 Baum, *Judges and Their Audiences,* 15-19.
100 Ibid, 20-21.
101 Ibid, 22 [emphasis added].
102 Gerald Baier, *Courts and Federalism: Judicial Doctrine in the United States, Australia, and Canada* (Vancouver: UBC Press, 2006).
103 Christopher P. Manfredi, *Feminist Activism in the Supreme Court: Legal Mobilization and the Women's Legal Education and Action Fund* (Vancouver: UBC Press, 2004).
104 Janet Hiebert, *Limiting Rights: The Dilemma of Judicial Review* (Montreal and Kingston: McGill-Queen's University Press, 1996).
105 Miriam Smith, "Institutionalism in the Study of Canadian Politics," in *New Institutionalism: Theory and Analysis,* edited by André Lecours (Toronto: University of Toronto Press, 2005), 110-12.
106 Alan Cairns, "The Judicial Committee and Its Critics," *Canadian Journal of Political Science* 4(3) (1971), 343.
107 Alan Cairns, *Charter versus Federalism: The Dilemmas of Constitutional Reform* (Montreal and Kingston: McGill-Queen's University Press, 1992).
108 Smith, "Institutionalism in the Study of Canadian Politics," 112.
109 For some notable examples of this new interdisciplinary dialogue, see Frank B. Cross, "Political Science and the New Legal Realism: A Case of Unfortunate Interdisciplinary Ignorance," *Northwestern University Law Review* 92(1) (1997), 251-326; Lee Epstein and Gary King, "The Rules of Inference," *University of Chicago Law Review* 69(1) (2002), 1-133; Stephen M. Feldman, "The Rule of Law or the Rule of Politics? Harmonizing the Internal and External Views of Supreme Court Decision Making," *Law and Social Inquiry* 30(1) (2005), 89-135; Barry Friedman, "The Politics of Judicial Review," *Texas Law Review* 84(2) (2005), 257-337.
110 For a good example, see Sujit Choudhry and Claire E. Hunter, "Measuring Judicial Activism on the Supreme Court of Canada: A Comment on *Newfoundland (Treasury Board) v NAPE,*" *McGill Law Journal* 48 (2003), 525-62; Christopher P. Manfredi and James B. Kelly, "Misrepresenting the Supreme Court's Record? A Comment on Sujit Choudhry and Claire E. Hunter, "Measuring Judicial Activism on the Supreme Court of Canada," *McGill Law Journal* 49 (2004), 741-64.
111 Harold J. Spaeth, "Reflections about Judicial Politics," in *Oxford Handbook of Law and Politics,* edited by Keith Whittington, R. Daniel Keleman, and Gregory A. Caldeira (New York: Oxford University Press, 2008).

112 Paul Pierson and Theda Skocpol, "Historical Institutionalism in Contemporary Political Science," in *Political Science: The State of the Discipline,* edited by Ira Katznelson and George R. Milner (New York: W.W. Norton, 2002), 711 [emphasis added].

113 Ibid, citing Andrew Abbot, "Of Space and Time: The Contemporary Relevance of the Chicago School," *Social Forces* 75(4) (1997), 1171, n. 10.

114 Beverley McLachlin, "On Impartiality" (Address at the University of Waikato, Hamilton, New Zealand, 23 April 2003) [unpublished]; Rosalie Silberman Abella, "The Dynamic Nature of Equality," in *Equality and Judicial Neutrality,* edited by Sheilah L. Martin and Kathleen E. Mahoney (Agincourt, ON: Carswell, 1987).

Chapter 2: The Evolution of the Court and Its Justices

1 *Canadian Charter of Rights and Freedoms,* Part 1 of the *Constitution Act, 1982,* being Schedule B to the *Canada Act 1982* (U.K.), 1982, c. 11.

2 *Constitution Act, 1867,* (U.K.), 30 & 31 Vict., c. 3, reprinted in R.S.C. 1985, App. II, No. 5.

3 The Supreme Court of Canada was first referred to in the amendment formula in the *Constitution Act, 1982* and the first reference to judicial independence was made in section 11(d) of the *Charter.* There is no consensus about whether the Court enjoys constitutional status. Peter Russell, *The Judiciary in Canada: The Third Branch of Government* (Toronto: McGraw-Hill Ryerson, 1987), 67.

4 Peter H. Russell et al., *The Court and the Constitution: Leading Cases* (Toronto: Emond Montgomery Publications, 2008), 4.

5 77 of 159 of the Judicial Committee of the Privy Council's cases on the Canadian Constitution were *per saltum* appeals. Russell et al., *The Court and the Constitution,* 4.

6 James G. Snell and Frederick Vaughan, *The Supreme Court of Canada: History of the Institution* (Toronto: Osgoode Society for Canadian Legal History, 1985), 42.

7 Bora Laskin, "The Supreme Court of Canada: A Final Court of and for Canadians," *Canadian Bar Review* 29 (1951), 1075.

8 "The Supreme Court," *Canada Law Journal* 38(3) (1 February 1902), 61-65.

9 Laskin, "The Supreme Court of Canada," 1047.

10 *Statute of Westminster,* 1931 (UK), 22 & 23 Geo. V, c. 4, s. 2.

11 Peter Russell, *The Supreme Court of Canada as a Bilingual and Bicultural Institution* (Ottawa: Queen's Printer, 1969), 33.

12 Russell et al., *The Court and the Constitution,* 4.

13 For a more thorough discussion, see ibid, 167-69. *British North America Act,* 1867, (U.K.), 30-31 Vict., c. 3.

14 Ronald Cheffins writes that "by and large, the Supreme Court of Canada has acknowledged the doctrine of the supremacy of the legislature, and has refused to strike down as unconstitutional legislative action, except on the ground that it was outside the defined boundaries of legislative power as delineated by the British North America Act." Ronald Cheffins, "The Supreme Court of Canada: The Quiet Court in an Unquiet Country," *Osgoode Hall Law Journal* 4 (1966), 263-64. See also Dale Gibson, "And One Step Backward: The Supreme Court and Constitutional Law in the Sixties," *Canadian Bar Review* 53 (1975), 621-48; Paul Weiler, *In the Last Resort: A Critical Study of the Supreme Court of Canada* (Toronto: Carswell, 1974); Ian Bushnell, *The Captive Court: A Study of the Supreme Court of Canada* (Montreal and Kingston: McGill-Queen's University Press, 1992). *Canadian Bill of Rights,* S.C. 1960, c. 44.

15 *The Queen v Drybones,* [1970] S.C.R. 282.

16 Russell, *The Supreme Court of Canada as a Bilingual and Bicultural Institution,* 55-57.

17 Snell and Vaughan, *The Supreme Court of Canada,* 218. This point is also made by F.L. Morton, *Law, Politics and the Judicial Process in Canada,* 2nd edition (Calgary: University of Calgary Press, 1992), 87; Ian Brodie, "Lobbying the Supreme Court," in *Political Dispute and Judicial Review: Assessing the Work of the Supreme Court of Canada,* edited by Hugh Mellon and Martin Westmacott (Scarborough, ON: Nelson, 2000), 197.

18 Bushnell, *The Captive Court,* 343.

19 Snell and Vaughan, *The Supreme Court of Canada,* 225.

20 *Supreme Court Act,* R.S.C. 1985, c. S-26.
21 Appeals by right were limited to criminal appeals where a provincial court of appeal judge dissents on a question of law or whenever acquittals were overturned on appeal.
22 Russell, *The Supreme Court of Canada as a Bilingual and Bicultural Institution,* 58.
23 Peter McCormick, *Supreme at Last: The Evolution of the Supreme Court of Canada* (Toronto: James Lorimer), 87.
24 The section reads: "The Constitution of Canada is the supreme law of Canada, and any law that is inconsistent with the provisions of the Constitution is, to the extent of the inconsistency, of no force or effect." *Constitution Act, 1982* (U.K.), 1982, c. 11.
25 Russell et al., *The Court and the Constitution,* 11; *R. v Sparrow,* [1990] 1 S.C.R. 1075.
26 Lorne M. Sossin, *Boundaries of Judicial Review: The Law of Justiciability in Canada* (Toronto: Thomson Canada, 1999), 2.
27 F.L. Morton and Rainer Knopff, *The Charter Revolution and the Court Party* (Peterborough, ON: Broadview Press, 2000), 54; Ian Brodie, *Friends of the Court: The Privileging of Interest Group Litigants in Canada* (Albany, NY: State University of New York Press, 2002), 27.
28 Sossin, *Boundaries of Judicial Review,* 5-6.
29 Ibid, 203, citing *Finlay v Canada (Minister of Finance),* [1986] 2 S.C.R. 607 *[Finlay].*
30 Robert J. Sharpe and Kent Roach, *The Charter of Rights and Freedoms,* 3rd edition (Toronto: Irwin Law, 2005), 110-11.
31 *Thorson v Canada (Attorney General) (No. 2),* [1975] 1 S.C.R. 138; *McNeil v Nova Scotia (Board of Censors),* [1976] 2 S.C.R. 265 (S.C.C.); *Minister of Justice (Can.) v Borowski,* [1981] 2 S.C.R. 575 *[Borowski].*
32 *Borowski,* 598.
33 Brodie, *Friends of the Court,* 27.
34 *Canadian Council of Churches v Canada (Minister of Employment and Immigration),* [1992] 1 S.C.R. 236.
35 *Finlay* extended public interest standing to challenge an exercise of administrative authority in addition to legislation.
36 *A.A. v B.B.,* 2007 ONCA 2. The case involved a lesbian couple that, with the assistance of a male friend, decided to start a family. The partner of the child's biological mother sought a declaration that she was the child's parent in addition to the child's biological parents. The appeal court ruled in her favour.
37 *Alliance for Marriage and Family v A.A.,* 2007 SCC 40, [2007] 3 S.C.R. 124 [emphasis in original].
38 *Borowski v Canada (Attorney General),* [1989] 1 S.C.R. 342. *R. v Morgentaler,* [1988] 1 S.C.R. 30. *Criminal Code,* R.S.C. 1985, c. C-46.
39 Brian A. Crane and Henry S. Brown, *Supreme Court of Canada Practice* (Toronto: Thomson Canada, 2008), 24. One notable case, *Tremblay v Daigle,* [1989] 2 S.C.R. 530, concerned an injunction sought by the former boyfriend of the respondent, Chantal Daigle, preventing her from having an abortion, was allowed to proceed after the Court was told during recess that Daigle had the abortion prior to the hearing. For a list of other examples, see Crane and Brown, *Supreme Court of Canada Practice,* 24-25.
40 Sossin, *Boundaries of Judicial Review,* 103, 130.
41 Ibid, 48.
42 *Operation Dismantle v The Queen,* [1985] 1 S.C.R. 441.
43 Ibid, para. 38.
44 Ibid, para. 64.
45 Ibid, para. 104.
46 Sossin, *Boundaries of Judicial Review,* 149.
47 Sossin, *Boundaries of Judicial Review,* 155. *Reference re Secession of Quebec,* [1998] 2 S.C.R. 217.
48 Sossin, *Boundaries of Judicial Review,* 168. Janet Hiebert's analysis of the reasonable limits clause provides a much more comprehensive examination of this point. See Janet Hiebert, *Limiting Rights: The Dilemma of Judicial Review* (Montreal and Kingston: McGill-Queen's University Press, 1996).
49 *Chaoulli v Quebec (Attorney General),* 2005 SCC 35, [2005] 1 S.C.R. 791.
50 Ibid, para. 183.

51 Dennis Baker has written a detailed discussion of separation of powers in the Canadian context. See chapters 3 and 4 of Dennis Baker, *Not Quite Supreme: The Courts and Coordinate Constitutional Interpretation* (Montreal and Kingston: McGill-Queen's University Press, 2010).

52 The Court acknowledged as much in justifying its decision to tackle the issues in the Quebec secession reference. *Reference re Secession of Quebec*, para. 15.

53 The United Kingdom's *Human Rights Act 1998*, c. 42, is an act of Parliament, which came into effect in 2000. It is possible that over time the UK courts may see fit to loosen the rules of justiciability.

54 Frank Iacobucci, "The Charter: Twenty Years Later," *Supreme Court Law Review*, 2nd series, 19 (2003), 393.

55 *Borowski*. Ian Brodie writes: "Laskin has been lionized for his work in broadening the Court's approach to interest groups, but he became less enthusiastic about intervention and standing later in his career." Brodie, *Friends of the Court*, 27.

56 Sossin, *Boundaries of Judicial Review*, 233.

57 Iacobucci, "The Charter," 394.

58 *Rodriguez v British Columbia (Attorney General)*, [1993] 3 S.C.R. 519.

59 The justice did note, however, that there were reasons not to take certain cases, such as those that lack a factual basis.

60 Cristin Schmitz, "Leaving after Fifteen Years on the Bench, Justice L'Heureux-Dubé Says She's 'Extremely Serene,'" *Lawyers Weekly* 22(2) (2002). At the same time, L'Heureux-Dubé J noted she did not regret her position in dissent.

61 Brodie, *Friends of the Court*, 26. The cases are *A-G Canada v Lavell, Isaac et al. v Bedard*, [1974] S.C.R. 1349, and *R. v Morgentaler*, [1976] 1 S.C.R. 616.

62 Ellen Anderson writes that the "original neutral 'friend of the court' concept was rapidly evolving into a strategic litigation movement paralleling the political lobbying by interest groups pressure for substantive legislative change." Ellen Anderson, *Judging Bertha Wilson: Law as Large as Life* (Toronto: University of Toronto Press, 2001), 295; Brodie, *Friends of the Court*, 33.

63 Robert J. Sharpe and Kent Roach, *Brian Dickson: A Judge's Journey* (Toronto: Osgoode Society for Canadian Legal History, 2003), 384.

64 Katherine E. Swinton, *The Supreme Court and Canadian Federalism: The Laskin-Dickson Years* (Toronto: Carswell, 1990), 73-74.

65 Brodie, *Friends of the Court*, xviii-xix.

66 Sharpe and Roach, *Brian Dickson*, 384.

67 Anderson, *Judging Bertha Wilson*, 294.

68 Quoted in Sharpe and Roach, *Brian Dickson*, 387.

69 Bertha Wilson, "Decision-Making in the Supreme Court," *University of Toronto Law Journal* 36 (1986), 242-43.

70 Sharpe and Roach, *Brian Dickson*, 388.

71 The Court received open letters or submissions from the Canadian Civil Liberties Association, the Women's Legal Education and Action Fund (LEAF), the British Columbia Civil Liberties Association, and the Ontario Public Advocacy Centre.

72 Brodie, *Friends of the Court*, 34.

73 Ibid, 42.

74 Although Lamer J held in dismissing an application by the National Metis Council in *Dumont v Canada (Attorney General)*, [1989] 1 S.C.R. 279, that there must be a specific interest not represented by the existing parties. Crane and Brown, *Supreme Court of Canada Practice*, 343.

75 Brodie, *Friends of the Court*, 67. Citing *Reference re Workers' Compensation Act, 1983 (Nfld.) (Application to intervene)*, [1989] 2 S.C.R. 335.

76 In *M.(K.) v M.(H.)*, [1992] 3 S.C.R. 3 *[M.K.]*, and *Norberg v Wynrib*, [1992] 2 S.C.R. 224 *[Norberg]*, the Court has also allowed the admission of fresh evidence by interveners: "Generally speaking, interveners are expected to take the case as they find it and cannot introduce new evidence. However, in public law cases where the evidence may be in the nature of 'legislative facts,' the Court is more generous." Crane and Brown, *Supreme Court of Canada Practice*, 353.

77 Crane and Brown, *Supreme Court of Canada Practice*, 343.

78 In *R. v Zundel*, [1992] 2 S.C.R. 731, the Canadian Civil Liberties Association, the Canadian Jewish Congress, and the League for Human Rights of the B'Nai Brith were allowed to intervene, while the Canadian Holocaust Remembrance Association and Simon Weisenthal were not. In *R. v Morgentaler*, [1993] 3 S.C.R. 463, Sopinka J refused to allow the Canadian Abortion Rights Action League to add a new ground to the list of constitutional challenges already raised in the case, after allowing LEAF to do so in the *M(K)* and *Norberg* cases. And in *Lavigne v Ontario Public Service Employees Union*, [1991] 2 S.C.R. 211, the Court forced the National Citizens Coalition to pay the costs of four trade union federations that intervened to defend the law being challenged. On this latter case, Brodie writes that "it is hard to avoid concluding that the Court will let LEAF push the envelope on intervention but penalize the NCC for challenging the power of Canada's trade unions." Brodie, *Friends of the Court*, 69-71.

79 John C. Major, "Interveners and the Supreme Court of Canada," *National* 8(3) (1999), 27. Cited in Crane and Brown, *Supreme Court of Canada Practice*, 343.

80 Luiza Chwialkowska, "Rein in Lobby Groups, Senior Judges Suggest," *National Post* (6 April 2000), A1-2. Cited in Anderson, *Judging Bertha Wilson*, 299.

81 John Jaffey, "Charter Has 'Enhanced Democracy,' Iacobucci Tells Toronto Audience," *Lawyers Weekly* 23(44) (2004).

82 Brodie, for example, argues that the Court's acceptance of third party interveners and the political nature of judicial review make the "legalistic" justifications for judicial review problematic. Brodie, *Friends of the Court*, 73-74.

83 Christopher P. Manfredi, *Feminist Activism in the Supreme Court: Legal Mobilization and the Women's Legal Education and Action Fund* (Vancouver: UBC Press, 2004), 151.

84 *Reference re Anti-Inflation Act*, [1976] 2 S.C.R. 373.

85 Iacobucci, "The Charter," 385 [emphasis in original].

86 Ibid, 397.

87 *R. v Oakes*, [1986] 1 S.C.R. 103.

88 Sharpe and Roach, *The Charter of Rights and Freedoms*, 84.

89 Jaffey, "Charter Has 'Enhanced Democracy.'"

90 Iacobucci, "The Charter," 389.

91 Sharpe and Roach, *The Charter of Rights and Freedoms*, 84, citing *RJR-MacDonald v Canada (Attorney General)*, [1995] 3 S.C.R. 199.

92 Sharpe and Roach, *The Charter of Rights and Freedoms*, 84, citing *R. v Edwards Books and Art*, [1986] 2 S.C.R. 713.

93 The clerk also suggested that the Court might better be equipped to evaluate social science evidence if it had an institutionalized mechanism, such as a committee of different experts it could consult. The clerk admitted, however, that this solution would possibly present problems related to judicial independence (Interview).

94 Bertha Wilson, "We Didn't Volunteer," in *Judicial Power and Canadian Democracy*, edited by Paul Howe and Peter Russell (Montreal and Kingston: McGill-Queen's University Press, 2001).

95 Swinton, *The Supreme Court and Canadian Federalism*, 320.

96 Rosalie Silberman Abella, "The Dynamic Nature of Equality," in *Equality and Judicial Neutrality*, edited by Sheilah L. Martin and Kathleen E. Mahoney (Toronto: Carswell, 1987), 8-9.

97 Michel Bastarache, "The Challenge of Law in the New Millenium," *Manitoba Law Journal* 25 (1997-98), 412.

98 Kirk Makin, "Plain-Talking Estey: After Eleven Years Sitting on the Supreme Court, Retiring Justice Plans Clean Break with Law," *Globe and Mail* (27 April 1988), A1.

99 Bastarache, "The Challenge of Law in the New Millenium," 412.

100 Parliament of Canada, Standing Committee on Justice, Human Rights, Public Safety and Emergency Preparedness, *Evidence*, Meeting No. 8, 37th Parliament, 3rd Session (30 March 2004), http://www.parl.gc.ca/committee/CommitteePublication.aspx?SourceId=76982.

101 Philip Girard, *Bora Laskin: Bringing Law to Life* (Toronto: Osgoode Society for Canadian Legal History, 2005), 97.

102 Ibid, 101, citing Jerome Frank, *Law and the Modern Mind* (London: Stevens, 1930).

103 Girard, *Bora Laskin,* citing Bora Laskin, *The Institutional Character of the Judge* (Jerusalem, Israel: Jerusalem Post Press, 1972).

104 Girard, *Bora Laskin,* 366.

105 Beverley McLachlin, "The Charter of Rights and Freedoms: A Judicial Perspective," *University of British Columbia Law Review* 23 (1989), 579-90; Beverley McLachlin, "The Charter: A New Role for the Judiciary?" *Alberta Law Review* 29(3) (1991), 540-59; Beverley McLachlin, "The Demystification of the Judiciary" (Speech to the McGill Law Journal Seventh Annual Alumni Lecture, Montreal, 19 February 1991); Beverley McLachlin, "Rules and Discretion in the Governance of Canada," *Saskatchewan Law Review* 56 (1992), 167-79; Beverley McLachlin, "The Role of Judges in Modern Commonwealth Society," *Law Quarterly Review* 110 (1994), 260-69; Beverley McLachlin, "The Supreme Court and the Public Interest," *Saskatchewan Law Review* 64 (2001), 309-21; Beverley McLachlin, "On Impartiality" (Address at University of Waikato, Hamilton, New Zealand, 23 April 2003).

106 McLachlin, "On Impartiality."

107 McLachlin, "The Supreme Court and the Public Interest," 316.

108 McLachlin, "On Impartiality."

109 Ibid.

110 Though McLachlin J admits that in such instances, "the weight one assigns to different factors often depends, at least in part, on one's own values, and on which other individuals' or groups' perspectives one is acquainted with." Ibid.

111 C.L. Ostberg and Matthew Wetstein, *Attitudinal Decision-Making in the Supreme Court of Canada* (Vancouver: UBC Press, 2007), 45.

112 Cristin Schmitz, "Bastarache Explains Dissents in One-Third of SCC Decisions," *Lawyer's Weekly* 20(34) (19 January 2001).

113 W.H. McConnell, *William R. McIntyre: Paladin of Common Law* (Montreal and Kingston: McGill-Queen's University Press, 2000).

114 Cristin Schmitz, "Former Chief Justice Offers a View from the Top," *Lawyer's Weekly* 21(44) (29 March 2002).

115 Quoted in Cristin Schmitz, "Justice Jack Major Reflects on Dealing with Life, Death as a Supreme Court Judge," *Lawyer's Weekly* 22(34) (17 January 2003).

116 Quoted in Cristin Schmitz, "Our One-on-One with Justice Claire L'Heureux-Dubé," *Lawyer's Weekly* 22(3) (17 May 2002).

117 Ostberg and Wetstein, *Attitudinal Decision-Making in the Supreme Court of Canada.*

118 L'Heureux-Dubé J was the only justice for whom this distinction was made, according to the newspaper reports Ostberg and Wetstein relied on to score judicial ideologies.

119 McLachlin, "The Charter: A New Role for the Judiciary?" 547-48.

120 *Egan v Canada,* [1995] 2 S.C.R. 513; *Vriend v Alberta,* [1998] 1 S.C.R. 493; *M. v H.,* [1999] 2 S.C.R. 3.

121 *Auton (Guardian ad litem of) v British Columbia (Attorney General),* 2004 SCC 78, [2004] 3 S.C.R. 657; *Newfoundland (Treasury Board) v N.A.P.E.,* 2004 SCC 66, [2004] 3 S.C.R. 381.

122 *Irwin Toy ltd. v Quebec (Attorney general),* [1989] 1 S.C.R. 927.

123 Matthew E. Wetstein et al., "Ideological Consistency and Attitudinal Conflict: A Comparative Analysis of the U.S. and Canadian Supreme Courts," *Comparative Political Studies* 42(6) (2009), 767.

124 Ibid, 772.

125 Ibid, 780.

126 Ibid, 782-83.

127 Ibid, 783.

128 Ibid.

129 Carol Gilligan, *In a Different Voice: Psychological Theory and Women's Development* (Cambridge, MA: Harvard University Press, 1982).

130 Bertha Wilson, "Will Women Judges Really Make a Difference?" *Osgoode Hall Law Journal* 28 (1990), 507-22 [emphasis in original].

131 Donald R. Songer, *The Transformation of the Supreme Court of Canada: An Empirical Analysis* (Toronto: University of Toronto Press, 2008), 206-9.

132 Ostberg and Wetstein, *Attitudinal Decision Making in the Supreme Court of Canada,* 120.

133   Ibid, 134-39.
134   Ibid, 144, 157.
135   *R. v Lavallee,* [1990] 1 S.C.R. 852.
136   Donna Martinson, *"Lavallee v. R.:* The Supreme Court of Canada Addresses Gender Bias in the Courts," *University of British Columbia Law Review* 24(2) (1990), 381.
137   Quoted in Tracey Tyler, "The Legal 'Sticky Floor,'" *Toronto Star* (15 August 2006), A09.
138   Peter McCormick and Ian Greene, *Judges and Judging: Inside the Canadian Judicial System* (Toronto: James Lorimer, 1990), 203.
139   Daved Muttart, *The Empirical Gap in Jurisprudence: A Comprehensive Study of the Supreme Court of Canada* (Toronto: University of Toronto Press, 2007), 88.
140   Justices were coded liberal, moderate, or conservative based on Ostberg and Wetstein's newspaper scores, where justices scoring in the middle range (from 0.499 to –0.499) are labelled moderate. Dickson and Beetz JJ are not included in the table, as there was no ideological commentary in the newspapers. Scores for Abella, Charron, Rothstein, Cromwell, Moldaver, and Karakatsanis JJ were tabulated by approximating the methodology described in Ostberg and Wetstein, *Attitudinal Decision Making in the Supreme Court of Canada,* 52-54.
141   Only six of the *Charter*-era justices have voting records in criminal cases that are more conservative than that of La Forest J, according to Ostberg and Wetstein, *Attitudinal Decision Making in the Supreme Court of Canada,* 76.

Chapter 3: Setting the Stage

  1   The first comprehensive description of the Court's administration in the scholarly literature was published drawing on research conducted for this book. See Emmett Macfarlane, "Administration at the Supreme Court of Canada: Challenges and Change in the Charter Era," *Canadian Public Administration* 52(1) (2009), 1-21.
  2   This, despite the fact the "puisne" is derived from the old French term for "junior" or "inferior in rank."
  3   Peter McCormick, "Assessing Leadership on the Supreme Court of Canada: Towards a Typology of Chief Justice Performance," *Supreme Court Law Review* 4 (1993), 419.
  4   Ibid, 421.
  5   Jack Batten, *Judges* (Toronto: Macmillan of Canada, 1986), 307.
  6   The puisne judges of the Court can also perform this latter function, if necessary.
  7   James MacPherson, "Working within the Dickson Court," in *The Dickson Legacy,* edited by Roland Penner (Winnipeg, MB: Legal Research Institute, University of Manitoba, 1992), 271.
  8   Philip Girard, *Bora Laskin: Bringing Law to Life* (Toronto: Osgoode Society for Canadian Legal History, 2005), 431.
  9   *Canadian Charter of Rights and Freedoms,* Part 1 of the *Constitution Act, 1982,* being Schedule B to the *Canada Act 1982* (U.K.), 1982, c. 11.
 10   Mitchell McInnes, Janet Bolton, and Natalie Derzko, "Clerking at the Supreme Court of Canada," *Alberta Law Review* 33(1) (1994), 61.
 11   McInnes, Bolton, and Derzko describe the actual process after interviews are conducted: "By right of position, the Chief Justice is entitled to hire three clerks immediately. Among the puisne judges, the remaining process very much resembles a draft in a sports league. Each judge is permitted to select one candidate at a time, in descending order of seniority with the Court. Thus, once the most junior judge has announced his or her first pick, the most senior judge is permitted a second selection, and so on until all positions have been filled." Ibid, 64.
 12   Robert J. Sharpe and Kent Roach, *Brian Dickson: A Judge's Journey* (Toronto: University of Toronto Press, 2003), 371.
 13   Brian A. Crane and Henry S. Brown, *Supreme Court of Canada Practice* (Toronto: Thomson Canada, 2008), 5.
 14   James G. Snell and Frederick Vaughan, *The Supreme Court of Canada: History of the Institution* (Toronto: Osgoode Society for Canadian Legal History, 1985), 240n17.
 15   Claire L'Heureux-Dubé, "The Length and Plurality of Supreme Court of Canada Decisions," *Alberta Law Review* 28 (1990), 585.

16 Daved Muttart, *The Empirical Gap in Jurisprudence: A Comprehensive Study of the Supreme Court of Canada* (Toronto: University of Toronto Press, 2007), 102; Donald Songer finds that the length of the Court's opinions increased dramatically after the *Charter,* across all areas of law. Donald Songer, *The Transformation of the Supreme Court of Canada: An Empirical Analysis* (Toronto: University of Toronto Press, 2008), 153.

17 Lorne Sossin, "The Sounds of Silence: Law Clerks, Policy Making and the Supreme Court of Canada," *University of British Columbia Law Review* 30(2) (1996), 279-308; F.L. Morton and Rainer Knopff, *The Charter Revolution and the Court Party* (Peterborough, ON: Broadview Press, 2000), 146-47.

18 Sharpe and Roach, *Brian Dickson,* 370-75.

19 Ibid, 374.

20 Carl Baar, "The Chief Justice as Court Administrator 1984-1990," in *Brian Dickson at the Supreme Court of Canada: 1973-1990,* edited by DeLloyd J. Guth (Winnipeg, MB: Canadian Legal History Project, 1998), 313.

21 Ibid, 316.

22 Cristin Schmitz, "SCC's Resources Now 'Stretched to the Limit,' McLachlin Tells CBA," *Lawyer's Weekly* 21(15) (24 August 2001).

23 In 1997, changes to the *Supreme Court Act,* R.S.C. 1985, c. S-26, eliminated appeals by right in criminal cases where acquittals were overturned on appeal, cutting the number of appeals by right by about half.

24 Cristin Schmitz, "Chief Justice McLachlin Discusses Terrorism, Liberty, Live Webcasting of Appeals," *Lawyer's Weekly* 21(33) (11 January 2002).

25 Canadian Press, "New Justice Building to Honour Trudeau," *Globe and Mail* (3 December 2003), A7.

26 Courts Administration Service, *Departmental Performance Report: 2006-2007* (Ottawa: Treasury Board of Canada, 2007), 20.

27 Supreme Court of Canada, *Bulletin of Proceedings: Special Edition Statistics 1996-2006* (Ottawa: Treasury Board of Canada, 2007), 4.

28 Cristin Schmitz, "'McLachlin Court' Sets Record Time for Rendering Judgment in 2004," *Lawyer's Weekly* 24(41) (11 March 2005).

29 Supreme Court of Canada, *Performance Report: For the Period Ending March 31, 2007* (Ottawa: Treasury Board of Canada, 2007), 5.

30 Bertha Wilson, "Decision-Making in the Supreme Court," *University of Toronto Law Journal* 36 (1986), 237.

31 The remaining cases are certain criminal appeals as of right and government references, explored later in this chapter.

32 Morton and Knopff, *The Charter Revolution and the Court Party.*

33 The controversy took place after Justice Douglas Abbott, recently appointed from the federal cabinet and with no prior judicial experience, refused to grant leave in a widely covered murder case. *R. v Coffin,* [1956] S.C.R. 191. Cited in Brian A. Crane and Henry S. Brown, *Supreme Court of Canada Practice* (Toronto: Thomson Canada, 2008), 5, n. 36. For details on the case and the ensuing controversy, see Snell and Vaughan, *The Supreme Court of Canada,* 209-10. *Criminal Code,* R.S.C. 1985, c. C-46. *Supreme Court Act,* R.S.C. 1985, c. S-26.

34 Crane and Brown, *The Supreme Court of Canada Practice,* 96.

35 Ibid, 30.

36 *Civil Code of Québec,* S.Q. 1991, c. 64 (CCQ).

37 Roy B. Flemming, *Tournament of Appeals: Granting Judicial Review in Canada* (Vancouver: UBC Press, 2004), 15.

38 Crane and Brown, *The Supreme Court of Canada Practice,* 96.

39 Text of a speech delivered by Justice John Sopinka, "The Supreme Court of Canada" (Toronto, 10 April 1997), reprinted with permission in Crane and Brown, *The Supreme Court of Canada Practice,* 482.

40 Ian Greene et al., *Final Appeal: Decision-Making in Canadian Courts of Appeal* (Toronto: James Lorimer, 1998), 108.

41 Crane and Brown, *The Supreme Court of Canada Practice,* 96-97.

42 Flemming, *Tournament of Appeals,* 3-4.

43 Ibid, 4.

44 Ibid, 57.

45 Flemming cites Peter McCormick, "Party Capability Theory and Appellate Success in the Supreme Court of Canada, 1949-1992," *Canadian Journal of Political Science* 26(3) (1993), 523-40, and F.L. Morton and Avril Allen, "Feminists and the Courts: Measuring Success in Interest Group Litigation in Canada," *Canadian Journal of Political Science* 34(1) (2001), 55-84. See also Christopher P. Manfredi, *Feminist Activism in the Supreme Court of Canada: Legal Mobilization and the Women's Legal Education and Action Fund* (Vancouver: UBC Press, 2004).

46 Flemming, *Tournament of Appeals*, 58.

47 Ibid, 40.

48 Ibid, 100.

49 Ibid, 83.

50 Ibid, 95.

51 Quoted in Crane and Brown, *The Supreme Court of Canada Practice*, 19, citing *R. v Hinse*, [1995] 4 S.C.R. 597 at 609.

52 Sopinka, "The Supreme Court of Canada," 482.

53 Flemming, *Tournament of Appeals*, 68-70.

54 Sopinka, "The Supreme Court of Canada," 481. One example was the issue of unreasonable delay in trial proceedings in *R. v Askov*, [1990] 2 S.C.R. 1199 *[Askov]*, in which the Court's ruling prompted the lower courts to dismiss thousands of cases. The Court revisited the issue in *R. v Morin*, [1992] 1 S.R.C. 771. See Carl Baar, "Court Delay Data as Social Science Evidence: The Supreme Court of Canada and 'Trial within a Reasonable Time,'" *Justice System Journal* 19(2) (1997), 123-44.

55 John Sopinka and Mark A. Gelowitz, *The Conduct of an Appeal* (Toronto: Butterworths Canada, 1993), 167.

56 Bertha Wilson, "Leave to Appeal to the Supreme Court of Canada," *Advocates' Quarterly* 4(1) (1983), 2.

57 Ibid, 3. Wilson appears to be in the minority in this thinking. Writing in 1993, Sopinka J contends that "[o]n a fundamental level, whether or not the Court of Appeal was 'wrong' has little if anything to do with whether the case is one of public importance." Sopinka and Gelowitz, *The Conduct of an Appeal*, 166-67.

58 Flemming, *Tournament of Appeals*, 91.

59 Ibid, 97.

60 According to his biographer, Laskin CJ "often" insisted on granting leave to cases out of personal interest, something that bothered his colleagues. There is no evidence, anecdotal or otherwise, that any justices serving more recently took a similar approach. Girard, *Bora Laskin*, 428.

61 Mitchell McInnes, Janet Bolton, and Natalie Derzko, "Clerking at the Supreme Court of Canada," *Alberta Law Review* 33(1) (1994), 61-62.

62 Ibid, 71.

63 McInnes, Bolton, and Derzko note that at the time of their writing in 1994, only one justice on the Court required this. Ibid, 72. Wilson J, who retired earlier than then, is said to have required memos for applications for leave to appeal at a time when many of the other justices did not require them of their own clerks. See Ellen Anderson, *Judging Bertha Wilson: Law as Large as Life* (Toronto: University of Toronto Press, 2001), 160.

64 McInnes, Bolton, and Derzko, "Clerking at the Supreme Court of Canada," 73.

65 Sossin, "The Sounds of Silence," 290.

66 Ibid.

67 Flemming, *Tournament of Appeals*, 12.

68 The average number of appeals by right was fifty-three per year in the five years leading up to the change, down to an average of nineteen per year from 1998 to 2002.

69 Schmitz, "Chief Justice McLachlin Discusses Terrorism, Liberty, Live Webcasting of Appeals."

70 Schmitz, "SCC's Resources Now 'Stretched to the Limit,' McLachlin Tells CBA."

71 Bora Laskin, *The Institutional Character of the Judge* (Jerusalem, Israel: Jerusalem Post Press, 1972), 14.

72 Anderson, *Judging Bertha Wilson,* 243.

73 Ibid, 243.

74 Cristin Schmitz, "Leaving after Fifteen Years on Bench, Justice L'Heureux-Dubé Says She's 'Extremely Serene,'" *Lawyer's Weekly* 22(2) (10 May 2002).

75 W.H. McConnell, *William R. McIntyre: Paladin of Common Law* (Montreal and Kingston: McGill-Queen's University Press, 2000), 90; Kirk Makin, "Supreme Court in the Spotlight: In the Post-Charter Era, Judges Face More Pressure and Plenty of Second Guessing," *Globe and Mail* (17 April 2002), A10.

76 Cristin Schmitz, "Chief Justice Defends Supreme Court and Legal Profession," *Lawyers Weekly* 27(15) (24 August 2007).

77 This power is laid out in section 53 of the *Supreme Court Act.*

78 The High Court of Australia's refusal was based on this reason. *Re Judiciary and Navigation Act,* (1921) 29 C.L.R. 257. The Supreme Court of the United States refused through informal communication between the justices and President Washington in 1793. It is believed the "cases" and "controversies" requirements under the judicial functions outlined under Article III of the United States Constitution precludes advisory opinions. See Peter W. Hogg, *Constitutional Law of Canada* (Scarborough, ON: Thomson Canada, 2003), 242.

79 See *A.-G. Ont. v A.-G. Can (Local Prohibition),* [1896] A.C. 348, 370; *Re Objection by Que. to Resolution to Amend the Constitution,* [1982] 2 S.C.R. 793, 806; *Re Can. Assistance Plan* [1991] 2 S.C.R. 524 at 545; *McEvoy v A.-G. N.B.,* [1983] 1 S.C.R. 704, 705-15, cited by Hogg, *Constitutional Law of Canada,* 243-44.

80 As acknowledged by the Court itself in *Reference re Same-Sex Marriage,* 2004 SCC 79, [2004] 3 S.C.R. 698, para. 61.

81 *Reference re Goods and Services Tax,* [1992] 2 S.C.R. 445, para. 485; *Reference re Remuneration of Judges of the Provincial Court of Prince Edward Island,* [1997] 3 S.C.R. 3, para. 256, cited in *Reference re Same-Sex Marriage,* para. 63.

82 *Reference re Authority of Parliament in Relation to the Upper House,* [1980] 1 S.C.R. 54, 75-77; *Reference re Remuneration of Judges of the Provincial Court of Prince Edward Island,* para. 257, cited in *Reference re Same-Sex Marriage,* para. 63.

83 John McEvoy, "Separation of Powers and the Reference Power: Is There a Right to Refuse?" *Supreme Court Law Review* 10 (1988), 429; John McEvoy, "Refusing to Answer: The Supreme Court and the Reference Power Revisited," *University of New Brunswick Law Journal* 29 (2005), 29. See also Grant Huscroft, "Political Litigation and the Role of the Court," *Supreme Court Law Review* 34 (2006), 35-56.

84 Hogg, *Constitutional Law of Canada,* 243.

85 *Reference re Same-Sex Marriage.*

86 Ibid, para. 70.

87 Ibid, para. 68.

88 Hogg, *Constitutional Law of Canada,* 244, citing *Re Resolution to Amend the Constitution,* [1981] 1 S.C.R. 753, and *Re Objection by Que. to Resolution to Amend the Constitution.*

89 Hogg, *Constitutional Law of Canada,* 244.

90 Huscroft, "Political Litigation and the Role of the Court."

91 Ibid, 45.

92 Peter Russell, *The Supreme Court of Canada as a Bilingual and Bicultural Institution* (Ottawa: Queen's Printer, 1969), 80.

93 Sharpe and Roach, *Brian Dickson,* 295. The authors note that Estey J wrote in a memo to his colleagues that long hearings were a "microcosm" of the "problem of this Court."

94 Some of the clerks I interviewed who served in the 1980s and early 1990s indicated that they rarely had time to attend the hearings. This may be the result of the clerks' having to work on applications for leave until 1996. All of the clerks I interviewed who served on the Court since then normally attend the hearings.

95 Michael John Herman, "Law Clerking at the Supreme Court of Canada," *Osgoode Hall Law Journal* 13(2) (1975), 280-81.

96 Sharpe and Roach, *Brian Dickson,* 209.

97 This conclusion is also reached by Sossin, "The Sounds of Silence," 292.

98   Lori Hausegger and Stacia Haynie, "Judicial Decisionmaking and the Use of Panels in the Canadian Supreme Court and the South African Appellate Division," *Law and Society Review* 37(3) (2003), 635-57.

99   Ibid, 651.

100   Ibid.

101   Greene et al., *Final Appeal*, 115.

102   Songer, *The Transformation of the Supreme Court of Canada*, 116.

103   Snell and Vaughan, *The Supreme Court of Canada*, 44.

104   According to Snell and Vaughan, the Court first instituted restrictions on oral hearings in 1907, when a new rule limited the number of counsel to be heard for each side to two and the time of argument to three hours. Ibid, 100. By the 1970s and 1980s, this rule seems to have evolved into a system by which lawyers would advise the Court registrar of the amount of time they required for oral argument. The policy came to frustrate the justices, particularly Estey J, who, in the midst of the case backlog, noted in a memo to colleagues that never-ending hearings were a "microcosm" of the "problem of this Court." Sharpe and Roach, *Brian Dickson*, 295.

105   John Sopinka, "Advocacy in the Top Court," *National* 4(4) (1995), 42.

106   Saul Brenner, "Fluidity on the United States Supreme Court: A Re-Examination," *American Journal of Political Science* 24 (1980), 380-86.

107   Clerks were asked how often their justice changed their minds during the course of deciding a case. Six clerks interviewed refused to answer the question on the basis of confidentiality. Of the remaining fifteen, only one clerk did not recall the justice ever changing his or her mind, and two clerks indicated not being privy to their justices' mindset going into oral hearings.

108   Indeed, until recently, the oral arguments at the Supreme Court of the United States were largely treated as unimportant by scholars of judicial behaviour. See Timothy R. Johnson, *Oral Arguments and Decision Making on the United States Supreme Court* (Albany, NY: State University of New York Press, 2004); Lawrence S. Wrightsman, *Oral Arguments before the Supreme Court: An Empirical Approach* (New York: Oxford University Press, 2008).

109   Lawrence Baum, *The Puzzle of Judicial Behavior* (Ann Arbor, MI: University of Michigan Press, 1997), 105-9.

110   Michel Bastarache, "Passion and Advocacy in the Supreme Court of Canada" (Address to the Joint Conference of the Canadian Bar Association's National Aboriginal Law Section and the Indigenous Bar Association, Ottawa, 5 March 2005).

111   Ibid.

112   John Sopinka, "Advocacy in the Top Court," *National* 4(4) (1995), 40.

113   Antonin Scalia and Bryan A. Garner have written about the oral hearing in the American context. Antonin Scalia and Bryan A. Garner, *Making Your Case: The Art of Persuading Judges* (St. Paul, MN: Thomson West, 2008).

114   Peter McCormick and Ian Greene, *Judges and Judging: Inside the Canadian Judicial System* (Toronto: James Lorimer, 1990), 200.

115   *Askov.*

116   *Reference re Secession of Quebec,* [1998] 2 S.C.R. 217.

117   Wilson, "The Decision-Making Process in the Supreme Court of Canada."

Chapter 4: The Decision

1   *Canadian Charter of Rights and Freedoms,* Part 1 of the *Constitution Act, 1982,* being Schedule B to the *Canada Act 1982* (U.K.), 1982, c. 11.

2   "The Supreme Court," *Canada Law Journal* 38(3) (1902), 63.

3   James G. Snell and Frederick Vaughan, *The Supreme Court of Canada: History of the Institution* (Toronto: Osgoode Society for Canadian Legal History, 1985), 35.

4   Ibid, 76.

5   Donald E. Fouts, "Policy-Making in the Supreme Court of Canada, 1950-1960," in *Comparative Judicial Behavior: Cross-Cultural Studies of Political Decision-Making in the East and West,* edited by Glendon Schubert and David J. Danelski (New York: Oxford University Press, 1969), 263.

6 Peter McCormick, *Supreme at Last: The Evolution of the Supreme Court of Canada* (Toronto: James Lorimer, 2000), 64.

7 Bertha Wilson, "Decision-Making in the Supreme Court," *University of Toronto Law Journal* 36 (1986), 236.

8 Peter McCormick and Ian Greene, *Judges and Judging: Inside the Canadian Judicial System* (Toronto: James Lorimer, 1990), 203.

9 Robert J. Sharpe and Kent Roach, *Brian Dickson: A Judge's Journey* (Toronto: Osgoode Society for Canadian Legal History, 2003), 301-3.

10 Ibid, 301-3.

11 Peter H. Russell, *The Judiciary in Canada: The Third Branch of Government* (Toronto: McGraw-Hill Ryerson, 1987), 26.

12 Sharpe and Roach's access to Court papers leads them to conclude that some justices were very blunt in the discussion (Ronald Martin, Louis-Phillippe Pigeon, and Bora Laskin JJ), others were slow to make firm decisions (Jean Beetz J), and others rarely spoke (Wilfred Judson J). Sharpe and Roach, *Brian Dickson*, 144.

13 Philip Girard, *Bora Laskin: Bringing Law to Life* (Toronto: Osgoode Society for Canadian Legal History, 2005), 432.

14 Cristin Schmitz, "The Bastarache Interview: 'Overall, This Is Not a Frustrating Job,'" *Lawyer's Weekly* 20(36) (2 February 2001).

15 McCormick, *Supreme at Last*, 134-35.

16 C.L. Ostberg and Matthew Wetstein, *Attitudinal Decision-Making in the Supreme Court of Canada* (Vancouver: UBC Press, 2007), 211.

17 Ellen Anderson, *Judging Bertha Wilson: Law as Large as Life* (Toronto: University of Toronto Press, 2001), 152.

18 Donald R. Songer, *The Transformation of the Supreme Court of Canada: An Empirical Examination* (Toronto: University of Toronto Press, 2008), 128-29.

19 Brian Dickson, "A Life in the Law: The Process of Judging," *Saskatchewan Law Review* 63 (2000), 382-83 (from an address given in 1992).

20 Anderson, *Judging Bertha Wilson*, 152.

21 Peter McCormick, "Judicial Career Patterns and the Delivery of Reasons for Judgment in the Supreme Court of Canada, 1949-1993," *Supreme Court Law Review* 5 (1994), 514.

22 *Reference re Public Service Employee Relations Act (Alta.)*, [1987] 1 S.C.R. 313; *PSAC v Canada*, [1987] 1 S.C.R. 424; *RWDSU v Saskatchewan*, [1987] 1 S.C.R. 460.

23 Sharpe and Roach, *Brian Dickson*, 358.

24 Bob Woodward and Scott Armstrong, *The Brethren: Inside the Supreme Court* (New York: Avon Books, 1979), 71 and 201.

25 F.L. Morton and Rainer Knopff, *The Charter Revolution and the Court Party* (Toronto: Broadview Press, 2000), 110.

26 Ibid.

27 Sharpe and Roach, *Brian Dickson*, 334. See also *R. v Oakes*, [1986] 1 S.C.R. 103.

28 Ibid, 359.

29 Ibid, 202.

30 Anderson, *Judging Bertha Wilson*, 161 [emphasis in original].

31 Bob Babinski, "Backstage at the Supreme Court," *Canadian Lawyer* 17(3) (1993), 11.

32 *R. v Vaillancourt*, [1987] 2 S.C.R. 636. *Criminal Code*, R.S.C. 1985, c. C-46.

33 *R. v Martineau*, [1990] 2 S.C.R. 633.

34 Babinski, "Backstage at the Supreme Court," 11.

35 See, for example, Lee Epstein and Jack Knight, *The Choices Justices Make* (Washington, DC: Congressional Quarterly, 1998), 65-79.

36 Schmitz, "The Bastarache Interview."

37 John Sopinka, "Advocacy in the Top Court," *National* 4(4) (1995), 42.

38 Parliament of Canada, Standing Committee on Justice, Human Rights, Public Safety and Emergency Preparedness, *Evidence*, Meeting No. 8, 37th Parliament, 3rd Session (30 March 2004) at 1545, http://www.parl.gc.ca/committee/.

39 Sharpe and Roach, *Brian Dickson*.

40 *Borowski v Canada (Attorney General)*, [1989] 1 S.C.R. 342.

41 Sharpe and Roach, *Brian Dickson*, 391-92.
42 *R. v. Morgentaler*, [1988] 1 S.C.R. 30.
43 Sharpe and Roach, *Brian Dickson*, 352. *R. v Edwards Books and Art*, [1986] 2 S.C.R. 713.
44 Sharpe and Roach, *Brian Dickson*, 405. *R. v Ogg-Moss*, [1984] 2 S.C.R. 173.
45 Sharpe and Roach, *Brian Dickson*, 406. *R. v Lavallee*, [1990] 1 S.C.R. 852.
46 Ian Greene et al., *Final Appeal: Decision-Making in Canadian Courts of Appeal* (Toronto: James Lorimer, 1998), 121.
47 Sharpe and Roach, *Brian Dickson*, xi.
48 Anderson, *Judging Bertha Wilson*, 162-63; Lorne Sossin, "The Sounds of Silence: Law Clerks, Policy Making and the Supreme Court of Canada," *University of British Columbia Law Review* 30(2) (1996), 295n48.
49 Anderson, *Judging Bertha Wilson*, 162-63.
50 Ibid, 164.
51 Ibid.
52 Cristin Schmitz, "Former Chief Justice Lamer Reflects on His Brightest, Darkest Moments as Canada's Top Jurist," *Lawyer's Weekly* 21(44) (29 March 2002).
53 Kirk Makin, "Lobbying Hurt Court, Book Says Backroom Deals among Top-Court Judges Threatened Charter, Wilson felt," *Globe and Mail* (11 March 2002), A9.
54 Anderson, *Judging Bertha Wilson*, 164-65.
55 Ibid, 415n12.
56 Ibid, 165.
57 Wilson, "Decision-Making at the Supreme Court," 237.
58 Sossin, "The Sounds of Silence," 295n48.
59 Ibid, 294-95.
60 Anderson, *Judging Bertha Wilson*, 164.
61 McCormick, *Supreme at Last*, 92.
62 Ibid, 134-35, 155-56. See also Kirk Makin, "It Fundamentally Changed the Justice System," *Globe and Mail* (10 April 2007), A7.
63 Makin, "Lobbying Hurt Court," A9.
64 Peter McCormick, "Blocs, Swarms, and Outliers: Conceptualizing Disagreement on the Modern Supreme Court of Canada," *Osgoode Hall Law Journal* 42(1) (2004), 134. See also Daved Muttart, *The Empirical Gap in Jurisprudence: A Comprehensive Study of the Supreme Court of Canada* (Toronto: University of Toronto Press, 2007).
65 Cristin Schmitz, "Our One-On-One with Justice Claire L'Heureux-Dubé," *Lawyer's Weekly* 22(3) (17 May 2002).
66 McCormick, "Blocs, Swarms, and Outliers," 135.
67 Ostberg and Wetstein, *Attitudinal Decision-Making in the Supreme Court of Canada*, 212.
68 Kirk Makin, "'We Are Not Gunslingers,'" *Globe and Mail* (9 April 2002), A4.
69 In *Judging Bertha Wilson*, Ellen Anderson makes the distinction between "collegiality" and "congeniality" (153).
70 Sharpe and Roach, *Brian Dickson*, 312.
71 *Reference re Secession of Quebec*, [1998] 2 S.C.R. 217.
72 Kirk Makin, "Judicial Activism Debate on Decline, Top Judge Says," *Globe and Mail* (8 January 2005), A1.
73 Which the measures obtained by Ostberg and Wetstein's study clearly do not. Ostberg and Wetstein, *Attitudinal Decision Making in the Supreme Court of Canada*, 55.
74 Donald R. Songer and Julia Siripurapu, "The Unanimous Cases of the Supreme Court of Canada as a Test of the Attitudinal Model," *Canadian Journal of Political Science* 42(1) (2009), 65-92.
75 Wilson, "Decision-Making in the Supreme Court," 235-36.
76 L'Heureux-Dubé J has also written about this tension. Claire L'Heureux-Dubé, "The Length and Plurality of Supreme Court of Canada Decisions," *Alberta Law Review* 28 (1989-90), 586.
77 Cristin Schmitz, "Communication, Consensus among McLachlin's Targets," *Lawyer's Weekly* 19(27) (19 November 1999).

78 Supreme Court of Canada, *Statistics 1999-2009* (Ottawa: Supreme Court of Canada, 2010).
79 Songer, *The Transformation of the Supreme Court of Canada,* 213.
80 Richard A. Posner, *How Judges Think* (Cambridge, MA: Harvard University Press, 2008), 50.
81 McCormick, "Blocs, Swarms, and Outliers," 107.
82 Ibid, 123.
83 Ibid, 127.
84 Correspondence with Peter McCormick (13 July 2009), drawing on his Supreme Court of Canada database from the start of McLachlin CJ's term as chief justice to *Greater Vancouver Transportation Authority v Canadian Federation of Students - British Columbia Component,* 2009 SCC 31.
85 Songer, *The Transformation of the Supreme Court of Canada,* 116.
86 McCormick, "Blocs, Swarms, and Outliers," 130.
87 Schmitz, "The Bastarache Interview."
88 Ibid.
89 Anderson, *Judging Bertha Wilson,* 164.
90 Songer, *The Transformation of the Supreme Court of Canada,* 213; Muttart, *The Empirical Gap in Jurisprudence,* 109.
91 L'Heureux-Dubé J explains there are "strong pressures" for the Court to speak collectively "and usually in the most important cases." L'Heureux-Dubé, "The Length and Plurality of Supreme Court of Canada Decisions," 586.
92 Dickson, "A Life in the Law," 385 (from his address delivered in 1992).
93 Songer and Siripurapu, "Unanimous Decisions of the Supreme Court of Canada as a Test of the Attitudinal Model," 87.
94 Wilson, "Decision-Making in the Supreme Court," 235.
95 Schmitz, "The Bastarache Interview."
96 Sujit Choudhry and Robert Howse, "Constitutional Theory and the *Quebec Secession Reference,*" *Canadian Journal of Law and Jurisprudence* 13(2) (2000), 166.
97 Robert A. Young, *The Struggle for Quebec* (Montreal and Kingston: McGill-Queen's University Press, 1999), 146.
98 Peter H. Russell et al., *The Court and the Constitution: Leading Cases* (Toronto: Emond Montgomery Publications, 2008), 543.
99 Ibid, 542.
100 *Reference re Secession of Quebec,* [1998] 2 S.C.R. 217, para. 153.
101 Peter Leslie, "Canada: The Supreme Court Sets Rules for the Secession of Quebec," *Publius* 29(2) (1999), 149-50.
102 Young, *The Struggle for Quebec,* 147; Russell et al., *The Court and the Constitution,* 543; Choudhry and Howse, "Constitutional Theory and the *Quebec Secession Reference,*" 166.
103 *Reference re Secession of Quebec,* para. 98 [emphasis in original].
104 Ibid, para. 100.
105 *Tremblay v Daigle,* [1989] 2 S.C.R. 530.
106 *Charter of Human Rights and Freedoms,* R.S.Q., c. C-12, s. 10.
107 Sharpe and Roach, *Brian Dickson,* 394-95.
108 *Law v Canada (Minister of Employment and Immigration),* [1999] 1 S.C.R. 497.
109 *Andrews v Law Society of British Columbia,* [1989] 1 S.C.R. 143. The justices were unanimous on the approach but divided over the outcome of the particular case.
110 The grounds enumerated in section 15(1) are race, national or ethnic origin, colour, religion, sex, age, or mental or physical disability. Over the years, the Court has identified several analogous grounds: marital status (*Miron v Trudel,* [1995] 2 S.C.R. 418); sexual orientation (*Egan v Canada,* [1995] 2 S.C.R. 513) citizenship/non-citizenship (*Andrews*); and off-reserve residence for Aboriginals (*Corbere v Canada [Minister of Indian and Northern Affairs]*), [1999] 2 S.C.R. 203).
111 See *Egan* and *Miron.*
112 *Law,* para. 53.
113 Ibid, para. 54.
114 Ibid, para. 88.

115   Debra M. McAllister, "Section 15: The Unpredictability of the *Law* Test," *National Journal of Constitutional Law* 15 (2003), 35; Robert J. Sharpe and Kent Roach, *The Charter of Rights and Freedoms*, 3rd edition (Toronto: Irwin Law, 2005), 293; Cristin Schmitz, "Mixed Reviews for 20th Anniversary of Section 15," *Lawyer's Weekly* 24(48) (29 April 2005); Sheila McIntyre and Sanda Rodgers, eds. *Diminishing Returns: Inequality and the Canadian Charter of Rights and Freedoms* (Markham, ON: LexisNexis Canada, 2006).

116   *Lavoie v Canada*, 2002 SCC 23, [2002] 1 S.C.R. 769.

117   Sonia Lawrence, "Section 15(1) at the Supreme Court 2001-2002: Caution and Conflict in Defining 'The Most Difficult Right,'" *Supreme Court Law Review* 16 (2002), 110.

118   *M. v H.*, [1999] 2 S.C.R. 3; *Nova Scotia (Attorney General) v Walsh*, 2002 SCC 83, [2002] 4 S.C.R. 325; *Canadian Foundation for Children, Youth and the Law v Canada (Attorney General)*, 2004 SCC 4, [2004] 1 S.C.R. 76. Cited by Peter Hogg, "What Is Equality? The Winding Course of Judicial Interpretation," *Supreme Court Law Review* 29 (2005), 57.

119   Sharpe and Roach, *Brian Dickson*, 292-93.

120   *R. v Kapp*, 2008 SCC 41. Bastarache J wrote a concurring opinion relating specifically to section 25 but signalled agreement with the restatement of the application of section 15 found in the majority reasons.

121   Ibid, para. 22.

122   Emmett Macfarlane, "Failing to Walk the Rights Talk? Post-9/11 Security Policy and the Supreme Court of Canada," *Review of Constitutional Studies* 16(2) (2012), 159-79.

Chapter 5: A Question of Competence

1   Allan C. Hutchinson, *Waiting for CORAF: A Critique of Law and Rights*, (Toronto: University of Toronto Press, 1995), 39; Jeremy Waldron, *Law and Disagreement* (New York: Oxford University Press, 1999).

2   *Canadian Charter of Rights and Freedoms*, Part 1 of the *Constitution Act, 1982*, being Schedule B to the *Canada Act 1982* (U.K.), 1982, c. 11.

3   *Harrison v Carswell*, [1976] 2 S.C.R. 200, 218, cited in Janet Hiebert, *Limiting Rights: The Dilemma of Judicial Review* (Montreal and Kingston: McGill-Queen's University Press, 1996), 57.

4   *R. v Morgentaler*, [1988] 1 S.C.R. 30, 137 *[Morgentaler]*.

5   *Sauvé v Canada (Chief Electoral Officer)*, 2002 SCC 68, [2002] 3 S.C.R. 519, para. 67.

6   Peter H. Russell, "The Political Purposes of the Canadian Charter of Rights and Freedoms," *Canadian Bar Review* 61 (1983), 52. See also Ran Hirschl, *Towards Juristocracy: The Origins and Consequences of the New Constitutionalism* (Cambridge, MA: Harvard University Press, 2004).

7   See F.L. Morton and Rainer Knopff, *The Charter Revolution and the Court Party* (Peterborough, ON: Broadview Press, 200), 142-43; Allan C. Hutchinson, "'Condition Critical': The Constitution and Health Care," in *Access to Care, Access to Justice: The Legal Debate over Private Health Insurance in Canada*, edited by Colleen M. Flood, Kent Roach, and Lorne Sossin (Toronto: University of Toronto Press, 2005), 112-13.

8   Jeremy Waldron, "The Core of the Case against Judicial Review," *Yale Law Journal* 115 (2006), 1368-69.

9   *Sauvé v Canada (Attorney General)*, [1993] 2 S.C.R. 438.

10   In section 7 cases, the reasonable limits analysis is often embedded in a consideration of whether a law accords with "the principles of fundamental justice." The Court has said that section 1 justifications for section 7 violations will be "rare." *United States v Burns*, [2001] SCC 7, [2001] 1 S.C.R. 283, para. 133.

11   *R. v Oakes*, [1986] 1 S.C.R. 103 *[Oakes]*.

12   The government succeeded in 97 percent of cases at justifying its objective as "pressing and substantial" and in 86 percent of cases at justifying that the measures to do so were rational. Leon E. Trakman, William Cole-Hamilton, and Sean Gatien, "*R. v. Oakes* 1986-1997: Back to the Drawing Board," *Osgoode Hall Law Journal* 36(1) (1998), 100.

13   Ibid, 103.

14   Marshall Rothstein, "Section 1: Justifying Breaches of Charter Rights and Freedoms," *Manitoba Law Journal* 27 (1999-2000), 171-83. For an in-depth examination of the development of the Court's approach to reasonable limits, see Hiebert, *Limiting Rights*.

15 Lorraine E. Weinrib, "The Supreme Court of Canada in the Age of Rights: Constitutional Democracy, the Rule of Law and Fundamental Rights under Canada's Constitution," *Canadian Bar Review,* 80 (2001), 699-748.

16 Christopher P. Manfredi, *Judicial Power and the Charter: Canada and the Paradox of Liberal Constitutionalism* (Toronto: Oxford University Press, 2001), 153-63.

17 Hiebert, *Limiting Rights,* 70.

18 Ibid, 71.

19 Ibid, 77-78.

20 An oft-cited study in this vein was conducted in the American context in 1977. See Donald Horowitz, *The Courts and Social Policy* (Washington, DC: Brookings Institution, 1977).

21 Ibid, 33-38.

22 Mahmud Jamal, "Legislative Facts in Charter Litigation: Where Are We Now?" *National Journal of Constitutional Law* 17 (2005), 16-17.

23 Danielle Pinard, "Institutional Boundaries and Judicial Review: Some Thoughts on How the Court Is Going about Its Business – Desperately Seeking Coherence," *Supreme Court Law Review* 25(2d) (2004), 217.

24 *Figueroa v Canada (Attorney General),* 2003 SCC 37, [2003] 1 S.C.R. 912. *Canada Elections Act,* S.C. 2000, c. 9.

25 Pinard, "Institutional Boundaries and Judicial Review," 222.

26 Janice Tibbetts, "Judges Ignorant of Science: Binnie," *Ottawa Citizen* (8 March 2003), A6.

27 Frank Iacobucci, "The Charter: Twenty Years Later," *Supreme Court Law Review* 19(2d) (2003), 405.

28 Claire L'Heureux-Dubé, "Re-Examining the Doctrine of Judicial Notice in the Family Law Context," *Ottawa Law Review* 26 (1995), 558.

29 Louise Arbour, *Dialogue on Democracy,* edited by Rudyard Griffiths (Toronto: Penguin Group, 2006), 175.

30 The Charter framers are said to have used "fundamental justice" instead of "due process" to avoid substantive interpretation that had long plagued debates in the United States. Thomas M.J. Bateman et al., *The Court and the Charter: Leading Cases* (Toronto: Emond Montgomery, 2008), 195.

31 *Re B.C. Motor Vehicle Act,* [1985] 2 S.C.R. 486.

32 Ibid, para. 18.

33 Ibid, para. 19.

34 Ibid, para. 31.

35 Robert J. Sharpe and Kent Roach, *The Charter of Rights and Freedoms,* 3rd edition (Toronto: Irwin Law, 2005), 231.

36 Jamie Cameron, "Positive Obligations under Sections 15 and 7 of the Charter: A Comment on *Gosselin v. Quebec,*" *Supreme Court Law Review* 20(2d) (2003), 70, citing Reference re ss. 193 and 195.1(1)(C) of the *Criminal Code* (Man.), [1990] 1 S.C.R. 1123.

37 Jamie Cameron, "From the MVR to Chaoulli v. Quebec: The Road Not Taken and the Future of Section 7," *Supreme Court Law Review* 34(2d) (2006), 105-68.

38 *Gosselin v Québec (Attorney General),* 2002 SCC 84, [2002] 4 S.C.R. 429.

39 Ibid, para. 213.

40 Ibid, para. 82.

41 Cameron, "Positive Obligations under Sections 15 and 7 of the Charter," 90.

42 Ibid, 91.

43 *Chaoulli v Quebec (Attorney General),* 2005 SCC 35, [2005] 1 S.C.R. 791 *[Chaoulli].*

44 *Re B.C. Motor Vehicle Act,* para. 31.

45 Sharpe and Roach, *The Charter of Rights and Freedoms,* 76.

46 *Auton (Guardian ad litem of) v British Columbia (Attorney General),* 2004 SCC 78, [2004] 3 S.C.R. 657 *[Auton].*

47 *Rodriguez v British Columbia (Attorney General),* [1993] 3 S.C.R. 519 *[Rodriguez].*

48 *R. v Askov,* [1990] 2 S.C.R. 1199.

49 The actual figure appears to be in dispute. Carl Baar puts the number at 40,000. Carl Baar, "Social Facts, Court Delay and the Charter," in *Law, Politics and the Judicial Process in Canada,* edited by F.L. Morton, 3rd edition (Calgary: University of Calgary Press, 2002),

375. Kent Roach claims the actual figure is closer to 25,000. Kent Roach, *The Supreme Court on Trial: Judicial Activism or Democratic Dialogue* (Toronto: Irwin Law, 2001), 181.

50 Roach, *The Supreme Court on Trial*, 181. Roach acknowledges the problematic outcome of the case but argues that the deleterious effects of the case were exaggerated in the media and by the Court's critics.

51 Baar, "Social Facts, Court Delay and the Charter," 375.

52 Ibid, 377.

53 *R. v Morin*, [1992] 1 S.C.R. 771; *R. v Sharma*, [1992] 1 S.C.R. 814.

54 Barbara Billingsley, "*Oakes* at 100: A Snapshot of the Supreme Court's Application of the *Oakes* Test in Social Policy v. Criminal Policy Cases," *Supreme Court Law Review* 35(2d) (2006), 347-411.

55 *Rocket v Royal College of Dental Surgeons of Ontario*, [1990] 2 S.C.R. 232, which involved professional advertising regulations (a restriction of freedom of expression under section 2), is thus excluded from this analysis, despite its status as a "health care" decision.

56 *Morgentaler; Rodriguez*.

57 *Eldridge v British Columbia (Attorney General)*, [1997] 3 S.C.R. 624 *[Eldridge]; Auton*.

58 *Canada (Attorney General) v PHS Community Services Society*, 2011 SCC 44, [2011] 3 S.C.R. 134 *[PHS Community Services Society]*.

59 *Morgentaler*, 171.

60 Cameron, "From the MVR to *Chaoulli v Quebec*," 121.

61 *Morgentaler*, 142.

62 Ibid, 140-41.

63 *R. v Morgentaler*, [1976] 1 S.C.R. 616, 632, cited in Bateman et al., *The Court and the Charter*, 214.

64 *Report of the Committee on the Operation of the Abortion Law (Badgley Report)* (Ottawa: Minister of Supply and Services, 1977).

65 Bateman et al., *The Court and the Charter*, 215.

66 Christopher P. Manfredi, *Feminist Activism in the Supreme Court: Legal Mobilization and the Women's Legal Education and Action Fund* (Vancouver: UBC Press, 2004), 180.

67 Ibid, 181.

68 *Rodriguez*, 104.

69 In another dissenting opinion, Lamer CJ argued that the law violated the equality rights of the disabled under section 15. Cory J's short dissenting opinion agreed with both McLachlin J and Lamer CJ.

70 Cameron, "The Future of Section 7," 122.

71 Cameron, "Positive Obligations under Sections 15 and 7 of the Charter."

72 *Eldridge*.

73 *Auton*.

74 *Newfoundland (Treasury Board) v N.A.P.E.*, 2004 SCC 66, [2004] 3 S.C.R. 381.

75 *Eldridge*, para. 87; *Oakes*.

76 *Eldridge*, para. 92.

77 Manfredi, *Feminist Activism in the Supreme Court*, 106.

78 Ibid.

79 Cameron, "Positive Obligations under Sections 15 and 7 of the Charter," 74.

80 *Auton*, para. 38.

81 Ibid, para. 55.

82 Ibid, para. 7.

83 Christopher P. Manfredi and Antonia Maioni, "Reversal of Fortune: Litigating Health Care Reform in *Auton v. British Columbia*," *Supreme Court Law Review* 29(2d) (2005), 130.

84 Ibid, 123.

85 Ibid, 126, citing *Auton*, 31-32.

86 Ibid, 130.

87 *Chaoulli*.

88 Ibid, para. 183.

89 *Charter of Human Rights and Freedoms*, R.S.Q., c. C-12, s. 10.

90 Canada, Senate, *The Health of Canadians: The Federal Role – Final Report of the Standing Senate Committee on Social Affairs, Science and Technology* (Ottawa: Senate, 2002).

91 Theodore R. Marmor, "Canada's Supreme Court and Its National Health Insurance Program: Evaluating the Landmark *Chaoulli* Decision from a Comparative Perspective," *Osgoode Hall Law Journal* 44(2) (2006), 312-13.

92 These expert testimonies included a former Quebec minister of health and various professors of medicine and public policy. Jeff A. King, "Constitutional Rights and Social Welfare: A Comment on the Canadian *Chaoulli* Health Care Decision," *Modern Law Review* 69(4) (2006), 637.

93 David Schneiderman, "Common Sense and the Charter," *Supreme Court Law Review* 45(2d) (2009), 13.

94 Colleen M. Flood, Mark Stabile, and Sasha Kontic, "Finding Health Policy 'Abritrary': The Evidence on Waiting, Dying, and Two-Tier Systems," in *Access to Care, Access to Justice: The Legal Debate over Private Health Insurance in Canada,* edited by Colleen M. Flood, Kent Roach, and Lorne Sossin (Toronto: University of Toronto Press, 2005), 315.

95 Ibid, 298.

96 *Chaoulli,* para. 163.

97 Ibid, para. 164.

98 Ibid, para. 214.

99 Ibid, para. 230 [emphasis in original].

100 Ibid, para. 166.

101 Ibid, para. 108.

102 Ibid, paras. 96 and 97.

103 Robert E. Charney, "Evidence in Charter Cases: Expert Evidence and Proving Purpose," *National Journal of Constitutional Law* 16 (2004-05), 5.

104 *Chaoulli,* para. 155.

105 Arbour, *Dialogue on Democracy,* 175.

106 Horowitz, *The Courts and Social Policy,* 298.

107 Christopher P. Manfredi, "Déjà Vu All Over Again: *Chaoulli* and the Limits of Judicial Policymaking," in *Access to Care, Access to Justice: The Legal Debate over Private Health Insurance in Canada,* edited by Colleen M. Flood, Kent Roach, and Lorne Sossin (Toronto: University of Toronto Press, 2005), 140.

108 *Chaoulli,* paras. 118-21.

109 Ibid, para. 167.

110 Cameron, "From the MVR to *Chaoulli v. Quebec,*" 141-42.

111 *Chaoulli,* para. 196.

112 Grant Huscroft, "Political Litigation and the Role of the Supreme Court," *Supreme Court Law Review* 34 (2006), 50, n. 45.

113 *Controlled Drugs and Substances Act,* S.C. 1996, c. 19.

114 *PHS Community Services Society,* para. 140.

115 Kavanagh explores a number of reasons for deference. See Aileen Kavanagh, "Deference or Defiance? The Limits of the Judicial Role in Constitutional Adjudication," in *Expounding the Constitution: Essays in Constitutional Theory,* edited by Grant Huscroft (Cambridge: Cambridge University Press, 2008).

Chapter 6: The Court in Government and Society

1 *Canadian Charter of Rights and Freedoms,* Part 1 of the *Constitution Act, 1982,* being Schedule B to the *Canada Act 1982* (U.K.), 1982, c. 11.

2 Peter Hogg and Allison Bushell, "The Charter Dialogue between Courts and Legislatures: (Or Perhaps The Charter of Rights Isn't Such a Bad Thing after All)," *Osgoode Hall Law Journal* 35(1) (1997), 75-124. Kent Roach has also contributed a great deal to the development of the metaphor. Kent Roach, *The Supreme Court on Trial: Judicial Activism or Democratic Dialogue* (Toronto: Irwin Law, 2001).

3 Hogg and Bushell, "The Charter Dialogue between Courts and Legislatures," 105.

4 Ibid, 82.

5 Ibid, 81.

6   Christopher Manfredi and James Kelly, "Six Degrees of Dialogue: A Response to Hogg and Bushell," *Osgoode Hall Law Journal* 37(3) (1999), 513-27; F.L. Morton, "Dialogue or Monologue?" in *Judicial Power and Canadian Democracy,* edited by Paul Howe and Peter H. Russell (Montreal and Kingston: McGill-Queen's University Press, 2001); Janet Hiebert, *Charter Conflicts: What Is Parliament's Role?* (Montreal and Kingston: McGill-Queen's University Press, 2002) 50; Dennis Baker and Rainer Knopff, "Minority Retort: A Parliamentary Power to Resolve Judicial Disagreement in Close Cases," *Windsor Yearbook of Access to Justice* 21 (2002), 347-60; Mark Tushnet, "Judicial Activism or Restraint in a Section 33 World," *University of Toronto Law Journal* 53 (2003), 89-100; Christopher Manfredi, "The Life of a Metaphor: Dialogue in the Supreme Court, 1998-2003," in *Constitutionalism in the Charter Era,* edited by Grant Huscroft and Ian Brodie (Markham, ON: LexisNexis Canada, 2004); Christopher Manfredi, "The Day the Dialogue Died: A Comment on *Sauvé v. Canada,*" *Osgoode Hall Law Journal* 45(1) (2007), 105-23; Andrew Petter, "Taking Dialogue Theory Much Too Seriously (Or Perhaps Dialogue Isn't Such a Good Thing after All)," *Osgoode Hall Law Journal* 45(1) (2007), 147-67; Grant Huscroft, "Rationalizing Judicial Power: The Mischief of Dialogue Theory," in *Contested Constitutionalism: Reflections on the Canadian Charter of Rights and Freedoms,* edited by James B. Kelly and Christopher P. Manfredi (Vancouver: UBC Press, 2009); Emmett Macfarlane, "Dialogue or Compliance? Measuring Legislatures' Policy Responses to Court Rulings on Rights," *International Political Science Review* (prepublished 13 April 2012), DOI: 10.1177/0192512111432565.
7   Morton, "Dialogue or Monologue?"
8   Baker and Knopff, "Minority Retort," 348.
9   Hiebert, *Charter Conflicts.*
10   Dennis Baker, *Not Quite Supreme: The Courts and Coordinate Constitutional Interpretation* (Montreal and Kingston: McGill-Queen's University Press, 2010).
11   Peter Hogg, "Discovering Dialogue," in *Constitutionalism in the Charter Era,* edited by Grant Huscroft and Ian Brodie (Markham, ON: LexisNexis Canada, 2004), 4.
12   Peter W. Hogg, Allison A. Bushell Thornton, and Wade K. Wright, "Charter Dialogue Revisited Or 'Much Ado about Metaphors,'" *Osgoode Hall Law Journal* 45(1) (2007), 26.
13   Manfredi and Kelly, "Six Degrees of Dialogue," 515-16, 521.
14   Hogg, Thornton, and Wright. "Charter Dialogue Revisited," 40.
15   Peter Russell, "The Notwithstanding Clause: The Charter's Homage to Parliamentary Democracy," *Policy Options* 28(2) (2007), 65-68. See also Janet L. Hiebert, "Is It Too Late to Rehabilitate Canada's Notwithstanding Clause?" *Supreme Court Law Review* 23(2d) (2004), 169-89.
16   Tsvi Kahana, "The Notwithstanding Mechanism and Public Discussion: Lessons from the Ignored Practice of Section 33 of the Charter," *Canadian Public Administration* 44(3) (2001), 255.
17   This point is also made by Jeremy Waldron, "Some Models of Dialogue between Judges and Legislators," *Supreme Court Law Review* 23(2d) (2004), 7.
18   Russell, "The Notwithstanding Clause," 68.
19   Mark Tushnet, "New Forms of Judicial Review and the Persistence of Rights- and Democracy-Based Worries," *Wake Forest Law Review* 38 (2003), 832-33.
20   Quoted in Janice Tibbetts, "Justice Warns against Overriding Supremes: Iacobucci Retiring," *National Post* (22 June 2004), A10.
21   Roach, *The Supreme Court on Trial,* 193.
22   Manfredi and Kelly, "Six Degrees of Dialogue," 521.
23   Hogg and Bushell, "The Charter Dialogue between Courts and Legislatures," 98.
24   The predominant view of the clause as an "override" of rights has been confirmed in an analysis of media coverage. See Emmett Macfarlane, "Terms of Entitlement: Is There a Distinctly Canadian 'Rights Talk'?" *Canadian Journal of Political Science* 41(2) (2008), 303-28.
25   Matthew Hennigar, "Expanding the 'Dialogue' Debate: Canadian Federal Government Responses to Lower Court Charter Decisions," *Canadian Journal of Political Science* 37(1) (2004), 16-17.
26   Ibid, 8.

27 Ibid.
28 *Canada (Attorney General) v JTI-Macdonald Corp.,* 2007 SCC 30, [2007] 2 S.C.R. 610 *[JTI-Macdonald Corp.],* in reference to *RJR-MacDonald v Canada (Attorney General),* [1995] 3 S.C.R. 199.
29 Huscroft, "Rationalizing Judicial Power," 60.
30 Hogg and Bushell, "The Charter Dialogue between Courts and Legislatures."
31 Manfredi and Kelly, "Six Degrees of Dialogue."
32 Macfarlane, "Dialogue or Compliance?"
33 Tushnet, "New Forms of Judicial Review," 835 [emphasis in original].
34 Huscroft, "Rationalizing Judicial Power," 54.
35 *R. v Morgentaler,* [1988] 1 S.C.R. 30.
36 Hennigar, "Expanding the 'Dialogue' Debate," 12.
37 *Vriend v Alberta,* [1998] 1 S.C.R. 493. *Individual's Rights Protection Act,* R.S.A. 1980, c. I-2.
38 Manfredi, "The Life of a Metaphor."
39 Hogg, Bushell Thornton, and Wright acknowledge that in this respect, *Vriend* was "unusual." Hogg, Bushell Thornton, and Wright, "Charter Dialogue Revisited," 40.
40 Manfredi, "The Life of a Metaphor," 110.
41 *R. v Mills,* [1999] 3 S.C.R. 668 *[Mills].*
42 *R. v O'Connor,* [1995] 4 S.C.R. 411.
43 For more details, see Hiebert, *Charter Conflicts,* 107-16.
44 *Mills,* para. 58.
45 Christopher P. Manfredi and James B. Kelly, "Dialogue, Deference and Restraint: Judicial Independence and Trial Procedures," *Saskatchewan Law Review* 64 (2001), 336.
46 Roach, *The Supreme Court on Trial,* 280-81.
47 Manfredi, "The Life of a Metaphor," 117.
48 Hogg, Bushell Thornton, and Wright, "Charter Dialogue Revisited," 31, citing Larry Alexander and Frederick Schauer, "On Extrajudicial Constitutional Interpretation," *Harvard Law Review* 110 (1997), 1359.
49 Manfredi and Kelly explain the distinction between deference and restraint as a difference between the outcome of a particular case and whether or not that case still advances judicial autonomy or power. In other words, they argue, the Court can show deference by upholding provisions in the *Criminal Code,* but where those provisions pertain to judicial discretion over trial procedures, a deferential approach is not necessarily a "restrained" approach. Manfredi and Kelly, "Dialogue, Deference and Restraint," 338. Notwithstanding this distinction, it is fair to say that in many instances deference and restraint overlap.
50 *R. v Hall,* [2002] 3 S.C.R. 309, referring to *R. v Morales,* [1992] 3 S.C.R. 711. *Criminal Code,* R.S.C. 1985, c. C-46.
51 *Hall,* para. 43.
52 Ibid, para. 127.
53 Ibid.
54 *Sauvé v Canada (Attorney General),* [1993] 2 S.C.R. 438.
55 *Canada Elections Act,* S.C. 2000, c. 9.
56 *Sauvé v Canada (Chief Electoral Officer),* [2002] 3 S.C.R. 519, para. 17.
57 Ibid, para. 104 [emphasis in original].
58 McLachlin CJ writes: "The framers of the *Charter* signaled the special importance of this right not only by its broad, untrammeled language, but by exempting it from legislative override under s. 33's notwithstanding clause." Ibid, para. 11.
59 Manfredi, "The Day the Dialogue Died," 117 [emphasis in original]. Hogg, Bushell Thornton, and Wright acknowledge that it appears in *Sauvé* no dialogue can take place. Hogg, Bushell Thornton, and Wright, "A Reply on 'Charter Dialogue Revisited,'" *Osgoode Hall Law Journal* 45(1) (2007), 198.
60 Christopher P. Manfredi, "Strategic Behaviour and the Canadian Charter of Rights and Freedoms," in *The Myth of the Sacred: The Charter, the Courts, and the Politics of the Constitution in Canada,* edited by Patrick James, Donald E. Abelson and Michael Lusztig (Montreal and Kingston: McGill-Queen's University Press, 2002).

61　*Harper v Canada (Attorney General)*, [2004] 1 S.C.R. 827 *[Harper]*.

62　*Libman v Quebec (Attorney General)*, [1997] 3 S.C.R. 569.

63　*Harper*, para. 63.

64　Ibid, para. 37.

65　See, for example, *M. v H.*, [1999] 2 S.C.R. 3, para. 78.

66　*Doucet-Boudreau v Nova Scotia (Minister of Education)*, 2003 SCC 62, [2003] 3 S.C.R. 3.

67　Ibid, para. 53

68　*JTI-Macdonald Corp.*, para. 11.

69　Hogg, Bushell Thornton, and Wright, "A Reply on 'Charter Dialogue Revisited,'" 202.

70　Richard Haigh and Michael Sobkin, "Does the Observer Have an Effect? An Analysis of the Use of the Dialogue Metaphor in Canada's Courts," *Osgoode Hall Law Journal* 45(1) (2007), 71.

71　Hiebert, *Charter Conflicts*, 94.

72　Ibid, 95.

73　*Re Manitoba Language Rights*, [1985] 1 S.C.R. 721. Hogg, Bushell Thornton, and Wright, "Charter Dialogue Revisited," 14-15, citing Sujit Choudhry and Kent Roach, "Putting the Past behind Us?" *Supreme Court Law Review* 21(2d) (2003), 205-66. The Court connected the remedy to the notion of dialogue in *Corbiere v Canada (Minister of Indian and Northern Affairs)*, [1999] 2 S.C.R. 203.

74　Mike De Souza, "Private Care on Hold for a Year," *Montreal Gazette* (5 August 2005), A8. *Chaoulli v Quebec (Attorney General)*, [2005] SCC 35, [2005] 1 S.C.R. 791.

75　Kent Roach, "Sharpening the Dialogue Debate: The Next Decade of Scholarship," *Osgoode Hall Law Journal* 45(1) (2007), 185.

76　Macfarlane, "Dialogue or Compliance?"

77　See Joseph F. Fletcher and Paul Howe, "Public Opinion and Canada's Courts," in *Judicial Power and Canadian Democracy*, edited by Paul Howe and Peter H. Russell (Montreal and Kingston: McGill-Queen's University Press, 2001); Nik Nanos, "Charter Values Don't Equal Canadian Values: Strong Support for Same-Sex and Property Rights," *Policy Options* 28(2) (2007), 50.

78　Lori Hausegger and Troy Riddell, "The Changing Nature of Public Support for the Supreme Court of Canada," *Canadian Journal of Political Science* 37(1) (2004), 23-50.

79　Elizabeth Goodyear-Grant, Janet Hiebert, and J. Scott Matthews, "The Courts/Parliament Trade-off: The View from the Canadian Election Study" (Paper presented at the Annual Meeting of the Canadian Political Science Association, Montreal, 2010).

80　Ian Greene et al., *Final Appeal: Decision-Making in Canadian Courts of Appeal* (Toronto: James Lorimer, 1998), 182.

81　Ellen Anderson, *Judging Bertha Wilson: Law as Large as Life* (Toronto: University of Toronto Press, 2001), 431n5.

82　Roach, *The Supreme Court on Trial*, 88.

83　Beverley McLachlin, "The Role of Judges in Modern Commonwealth Society," *Law Quarterly Review* 110 (1994), 260-69; Beverley McLachlin, "Charter Myths," *University of British Columbia Law Review* 33(1) (1999-2000), 23-36; Beverley McLachlin, "The Supreme Court and the Public Interest," *Saskatchewan Law Review* 64 (2001), 309-21; Frank Iacobucci, "The Charter: Twenty Years Later," *Supreme Court Law Review* 19(2d) (2003), 405; Michel Bastarache, "The Challenge of Law in the New Millenium," *Manitoba Law Journal* 25 (1997-98), 411-19.

84　Quoted in John Jaffey, "Charter Has 'Enhanced Democracy,' Iacobucci Tells Toronto Audience," *Lawyer's Weekly* 23(44) (26 March 2004).

85　Cristin Schmitz, "Dubé Speaks Out on Ewanchuk Controversy," *Lawyers Weekly* 22(2) (2002).

86　Cristin Schmitz, "Former Chief Justice Lamer Reflects on His Brightest, Darkest Moments as Canada's Top Jurist," *Lawyer's Weekly* 21(44) (29 March 2002). See Cristin Schmitz, "The Bastarache Interview: Reasoning to Results at SCC," *Lawyer's Weekly* 20(35) (26 January 2001).

87　For a discussion on this topic by a former Supreme Court of Canada justice, see John Sopinka, "Must a Judge Be a Monk: Revisited," *University of New Brunswick Law Journal* 45 (1996), 167-74.

88 Quoted in Cristin Schmitz, "Bastarache Explains Dissents in One-Third of SCC Decisions," *Lawyer's Weekly* 20(34) (19 January 2001).
89 G.V. La Forest, "Judicial Lawmaking, Creativity and Constraints," in *Gérard V. La Forest at the Supreme Court of Canada 1985-1997*, edited by Rebecca Johnson, John P. McEvoy, Thomas Kuttner, and H. Wade MacLachlan (Winnipeg: Supreme Court of Canada Historical Society, 1998), 9.
90 Roach, *The Supreme Court on Trial*, 89.
91 Ibid, 92.
92 Sharpe and Roach, *Brian Dickson*, 388.
93 Morton and Knopff, *The Charter Revolution and the Court Party*, 51, citing Stephen Bindman, "Thank God for the Charter," *Ottawa Citizen* (17 April 1997), A1.
94 Sharpe and Roach, *Brian Dickson*, 216.
95 Kirk Makin, "Judicial Activism Debate on Decline, Top Judge Says," *Globe and Mail* (8 January 2005), A1.
96 Quoted in Cristin Schmitz, "Our One-on-One with Justice Claire L'Heureux-Dubé," *Lawyer's Weekly* 22(3) (17 May 2002).
97 *Brown v Board of Education*, 347 U.S. 483 [1954].
98 Rosalie Silberman Abella, "Public Opinion, the Courts, and Rights: The Charter in Context," *Supreme Court Law Review* 19(2d) (2003), 434.
99 Bora Laskin CJ sat for a couple of the first Charter cases but did not participate in any of the judgments. He died in 1984.
100 Florian Sauvageau, David Schneiderman, and David Taras, *The Last Word: Media Coverage of the Supreme Court of Canada* (Vancouver: UBC Press, 2006), 12 and 199.
101 Peter Calamai, "The Media and the Court's Public Accountability," in *Brian Dickson at the Supreme Court of Canada: 1973-1990*, edited by DeLloyd J. Guth (Winnipeg: Canadian Legal History Project, 1998), 292.
102 Robert J. Sharpe and Kent Roach, *Brian Dickson: A Judge's Journey* (Toronto: University of Toronto Press, 2003), 292.
103 Calamai, "The Media and the Court's Public Accountability," 293.
104 Cristin Schmitz, "'Supreme Court Agrees to Test Pre-Release Media Lockups," *Lawyer's Weekly* 22(34) (17 January 2003).
105 Cristin Schmitz, "Communication, Consensus among McLachlin's Targets," *Lawyer's Weekly* 19(27) (24 August 1999).
106 Schmitz, "Supreme Court Agrees to Test Pre-Release Media Lockups."
107 Cristin Schmitz, "SCC Held First Media Lockup for Its Spanking Judgment," *Lawyer's Weekly* 23(38) (13 February 2004).
108 Sauvageau, Schneiderman, and Taras, *The Last Word*, 201.
109 Ibid, 202.
110 Macfarlane, "Terms of Entitlement," 303-28.

Conclusion

1 *Canadian Charter of Rights and Freedoms*, Part 1 of the *Constitution Act, 1982*, being Schedule B to the *Canada Act* 1982 (U.K.), 1982, c. 11.
2 See, for example, Bertha Wilson, "We Didn't Volunteer," in *Judicial Power and Canadian Democracy*, edited by Paul Howe and Peter H. Russell (Montreal and Kingston: McGill-Queen's University Press, 2001).
3 *Constitution Act, 1982* (U.K.), 1982, c. 11.
4 Lorne Sossin, "The Sounds of Silence: Law Clerks, Policy Making and the Supreme Court of Canada," *University of British Columbia Law Review* 30(2) (1996), 279-308.
5 See, for example, Lori Hausegger, Matthew Hennigar, and Troy Riddell, *Canadian Courts: Law, Politics, and Process* (Don Mills, ON: Oxford University Press, 2009), 141-43.
6 Included among these is Chief Justice Beverley McLachlin. See Cristin Schmitz, "McLachlin Enjoys Job, Has No Thought of Retirement," *Lawyers Weekly* 24(15) (2004).
7 James B. Kelly, *Governing with the Charter: Legislative and Judicial Activism and Framers' Intent* (Vancouver: UBC Press, 2005); Janet Hiebert, *Charter Conflicts: What Is Parliament's Role?* (Montreal and Kingston: McGill-Queen's University Press, 2002).

8 *Chaoulli v Quebec* (Attorney General) [2005] SCC 35, [2005] 1 S.C.R. 791.
9 *R. v Morgentaler,* [1988] 1 S.C.R. 30. *Rodriguez v British Columbia (Attorney General)* [1993] 3 S.C.R. 519.
10 *Canada (Attorney General) v PHS Community Services Society,* 2011 SCC 44, [2011] 3 S.C.R. 134.
11 *Controlled Drugs and Substances Act,* S.C. 1996, c. 19.
12 Kirk Makin, "Top Court Orders Clerks to Keep Quiet: U.S. Scholar asking 'Inappropriate' Questions about Judges and Their Cases," *Globe and Mail* (19 June 2009), A4.
13 James L. Gibson, "From Simplicity to Complexity: The Development of Theory in the Study of Judicial Behavior," *Political Behavior* 5(1) (1983), 9.

Bibliography

Abella, Rosalie Silberman. "The Dynamic Nature of Equality." In *Equality and Judicial Neutrality,* edited by Sheilah L. Martin and Kathleen E. Mahoney. Agincourt, ON: Carswell, 1987.

–. "Public Opinion, the Courts, and Rights: The Charter in Context." *Supreme Court Law Review* 19(2d) (2003), 421-35.

Abbot, Andrew. "Of Space and Time: The Contemporary Relevance of the Chicago School." *Social Forces* 75(4) (1997), 1149-82.

Alexander, Larry, and Frederick Schauer. "On Extrajudicial Constitutional Interpretation." *Harvard Law Review* 110 (1997), 1359-87.

Anderson, Ellen. *Judging Bertha Wilson: Law as Large as Life.* Toronto: Osgoode Society for Canadian Legal History, 2001.

Arbour, Louise. *Dialogue on Democracy,* edited by Rudyard Griffiths. Toronto: Penguin Group, 2006.

Baar, Carl. "The Chief Justice as Court Administrator 1984-1990." In *Brian Dickson at the Supreme Court of Canada: 1973-1990,* edited by DeLloyd J. Guth. Winnipeg, MB: Canadian Legal History Project, 1998.

–. "Court Delay Data as Social Science Evidence: The Supreme Court of Canada and 'Trial within a Reasonable Time.'" *Justice System Journal* 19(2) (1997), 123-44.

–. "Social Facts, Court Delay and the Charter." In *Law, Politics and the Judicial Process in Canada,* edited by F.L. Morton, 3rd edition. Calgary, AB: University of Calgary Press, 2002.

Babinski, Bob. "Backstage at the Supreme Court." *Canadian Lawyer* 17(3) (1993), 11.

Baier, Gerald. *Courts and Federalism: Judicial Doctrine in the United States, Australia, and Canada.* Vancouver: UBC Press, 2006.

Baker, Dennis. *Not Quite Supreme: The Courts and Coordinate Constitutional Interpretation.* Montreal and Kingstom: McGill-Queen's University Press, 2010.

Baker, Dennis, and Rainer Knopff. "Minority Retort: A Parliamentary Power to Resolve Judicial Disagreement in Close Cases." *Windsor Yearbook of Access to Justice* 21 (2002), 347-60.

Barnett, Randy E. *Restoring the Lost Constitution: The Presumption of Liberty.* Princeton, NJ: Princeton University Press, 2003.

Bastarache, Michel. "The Challenge of Law in the New Millenium." *Manitoba Law Journal* 25 (1997), 411-19.

–. "Passion and Advocacy in the Supreme Court of Canada." Address to the Joint Conference of the Canadian Bar Association's National Aboriginal Law Section and the Indigenous Bar Association, Ottawa, 5 March 2005.

Bateman, Thomas M.J., Janet L. Hiebert, Rainer Knopff, and Peter H. Russell. *The Court and the Charter: Leading Cases.* Toronto: Emond Montgomery, 2008.

Batten, Jack. *Judges.* Toronto: Macmillan of Canada, 1986.

Baum, Lawrence. *Judges and Their Audiences: A Perspective on Judicial Behavior.* Princeton, NJ: University of Princeton Press, 2006.

–. *The Puzzle of Judicial Behavior.* Ann Arbor, MI: University of Michigan Press, 1997.

Becker, Theodore L. *Comparative Judicial Politics: The Political Functionings of Courts.* Chicago: Rand McNally, 1970.

–. *Political Behavioralism and Modern Jurisprudence: A Working Theory and Study in Judicial Decision-Making.* Chicago: Rand McNally, 1964.

Benesh, Sara. "Harold J. Spaeth: The Supreme Court Computer." In *The Pioneers of Judicial Behavior,* edited by Nancy Maveety. Ann Arbor, MI: University of Michigan Press, 2003.

Bernstein, Claire. "How Top Judges Came to Grips with the Charter." *Toronto Star* (20 May 1990), B1.

Bickel, Alexander. *The Least Dangerous Branch: The Supreme Court at the Bar of Politics.* Indianapolis, IN: Bobbs-Merrill, 1962.

Billingsley, Barbara. "*Oakes* at 100: A Snapshot of the Supreme Court's Application of the *Oakes* Test in Social Policy v. Criminal Policy Cases." *Supreme Court Law Review* 35(2d) (2006), 347-411.

Bindman, Stephen. "Thank God for the Charter." *Ottawa Citizen* (17 April 1997), A1.

Brenner, Saul. "Fluidity on the United States Supreme Court: A Re-Examination." *American Journal of Political Science* 24 (1980), 380-86.

Brodie, Ian. *Friends of the Court: The Privileging of Interest Group Litigants in Canada.* Albany, NY: State of New York Press, 2002.

–. "Lobbying the Supreme Court." In *Political Dispute and Judicial Review: Assessing the Work of the Supreme Court of Canada,* edited by Hugh Mellon and Martin Westmacott. Scarborough, ON: Nelson, 2000.

Bushnell, Ian. *The Captive Court: A Study of the Supreme Court of Canada.* Montreal and Kingston: McGill-Queen's University Press, 1992.

Cairns, Alan. *Charter versus Federalism: The Dilemmas of Constitutional Reform.* Montreal and Kingston: McGill-Queen's University Press, 1992.

–. "The Judicial Committee and Its Critics." *Canadian Journal of Political Science* 4(3) (1971), 301-45.

Calabresi, Steven G., ed. *Originalism: A Quarter-Century of Debate.* (Washington, DC: Regnery Publishing, 2007).

Calamai, Peter. "The Media and the Court's Public Accountability." In *Brian Dickson at the Supreme Court of Canada: 1973-1990,* edited by DeLloyd J. Guth. Winnipeg, MB: Canadian Legal History Project, 1998.

Cameron, Jamie. "From the *MVR* to *Chaoulli v. Quebec:* The Road Not Taken and the Future of Section 7." *Supreme Court Law Review* 34(2d) (2006), 105-68.

–. "Positive Obligations under Sections 15 and 7 of the Charter: A Comment on *Gosselin v. Quebec.*" *Supreme Court Law Review* 20(2d) (2003), 65-91.

Canada. Senate. *The Health of Canadians: The Federal Role – Final Report of the Standing Senate Committee on Social Affairs, Science and Technology.* Ottawa: Senate, 2002.

Canadian Press. "New Justice Building to Honour Trudeau." *Globe and Mail* (3 December 2003), A7.

Charney, Robert E. "Evidence in Charter Cases: Expert Evidence and Proving Purpose." *National Journal of Constitutional Law* 16 (2004-05), 1-25.

Cheffins, Ronald. "The Supreme Court of Canada: The Quiet Court in an Unquiet Country." *Osgoode Hall Law Journal* 4 (1966), 259-75.

Choudhry, Sujit, and Robert Howse. "Constitutional Theory and the *Quebec Secession Reference.*" *Canadian Journal of Law and Jurisprudence* 13(2) (2000), 143-69.

Choudhry, Sujit, and Claire E. Hunter. "Measuring Judicial Activism on the Supreme Court of Canada: A Comment on *Newfoundland (Treasury Board) v. NAPE.*" *McGill Law Journal* 48 (2003), 525-62.

Choudhry, Sujit, and Kent Roach. "Putting the Past Behind Us?" *Supreme Court Law Review* 21(2d) (2003), 205-66.

Chwialkowska, Luiza. "Rein in Lobby Groups, Senior Judges Suggest." *National Post* (6 April 2000), A1-2.

Clayton, Cornell W. "The Supreme Court and Political Jurisprudence: New and Old Institutionalism." In *Supreme Court Decision-Making: New Institutionalist Approaches,* edited by Cornell W. Clayton and Howard Gillman. Chicago: University of Chicago Press, 1999.

Clayton, Cornell, and David A. May. "A Political Regimes Approach to the Analysis of Legal Decisions." *Polity* 32(2) (1999), 233-52.

"The Court's Arrogant Judgment on Medicare." *Globe and Mail* (18 June 2005), A16.

Courts Administration Service. *Departmental Performance Report: 2006-2007.* Ottawa: Treasury Board of Canada, 2007.

Crane, Brian A., and Henry S. Brown. *Supreme Court of Canada Practice.* Toronto: Thomson Canada, 2008.

Crosariol, Beppi. "The Clerk's Tale Is a Supreme Story." *Globe and Mail* (17 August 2005), B7.

Cross, Frank B. "Political Science and the New Legal Realism: A Case of Unfortunate Interdisciplinary Ignorance." *Northwestern University Law Review* 92(1) (1997), 251-326.

De Souza, Mike. "Private Care on Hold for a Year." *Montreal Gazette* (5 August 2005), A8.

Dickson, Brian. "A Life in the Law: The Process of Judging." *Saskatchewan Law Review* 63 (2000), 373-88.

Dickson, Brian, and DeLloyd J. Guth. "Securing Canada's Judicial Heritage." In *Brian Dickson at the Supreme Court of Canada: 1973-1990,* edited by DeLloyd J. Guth. Winnipeg, MB: Supreme Court of Canada Historical Society, 1998.

Dworkin, Ronald. *Law's Empire.* Cambridge, MA: Harvard University Press, 1986.

–. *Taking Rights Seriously.* Cambridge, MA: Harvard University Press, 1978.

Editorial. "The Court's Arrogant Judgment on Medicare." *Globe and Mail* (18 June 2005), A16.

Edwards, Harry T. "The Effects of Collegiality on Judicial Decision-Making." *University of Pennsylvania Law Review* 151(5) (2003), 1639-90.

Ely, John Hart. *Democracy and Distrust: A Theory of Judicial Review.* Cambridge, MA: Harvard University Press, 1980.

Epstein, Lee, Valerie Hoeksra, Jeffrey A. Segal, and Harold J. Spaeth. "Do Political Preferences Change? A Longitudinal Study of U.S. Supreme Court Justices." *Journal of Politics* 60(3) (1998), 801-18.

Epstein, Lee, and Gary King. "The Rules of Inference." *University of Chicago Law Review* 69(1) (2002), 1-133.

Epstein, Lee, and Jack Knight. *The Choices Justices Make.* Washington, DC: Congressional Quarterly, 1998.

–. "Toward a Strategic Revolution in Judicial Politics: A Look Back, A Look Ahead." *Political Research Quarterly* 53(3) (2000), 625-61.

Epstein, Lee, and Joseph F. Kobylka. *The Supreme Court and Legal Change: Abortion and the Death Penalty.* Chapel Hill, NC: University of North Carolina Press, 1992.

Epstein, Lee, Andrew D. Martin, Kevin M. Quinn, and Jeffrey A. Segal. "Ideological Drift among Supreme Court Justices: Who, When, and How Important." *Northwestern University Law Review* 101(4) (2007), 1483-1541.

Feldman, Stephen M. "The Rule of Law or the Rule of Politics? Harmonizing the Internal and External Views of Supreme Court Decision Making." *Law and Social Inquiry* 30(1) (2005), 89-135.

Flemming, Roy B. *Tournament of Appeals: Granting Judicial Review in Canada.* Vancouver: UBC Press, 2004.

Fletcher, Joseph F., and Paul Howe. "Public Opinion and Canada's Courts." *Judicial Power and Canadian Democracy,* edited by Paul Howe and Peter H. Russell. Montreal and Kingston: McGill-Queen's University Press, 2001.

Flood, Colleen M., Kent Roach, and Lorne Sossin, eds. *Access to Care, Access to Justice: The Legal Debate over Private Health Insurance in Canada.* Toronto: University of Toronto Press, 2005.

Flood, Colleen M., Mark Stabile, and Sasha Kontic. "Finding Health Policy 'Abritrary': The Evidence on Waiting, Dying, and Two-Tier Systems." In *Access to Care, Access to Justice: The Legal Debate over Private Health Insurance in Canada,* edited by Colleen M. Flood, Kent Roach, and Lorne Sossin. Toronto: University of Toronto Press, 2005.

Fouts, Donald E. "Policy-Making in the Supreme Court of Canada, 1950-1960." In *Comparative Judicial Behavior: Cross-Cultural Studies of Decision-Making in the East and West*, edited by Glendon Schubert and David Danelski. New York: Oxford University Press, 1969.

Frank, Jerome. *Law and the Modern Mind*. London: Stevens, 1930.

Friedman, Barry. "The Politics of Judicial Review." *Texas Law Review* 84(2) (2005), 257-337.

Gibson, Dale. "And One Step Backward: The Supreme Court and Constitutional Law in the Sixties." *Canadian Bar Review* 53 (1975), 621-48.

Gibson, James L. "From Simplicity to Complexity: The Development of Theory in the Study of Judicial Behavior." *Political Behavior* 5(1) (1983), 7-49.

–. "Judges' Role Orientations, Attitudes, and Decisions: An Interactive Model." *American Political Science Review* 72(3) (1978), 911-24

Gilligan, Carol. *In a Different Voice: Psychological Theory and Women's Development*. Cambridge, MA: Harvard University Press, 1982.

Gillman, Howard. "What's Law Got to Do with It? Judicial Behavioralists Test the 'Legal Model' of Judicial Decision Making." *Law and Social Inquiry* 26(2) (2001), 465-504.

Gillman, Howard, and Cornell W. Clayton. "Beyond Judicial Attitudes: Institutional Approaches to Supreme Court Decision-Making." In *Supreme Court Decision-Making: New Institutionalist Approaches*, edited by Cornell W. Clayton and Howard Gillman. Chicago: University of Chicago Press, 1999.

Girard, Philip. *Bora Laskin: Bringing Law to Life*. Toronto: Osgoode Society for Canadian Legal History, 2005.

Glendon, Mary Ann. *Rights Talk: The Impoverishment of Political Discourse*. New York: Free Press, 1991.

Goodyear-Grant, Elizabeth, Janet Hiebert, and J. Scott Matthews. "The Courts/Parliament Trade-off: The View from the Canadian Election Study." Paper presented at the Annual Meeting of the Canadian Political Science Association, Montreal, 2010.

Green, Donald, and Ian Shapiro. *Pathologies of Rational Choice Theory: A Critique of Applications in Political Science*. New Haven, CT: Yale University Press, 1994.

Greene, Ian, Carl Baar, Peter McCormick, George Szablowski, and Martin Thomas. *Final Appeal: Decision-Making in Canadian Courts of Appeal*. Toronto: James Lorimer, 1998.

Hagle, Timothy M., and Harold J. Spaeth. "Voting Fluidity and the Attitudinal Model of Supreme Court Decision Making." *Western Political Quarterly* 44(1) (1991), 119-28.

Haigh Richard, and Michael Sobkin. "Does the Observer Have an Effect? An Analysis of the Use of the Dialogue Metaphor in Canada's Courts." *Osgoode Hall Law Journal* 45(1) (2007), 67-90.

Hall, Melinda Gann, and Paul Brace. "Order in the Courts: A Neo-Institutional Approach to Judicial Consensus." *Western Political Quarterly* 42(3) (1989), 391-407.

Hart, H.L.A. *The Concept of Law*. New York: Oxford University Press, 1961.

Hausegger, Lori, and Stacia Haynie. "Judicial Decisionmaking and the Use of Panels in the Canadian Supreme Court and the South African Appellate Division." *Law and Society Review* 37(3) (2003), 635-57.

Hausegger, Lori, Matthew Hennigar, and Troy Riddell. *Canadian Courts: Law, Politics, and Process*. Toronto: Oxford University Press, 2009.

Hausegger, Lori, and Troy Riddell. "The Changing Nature of Public Support for the Supreme Court of Canada." *Canadian Journal of Political Science* 37(1) (2004), 23-50.

Hennigar, Matthew. "Expanding the 'Dialogue' Debate: Canadian Federal Government Responses to Lower Court Charter Decisions." *Canadian Journal of Political Science* 37(1) (2004), 3-21.

Herman, Michael John. "Law Clerking at the Supreme Court of Canada." *Osgoode Hall Law Journal* 13(2) (1975), 279-92.

Hiebert, Janet. *Charter Conflicts: What Is Parliament's Role?* Montreal and Kingston: McGill-Queen's University Press, 2002.

–. "Is It Too Late to Rehabilitate the Notwithstanding Clause?" *Supreme Court Law Review* 23(2d) (2004), 169-89.

–. *Limiting Rights: The Dilemma of Judicial Review*. Montreal and Kingston: McGill-Queen's University Press, 1996.

Hirschl, Ran. *Towards Juristocracy: The Origins and Consequences of the New Constitutionalism*. Cambridge, MA: Harvard University Press, 2004.

Hogg, Peter. *Constitutional Law of Canada*. Scarborough, ON: Thomson Canada, 2003.

–. "Discovering Dialogue." In *Constitutionalism in the Charter Era*, edited by Grant Huscroft and Ian Brodie. Markham, ON: LexisNexis Canada, 2004.

–. "What Is Equality: The Winding Course of Judicial Interpretation." *Supreme Court Law Review* 29 (2005), 39-62.

Hogg, Peter, and Allison Bushell. "The *Charter* Dialogue between Courts and Legislatures: (Or Perhaps The *Charter Of Rights* Isn't Such a Bad Thing After All)." *Osgoode Hall Law Journal* 35(1) (1997), 75-124.

Hogg, Peter W., and Allison A. Bushell Thornton, and Wade K. Wright. "*Charter* Dialogue Revisited: Or 'Much Ado about Metaphors,'" *Osgoode Hall Law Journal* 45(1) (2007), 1-65.

–. "A Reply on '*Charter* Dialogue Revisited.'" *Osgoode Hall Law Journal* 45(1) (2007), 193-202.

Horowitz, Donald. *The Courts and Social Policy*. Washington, DC: Brookings Institution, 1977.

Howard, J. Woodford Jr. "On the Fluidity of Judicial Choice." *American Political Science Review* 62(1) (1968), 43-56.

–. "Role Perceptions and Behavior in Three U.S. Courts of Appeals." *Journal of Politics* 39(4) (1977), 916-38.

Huscroft, Grant. "Political Litigation and the Role of the Court." *Supreme Court Law Review* 34 (2006), 35-56.

–. "Rationalizing Judicial Power: The Mischief of Dialogue Theory." In *Contested Constitutionalism: Reflections on the Canadian Charter of Rights and Freedoms*, edited by James B. Kelly and Christopher P. Manfredi. Vancouver: UBC Press, 2009.

Hutchinson, Allan C. "'Condition Critical': The Constitution and Health Care." In *Access to Care, Access to Justice: The Legal Debate over Private Health Insurance in Canada*, edited by Colleen M. Flood, Kent Roach, and Lorne Sossin. Toronto: University of Toronto Press, 2005.

–. *Waiting for CORAF: A Critique of Law and Rights*. Toronto: University of Toronto Press, 1995.

Iacobucci, Frank. "The Charter: Twenty Years Later." *Supreme Court Law Review* 19(2d) (2003), 3-32.

Ignatieff, Michael. *The Rights Revolution*. Toronto: House of Anansi Press, 2000.

Jaffey, John. "Charter Has 'Enhanced Democracy,' Iacobucci Tells Toronto Audience." *Lawyers Weekly* 23(44) (26 March 2004).

Jamal, Mahmud. "Legislative Facts in Charter Litigation: Where Are We Now?" *National Journal of Constitutional Law* 17 (2005), 1-18.

Johnson, James. "Conceptual Problems as Obstacles to Progress in Political Science: Four Decades of Political Culture Research." *Journal of Theoretical Politics* 15(1) (2003), 87-115.

–. "Consequences of Positivism: A Pragmatist Assessment." *Comparative Political Studies* 39(2) (2006), 224-52.

Johnson, Timothy R. *Oral Arguments and Decision Making on the United States Supreme Court*. Albany, NY: State University of New York Press, 2004.

Kahana, Tsvi. "The Notwithstanding Mechanism and Public Discussion: Lessons from the Ignored Practice of Section 33 of the Charter." *Canadian Public Administration* 44(3) (2001), 255-91.

Kavanagh, Aileen. "Deference or Defiance? The Limits of the Judicial Role in Constitutional Adjudication." *Expounding the Constitution: Essays in Constitutional Theory*, edited by Grant Huscroft. Cambridge: Cambridge University Press, 2008.

Kelly, James B. *Governing with the Charter: Legislative and Judicial Activism and Framers' Intent*. Vancouver: UBC Press, 2005.

Kennedy, Mark. "Canadians Rue Medicare's Decline, but Eager for Private System: Poll." *Ottawa Citizen* (18 June 2005), A3.

King, Jeff A. "Constitutional Rights and Social Welfare: A Comment on the Canadian *Chaoulli* Health Care Decision." *Modern Law Review* 69(4) (2006), 631-43.

Kostal, R.W. "Shilling for Judges: Brian Dickson and His Biographers." *McGill Law Journal* 51 (2006), 199-208.

Kritzer, Herbert M., and Mark J. Richards. "Jurisprudential Regimes and Supreme Court Decisionmaking: The *Lemon* Regime and Establishment Clause Cases." *Law and Society Review* 37(4) (2003), 827-40.

–. "Taking and Testing Jurisprudential Regimes Seriously: A Response to Lax and Rader." *Journal of Politics* 72(2) (2010), 285-88.

L'Heureux-Dubé, Claire. "The Length and Plurality of Supreme Court of Canada Decisions." *Alberta Law Review* 28 (1990), 581-88.

–. "Re-Examining the Doctrine of Judicial Notice in the Family Law Context." *Ottawa Law Review* 26(3) (1994), 551-77.

La Forest, G.V. "Judicial Lawmaking, Creativity and Constraints." In *Gérard V. La Forest at the Supreme Court of Canada 1985-1997,* edited by Rebecca Johnson, John P. McEvoy, Thomas Kuttner, and H. Wade MacLachlan. Winnipeg, MB: Supreme Court of Canada Historical Society, 1998.

Laskin, Bora. *The Institutional Character of the Judge.* Jerusalem, Israel: Jerusalem Post Press, 1972.

–. "The Supreme Court of Canada: A Final Court of and for Canadians." *Canadian Bar Review* 29 (1951), 1038-79.

Lawrence, Sonia. "Section 15(1) at the Supreme Court 2001-2002: Caution and Conflict in Defining 'The Most Difficult Right.'" *Supreme Court Law Review* 16(2d) (2002), 103-20.

Lax, Jeffrey R., and Kelly T. Rader. "Legal Constraints on Supreme Court Decision Making: Do Jurisprudential Regimes Exist?" *Journal of Politics* 72(2) (2010), 273-84.

Lazarus, Edward. *Closed Chambers: The Rise, Fall, and Future of the Modern Supreme Court.* New York: Penguin Books, 1998.

Leishman, Rory. *Against Judicial Activism: The Decline of Freedom and Democracy in Canada.* Montreal and Kingston: McGill-Queen's University Press, 2006.

Leslie, Peter. "Canada: The Supreme Court Sets Rules for the Secession of Quebec." *Publius* 29(2) (1999), 135-51.

Lewis, Neil A. "Senate Panel Endorses Sotomayor on a Partisan Vote." *New York Times* (29 July 2009), 12.

Macfarlane, Emmett. "Administration at the Supreme Court of Canada: Challenges and Change in the Charter Era." *Canadian Public Administration* 52(1) (2009), 1-21.

–. "Attitudinal Decision Making in the Supreme Court of Canada." *Queen's Law Journal* 33(1) (2007), 249-59.

–. "Consensus and Unanimity at the Supreme Court of Canada," *Supreme Court Law Review* 52(2010), 379-410.

–. "Dialogue or Compliance? Measuring Legislatures' Policy Responses to Court Rulings on Rights." *International Political Science Review* (prepublished 19 April 2012), DOI: 10.1177/0192512111432565.

–. "Failing to Walk the Rights Talk? Post-9/11 Security Policy and the Supreme Court of Canada." *Review of Constitutional Studies* 16(2) (2012), 159-79.

–. "Terms of Entitlement: Is There a Distinctly Canadian 'Rights Talk'?" *Canadian Journal of Political Science* 41(2) (2008), 303-28.

MacIvor, Heather. *Canadian Politics and Government in the Charter Era*. Toronto: Thomson Nelson, 2006.

MacPherson, James. "Working within the Dickson Court." *Dickson Legacy,* edited by Roland Penner. Winnipeg, MB: Legal Research Institute of the University of Manitoba, 1992.

Major, John C. "Interveners and the Supreme Court of Canada." *National* 8(3) (1999), 27.

Makin, Kirk. "It Fundamentally Changed the Justice System." *Globe and Mail* (10 April 2007), A7.

–. "Judicial Activism Debate on Decline, Top Judge Says." *Globe and Mail* (8 January 2005), A1.

–. "Lobbying Hurt Court, Book Says Backroom Deals among Top-Court Judges Threatened Charter, Wilson Felt." *Globe and Mail* (11 March 2002), A9.

–. "Plain-Talking Estey: After Eleven Years Sitting on the Supreme Court, Retiring Justice Plans Clean Break with Law." *Globe and Mail* (27 April 1988), A1.

–. "Supreme Court in the Spotlight: In the Post-Charter Era, Judges Face More Pressure and Plenty of Second Guessing." *Globe and Mail* (17 April 2002), A10.

–. "Top Court Orders Clerks to Keep Quiet: U.S. Scholar asking 'Inappropriate' Questions about Judges and Their Cases." *Globe and Mail* (19 June 2009), A4.

–. "'We Are Not Gunslingers.'" *Globe and Mail* (9 April 2002), A4.

Maltzman, Forrest, James F. Spriggs II, and Paul J. Wahlbeck. *Crafting Law on the Supreme Court: The Collegial Game*. New York: Cambridge University Press, 2000.

Mandel, Michael. *The Charter of Rights and the Legalization of Politics in Canada*. Toronto: Wall and Thompson, 1989.

Manfredi, Christopher. "The Day the Dialogue Died: A Comment on *Sauvé v. Canada*." *Osgoode Hall Law Journal* 45(1) (2007), 105-23.

–. "Déjà Vu All Over Again: *Chaoulli* and the Limits of Judicial Policymaking." In *Access to Care, Access to Justice: The Legal Debate over Private Health Insurance in Canada*, edited by Colleen M. Flood, Kent Roach, and Lorne Sossin. Toronto: University of Toronto Press, 2005.

–. *Feminist Activism in the Supreme Court: Legal Mobilization and the Women's Legal Education and Action Fund*. Vancouver: UBC Press, 2004.

–. *Judicial Power and the Charter: Canada and the Paradox of Liberal Constitutionalism*. Don Mills, ON: Oxford University Press, 2001.

–. "The Life of a Metaphor: Dialogue in the Supreme Court, 1998-2003." In *Constitutionalism in the Charter Era*, edited by Grant Huscroft and Ian Brodie. Markham, ON: LexisNexis Canada, 2004.

–. "Strategic Behavior and the Canadian Charter of Rights and Freedoms." In *The Myth of the Sacred: The Charter, the Courts and the Politics of the Constitution in Canada*, edited by Patrick James, Donald E. Abelson, and Michael Lusztig. Montreal and Kingston: McGill-Queen's University Press, 2002.

Manfredi, Christopher, and James Kelly. "Dialogue, Deference and Restraint: Judicial Independence and Trial Procedures." *Saskatchewan Law Review* 64 (2001), 323-46.

–. "Misrepresenting the Supreme Court's Record? A Comment on Choudhry and Hunter, 'Measuring Judicial Activism on the Supreme Court of Canada.'" *McGill Law Journal* 49(3) (2004), 741-64.

–. "Six Degrees of Dialogue: A Response to Hogg and Bushell." *Osgoode Hall Law Journal* 37(3) (1999), 513-27.

Manfredi, Christopher P., and Antonia Maioni. "Reversal of Fortune: Litigating Health Care Reform in *Auton v. British Columbia*." *Supreme Court Law Review* 29(2d) (2005), 111-36.

March, James G., and Johan P. Olsen. "The New Institutionalism: Organizational Factors in Political Life." *American Political Science Review* 78(3) (1984), 734-49.

Marmor, Theodore R. "Canada's Supreme Court and Its National Health Insurance Program: Evaluating the Landmark Chaoulli Decision from a Comparative Perspective." *Osgoode Hall Law Journal* 44(2) (2006), 311-25.

Martin, Andrew D., and Kevin M. Quinn. "Assessing Preference Change on the U.S. Supreme Court." *Journal of Law, Economics and Organization* 23(2) (2007), 365-85.

Martinson, Donna. "*Lavallee v. R.:* The Supreme Court of Canada Addresses Gender Bias in the Courts." *University of British Columbia Law Review* 24(2) (1990), 381-86.

Maveety, Nancy, ed. *The Pioneers of Judicial Behavior*. Ann Arbor, MI: University of Michigan Press, 2003.

McAllister, Debra M. "Section 15: The Unpredictability of the *Law* Test." *National Journal of Constitutional Law* 15 (2003), 35-106.

McConnell, W.H. *William R. McIntyre: Paladin of Common Law*. Montreal and Kingston: McGill-Queen's University Press, 2000.

McCormick, Peter. "Assessing Leadership on the Supreme Court of Canada: Towards a Typology of Chief Justice Performance." *Supreme Court Law Review* 4 (1993), 409-29.

–. "Blocs, Swarms, and Outliers: Conceptualizing Disagreement on the Modern Supreme Court of Canada." *Osgoode Hall Law Journal* 42(1) (2004), 99-138.

–. *Canada's Courts.* Toronto: James Lorimer, 1994.

–. "Judicial Career Patterns and the Delivery of Reasons for Judgment in the Supreme Court of Canada, 1949-1993." *Supreme Court Law Review* 5 (1994), 499-522.

–. "Party Capability Theory and Appellate Success in the Supreme Court of Canada, 1949-1992." *Canadian Journal of Political Science* 26(3) (1993), 523-40.

–. "Standing Apart: Separate Concurrence and the Modern Supreme Court of Canada, 1984-2006." *McGill Law Journal* 53 (2008), 137-66.

–. *Supreme at Last: The Evolution of the Supreme Court of Canada.* Toronto: James Lorimer, 2000.

–. "What Supreme Court Cases Does the Supreme Court Cite? Follow-Up Citations on the Supreme Court of Canada, 1989-1993." *Supreme Court Law Review* 7 (1996), 451.

McCormick, Peter, and Ian Greene. *Judges and Judging: Inside the Canadian Judicial System.* Toronto: James Lorimer, 1990.

McEvoy, John. "Refusing to Answer: The Supreme Court and the Reference Power Revisited." *University of New Brunswick Law Journal* 29 (2005), 29-42.

–. "Separation of Powers and the Reference Power: Is There a Right to Refuse?" *Supreme Court Law Review* 10 (1988), 429.

McInnes, Mitchell, Janet Bolton, and Natalie Derzko. "Clerking at the Supreme Court of Canada." *Alberta Law Review* 33(1) (1994), 58-79.

McIntyre, Sheila, and Sanda Rodgers, eds. *Diminishing Returns: Inequality and the Canadian Charter of Rights and Freedoms.* Markham, ON: LexisNexis Canada, 2006.

McLachlin, Beverley. "The Charter: A New Role for the Judiciary?" *Alberta Law Review* 29(3) (1991), 540-59.

–. "Charter Myths." *University of British Columbia Law Review* 33(1) (1999-2000), 23-36.

–. "The Charter of Rights and Freedoms: A Judicial Perspective." *University of British Columbia Law Review* 23 (1989), 579-90.

–. "The Demystification of the Judiciary." Speech to the McGill Law Journal Seventh Annual Alumni Lecture, Montreal, 19 February 1991.

–. "On Impartiality." Address at University of Waikato, Hamilton, New Zealand, 23 April 2003 [unpublished].

–. "The Role of Judges in Modern Commonwealth Society." *Law Quarterly Review* 110 (1994), 260-69.

–. "Rules and Discretion in the Governance of Canada." *Saskatchewan Law Review* 56 (1992), 167-79.

–. "The Supreme Court and the Public Interest." *Saskatchewan Law Review* 64 (2001), 309-21.

Morton, F.L. "Dialogue or Monologue?" In *Judicial Power and Canadian Democracy,* edited by Paul Howe and Peter H. Russell. Montreal and Kingston: McGill-Queen's University Press, 2001.

–. *Law, Politics and the Judicial Process in Canada,* 3rd edition. Calgary: University of Calgary Press, 2002.

Morton, F.L., and Avril Allen. "Feminists and the Courts: Measuring Success in Interest Group Litigation in Canada." *Canadian Journal of Political Science* 34(1) (2001), 55-84.

Morton, F.L., and Rainer Knopff. *The Charter Revolution and the Court Party.* Peterborough, ON: Broadview Press, 2000.

Murphy, Walter F. *Elements of Judicial Strategy.* Chicago: University of Chicago Press, 1964.

Muttart, Daved. *The Empirical Gap in Jurisprudence: A Comprehensive Study of the Supreme Court of Canada.* Toronto: University of Toronto Press, 2007.

Nanos, Nik. "Charter Values Don't Equal Canadian Values: Strong Support for Same-Sex and Property Rights." *Policy Options* 28(2) (2007), 50-55.

Ostberg, C.L., and Matthew E. Wetstein. *Attitudinal Decision Making in the Supreme Court of Canada.* Vancouver: UBC Press, 2007.

–. "Dimensions of Attitudes Underlying Search and Seizure Decisions of the Supreme Court of Canada." *Canadian Journal of Political Science* 31 (1998), 767-87.

Ostberg, C.L., Matthew E. Wetstein, and Craig R. Ducat. "Attitudinal Dimensions of Supreme Court Decision Making in Canada: The Lamer Court, 1991-1995." *Political Research Quarterly* 55(1) (2002), 235-56.

Peacock, Anthony A. "Strange Brew: Tocqueville, Rights, and the Technology of Equality." *Rethinking the Constitution: Perspectives on Canadian Constitutional Reform, Interpretation, and Theory,* edited by Anthony A. Peacock. Don Mills, ON: Oxford University Press, 1996.

Peck, Sidney. "A Scalogram Analysis of the Supreme Court of Canada, 1958-1967." *Comparative Judicial Behavior: Cross-Cultural Studies of Decision-Making in the East and West,* edited by Glendon Schubert and David Danelski. New York: Oxford University Press, 1969.

Petter, Andrew. *The Politics of the Charter: The Illusive Promise of Constitutional Rights.* Toronto: University of Toronto Press, 2010.

–. "Taking Dialogue Theory Much Too Seriously (Or Perhaps Dialogue Isn't Such a Good Thing After All)." *Osgoode Hall Law Journal* 45(1) (2007), 147-67.

Philp, Margaret. "Angry Parents Threaten to Leave Country." *Globe and Mail* (20 November 2004), A11.

Pierson, Paul, and Theda Skocpol. "Historical Institutionalism in Contemporary Political Science." In *Political Science: State of the Discipline,* edited by Ira Katznelson and George R. Milner, eds. New York: W.W. Norton, 2002.

Pinard, Danielle. "Institutional Boundaries and Judicial Review: Some Thoughts on How the Court Is Going about Its Business: Desperately Seeking Coherence." *Supreme Court Law Review* 25(2d) (2004), 213-40.

Posner, Richard A. *How Judges Think.* Cambridge, MA: Harvard University Press, 2008.

–. "What Do Judges and Justices Maximize? (The Same Thing as Everybody Else Does)." *Supreme Court Economic Review* 3 (2003), 1-41.

Pritchett, C. Herman. *Civil Liberties and the Vinson Court.* Chicago: University of Chicago Press, 1954.

–. "Divisions of Opinions among Justices of the U.S. Supreme Court, 1939-1941." *American Political Science Review* 35 (1941), 890-98.

Richards, Mark J., and Herbert M. Kritzer. "Jurisprudential Regimes in Supreme Court Decision Making." *American Political Science Review* 96(2) (2002), 305-20.

Roach, Kent. "Sharpening the Dialogue Debate: The Next Decade of Scholarship." *Osgoode Hall Law Journal* 45(1) (2007), 169-91.

–. *The Supreme Court on Trial: Judicial Activism or Democratic Dialogue.* Toronto: Irwin Law, 2001.

Rothstein, Marshall. "Section 1: Justifying Breaches of Charter Rights and Freedoms." *Manitoba Law Journal* 27 (2000), 171-83.

Russell, Peter H. "Canadian Constraints on Judicialization from Without." In *The Global Expansion of Judicial Power,* edited by C. Neal Tate and Torbjorn Vallinder. New York: New York University Press, 1995.

–. *The Judiciary in Canada: The Third Branch of Government.* Toronto: McGraw-Hill Ryerson, 1987.

–. "The Notwithstanding Clause: The Charter's Homage to Parliamentary Democracy." *Policy Options* 28(2) (2007), 65-68.

–. "The Political Purposes of the Canadian Charter of Rights and Freedoms." *Canadian Bar Review* 61 (1983), 30-54.

–. *The Supreme Court of Canada as a Bilingual and Bicultural Institution.* Ottawa: Queen's Printer, 1969.

Russell, Peter H., Rainer Knopff, Thomas M.J. Bateman, and Janet Hiebert. *The Court and the Constitution: Leading Cases.* Toronto: Emond Montgomery, 2008.

Sauvageau, Florian, David Schneiderman, and David Taras. *The Last Word: Media Coverage of the Supreme Court of Canada.* Vancouver: UBC Press, 2006.

Scalia, Antonin, and Bryan A. Garner. *Making Your Case: The Art of Persuading Judges.* St. Paul, MN: Thomson West, 2008.

Scheb, John M., II, Thomas D. Ungs, and Allison L. Hayes. "Judicial Role Orientations, Attitudes and Decision Making: A Research Note." *Western Political Quarterly* 42(3) (1989), 427-35.

Schmitz, Cristin. "Bastarache Explains Dissents in One-Third of SCC Decisions." *Lawyer's Weekly* 20(34) (2001).

–. "The Bastarache Interview: 'Overall, This Is Not a Frustrating Job.'" *Lawyer's Weekly* 20(36) (2 February 2001).

–. "The Bastarache Interview: Reasoning to Results at SCC." *Lawyer's Weekly* 20(35) (26 January 2001).

–. "Chief Justice Defends Supreme Court and Legal Profession." *Lawyers Weekly* 27(15) (24 August 2007).

–. "Chief Justice McLachlin Discusses Terrorism, Liberty, Live Webcasting of Appeals." *Lawyers Weekly* 21(33) (11 January 2002).

–. "Communication, Consensus among McLachlin's Targets." *Lawyer's Weekly* 19(27) (19 November 1999).

–. "Dubé Speaks Out on Ewanchuk Controversy." *Lawyer's Weekly* 22(2) (10 May 2002).

–. "Former Chief Justice Lamer Reflects on His Brightest, Darkest Moments as Canada's Top Jurist." *Lawyer's Weekly* 21(44) (2002).

–. "Former Chief Justice Offers a View from the Top." *Lawyer's Weekly* 21(44) (29 March 2002).

–. "Justice Jack Major Reflects on Dealing with Life, Death as a Supreme Court Judge." *Lawyer's Weekly* 22(34) (17 January 2003).

–. "Leaving after Fifteen Years on Bench, Justice L'Heureux-Dubé Says She's 'Extremely Serene.'" *Lawyer's Weekly* 22(2) (2002).

–. "'McLachlin Court' Sets Record Time for Rendering Judgment in 2004." *Lawyer's Weekly* 24(41) (11 March 2005).

–. "McLachlin Enjoys Job, Has No Thought of Retirement." *Lawyers Weekly* 24(15) (27 August 2004).

–. "Mixed Reviews for 20th Anniversary of Section 15." *Lawyer's Weekly* 24(48) (29 April 2005).

–. "Our One-on-One with Justice Claire L'Heureux-Dubé." *Lawyer's Weekly* 22(3) (17 May 2002).

–. "SCC Held First Media Lockup for Its Spanking Judgment." *Lawyer's Weekly* 23(38) (13 February 2004).

–. "SCC's Resources Now 'Stretched to the Limit,' McLachlin Tells CBA." *Lawyers Weekly* 21(15) (24 August 2001).

–. "'Supreme Court Agrees to Test Pre-Release Media Lockups." *Lawyer's Weekly* 22(34) (17 January 2003).

Schneiderman, David. "Common Sense and the Charter." *Supreme Court Law Review* 45(2d) (2009), 3-18.

Schubert, Glendon. *The Judicial Mind*. Evanston, IL: Northwestern University Press, 1965.

Schwartz, Bernard. *Decision: How the Supreme Court Decides Cases*. New York: Oxford University Press, 1996.

Segal, Jeffrey A. "Judicial Behavior." In *The Oxford Handbook of Law and Politics*, edited by Keith Whittington, Daniel Keleman, and Gregory A. Caldeira. New York: Oxford University Press, 2008.

Segal, Jeffrey A., and Harold J. Spaeth. *The Supreme Court and the Attitudinal Model*. New York: Cambridge University Press, 1993.

–. *The Supreme Court and the Attitudinal Model Revisited*. New York: Cambridge University Press, 2002.

Sharpe, Robert J., and Kent Roach. *Brian Dickson: A Judge's Journey*. Toronto: Osgoode Society for Canadian Legal History, 2003.

–. *The Charter of Rights and Freedoms*, 3rd edition. Toronto: Irwin Law, 2005.

Simpson, Jeffrey. "Rights Talk: The Effect of the Charter on Canadian Political Discourse." In *Protecting Rights and Freedoms: Essays on the Charter's Place in Canada's Political, Legal, and Intellectual Life*, edited by Philip Bryden, Steven Davis, and Peter Russell. Toronto: University of Toronto Press, 1994.

Slayton, Philip. *Mighty Judgment: How the Supreme Court of Canada Runs Your Life*. Toronto: Penguin Group, 2011.

Smith, Miriam. "Institutionalism in the Study of Canadian Politics." In *New Institutionalism: Theory and Analysis*, edited by André Lecours. Toronto: University of Toronto Press, 2005.

–. *Political Institutions and Lesbian and Gay Rights in the United States and Canada.* New York: Routledge, 2008.

Smith, Rogers M. "Political Jurisprudence, the 'New Institutionalism,' and the Future of Public Law." *American Political Science Review* 82(1) (1988), 89-108.

Snell, James G., and Frederick Vaughan. *The Supreme Court of Canada: History of the Institution.* Toronto: Osgoode Society for Canadian Legal History, 1985.

Songer, Donald R. *The Transformation of the Supreme Court of Canada: An Empirical Examination.* Toronto: University of Toronto Press, 2008.

Songer, Donald R., and Susan W. Johnson. "Judicial Decision Making in the Supreme Court of Canada: Updating the Personal Attribute Model." *Canadian Journal of Political Science* 40(4) (2007), 911-34.

Songer, Donald R., and Julia Siripurapu. "The Unanimous Cases of the Supreme Court of Canada as a Test of the Attitudinal Model." *Canadian Journal of Political Science* 42(1) (2009), 65-92.

Sopinka, John. "Advocacy in the Top Court." *National* 4(4) (1995), 38-42.

–. "Must a Judge Be a Monk: Revisited." *University of New Brunswick Law Journal* 45 (1996), 167-74.

–. "The Supreme Court of Canada." In *Supreme Court of Canada Practice,* edited by Brian A. Crane and Henry S. Brown. Toronto: Thomson Canada, 2008.

Sopinka, John, and Mark A. Gelowitz. *The Conduct of an Appeal.* Toronto: Butterworths Canada, 1993.

Sossin, Lorne M. *Boundaries of Judicial Review: The Law of Justiciability in Canada.* Toronto: Thomson Canada, 1999.

–. "The Sounds of Silence: Law Clerks, Policy Making and the Supreme Court of Canada." *University of British Columbia Law Review* 30(2) (1996), 279-308.

Spaeth, Harold J. "Reflections about Judicial Politics." *Oxford Handbook of Law and Politics,* edited by Keith Whittington, R. Daniel Keleman, and Gregory A. Caldeira. New York: Oxford University Press, 2008.

Spaeth, Harold J., and Jeffrey A. Segal. *Majority Rule or Minority Will.* New York: Cambridge University Press, 1999.

"The Supreme Court." *Canada Law Journal* 38(3) (1 February 1902), 61-65.

Supreme Court of Canada, *Bulletin of Proceedings: Special Edition Statistics 1996-2006.* Ottawa: Treasury Board of Canada, 2007.

–. *Performance Report: For the Period Ending March 31, 2007.* Ottawa: Treasury Board of Canada, 2007.

–. *Statistics 1999-2009.* Ottawa: Supreme Court of Canada, 2010.

–. *Statistics 2001-2011.* Ottawa: Supreme Court of Canada, 2012.

Swinton, Katherine. *The Supreme Court and Canadian Federalism: The Laskin-Dickson Years.* Toronto: Carswell, 1990.

Tamanaha, Brian Z. *Beyond the Formalist-Realist Divide: The Role of Politics in Judging.* Princeton, NJ: Princeton University Press, 2010.

Tate, C. Neil. "Why the Expansion of Judicial Power?" In *The Global Expansion of Judicial Power,* edited by C. Neal Tate and Torbjorn Vallinder. New York: New York University Press, 1995.

Tate, C. Neal, and Panu Sittiwong. "Decision Making in the Canadian Supreme Court: Extending the Personal Attributes Model across Nations." *Journal of Politics* 51(4) (1989), 900-16.

Tibbetts, Janice. "Judges Ignorant of Science: Binnie." *Ottawa Citizen* (8 March 2003), A6.

–. "Justice Warns against Overriding Supremes: Iacobucci Retiring." *National Post* (22 June 2004), A10.

Toobin, Jeffrey. *The Nine: Inside the Secret World of the Supreme Court.* New York: Random House, 2007.

Trakman, Leon E., William Cole-Hamilton, and Sean Gatien. "*R. v. Oakes* 1986-1997: Back to the Drawing Board." *Osgoode Hall Law Journal* 36(1) (1998), 83-149.

Tushnet, Mark. "Judicial Activism or Restraint in a Section 33 World." *University of Toronto Law Journal* 53 (2003), 89-100.

–. "New Forms of Judicial Review and the Persistence of Rights- and Democracy-Based Worries." *Wake Forest Law Review* 38 (2003), 813-38.

Tyler, Tracey. "The Legal 'Sticky Floor.'" *Toronto Star* (15 August 2006), A09.

Waldron, Jeremy. "The Core of the Case against Judicial Review." *Yale Law Journal* 115 (2006), 1346-1406.

–. *Law and Disagreement.* New York: Oxford University Press, 1999.

–. "Some Models of Dialogue between Judges and Legislators." *Supreme Court Law Review* 23 (2004), 7.

Weiler, Paul. *In the Last Resort: A Critical Study of the Supreme Court of Canada.* Toronto: Carswell, 1974.

Weinrib, Lorraine E. "The Supreme Court of Canada in the Age of Rights: Constitutional Democracy, the Rule of Law and Fundamental Rights under Canada's Constitution." *Canadian Bar Review* 80 (2001), 699-748.

Wetstein, Matthew E., and C.L. Ostberg. "Search and Seizure Cases in the Supreme Court of Canada: Extending an American Model of Judicial Decision Making across Countries." *Social Science Quarterly* 80(4) (1999), 757-74.

–. "Strategic Leadership and Political Change on the Canadian Supreme Court: Analyzing the Transition to Chief Justice." *Canadian Journal of Political Science* 38(3) (2005), 653-73.

Wetstein, Matthew E., C.L. Ostberg, Donald R. Songer, and Susan W. Johnson. "Ideological Consistency and Attitudinal Conflict: A Comparative Analysis of the U.S. and Canadian Supreme Courts." *Comparative Political Studies* 42(6) (2009), 763-92.

White, Linda, Richard Simeon, Robert Vipond, and Jennifer Wallner, eds. *The Comparative Turn in Canadian Political Science.* Vancouver: UBC Press, 2008.

Whittington, Keith E. "Once More unto the Breach: PostBehavioralist Approaches to Judicial Politics." *Law and Social Inquiry* 25 (2000), 601-34.

Wilson, Bertha. "Decision-Making in the Supreme Court." *University of Toronto Law Journal* 36 (1986), 227-48.

–. "Leave to Appeal to the Supreme Court of Canada." *The Advocates' Quarterly* 4(1) (1983), 1-9.

–. "We Didn't Volunteer." In *Judicial Power and Canadian Democracy,* edited by Paul Howe and Peter Russell. Montreal and Kingston: McGill-Queen's University Press, 2001.

–. "Will Women Judges Really Make a Difference?" *Osgoode Hall Law Journal* 28 (1990), 507-22.

Wold, John T. "Political Orientations, Social Backgrounds, and Role Perceptions of State Supreme Court Judges." *Western Political Quarterly* 27(2) (1974), 239-48.

Woodward, Bob, and Scott Armstrong. *The Brethren: Inside the Supreme Court.* New York: Avon Books, 1979.

Wrightsman, Lawrence S. *Oral Arguments before the Supreme Court: An Empirical Approach.* New York: Oxford University Press, 2008.

Young, Robert A. *The Struggle for Quebec.* Montreal and Kingston: McGill-Queen's University Press, 1999.

Cases Cited

A.A. v B.B., 2007 ONCA 2.

A.-G. Ont. v A.-G. Can. (Local Prohibition), [1896] A.C. 348.

A-G Canada v Lavell, Isaac et al. v Bedard, [1974] S.C.R. 1349.

Alliance for Marriage and Family v A.A., 2007 SCC 40, [2007] 3 S.C.R. 124.

Andrews v Law Society of British Columbia, [1989] 1 S.C.R. 143.

Auton (Guardian ad litem of) v British Columbia (Attorney General), 2004 SCC 78, [2004] 3 S.C.R. 657.

Borowski v A.G. (Can.), [1989] 1 S.C.R. 342.

Brown v Board of Education, 347 U.S. 483 [1954].

Canada (Attorney General) v JTI-Macdonald Corp., 2007 SCC 30, [2007] 2 S.C.R. 610.

Canada (Attorney General) v PHS Community Services Society, 2011 SCC 44, [2011] 3 S.C.R. 134.

Canadian Council of Churches v Canada (Minister of Employment and Immigration), [1992] 1 S.C.R. 236.

Canadian Foundation for Children, Youth and the Law v Canada (Attorney General), 2004 SCC 4, [2004] 1 S.C.R. 76.

Chaoulli v Quebec (Attorney General), [2005] SCC 35, [2005] 1 S.C.R. 791.

Corbiere v Canada (Minister of Indian and Northern Affairs), [1999] 2 S.C.R. 203.

Doucet-Boudreau v Nova Scotia (Minister of Education), 2003 SCC 62, [2003] 3 S.C.R. 3.

Dumont v Canada (Attorney General), [1990] 1 S.C.R. 279.

Egan v Canada, [1995] 2 S.C.R. 513.

Eldridge v British Columbia (Attorney General), [1997] 3 S.C.R. 624.

Figueroa v Canada (Attorney General), 2003 SCC 37, [2003] 1 S.C.R. 912.

Finlay v Canada (Minister of Finance), [1993] 1 S.C.R. 1080.

Ford v Quebec (Attorney General), [1988] 2 S.C.R. 712.

Gosselin v Québec (Attorney General), 2002 SCC 84, [2002] 4 S.C.R. 429.

Greater Vancouver Transportation Authority v Canadian Federation of Students - British Columbia Component, 2009 SCC 31.

Harper v Canada (Attorney General), 2004 SCC 33, [2004] 1 S.C.R. 827.

Harrison v Carswell, [1976] 2 S.C.R 200.

Irwin Toy Ltd. v Quebec (Attorney General), [1989] 1 S.C.R. 927.

Lavigne v Ontario Public Service Employees Union, [1991] 2 S.C.R. 211.

Lavoie v Canada, 2002 SCC 23, [2002] 1 S.C.R. 769.

Law v Canada (Minister of Employment and Immigration), [1999] 1 S.C.R. 497.

Libman v Quebec (Attorney General), [1997] 3 S.C.R. 569.

M. v H., [1999] 2 S.C.R. 3.

M.(K.) v M.(H.), [1992] 3 S.C.R. 3.

McEvoy v A.-G. N.B., [1983] 1 S.C.R. 704.

McNeil v Nova Scotia (Board of Censors), [1976] 2 S.C.R. 265.

Minister of Justice (Can.) v Borowski, [1981] 2 S.C.R. 575.

Miron v Trudel, [1995] 2 S.C.R. 418

Newfoundland (Treasury Board) v N.A.P.E., 2004 SCC 66, [2004] 3 S.C.R. 381.

Norberg v Wynrib, [1992] 2 S.C.R. 224.

Nova Scotia (Attorney General) v Walsh, 2002 SCC 83, [2002] 4 S.C.R. 325.

Operation Dismantle v The Queen, [1985] 1 S.C.R. 441.

PSAC v Canada, [1987] 1 S.C.R. 424.

The Queen v Drybones, [1970] S.C.R. 282.

R. v Askov, [1990] 2 S.C.R. 1199.

R. v Coffin, [1956] S.C.R. 191.

R. v Edwards Books and Art, [1986] 2 S.C.R. 713.

R. v Hall, [2002] 3 S.C.R. 309.

R. v Hinse, [1995] 4 S.C.R. 597.

R. v Kapp, 2008 SCC 41.

R. v Lavallee, [1990] 1 S.C.R. 852.

R. v Martineau, [1990] 2 S.C.R. 633.

R. v Mills, [1999] 3 S.C.R. 668.

R. v Morales, [1992] 3 S.C.R. 711.

R. v Morin, [1992] 1 S.R.C. 771.

R. v Morgentaler, [1976] 1 S.C.R. 616.

R. v Morgentaler, [1988] 1 S.C.R. 30.

R. v Morgentaler, [1993] 3 S.C.R. 463.

R. v O'Connor, [1995] 4 S.C.R. 411.

R. v Oakes, [1986] 1 S.C.R. 103.

R. v Ogg-Moss, [1984] 2 S.C.R. 171.

R. v Sharma, [1992] 1 S.C.R. 814.

R. v Sparrow, [1990] 1 S.C.R. 1075.

R. v Vaillancourt, [1987] 2 S.C.R. 636.

R. v Zundel, [1992] 2 S.C.R. 731.

Re B.C. Motor Vehicle Act, [1985] 2 S.C.R. 486.

Re Can. Assistance Plan, [1991] 2 S.C.R. 524.

Re Manitoba Language Rights, [1985] 1 S.C.R. 721.

Re Objection by Que. to Resolution to Amend the Constitution, [1982] 2 S.C.R. 793.

Re Resolution to Amend the Constitution, [1981] 1 S.C.R. 753.

Reference re Anti-Inflation Act, [1976] 2 S.C.R. 373.

Reference re Authority of Parliament in Relation to the Upper House, [1980] 1 S.C.R. 54

Reference re Goods and Services Tax, [1992] 2 S.C.R. 445.

Reference re Public Service Employee Relations Act (Alta.), [1987] 1 S.C.R. 313.

Reference re Remuneration of Judges of the Provincial Court of Prince Edward Island, [1997] 3 S.C.R. 3.

Reference re Same-Sex Marriage, 2004 SCC 79, [2004] 3 S.C.R. 698.

Reference re Secession of Quebec, [1998] 2 S.C.R. 217.

Reference re ss. 193 and 195.1(1)(C) of the Criminal Code (Man.), [1990] 1 S.C.R. 1123.

Reference re Workers' Compensation Act, 1983 (Nfld.) (Application to intervene), [1989] 2 S.C.R. 335.

RJR-MacDonald Inc. v Canada (Attorney General), [1995] 3 S.C.R. 199.

Rocket v Royal College of Dental Surgeons of Ontario, [1990] 2 S.C.R. 232.

Rodriguez v British Columbia (Attorney General), [1993] 3 S.C.R. 519.

RWDSU v Saskatchewan, [1987] 1 S.C.R. 460.

Sauvé v Canada (Attorney General), [1993] 2 S.C.R. 438.

Sauvé v Canada (Chief Electoral Officer), 2002 SCC 68, [2002] 3 S.C.R. 519.

Thorson v Canada (Attorney General) (No. 2), [1975] 1 S.C.R. 138.

Tremblay v Daigle, [1989] 2 S.C.R. 530

United States v Burns, 2001 SCC 7, [2001] 1 S.C.R. 283.

Vriend v Alberta, [1998] 1 S.C.R. 493.

Index

Abella, Rosalie: background, 67; on human dignity, 131; on judicial objectivity, 567; on public opinion, 176

Aboriginal rights, 42, 81, 86, 173, 188

abortion: and the *Charter*, 1-2, 11, 134-35, 144-46, 189; and dialogue, 164, 169; fetal rights, 44, 113; and judicial impartiality, 57; and public opinion, 172, 174; strategic behaviour, 30-31, 129

accountability, 101, 165, 173

Andrews v Law Society of British Columbia, 129-30, 211n110

Arbour, Louise: background, 67; caseload, 87; on dialogue, 168; on social and economic rights under section 7 of the *Charter*, 139-40, 154

assisted suicide, 1, 48, 142, 144, 146-47, 189

attitudinal model: applied to Supreme Court of Canada, 8, 22-23, 70, 101, 118, 133, 155, 158-59, 183-84, 186, 189-90; definition of 4, 21; limitations, 9-10, 16, 23-26, 32-34, 59-63, 78, 84, 95-96, 99-100, 113-14, 118, 122, 129, 131; and other approaches, 6, 12-13, 26-29, 32-38

Auton (Guardian ad litem of) v British Columbia (Attorney General), 15-17, 148-52, 154-55, 157-58

Baar, Carl, 143

Baier, Gerald, 35

Baker, Dennis, 162, 201n51

Bastarache, Michel: background, 67; on collegiality, 112, 123-24; complaint to Canadian Judicial Council, 173; on conferencing, 104; on consensus, 125-26; ideology, 59; on interveners, 51; on judi-

cial objectivity, 57; on oral hearings, 97; on public opinion, 173; on section 7 of the *Charter*, 140

Baum, Lawrence, 35

Beetz, Jean: on abortion, 145; background, 65; indecisiveness, 65, 75, 104

Bickel, Alexander, 2

Binnie, Ian: background, 67; on evidence, 138-39; on the prohibition of private health insurance, 151-52, 156

Borovoy, Alan, 49

Borowski v Canada (Attorney General), 44-45, 113-14

British North America Act, 41, 199n14. *See also Constitution Act, 1867*

Brodie, Ian, 44, 49-51, 201n55, 202n78, 202n82

Brown v Board of Education, 174-75

Cairns, Alan, 36

Cameron, Jamie, 140, 145, 147, 149, 155

Canada (Attorney General) v PHS Community Services Society, 144, 156-58, 189. *See also* Insite case

Canada Elections Act, 138, 168

Canadian Bar Association, 50, 86

Canadian Bill of Rights, 12, 41

Canadian Civil Liberties Association, 49

Canadian Council of Churches v Canada (Minister of Employment and Immigration), 44

Canadian Judicial Council, 71, 73, 173

capacity: of individual justices, 35, 54, 56; of the institution, 9, 14, 55, 61, 133-59, 171, 185; relation to justiciability, 47-8. *See also* competence

Cartwright, John, 71, 102

caseload, 11, 42, 73, 77-78, 86-87

David R. Boyd
The Right to a Healthy Environment: Revitalizing Canada's Constitution (2012)

David Milward
Aboriginal Justice and the Charter: Realizing a Culturally Sensitive Interpretation of Legal Rights (2012)

Shelley A.M. Gavigan
Hunger, Horses, and Government Men: Criminal Law on the Aboriginal Plains, 1870-1905 (2012)

Steven Bittle
Still Dying for a Living: Corporate Criminal Liability after the Westray Mine Disaster (2012)

Jacqueline D. Krikorian
International Trade Law and Domestic Policy: Canada, the United States, and the WTO (2012)

Michael Boudreau
City of Order: Crime and Society in Halifax, 1918-35 (2012)

Lesley Erickson
Westward Bound: Sex, Violence, the Law, and the Making of a Settler Society (2011)

David R. Boyd
The Environmental Rights Revolution: A Global Study of Constitutions, Human Rights, and the Environment (2011)

Elaine Craig
Troubling Sex: Towards a Legal Theory of Sexual Integrity (2011)

Laura DeVries
Conflict in Caledonia: Aboriginal Land Rights and the Rule of Law (2011)

Jocelyn Downie and Jennifer J. Llewellyn (eds.)
Being Relational: Reflections on Relational Theory and Health Law (2011)

Grace Li Xiu Woo
Ghost Dancing with Colonialism: Decolonization and Indigenous Rights at the Supreme Court of Canada (2011)

Fiona Kelly
Transforming Law's Family: The Legal Recognition of Planned Lesbian Motherhood (2011)

Colleen Bell
The Freedom of Security: Governing Canada in the Age of Counter-Terrorism (2011)

Andrew S. Thompson
In Defence of Principles: NGOs and Human Rights in Canada (2010)

Aaron Doyle and Dawn Moore (eds.)
Critical Criminology in Canada: New Voices, New Directions (2010)

Joanna R. Quinn
The Politics of Acknowledgement: Truth Commissions in Uganda and Haiti (2010)

Patrick James
Constitutional Politics in Canada after the Charter: Liberalism, Communitarianism, and Systemism (2010)

Louis A. Knafla and Haijo Westra (eds.)
Aboriginal Title and Indigenous Peoples: Canada, Australia, and New Zealand (2010)

Janet Mosher and Joan Brockman (eds.)
Constructing Crime: Contemporary Processes of Criminalization (2010)

Stephen Clarkson and Stepan Wood
A Perilous Imbalance: The Globalization of Canadian Law and Governance (2009)

Amanda Glasbeek
Feminized Justice: The Toronto Women's Court, 1913-34 (2009)

Kimb Brooks (ed.)
Justice Bertha Wilson: One Woman's Difference (2009)

Wayne V. McIntosh and Cynthia L. Cates
Multi-Party Litigation: The Strategic Context (2009)

Renisa Mawani
Colonial Proximities: Crossracial Encounters and Juridical Truths in British Columbia, 1871-1921 (2009)

James B. Kelly and Christopher P. Manfredi (eds.)
Contested Constitutionalism: Reflections on the Canadian Charter of Rights and Freedoms (2009)

Catherine Bell and Robert K. Paterson (eds.)
Protection of First Nations Cultural Heritage: Laws, Policy, and Reform (2008)

Hamar Foster, Benjamin L. Berger, and A.R. Buck (eds.)
The Grand Experiment: Law and Legal Culture in British Settler Societies (2008)

Richard J. Moon (ed.)
Law and Religious Pluralism in Canada (2008)

Catherine Bell and Val Napoleon (eds.)
First Nations Cultural Heritage and Law: Case Studies, Voices, and Perspectives (2008)

Douglas C. Harris
Landing Native Fisheries: Indian Reserves and Fishing Rights in British Columbia, 1849-1925 (2008)

Peggy J. Blair
Lament for a First Nation: The Williams Treaties of Southern Ontario (2008)

Lori G. Beaman
Defining Harm: Religious Freedom and the Limits of the Law (2007)

Stephen Tierney (ed.)
Multiculturalism and the Canadian Constitution (2007)

Julie Macfarlane
The New Lawyer: How Settlement Is Transforming the Practice of Law (2007)

Kimberley White
Negotiating Responsibility: Law, Murder, and States of Mind (2007)

Dawn Moore
Criminal Artefacts: Governing Drugs and Users (2007)

Hamar Foster, Heather Raven, and Jeremy Webber (eds.)
Let Right Be Done: Aboriginal Title, the Calder *Case, and the Future of Indigenous Rights* (2007)

Dorothy E. Chunn, Susan B. Boyd, and Hester Lessard (eds.)
Reaction and Resistance: Feminism, Law, and Social Change (2007)

Margot Young, Susan B. Boyd, Gwen Brodsky, and Shelagh Day (eds.)
Poverty: Rights, Social Citizenship, and Legal Activism (2007)

Rosanna L. Langer
Defining Rights and Wrongs: Bureaucracy, Human Rights, and Public Accountability (2007)

C.L. Ostberg and Matthew E. Wetstein
Attitudinal Decision Making in the Supreme Court of Canada (2007)

Chris Clarkson
Domestic Reforms: Political Visions and Family Regulation in British Columbia, 1862-1940 (2007)

Jean McKenzie Leiper
Bar Codes: Women in the Legal Profession (2006)

Gerald Baier
Courts and Federalism: Judicial Doctrine in the United States, Australia, and Canada (2006)

Avigail Eisenberg (ed.)
Diversity and Equality: The Changing Framework of Freedom in Canada (2006)

Randy K. Lippert
Sanctuary, Sovereignty, Sacrifice: Canadian Sanctuary Incidents, Power, and Law (2005)

James B. Kelly
Governing with the Charter: Legislative and Judicial Activism and Framers' Intent (2005)

Dianne Pothier and Richard Devlin (eds.)
Critical Disability Theory: Essays in Philosophy, Politics, Policy, and Law (2005)

Susan G. Drummond
Mapping Marriage Law in Spanish Gitano Communities (2005)

Louis A. Knafla and Jonathan Swainger (eds.)
Laws and Societies in the Canadian Prairie West, 1670-1940 (2005)

Ikechi Mgbeoji
Global Biopiracy: Patents, Plants, and Indigenous Knowledge (2005)

Florian Sauvageau, David Schneiderman, and David Taras, with Ruth Klinkhammer and Pierre Trudel
The Last Word: Media Coverage of the Supreme Court of Canada (2005)

Gerald Kernerman
Multicultural Nationalism: Civilizing Difference, Constituting Community (2005)

Pamela A. Jordan
Defending Rights in Russia: Lawyers, the State, and Legal Reform in the Post-Soviet Era (2005)

Anna Pratt
Securing Borders: Detention and Deportation in Canada (2005)

Kirsten Johnson Kramar
Unwilling Mothers, Unwanted Babies: Infanticide in Canada (2005)

W.A. Bogart
Good Government? Good Citizens? Courts, Politics, and Markets in a Changing Canada (2005)

Catherine Dauvergne
Humanitarianism, Identity, and Nation: Migration Laws in Canada and Australia (2005)

Michael Lee Ross
First Nations Sacred Sites in Canada's Courts (2005)

Andrew Woolford
Between Justice and Certainty: Treaty Making in British Columbia (2005)

John McLaren, Andrew Buck, and Nancy Wright (eds.)
Despotic Dominion: Property Rights in British Settler Societies (2004)

Georges Campeau
From UI to EI: Waging War on the Welfare State (2004)

Alvin J. Esau
The Courts and the Colonies: The Litigation of Hutterite Church Disputes (2004)

Christopher N. Kendall
Gay Male Pornography: An Issue of Sex Discrimination (2004)

Roy B. Flemming
Tournament of Appeals: Granting Judicial Review in Canada (2004)

Constance Backhouse and Nancy L. Backhouse
The Heiress vs the Establishment: Mrs. Campbell's Campaign for Legal Justice (2004)

Christopher P. Manfredi
Feminist Activism in the Supreme Court: Legal Mobilization and the Women's Legal Education and Action Fund (2004)

Annalise Acorn
Compulsory Compassion: A Critique of Restorative Justice (2004)

Jonathan Swainger and Constance Backhouse (eds.)
People and Place: Historical Influences on Legal Culture (2003)

Jim Phillips and Rosemary Gartner
Murdering Holiness: The Trials of Franz Creffield and George Mitchell (2003)

David R. Boyd
Unnatural Law: Rethinking Canadian Environmental Law and Policy (2003)

Ikechi Mgbeoji
Collective Insecurity: The Liberian Crisis, Unilateralism, and Global Order (2003)

Rebecca Johnson
Taxing Choices: The Intersection of Class, Gender, Parenthood, and the Law (2002)

John McLaren, Robert Menzies, and Dorothy E. Chunn (eds.)
Regulating Lives: Historical Essays on the State, Society, the Individual, and the Law (2002)

Joan Brockman
Gender in the Legal Profession: Fitting or Breaking the Mould (2001)

Printed and bound in Canada by Friesens

Set in Stone by Artegraphica Design Co. Ltd.

Copy editor: Stacy Belden

Proofreader: Dianne Tiefensee